Nation-Building, Ethnicity and
Language Politics in Transition Countries

Local Government
and Public Service
Reform Initiative

EUROPEAN CENTRE
FOR
MINORITY ISSUES

NATION-BUILDING, ETHNICITY AND LANGUAGE POLITICS IN TRANSITION COUNTRIES

Edited by

FARIMAH DAFTARY AND FRANÇOIS GRIN

LGI Books

First edition published by
Local Government and Public Service Reform Initiative
Open Society Institute

Nádor utca 11
H–1051 Budapest, Hungary

Telephone: (+36 1) 327 3104
Fax: (+36 1) 327 3105
http://lgi.osi.hu

Design & Production by Judit Kovács/Createch Ltd.

 OPEN SOCIETY INSTITUTE

The views expressed by the contributors to this book do not reflect the views of either LGI, ECMI or the editors
of the book, but are the sole responsibility of the authors.

ISBN: 963 9419 58 3
ISSN: 1586-1317

Printed in Hungary by Createch Ltd., May 2003

 Local Government
and Public Service
Reform Initiative

Local Government and Public Service Reform Initiative (LGI), as one of the programs of the Open Society Institute (OSI), is an international development and grant-giving organization dedicated to the support of good governance in the countries of Central and Eastern Europe (CEE) and the Commonwealth of Independent States (CIS). LGI seeks to fulfill its mission through the initiation of research and support of development and operational activities in the fields of decentralization, public policy formation and the reform of public administration.

With projects running in countries covering the region between the Czech Republic and Mongolia, LGI seeks to achieve its objectives through:

- development of sustainable regional networks of institutions and professionals engaged in policy analysis, reform-oriented training and advocacy;
- support and dissemination of in-depth comparative and regionally applicable policy studies tackling local government issues;
- support of country-specific projects and delivery of technical assistance to the implementation agencies;
- assistance to Soros foundations with the development of local government, public administration and/or public policy programs in their countries of the region;
- publication of books, studies and discussion papers dealing with the issues of decentralization, public administration, good governance, public policy and lessons learned from the process of transition in these areas;
- development of curricula and organization of training programs dealing with specific local government issues;
- support of policy centers and think tanks in the region.

Apart from its own projects, LGI works closely with a number of other international organizations (Council of Europe, Department for International Development, USAID, UNDP and the World Bank) and co-funds larger regional initiatives aimed at the support of reforms on the subnational level. The Local Government Information Network (LOGIN) and the Fiscal Decentralization Initiative (FDI) are two main examples of this cooperation.

For additional information or specific publications, please contact:

Local Government and Public Service Reform Initiative
P.O. Box 519
H–1397 Budapest,Hungary
E-mail: lgprog@osi.hu • http://lgi.osi.hu
Telephone: (+36 1) 327 3104 • Fax: (+36 1) 327 3105

Introduction to the Series

Nation-Building, Ethnicity and Language Politics in Transition Countries is the second volume in the ECMI/LGI Series on Ethnopolitics and Minority Issues. The Series is a joint venture of the European Centre for Minority Issues (ECMI) and the Local Government and Public Service Reform Initiative (LGI). ECMI conducts practice-oriented research, provides information and documentation, and offers advisory services concerning minority-majority relations in Europe; in addition, it engages in constructive conflict management through its action-oriented projects, particularly in the Balkans and the Baltics. LGI, a programme of the Open Society Institute, is a think tank specializing in improving governance practices and the provision of public services, especially at the local level.

The ECMI/LGI Series aims to provide a highly visible and accessible platform for ECMI's cutting-edge studies. These multi-author works are the result of the Centre's cooperative research projects, often lasting a number of years. While these projects were at times supported by conferences and seminars, the resulting books attempt to present a coherent and comprehensive picture of the area under investigation. In this way, the Series avoids the pitfalls of conference publications that often lack a clear focus and structure.

The Series also enables both ECMI and LGI to strengthen the link between their proactive work across Europe and the development of scholarly work that is geared towards influencing policy decisions. Through these studies, ECMI and LGI will raise awareness of crosscutting issues related to majority-minority relations and will analyze new issues and practices as they arise. In this way, the Series will advance the practical understanding of new challenges concerning minority issues while at the same time adding a dimension of theoretically based understanding.

The majority of countries in the former Eastern bloc, in particular in Central and Eastern Europe, feature multiethnic societies. Decentralization and the transition to a free market environment have made this characteristic of nation-states more visible and have raised the claim for a proactive approach toward multiethnic community management. The first step for countries that plan to solve ethnic conflicts in a peaceful way is to draft legislation on individual and collective minority rights. The second step is to implement these rules and manage the public sector in accordance with the accepted principles.

As there is a lack of relevant literature and research in this field, the ECMI/LGI Series intends to fill the gap by providing information and 'food for thought' for public officials and relevant professionals as well as practitioners. It is hoped that the ECMI/LGI publishing partnership will result in a significant addition to the study and practice of emerging policy issues related to minorities.

Marc Weller
European Centre for Minority Issues

Petra Kovács
Local Government and Public Service Reform Initiative

Also available in the Series

Contents

List of Contributors

Farimah Daftary received her Masters of International Affairs (M.I.A.) with a specialization in East Central Europe from the School of International and Public Affairs (SIPA), Columbia University, New York, in 1991. She is currently a Consultant on Minority Protection for the EU Accession Monitoring Program (EUMAP), Open Society Institute–Budapest. From 1997 to 2002, she worked as a Research Associate at the European Centre for Minority Issues (ECMI) in Flensburg, Germany, dealing with various aspects of interethnic relations and minority issues in Europe. Her research concerns conflict management through autonomy and power-sharing arrangements (notably in Corsica and in Macedonia), as well as language issues in transition countries. She has also had a long-standing interest in the development of minority protection regimes of the OSCE and the Council of Europe.

Helen M. Faller is a Ph.D. candidate in Anthropology at the University of Michigan. Her dissertation, entitled "Repossessing Kazan: Nation-Building After Socialism in Tatarstan, Russia" examines the social effects of Tatarstan's political movement for sovereignty. In particular, it demonstrates that increasing the domains of use of the Tatar language in Kazan has resulted in a divergence in the world views of the linguistic communities living there. Her publications so far argue for attention to linguistic practices in shaping the worlds people occupy. In addition to the political economy of languages and nationalisms, Faller's research interests include post-socialist gender relations and variation in models for creating racial difference.

Kinga Gál is Chief Advisor to the President of the Hungarian Academy of Sciences, and Senior Non-Resident Research Associate at the European Centre for Minority Issues (ECMI), Flensburg, Germany. She specializes in international human rights law and minority legislation, and bilateral treaties in Central and Eastern Europe.

Yagfar Z. Garipov is a professor at the Tatarstan Academy of Sciences' Institute of Social Sciences, Economics and Law and a docent at the Institute of Economics, Management and Law in Kazan, Tatarstan. He received a Ph.D. in applied sociology with a specialization in national affairs from the Sociology Institute of the Moscow Academy of Sciences in 1978. His research focuses on social politics, migration and demography, as well as ethnolinguistic and ethnological processes. He is the author of some 50 publications in those fields. His recent publications include "Ethnic Aspects of Education" (in *Urgent Problems of Education*, Moscow: Ministry of Education of the Russian Federation, 1999: 134–135) and "Tendencies of National and Language Development" (*Sociological Research*, Kazan, 2002: 3–13).

François Grin (Ph.D., Economics) is Professor of Economics at the Institute of Translation and Interpretation of the University of Geneva, Switzerland, and Adjunct Director of the Education Resarch Unit (SRED) and Senior Lecturer at the University of Geneva. From 1998 to 2001, he was Deputy Director of the European Centre for Minority Issues (ECMI), to which he remains affiliated as a Senior Fellow. His research focuses on the economics of language, the economics of education and the evaluation of language and education policies. He is the author of over 150 publications in those fields.

Ian F. Hancock served as UN representative for the International Romani Union from 1990 to 2000. He was recipient of the Norwegian Rafto Foundation's International Prize for Human Rights and past holder of the Gamaliel Chair in Peace and Justice. In 1997, President Bill Clinton appointed him as sole Romani member of the US Holocaust Memorial Council. He teaches at the University of Texas at Austin, where he is Director of The Romani Archives and Documentation Center. He has over 300 publications, including *The Pariah Syndrome: An Account of Gypsy Slavery and Persecution* (1987), *A Handbook of Vlax Romani* (1995) and *We Are the Romani People* (Hatfield: Hertfordshire University Press, 2002).

Priit Järve graduated from the University of Tartu, Estonia, and completed his Ph.D. in Philosophy of Science at the Institute of Philosophy of the Academy of Sciences in Moscow. From 1989 to 1997, he was the director of the Institute of International and Social Studies in Tallinn, Estonia. Under the auspices of the UNDP, he contributed to and edited the Estonian Human Development Reports of 1995, 1996 and 1997. From 1995 to 1997, he also served as the Plenipotentiary of the President of Estonia to the Estonian Roundtable of National Minorities. Dr. Järve joined the European Centre for Minority Issues (ECMI) in May 1997 as Senior Analyst. He has published on the democratization of transitional societies, multiculturalism and interethnic relations in the post-Soviet area.

Rouben Karapetyan (Ph.D., History) is the head of the group of scientific officers of the Institute of Archaeology and Ethnography of the National Academy of Science of Armenia, Senior Lecturer at the Armenian State Engineering University and Vice-President of the Armenian Sociological Association. His research focuses on the social and cultural aspects of migration, ethnic minorities and economic and socio-cultural problems in transition countries. He is the author of some 30 publications in those fields.

Carmen Kettley received her law degree from the University of Bucharest and taught international law at the Bucharest School of Economics (1993–1996). During 1990–1997, she was a researcher at the Bucharest Institute of Legal Sciences. From 1997 to 1998, Ms. Kettley was a Global Security Fellow at Wolfson College and at the Faculty of Social and Political Sciences, University of Cambridge. She is currently conducting her doctoral research at the Centre of International Studies in Cambridge on the prospects for power-sharing arrangements in Central and Eastern Europe. Ms. Kettley is a member of Wolfson College, Cambridge.

Will Kymlicka is the author of five books published by Oxford University Press: *Liberalism, Community and Culture* (1989), *Contemporary Political Philosophy* (1990; second edition 2002), *Multicultural Citizenship* (1995), *Finding Our Way: Rethinking Ethnocultural Relations in Canada* (1998) and *Politics in the Vernacular: Nationalism, Multiculturalism, Citizenship* (2001). He is also the editor of *The Rights of Minority Cultures* (Oxford University Press, 1995) and co-editor of *Ethnicity and Group Rights* (New York University Press, 1997), *Citizenship in Diverse Societies* (OUP, 2000), *Alternative Conceptions of Civil Society* (OUP, 2001) and *Can Liberal Pluralism Be Exported? Western Political Theory and Ethnic Relations in Eastern Europe* (OUP, 2001). He is currently a professor of philosophy at Queen's University, Canada, and a visiting professor in the Nationalism Studies program at the Central European University in Budapest.

Petra Roter is a Ph.D. candidate at the University of Cambridge, UK, and a Junior Research Fellow at the University of Ljubljana, Slovenia, Centre of International Relations. She obtained her M. Phil. degree in International Relations from the University of Cambridge, UK. In 1999, she was a DAAD (Deutscher Akademischer Austauschdienst) visiting researcher at the University of Tübingen, Germany, and in 2000, a visiting research associate at the European Centre for Minority Issues (ECMI) in Flensburg, Germany. Her research interests include minority-majority relations, nationalism, ethnic conflicts and ethnic conflict management, minority protection, international relations theory, the former Yugoslavia and its break-up. Her recent publications include: "Locating the 'Minority Problem' in Europe: a Historical Perspective" (*Journal of International Relations and Development*, 4(3), 2001: 221–249); and "Managing the 'Minority Problem' in Post-Cold War Europe Within the Framework of a Multilayered Regime for the Protection of National Minorities" (*European Yearbook of Minority Issues* 1, 2001/2, The Hague, London, New York: Kluwer Law International, 2003: 85–129).

Viktor Stepanenko received his Ph.D. at the University of Manchester in 1998. He is currently a Senior Fellow at the Institute of Sociology in Kyiv, Ukraine, where he has been working since 1992. From 1992 to 1995, he took part in the international project Neighbourhood of Cultures, established by the University of Bielefeld and the University of Warsaw. From 1997 to 1998, he was a Global Security Fellow at Wolfson College and at the Faculty of Social and Political Sciences, University of Cambridge. From 1999 to 2001, he was participating in the project Managing Multiethnic Communities, organized by the Local Government and Public Service Reform Initiative (LGI), at the Open Society Institute–Budapest. His fields of research are: ethnic issues, political sociology and public policy analysis. His recent publications include: *Construction of Identity and School Policy in Ukraine* (New York: Commack, 1999), chapters in Anna-Mária Bíró and Petra Kovács (eds.) *Diversity in Action. Local Public Management of Multi-ethnic Communities in Central and Eastern Europe* (Budapest: LGI/OSI, 2001) and in I. Kononov (ed.) *Civil Society and Contemporary Ukrainian Reality* (Lugansk–Geneva: Alma Mater, 2002).

List of Tables and Figures

Foreword

François Grin[1] and Farimah Daftary[2]

The idea for this book has grown out of the academic production and field work of the European Centre for Minority Issues (ECMI), which, since its creation in 1996 in Flensburg (Germany), has been active in practice-oriented research on various aspects of minority–majority relations in Europe.

Despite its cross-European scope, much of ECMI's activity concerns regions such as Central and Eastern Europe, Southeastern Europe and the Commonwealth of Independent States (CIS). What most countries of these regions have in common is that they are in 'transition'—that is, they possess a particular political history characterized by a certain number of years of communist rule (over seventy in the case of CIS countries, less than fifty for some of the others). The historical experience of communism has also translated into a specific discourse regarding ethnic and linguistic plurality. The regional emphasis just described also coincides with what is sometimes called 'the OSCE[3] region', a denomination reflecting the OSCE's core mission, namely, "to ensure security, in the broader sense of the term, including the protection and promotion of human rights, economic and environmental stability, as well as politico-military issues".

The action of the OSCE is therefore intended to help these countries manage a smooth transition from various types of communist regimes and centrally planned economies to the so-called 'Western' system combining representative democracy with market economy. As part of this mission, the OSCE is one of the many actors on the international scene (which includes not only international organizations, but also non-governmental organizations and, of course, the foreign services of many European countries) devoting particular attention to ethnopolitical issues and the way in which legal and institutional provisions in transition countries address these matters. Of distinct concern are issues such as the adequate representation of national minorities in legislative bodies, national and local administrations and the judiciary, as well as their effective participation in the political process. The OSCE's activity can be said to encourage state authorities' acknowledgement of minorities as legitimate components of the nation-state, even when the state is more closely associated with a 'titular nation'.

---

[1]   Education Research Unit (SRED) and University of Geneva.

[2]   EU Accession Monitoring Program (EUMAP), Open Society Institute–Budapest.

[3]   Organization for Security and Co-operation in Europe.

Much of this effort, by the OSCE and more generally, has been formulated in terms of the concept of 'rights', resulting in an emphasis on the drafting and enforcement of legal and constitutional provisions ensuring respect for minority rights. The attention devoted to the evolution of national (level) legislation in many transition countries went along with the development of international legal instruments pertaining to the position of minorities. Most of these instruments, in fact, reflect a given set of epistemological references (Grin, 2003) also structured around the concept of rights, the subjects of which are individuals belonging to 'national minorities'.[4]

However, this emphasis on national minorities risks overplaying ethnicity as the unquestioned and unchallenged organizing concept for the analysis of minority-majority relations. One of the difficulties associated with the notion of ethnicity (as well as the frequently associated assumption that 'ethnicity' and 'nation' are in a necessary mutual relation) is that collective identity may be taken for granted (May, 2001). The focus tends to be placed on what people 'are' (or are assumed to be) rather than on what they do. Consequently, a national minority simply 'is'—that is, it is assumed to necessarily have certain characteristics and aspirations.

This essentialist view of minorities may obscure the fact that reality is considerably more complex (Anderson, 1983); it may be more useful to look closely at what people do—as members of groups sharing particular characteristics related to language, culture and patrimony (Fishman, 1977). In this perspective, language emerges as a particularly important phenomenon, as has been known to sociolinguists for a long time. Therefore, society's intervention in the field of language requires closer attention as a fully legitimate object of study—not as a mere appendix to ethnicity and nationalism. Consequently, this book is intended as a review of cases showing how, in several transition countries, language issues, while still related to ethnicity, have emerged as political issues in their own right. By selecting this angle, this book intends to contribute, in a specific way, to the growing body of literature on language, ethnicity and politics (O'Reilly, 2001).

This book has also grown out of circumstance. ECMI had organized, at the 2000 convention of the Association for the Study of Nationalities (ASN), held on the campus of Columbia University in New York, a panel on "Language Laws: Nation-Building, Ethnic Containment or Diversity Management?". The papers presented at this panel, in which Will Kymlicka took part as discussant, have been consolidated into the present book together with additional contributions.

...

---

[4] Examples include the Council of Europe's Framework Convention for the Protection of National Minorities and a series of guidelines developed by the OSCE, in particular the Hague Recommendations Regarding the Education Rights of National Minorities, the Oslo Recommendations Regarding the Linguistic Rights of National Minorities, and the Lund Recommendations on the Effective Participation of National Minorities in Public Life. The major exception to this general pattern is the Council of Europe's European Charter for Regional or Minority Languages, which is not formulated in terms of rights (see Introduction).

The book opens with a theoretical overview of the issues by Will Kymlicka and François Grin—an introduction to contrasting, yet complementary perspectives on the political meaning of the development of language legislation. Contrary to what is often done elsewhere, this discussion does not focus on the links between language legislation and the apparatus of legal instruments and formal minority rights. Rather, the emphasis is on how legal texts regarding language relate to the principles of political theory on the one hand and policy analysis on the other hand. Both perspectives cast an original light on the process of legislative development regarding language issues.

In the first of three case studies of 'one state, one language' policy, Farimah Daftary and Kinga Gál's analysis of language politics in Slovakia demonstrates how sensitive demands for minority rights generally, and language rights in particular, can be when they are formulated during the early phases of state-building. The study also illustrates how language policies can be used to foster the identity of a dominant nation and promote the assimilation of minority citizens. The chapter also argues that, in Slovakia, these sensitivities persisted under the newly-elected coalition government which came to power in 1998 even though it included ethnic Hungarians, as demonstrated by the interplay between domestic and international processes impacting the content of the 1999 Minority Language Law.

Priit Järve examines the three Baltic states of Estonia, Latvia and Lithuania, testing the hypothesis that the aim of language policies evolves over time as state-building progresses, from serving the aim of (nation-)state-building to the ethnic containment of Russian-speakers and, eventually, to the management of diversity. In conclusion, Järve argues that, stimulated by the prospect of European integration, citizens of the Baltic states are increasingly preoccupied with learning English, which may defuse tensions over issues related to the legacy of Russian language dominance.

In his chapter on identities and language politics in Ukraine, Viktor Stepanenko examines attempts to revitalize the Ukrainian language and reverse trends of 'Russification' during the process of social transformation. He thus analyzes the tensions resulting from an official 'one state, one language' ideology and *laissez-faire* state policy of 'balance' between the official state language—Ukrainian—and the main language of communication in everyday life—Russian. However, Stepanenko argues that the real source of language tensions in Ukraine lies in the deep link between language and identity. Special attention is devoted to the particularly sensitive issue of language use in education where a 'Ukrainization' of Russian-language schools has been attempted with little success. He concludes with a hopeful prediction that Ukraine will realize that the path of interethnic and linguistic tolerance is preferable to the forced assimilation of its minorities which will inevitably generate conflict.

Opening the section on titular language promotion and bilingualism, Rouben Karapetyan's account of the development of Armenia's language legislation stresses the role of sociolinguistic and historical factors in the emergence of language legislation. In addition to the importance of the Armenian language as a marker of the identity of a small people, the fragmentation of the language (reinforced by emigration, particularly after the 1915 genocide) goes a long way towards explaining the relative importance of different issues in the contemporary debate over Armenian language legislation. Given also the high level of ethnolinguistic homogeneity in present-day Armenia, this translates into a particularly interesting linkage between matters of language corpus (such as lexical innovation or spelling) and the more explicitly political level of language status, which refers to the position of one language *vis-à-vis* other languages.

The chapter on Tatarstan by Yagfar Z. Garipov and Helen Faller offers an account of what remains a relatively little-known case, on which there exist few detailed studies in languages other than Russian. The authors analyze the Tatar language renaissance as a process that must be seen in the context of centuries of integration into the Russian empire, and, increasingly, assimilation into the Russian-speaking world. The ethnolinguistic context is marked by the presence of over one hundred nationalities in present-day Tatarstan. Unavoidably, Russian is the language of communication between people of different ethnic origin, and this dominant position will not be easily challenged. Against the backdrop set by this and similar examples, the recent decision (November 2002) of the Russian Duma to impose the Cyrillic script as the only alphabet acceptable for the writing of the official languages of component parts of the Federation seems difficult to trace back to any serious challenge to Russian as the language of inter-group communication.

The chapter on Kalmykia by François Grin surveys another little-researched case. As the only Buddhist people indigenous to Europe, the Kalmyks' experience is characterized by a highly original cultural background. Despite geographical remoteness and economic difficulties, the language legislation that Kalmykia has adopted in 1999 constitutes a surprisingly 'modern' example, in which what is at stake appears considerably closer to the well-known situations of 'unique' minority languages of Western Europe, such as Breton, Scottish Gaelic or Sardinian.[5] It remains to be seen, however, if this legislation will succeed in stopping or reversing longstanding patterns of language attrition, which were abetted by the wholesale deportation of the Kalmyk people under Stalin.

In a third section on Identity, Differentiation and Unification, Petra Roter examines the crucial role which Slovene has played in binding together the Slovenian nation and enhancing its sense of self-awareness in the absence of an independent state and, more recently, under the newly-independent state. Roter places the role of language in the processes of Slovenian nation-building and state-formation in a historical context, contending that attitudes towards language issues and language policies should be analyzed within the broader context of what she calls 'Slovenian smallness'. It is this perception of vulnerability, she argues, that has made language a particularly sensitive issue and shaped language policies towards minorities in contemporary Slovenia.

Carmen Kettley uses the example of the Hungarian minority in another officially monolingual country—Romania—to illustrate the sensitivity of demands for minority-language rights in the context of transition. She argues that the dynamics of the relationship between the Hungarian minority and Romanian political elites have set the tone of ethnic discourse and determined the development of the legal framework for the protection of minority rights in Romania. Interestingly, in analyzing the dynamics between Romania and Hungary over the same period, Kettley finds that the relationship between the kin-state and the host-state does not necessarily mirror the internal dynamics of majority minority relations as demonstrated by the controversies generated by the so-called Hungarian Status Law.

---

[5]   The concept of a 'unique' minority language refers to the situation of languages that are not used as a majority language, particularly in a so-called 'kin-state' across an international border.

The final chapter in this third section by Ian F. Hancock examines the process not of differentiation but of unification which might arise as a result of efforts to standardize the Romani language. Indeed, the emergence of a common language out of many dialects is expected to have the effect of generating a sense of belonging to a common nation amongst individuals scattered throughout Europe with no state of their own. Hancock analyzes attitudes towards Romani identity and language, both among Roma and non-Roma, and describes the issues surrounding the proposal of a standard dialect. In conclusion, Hancock calls for a greater involvement of Romani specialists in these issues to redress the current imbalance.

...

The realities described in these case studies will surely change as trade and exchange across international boundaries increase, younger generations enter the fray and new geopolitical forces emerge. Despite the (sometimes impressive) speed of change, it is our hope that this set of studies, as well as the integrative analytical perspective with which we have attempted to organize them, will prove to be a valuable tool for scholars and practitioners seeking to take stock of the complex interplay between language, politics and nation-building in transition countries.

The practical aspects of the production of this book have been coordinated by ECMI's publications officer, Ms. Marita Lampe. The editors are deeply indebted to Ms. Lampe for editorial assistance, and above all for helping keep this book on a steady course toward completion. The editors also wish to express their gratitude to other colleagues at ECMI, in particular Priit Järve for strategically timed phone calls to distant parts of the CIS.

Geneva and Budapest, December 2002

REFERENCES

Anderson, Benedict (1983) *Imagined Communities*. London: Verso.

Fishman, Joshua (1977) "Language and Ethnicity". In Howard Giles (ed.) *Language and Ethnicity in Intergroup Relations*. London and New York: Academic Press, pp.83–98.

Grin, François (2003) "Diversity as Paradigm, Analytical Device, and Policy Goal". In Will Kymlicka and Alan Patten (eds.) *Language Rights and Political Theory*. Oxford: Oxford University Press, pp.169–88.

May, Stephen (2001) *Language and Minority Rights. Ethnicity, Nationalism and the Politics of Language*. Harlow: Longman.

O'Reilly, Camille (ed.) (2001) *Language, Ethnicity and the State, Volume Two. Minority Languages in Eastern Europe, Post-1989*. London: Palgrave.

Will Kymlicka and François Grin

Assessing the Politics
of Diversity
in Transition Countries

Assessing the Politics of Diversity in Transition Countries

Will Kymlicka and François Grin

Assessing the Politics of Diversity in Transition Countries

Will Kymlicka and François Grin

INTRODUCTION

The nine case studies presented in this volume exemplify the wide range of experience found in transition countries regarding relations between majorities and minorities. This range of experience is reflected in the significant variation in legal status of majority and minority languages.

Very different core concerns come to the forefront in these texts, and they may be contrasted along different dimensions. A number of typologies of linguistic minorities have been published in recent years (e.g., Edwards, 1990; Nelde, Strubell and Williams, 1996), and we shall not attempt, in this introductory chapter, to develop yet one more typology on the basis of the cases presented here. However, some distinctions are worth keeping in mind. In particular, language policies that aim at promoting a titular language can be contrasted with those that aim at preserving non-titular languages. At the same time, another distinction may be made between policies that are primarily instruments of nation-building and those that are mainly viewed as tools for the preservation of linguistic diversity. We can find examples of all of these different types of language policies in the cases represented in this volume, although the clear tendency is towards the adoption of policies which are intended to both promote a titular language (rather than minority languages) and to promote nation-building (rather than to preserve linguistic diversity).

In cases such as Slovakia and Romania, for example, the legislation aims at enshrining the pre-eminence of a titular nation and its associated language over that of a group which is generally perceived (and tends to perceive itself) as a national minority. In these cases, this assertion of the privileged position of a titular language may be said to coincide with the traditional 'one state, one language' nation-building ideology.[1] The assertion or reassertion of a titular language, however, looks quite different depending on the relative demolinguistic sizes of the national majority, the national minority and, where applicable, the kin-state with which the national minority has close links through language, history or culture. Seen in this light, the case of the Baltic states and Ukraine, where there is rivalry between the titular language and once-dominant Russian, must be seen as distinct from that of, say, Romania, Slovenia or Slovakia.

---

[1]   However, this need not be the case. Following independence, many African states, though embracing the 'one state, one language' ideology, made official the language of the former colonial power rather than the language of one of the local groups. (Calvet, 1974).

In other cases, the chief concern is the revitalization of a threatened minority language (even if the latter may be titular at the sub-state level). This is particularly manifest in the case of Kalmyk and Tatar, which turn out to be closer to many Western European experiences with the protection and promotion of threatened languages.

In yet other cases, language policies that promote the titular language, as part of an ideology of nation-building, can simultaneously be interpreted as protecting an endangered language. Given the relatively small 'absolute' number of speakers of Estonian, Estonia would be an example. Policies aimed at privileging the Estonian language over the Russian language within Estonia are, in part, an attempt to privilege a majority titular language over a minority language. But they are also an attempt to protect a small, potentially threatened language confronted by a world language. Taking sociolinguistic realities into account, the situation of small titular languages like Estonian in competition with a world language like Russian is, in some ways, similar to the revitalization of threatened minority languages in Western Europe, like that of Catalan, Basque, Welsh or Gaelic, competing with world languages such as English and Spanish. This 'threatened language vs. world language' dynamic, along with its political and policy implications, may turn out to be as important as the 'titular language vs. national minority language' dynamic. In many of the cases presented in this volume, the policies being implemented reflect an intention to shake off traces of earlier submission to a former imperial power which is now the kin-state of a national minority.

Given the variability not only of situations, but also of the analytical perspectives in which they can be interpreted, we have thought it worthwhile to reconsider the case studies through the prism of two contrasting yet complementary approaches to the larger question of linguistic diversity in society—particularly in transition contexts. Our aim in this introductory chapter is to present these two approaches and to discuss how they link up with the case studies.

The first approach emphasizes key questions from normative political theory. The problems to be addressed include the following: Are there general normative principles that can guide us in the assessment of various institutional arrangements (as enshrined in legislation)? What is the relative weight that different principles appear to have been given, implicitly or explicitly, by the authorities that have adopted and implemented these legal texts? Of the institutional and legal arrangements presented, do some appear to be more or less compatible with such normative principles? Can some be said, in particular, to be more congruent with liberalism?

The second approach is derived from a policy analysis perspective on language policies. This perspective helps to structure the emerging field of research variously called 'diversity management' or 'linguistic governance'. One of its core concerns is to clarify the goals of policy intervention in the area of language and in particular to ascertain whether a given intervention can be said to be welfare-increasing. This in turn raises questions regarding the mode of delivery of the results expected. Some consideration must therefore be given to issues of effectiveness and costs, as well as to the (re)distributive implications of policy interventions.

We want to discuss these two approaches because they have been relatively neglected and offer important alternatives or supplements to the two approaches which currently dominate much of the literature, namely, the linguistic human rights approach and the legal-institutional approach. The 'linguistic human rights' approach, which is usually rooted in sociolinguistics (e.g., Skutnabb-Kangas, 2000; some contributions in Kontra *et al.*, 1999), can be characterized as follows: It seeks to formulate a minimal set of universal linguistic rights to be included in the list of universal human rights. It tends to assume that such rights can be demanded by all individuals—irrespective, for example, of the 'autochthonous vs. immigrant' distinction, or of the number of speakers concerned. The legal-institutional approach is usually rooted in international and constitutional law (e.g., de Varennes, 1996; some contributions in Guillorel and Koubi, 1999). Legal discourse on ethnic, linguistic and cultural diversity concentrates on issues such as the interpretation of international legal instruments, or on the examination of the compatibility between some aspect of national legislation and international legal standards.

The two approaches developed in this chapter are not necessarily inconsistent with the goals of either the linguistic human rights approach or the legal-institutional approach. Both normative political theory and policy analysis can support efforts to codify international legal standards relating to language. However, both approaches try to look beyond legal standards (or to side-step this type of issues), because they are grounded in other types of arguments, which, in turn, embody different epistemological perspectives.

Both the political theory and policy analysis approaches are relatively new. The targeted discussion of principles of normative political theory in the evaluation of language legislation is in fact a recent development (e.g., Patten, 2001; van Parijs, 2000), drawing on earlier work by political philosophers on multiculturalism, citizenship and minorities (e.g., Kymlicka, 1989, 1995a, 1995b). The development of a policy analysis approach to language policies, though suggested at regular intervals over the past thirty years (e.g., Jernudd, 1983; Pool, 1991), has also been the object of more work in recent years (e.g., Grin, 1996, 2000, 2002; de Swaan, 2001; van Parijs, 2001).[2]

The theoretical questions addressed by these two new approaches are complex, and it would therefore not be possible to do justice to them here. Rather, we shall confine ourselves to a characterization of the essential issues that they raise and then revisit them in the light of selected elements of the accounts presented in the case studies. In other words, our goal has been not so much to pass judgement on the experience of a number of transition countries (let alone on the actors involved in shaping this experience) as to assess what theoretical research can actually learn from this experience.

This chapter is organized as follows. Section 1 presents the essential aspects of the normative political philosophy approach, explores whether normative principles do come to the fore in the case studies and whether the latter can serve as valid illustrations of these principles.

A symmetrical exercise is attempted in Section 2, starting out instead from a policy analysis perspective. The latter queries the meaning of the notion of 'rights' as the actual rationalization behind the institutional arrangements described in the case studies. Within both Sections 1 and 2, we ask what light the approach sheds on the case studies, but also how these two approaches may be improved and refined in light of the case studies.

---

[2]   The work by van Parijs quoted in this chapter bridges aspects of political theory with aspects of policy analysis (e.g., the distributive effects of regulations regarding language use).

In a concluding section, we assess the possibility of combining these two approaches into a more adequate integrated framework for analyzing issues of language policy. We also examine whether the 'transition' situation common to all the case studies is likely to have an influence on these results, or whether they can be generalized to other studies in the 'politics of diversity'.

1.   NORMATIVE THEORIES OF LINGUISTIC JUSTICE

Western democracies pride themselves on being based on liberal-democratic principles and are pressuring countries of post-communist Europe to adopt the same principles as a pre-condition for 'rejoining Europe'. But what are these principles? And what do they imply for issues of language policy?

According to John Rawls, perhaps the foremost liberal philosopher of the twentieth century, the core value of liberal democracy is justice. As he puts it, justice "is the first virtue of social institutions" (Rawls, 1971: 3). So, from a liberal -democratic viewpoint, what does justice require in the sphere of language? This is a remarkably neglected question in the history of the liberal tradition. Most theorists (including Rawls) never raise the question. One explanation for this surprising omission is that language turns out to be rather embarrassing for liberals. Issues of language cannot easily be accommodated within the standard frame-work that liberals adopt for dealing with diversity.

Liberalism first grappled with the issue of diversity in the context of religious conflict. Indeed, Rawls suggests that liberalism emerged precisely in response to the horrific wars of religion that engulfed Western Europe in the sixteenth and seventeenth centuries. In order to resolve the unending battle between Catholics and Protestants over what the established church should be, liberals suggested the radical idea that there should not be any established church at all. They promoted the principle of the separation of church and state, according to which the state would neither promote nor hinder any particular religious group, so long as they all respected a common rule of law. Religion would be 'privatized'. Churches would be redefined as voluntary associations in civil society, and religious membership would be based on individual choice. Churches would grow or shrink in accordance with their ability to gain and maintain the voluntary adherence of individual members.

This model has proven remarkably successful in the West. Not only has it pacified re-ligious conflict, virtually eliminating religious differences as a source of political violence or instability, but it has done so in a way consistent with the two basic values that, according to Rawls, define a liberal conception of justice—namely, freedom and equality. It respects indi-vidual freedom since it respects freedom of conscience and protects the right of individuals to maintain or change their religious membership. It also respects equality since all religions are treated in an equal, non-discriminatory way. The state does not award or penalize people for their religious affiliation.

Not surprisingly, liberals have wanted to apply the same model to other areas of di-versity, in particular ethnocultural diversity. They have hoped to create a similar separation between state and ethnocultural groups. There should be no official or established culture; no public support for the culture, practices or identity of any particular group. Each ethnocul-tural group would grow or shrink in accordance with the free choices of individuals in civil society to maintain or change their ethnocultural allegiances and practices.

While this is an attractive model in theory, it cannot work in practice, and language is its Achilles' heel. There is no possibility of 'privatizing' language issues. The state must decide what will be the language(s) of public administration, the courts, the bureaucracy, the army, public schools, public media, road signs, town names and so on. And whichever language is chosen will obviously fare much better than those languages which are not chosen and thereby relegated to private life. State decisions about the language of public institutions are, therefore, *de facto* decisions about which linguistic groups will grow and which will diminish.

This is obviously in tension with the usual liberal conception of freedom and equality. This is clearest in countries where there is only one official language. In such countries, the state provides neither linguistic choice nor linguistic equality. Individuals have no choice about the language they use to communicate with public institutions, and there is no equality in the treatment accorded to different linguistic groups.

There can be a greater degree of linguistic choice and linguistic equality where the state recognizes two or more official languages and allows individuals to choose which they will use when communicating with public institutions. However, there are practical limits on the number of languages that can be recognized in this way. No state offers individuals an unlimited range of choices regarding the language they can use in public institutions. Indeed, most liberal democracies historically have been reluctant to adopt more than one official language.

We can see now why liberals have been embarrassed to discuss language policy. According to the standard liberal framework, the state achieves freedom and equality by taking a 'hands-off' attitude to diversity, by privatizing diversity and leaving it to the free choice of individuals in civil society. In the sphere of language, however, liberal states do not take a hands-off attitude, but rather select one or more languages as privileged languages and force citizens to use them when communicating with public institutions. State language policies directly contradict the usual liberal framework for accommodating diversity. Liberals have said it is a violation of freedom and equality to have an official state church, yet they have historically endorsed the idea of an official state language.

While most liberals have simply ignored this apparent contradiction, some have attempted to explain and justify it, typically in one of two ways. One strategy is to trivialize the issue, by claiming that language (unlike religion) has only instrumental value. Whereas people attach intrinsic importance to being able to pursue their particular religion, language is simply a tool for communicating one's thoughts and feelings. Since people's interest in language is simply that it enables one to communicate with others, people will only value any particular language insofar as it improves their communicative reach.

On this view, everyone who lives in a linguistically divided society has a common interest in converging on a single public language, since everyone will thereby gain greater communicative reach, which is the only reason to value language in the first place. Hence, imposing a common language cannot be seen to harm linguistic minorities, since they gain a more valuable tool of communication. Seen in this light, the choice of a common language is like the choice of which side of the road to drive on. Some people have an initial preference to drive on the right, while others will want to drive on the left, perhaps because they were taught that way. But these initial preferences are trivial compared to the overriding interest in having a common rule of the road. What really matters is that you can drive safely from

A to B without fear of oncoming cars; whether you drive on the left or the right should be a matter of relative indifference, at least so long as any transitional costs are covered (e.g., if a person originally owned a left-drive car, he or she should have the costs of re-fitting it to a right-hand drive covered).

So too, some argue, with language. Some speakers will have an initial preference to speak language A; others will have an initial preference to speak B, because of the way they were raised. But these initial preferences are trivial compared to the overriding interest in ensuring that there is a single language that maximizes one's communicative reach. What matters is the possibility to communicate thoughts and feelings with as many people as possible; whether one communicates them in language A or B should be a matter of relative indifference—again, so long as one-time transitional costs in learning the common language are covered.

On this view, then, imposing a common language is very different from imposing a common religion and closer to the case of imposing common road rules. Whereas imposing a common religion would restrict people's ability to pursue what they believe to be of intrinsic value (e.g., their beliefs about virtue, God and salvation), imposing a common language only affects people's ability to use something of instrumental value. Moreover, it does so in a way that actually offers better communicative tools. It is therefore a matter of promoting a common interest, not privileging one group arbitrarily over another.

This is a popular strategy for resolving the liberal conundrum about language policy, but the essays in this collection show that is not an accurate description of the real world of language conflict. In none of the case studies were people motivated solely by instrumental considerations of communicative reach. On the contrary, both majorities and minorities manifest a deep commitment to maintaining their own language, even at the expense of greater communicative reach. Czechs and Slovenians resisted pressure to give up their small language community and linguistically assimilate into the huge German-speaking world; Estonians, Latvians, Lithuanians, Tatars and Armenians resisted pressure to give up their small language community and assimilate into the huge Russian-speaking world.

Of course, the strength of this commitment varies across individuals and groups. Some individual members are willing to abandon their mother tongue and assimilate, typically for reasons of individual advancement. Yet in virtually all of the case studies, political parties or political movements dedicated to preserving national languages and resisting assimilation into much larger language communities have been able to gain enduring popular support.[3]

This suggests that people's interests in language go far beyond the single simple interest of communicative reach. And the studies in this volume give some hints at this wider range of interests. Many people view the maintenance of their language as crucial to their very survival as a nation and their claims to national self-determination. If Slovenians had linguistically assimilated into German, say, or Serbo-Croatian, on what basis could they continue to demand their own state or self-governing republic? If minorities linguistically assimilate, on what

---

[3] The only exception in these chapters might be the Roma, where the level of popular support within the Roma community for linguistic retention is difficult to gauge.

basis can they claim their own schools or cultural institutions? Maintaining a language is often the basis on which claims for political and institutional autonomy are made.[4]

Also, preserving the language is often seen as necessary to preserve the historic achievements of their culture, such as its literature and arts. If a group linguistically assimilates, who will read its old poets and chroniclers? Who will even remember the history of the group? Preserving the language is also often seen as a way of maintaining inter-generational links with one's ancestors and honouring those who fought to preserve the language in the past. In these and other ways, language becomes a key symbol of national identity, and protecting it becomes almost a sacred duty.

So when a language group fights to preserve its language, it is never just preserving a tool for communication: It is also preserving certain political claims, autonomous institutions, cultural products and practices, and national identities. Conversely, of course, when the state attempts to impose a dominant language on minorities, it is never just imposing a language: It is also imposing a set of political and cultural claims about the primacy of the state, the need for common rules and centralized institutions, the need to learn a new history and literature and the construction of new nation-state loyalties and identities. Language disputes are never just disputes over language.

In short, the view that language is simply valued as a tool for achieving communicative reach is not plausible. There are many other values and interests at stake. We could say, perhaps, that people often attach intrinsic importance to the use of their own language (Réaume, 2000). But it might be more accurate to say that even if language only has instrumental value, it nonetheless serves a wide range of values, beyond simply communicative reach. It also serves as an instrument for reinforcing group loyalties and solidarities, affirming identities and histories, reproducing culture and advancing political and institutional claims.[5] It is therefore quite rational for people to invest time and resources on language preservation, even if this yields no gain in communicative efficiency.

Once we recognize that language serves these multiple functions, the liberal strategy of trivializing language issues as simply technical questions of communicative reach will not work. Language policies impact on a wide range of people's interests, and assimilationist policies that promote a minority's communicative reach might nonetheless harm many other legitimate interests and thereby violate principles of justice.

However, there is a second liberal strategy for justifying the imposition of a single official language, one which relies precisely on the fact that language is connected to issues of loyalty and identity. According to some liberals, it is precisely because language helps to define

---

[4]   As Baubock notes, while nationalists typically claim that self-government is needed in order to protect a language and culture, the reverse is often more accurate: namely, nationalists seek to preserve a distinct language in order to justify claims to self-government (Baubock, 2000).

[5]   This tenacious commitment to maintaining national languages is sometimes said to be distinctive to the 'ethnic' nationalisms of Central and Eastern Europe. But in fact, the same phenomenon is found in the West. Here, too, both majorities and national minorities have historically resisted pressure to assimilate into larger language communities. Moreover, as in the East, national groups in the West have attempted to guarantee the survival of their language into the indefinite future by, for example, enshrining its official status in the constitution, and requiring immigrants to learn the language as a condition of citizenship.

national identities and group loyalties that democracy requires linguistic homogenization. As John Stuart Mill puts it, free institutions are "next to impossible" in a multilingual state:

> Among a people without fellow-feelings, especially if they read and speak differ-
> ent languages, the united public opinion necessary to the workings of representa-
> tive institutions cannot exist . . . [It] is in general a necessary condition of free
> institutions that the boundaries of government should coincide in the main with
> those of nationalities (Mill, 1972: 230, 233).

Needless to say, this approach is diametrically opposed to the first liberal strategy. The first strategy says that imposing a common language is permissible because language is simply a neutral medium for communicating pre-existing feelings and thoughts and hence does not privilege any particular set of beliefs or interests. By contrast, Mill's argument for imposing a common language is precisely that it is a way of 'shaping' people's feelings and 'creating' certain opinions. According to Mill, linguistic homogenization will help to create feelings of national identity and trust, shared sympathies and loyalties, and thereby eliminate any com-peting claims on people's political allegiances. A common language is not simply a neutral vehicle for debating who should exercise sovereignty or who has rights of self-government. Rather, imposing a common language resolves these questions, by creating a 'we' that is united as a single political community with a common sense of nationhood.

This is another ingenious theoretical attempt to get around the problem of official languages. Unlike the first strategy, it does not deny that imposing a common language in-volves privileging a dominant group over minority groups, with the ultimate consequence of diminishing the latter's ability to retain its own culture, history, national identity, autonomous institutions and political aspirations. Rather, it simply asserts that this sort of privileging is a regrettable but inevitable step in achieving a functioning liberal democracy. On this view, we cannot apply liberal tests of freedom and equality to the initial choice of an official language. Rather, we can only apply those tests after we first create a functioning democratic state, and this requires linguistic homogenization. Linguistic homogenization is then interpreted as prior to, and a precondition for, applying liberal justice.

The difficulty with this argument, long noted by sociolinguists, is that it does not seem to be true. There are many multilingual democracies. Indeed, some of the oldest and most prosperous democracies are multilingual, from Switzerland to Belgium, Finland and Canada. The multilingual constitution in Spain today is much more democratic than the monolingual constitution of Franco. In any event, even if a common public language is either necessary or desirable for democracy, this does not yet tell us about the appropriate level of public support for minority languages. In most of the case studies in this volume, minority groups accept the requirement that they should learn the majority language and use it in central political insti-tutions. They simply want the right to use their own language in certain spheres or at local levels, such as minority-language schools, bilingual signs, local town councils or minority-language media. They view this as supplementing, not replacing, the need to speak the official language in central political institutions. Mill's argument provides no clear guidance for resolving such claims.

In short, the orthodox liberal view about accommodating diversity has run into a conceptual dead end in the area of language policy. The original idea that the state should privatize diversity, relegating it to civil society and individual choice, is impossible in the case of language. Attempts to evade this problem by pretending that language is merely of instrumental value, or that a common language is a precondition of democracy, are unpersuasive. In the end, all of these liberal strategies simply avoid, rather than really address, the normative issues of justice raised by language policies.

There is increasing recognition, therefore, that liberal theory requires a new approach to issues of language. We need to recognize that people have a wide range of interests relating to language and that justice requires a fair accommodation of these interests. What would such a fair accommodation involve? If we apply the basic liberal norms of freedom and equality, the goal, presumably, would be to provide equitable treatment by the state of all linguistic groups, while preserving basic individual liberties, insofar as possible.

We are still at the first stages of trying to sort out what this would mean in practice. One way to develop such a theory would be to apply Rawls' own method of the "veil of ignorance". According to Rawls, we can identify what justice requires in a given situation by imagining that we do not know which position in the society we will occupy, and asking what rules we would adopt under this condition of uncertainty. In the past, Rawls and his followers have applied this method to ask what rules of justice we would choose for society if we did not know whether we were going to be born talented or infirm, white or black, male or female. However, of the several thousand articles written on Rawls, it is difficult to think of a single example where this method has been applied to the case of language.

Assume, then, that you do not know which linguistic group you will be born into, although you are aware of basic sociological facts, including the way that language policy can be used to promote or hinder a range of interests. What rules of linguistic justice would you choose for society? Without going into the details of Rawls' theory, he argues that a rational person will choose equality between the various positions in society, except where equality works to the benefit of the least well-off.

What would this require in the case of language? Presumably the default assumption is that all languages spoken in society are given an equal public status, and we then ask which deviations from that equal status work to everyone's benefit, including those whose language would then have a less-than-equal status. For example, some language groups may be too small or dispersed to be able to support in practice the full range of public institutions operating in their own language. If so, it would be to their own benefit to give up the right to such mother-tongue institutions and demand instead special help in integrating into institutions operating in the dominant language. Similarly, it may be in everyone's interest to have one or two languages singled out as *linguae francae* to enable interethnic communication. If so, it would be in minorities' interests to give up full equality of languages and to accept that one or two languages will be chosen for certain purposes as a public *lingua franca*, while still preserving as many of their own autonomous institutions as possible.

Obviously, there will be great difficulty in using this method to generate concrete policy recommendations. In order to determine which inequalities in the status of languages work to everyone's benefit, we need to know quite a bit about the size and territorial concentration of the various languages, their mutual comprehensibility and so on. But it is probably safe to say that this approach would lead to a much more ample scheme of minority-language rights than we see in most countries in Central and Eastern Europe, or indeed in the West.

In most countries, the default position is that there is only one language used in national public institutions, and any deviations or exemptions from that rule need to be justified. In the Rawlsian model, by contrast, the default position would presumably be equality of status for all languages, and it is deviations from equality that need to be justified (and justified in terms of benefits to those whose language has a lesser public status). The result is likely to be some sort of official multilingualism, particularly for those language groups that are large and concentrated enough to support a wide range of public institutions.

Some liberals find Rawls' method too vague and speculative. But we can find some real world circumstances that share key features of Rawls' approach. The crucial point of the veil of ignorance, for Rawls, is that it prevents people from using their unequal bargaining power to manipulate the results in their favour. Since people behind the veil of ignorance do not know which position they will occupy, or how much bargaining power they will possess in it, they have to choose principles of justice based on impartial concern for all of the different positions in society (since they may end up occupying any one of them).

There is no veil of ignorance in the real world. But there are circumstances where there is something like equality of bargaining power between different groups. The resulting negotiations are therefore likely to embody something close to equal concern for the members of both groups. For example, consider the bargaining between francophones and anglophones in Canada in 1867, when the country was first formed as a federation of former British colonies. Despite the British military victories over the French that had, in the second half of the eighteenth century, resulted in the British takeover of Canada, neither side had the power to impose a settlement on the other, so genuine consent was required. The same is true of negotiations more recently between the Flemish and Walloons in Belgium, or even between Castilians and Catalans in Spain during the transition to democracy. In all of these cases, no side was capable of dictating a solution, so something close to bargaining in good faith took place.

We can view this as a real-world test for the justice of language policies—i.e., that they would be agreed to by all parties under conditions of parity of bargaining power. Any proposal which could not achieve free consent under conditions of equal bargaining power is likely to be unjust.

If we now examine the outcome in such cases of consensual agreement between linguistic groups under conditions of parity of bargaining power, we see some common features. In all of these cases, we see some form of official status for the minority language, along with guarantees of a wide range of autonomous institutions operating in that language, typically through some form of territorial autonomy. That seems to be a precondition for linguistic groups to consent to new constitutional arrangements, wherever they have been given the choice. Since liberalism is premised on the view that political authority should be based on consent, this is a powerful argument for liberals to take minority-language rights seriously.

Here again, we need to reframe the question of linguistic justice. On this view, the question is not whether deviations from official monolingualism are justified. Rather the question is under what terms linguistic minorities would voluntarily consent to the constitution of the larger society.

If this is indeed the correct interpretation of the liberal conception of linguistic justice, then it seems clear that we are very far from achieving linguistic justice in most countries of

Central and Eastern Europe (or indeed in most Western countries). As the studies in this book show, post-communist states remain firmly wedded to the view that a 'normal' state has just one official language, and the burden of proof rests on anyone who demands 'exceptions' from this. Moreover, any such exceptions tend to be very modest, relating primarily to mother-tongue media and elementary education, not to recognition as a co-official language and not to the establishment of territorial autonomy.

In those few cases where more robust forms of minority-language rights have been adopted, they typically have arisen as a result, not of good-faith democratic negotiation, but of civil war in which the minority simply seized the levers of power (as in Bosnia, Kosovo, Abkhazia or Nagorno-Karabakh). Even the more modest forms of minority-language rights we find in peaceful countries have typically only arisen as a result of international pressure from the EU and the OSCE (as in Slovakia and Estonia), or as a result of concern for kin minorities abroad.[6] It is difficult to find any case in the region where the state's policy towards minorities was significantly influenced by considerations of liberal justice.

On the contrary, the studies in this collection reveal repeatedly that the underlying concern behind state language policies is not justice, but security. States in the region fear that granting minority-language rights, however 'fair' this might seem, is too dangerous, since it may lead to irredentist claims. It may encourage linguistic minorities to think that they 'own' a part of the country and therefore have a right to choose to break away from the state and join or rejoin their kin-state. This concern about irredentism arises in several of the studies (Ukraine, the Baltic states, Slovakia, Romania). Interestingly, however, it does not arise in the West, and this may be an important factor in explaining why minority-language rights tend to be more controversial in Central and Eastern Europe. States are unlikely to extend justice as defined here to groups which they view as disloyal and security threats. Indeed, the studies in the collection strongly suggest that considerations of liberal justice for linguistic minorities cannot take root until more basic fears about loyalty and security are somehow addressed.[7]

2. NATURE AND PRINCIPLES OF POLICY ANALYSIS

In the preceding section, we have reviewed the core aspects of an approach based on normative political theory, which stresses the reasons for adopting one or another rule to guide policy decisions. It should by now be clear that it differs from the 'linguistic human rights' approach in which claims to certain rights are usually postulated rather than reviewed critically. It is also distinct from the purely legal approach to language politics and policy, which mainly focuses on the compatibility of legal provisions with other, higher-order provisions,

---

[6]   See Roter's discussion of how Slovenia extended minority language rights to Italians and Hungarians in the hope that this would put pressure on neighbouring countries to extend minority-language rights to ethnic Slovenians. The same is true about Hungary's seemingly generous policy towards its minorities. The underlying motivation of the policy may in fact rest less on a concern for minorities within Hungary than on the intention to set a benchmark for the treatment of Hungarian minorities in other countries.

[7]   For further elaboration of this 'security vs. justice' problem, see Kymlicka and Opalski (2001).

but does not analyse why society should (as part of a coherent system of norms and values) do what it does—or should do something different. The normative political theory approach therefore raises central questions and provides the necessary concepts for assessing issues of language politics and language policy. Yet, one more perspective is required to complete this assessment, namely, the policy analysis perspective.

This perspective is conceptually located 'after', or 'downstream from' the others. In one way or another, the various approaches mentioned in the preceding paragraph address the question of what society should do, and therefore they revolve around norms. Normative political theory is particularly careful at establishing 'why' certain courses of action may be said to be more justified than others. However, after such issues are settled (even provisionally), it is also important to study 'how' society's goals can be reached, and if some way of reaching them is preferable to other ways. Handling this question in an orderly manner is the main contribution of policy analysis.

Despite its emphasis on 'how', policy analysis does not ignore the question of 'why'. However, it is approached in a perspective that is fundamentally different from that of those previously mentioned. Generally, the criterion for adopting a certain policy is that it promises to increase 'welfare' (or, equivalently, citizens' satisfaction). There is no *a priori* notion of what is actually welfare-enhancing; a policy analyst will in principle abstain from any judgement on the matter. Whereas moral considerations are central to all the other perspectives, they are peripheral in the policy analysis perspective. In line with the liberal tradition of political theory, mainstream policy analysis assumes that citizens know what they need, and that nobody is entitled to tell them what is good or bad. However, political theory analyses the contents and coherence of these norms, while the policy analysis perspective will usually take them as given—and hence keep well away from the question of which course of action is morally superior.

Since the concept of welfare can harbour different, possibly incompatible, desires, it is of limited help in formulating the overall goals of a policy, precisely because it is up to social actors to say what measures will increase that welfare, whatever these measures may be. However, the virtue of the policy analysis approach lies with the fact that it provides a logically clear structure for comparing alternative policies, while maintaining a profoundly liberal view of the role of social actors as legitimate masters of their own destiny. As regards practical usefulness, the main contribution of the policy analysis approach is that it helps to shift attention to a different plane and to address questions which all the preceding perspectives leave largely in the dark. More specifically, it helps to compare (and select between) different ways of reaching a certain goal—which will have been set as the result of a 'political', rather than 'policy' process.

There can be little doubt that this opens up a wide range of relevant questions. More specifically, it is necessary to examine *how* goals are to be reached, since not all ways of achieving these goals are equal. Some ways are more effective than others; some are more costly than others. In fact, the problem is often to reach certain goals as effectively as possible, but also as cheaply as possible. It generally proves very difficult to meet both requirements at the same time, and some degree of arbitration will usually be necessary. Finally, even if effectiveness and economy of means can be reconciled, the policies applied to reach these goals need to be reconsidered critically in light of a general principle of policy implementation. This principle is that of 'democracy' and raises the following questions: Is the policy truly democratic, not only in its *ex ante* aims and *ex post* results, but also in its actual operations? Or does it in fact appear as a technocratic device from which citizens (even though they may agree with the policy) are excluded?

The application of policy analysis approaches to language is a relatively recent phenomenon, and it is intimately connected with the development of language policy (or 'language planning') as a full-fledged area of specialization. Some authors make a sharp distinction between language policy and language planning, but in the more recent literature, this distinction appears to be fading, and no analytical distinction will be made here between those two terms.

Following Ricento's (2000) account, we may describe this field as having gone through three historical phases since the early 1960s. In the first phase, language policy was largely concerned with questions of decolonization. It endorsed relatively simple concepts of 'progress' and 'efficiency', according to which countries gaining independence from former colonial powers had to pick a European language (usually that of the former colonizer) as a means to overcome linguistic fragmentation, as well as the 'inadequate' level of development (lexical or otherwise) of their languages. In a second phase, specialists of language policy adopted more critical representations, stressing in particular the fact that all forms of language use (and hence of language policy) are socially embedded and enmeshed with power issues. Language policy models are therefore liable to carry limitations (which may, in fact, have had as much to do with the discourse in which they were embedded as with the courses of action they were actually inclined to recommend); in either case, such limitations were liable to preclude their applicability. In a third phase, which originated in the mid-1980s, the emphasis shifted again, this time towards ways of accommodating various new issues. It is not clear that there is any common pattern linking together these 'new issues'; however, examples are many, such as the effects of large-scale migration, or a more acute concern for the accelerating rate of extinction of small languages, which has been likened by some to a loss in biodiversity. At the same time, part of this discourse branched off into the 'discourse of linguistic human rights', which we have attempted to characterize at the beginning of this chapter.

Throughout the history of the development of language planning, some attempts have been made at linking up this field of research and action with more or less formal policy analysis procedures as outlined above. The first explicit call to this end is attributed to Jernudd (1971), opening up a line of argument consistently pursued through the years (see Jernudd, 1983, 2001). However, Jernudd's work constitutes something of an exception. Although sociolinguists and applied linguists have produced a considerable amount of literature on language policy or language planning, sometimes in books whose title uses the latter expression (e.g., Cooper, 1989; Kaplan and Baldauf, 1997), their emphasis is clearly on language 'politics', rather than 'policy' (e.g., Ricento, 2000; Schiffman, 1996). Keeping things simple, we may say that policy focuses more on implementation (and hence on 'how' something is done), whereas politics focuses more on the process whereby objectives are chosen. The difference between politics and policy so defined is certainly not always clear-cut; nonetheless, there is a tension between the two, and this tension between language politics and language policy (with a clear orientation towards the former) is probably instrumental in explaining why, according to Ricento's account, much of contemporary research on language politics and policy has embraced the discourse of "linguistic human rights" (e.g., Skutnabb-Kangas, 2000), leaving large tracts of language policy analysis to others.

In fact, much of the specific language policy analysis work is due to economists (Breton, 1978; Vaillancourt, 1978; Grin, 1996, 1999a, 1999b; Grin and Vaillancourt, 1999), or to political scientists (Pool, 1991; de Swaan, 2001). Recent work drawing on language economics as well as policy analysis is being used to evaluate language policy proposals *ex ante* as well as the *ex post* implementation of language policies, in particular in Western Europe (Grin, 2000; Grin and Moring, 2002). Much of this literature, taking the set of broad policy aims as a given derived from (earlier) political debate, focuses on matters of effective, cost-effective and democratic policies, whether in their selection, design or implementation.

The essays collated in this volume generally overlook these policy matters almost entirely. To the extent that the focus of this volume has deliberately been set on 'language politics', it is natural that politics rather than policy should be at the forefront. However, one would also expect issues of implementation to emerge, even as a second-rank concern. In this perspective, it is striking that so little thought appears to be given by decision-makers to matters of effectiveness and cost, which can only have a determining influence on the destiny of the languages which a legal act intends to support—or, on the contrary, to keep at bay. For example, the often rocky story of language legislation in the former Soviet Republics, whether in Armenia or in the Baltic region, seems to have developed with rather little concern for comparing the direct and indirect costs (meaning 'public' and 'private' costs, as well as 'market' and 'non-market' costs) of language policy alternatives. In the same way, the notion of 'effectiveness' hardly registers in the development of promotional policies for languages like Tatar and Kalmyk.

At a time when the likely consequences of other proposed forms of legislation (which may pertain to transportation, energy supply or education) are increasingly subjected to detailed evaluations, this oversight is surprising. Therefore, it seems safe to assume that in the future, the language politics debate will, with increasing frequency, call on concepts and analyses fed by a policy analysis approach. Such an evolution can already be detected, for example through the fact that a novel instrument such as the European Charter for Regional or Minority Languages does not even mention the word 'rights' (except in its Preamble) and then focuses entirely on practical measures in favour of these languages.

Language policy is only beginning to be seen as a form of public policy. This recognition is slowed down by the fact that most of the actors involved in language matters (whether they act as language activists, as nationalists trying to establish the claims of an ethnic movement, as national politicians or as officers of international organizations) are predominantly trained in law or international relations. It also reflects the intrinsically political nature of the issues at hand (which clearly are not confined to technical aspects). Interestingly, and even though it is common to hear that language policy is 'expensive' (particularly, experience suggests, in the eyes of majority language users assessing programmes for the promotion of minority languages), closer examination reveals that language policy is, in fact, relatively cheap. The costs of language policy is a matter on which one often hears wild (and usually unsubstantiated) claims, although the few cases where estimates have been carried out reveal rather modest figures. For example, moving from a monolingual to a bilingual education system implies an additional expenditure of less than five per cent to the education system; the cost of Quebec's very extensive language legislation (including the value of the time spent by managers who have to design and implement a plan to ensure that internal communication in their firm can take place in French) stands at around 0.48 per cent of provincial GDP; the supposedly frightening expenditure on translation to and from all the official languages of the EU currently stands at around € 1.82 per resident and year (Grin, 2003). It is true that the issue of language-policy costs has not yet been the object of systematic comparative study, but available evidence clearly indicates that costs are much lower than is commonly believed. If this were not the case, one can safely assume that much more attention would for a long time have been devoted to public policy analyses of language policies.

3. IMPLICATIONS FOR THE STUDY OF LANGUAGE POLICY

We can see from this brief survey that the study of language policy requires decidedly interdisciplinary treatment. Any approach that focuses only on sociolinguistic or legal aspects will fail to capture the full complexity of the issue, as will any approach that focuses only on normative theories of liberalism or nationalism. Such unidisciplinary approaches will be incapable of generating the types of policy recommendations that are needed.

One way to think about integrating the full range of issues would be to try to systematically analyse the sorts of constraints that impinge on language policy. States make language policy, but not under conditions of their own choosing. We can get a better picture of the choices facing countries if we review the various legal, international, political, economic, demographic, historical and cultural constrains that they face.

One important constraint which reappears continually in this volume is the emerging framework of international law regarding language rights, particularly as codified in the Council of Europe's 1992 Charter for Regional or Minority Languages, its 1995 Framework Convention for the Protection of National Minorities and in various guidelines developed under the aegis of the OSCE High Commissioner on National Minorities, such as the 1998 Oslo Recommendations Regarding the Linguistic Rights of National Minorities. These supranational norms are not legally enforceable, in the sense that no international court has the authority to overturn domestic laws or policies that violate these norms. Some commentators therefore describe these as 'soft law', to indicate their status as something more than mere exhortation but less than enforceable law. Yet it is clear that for most countries in the region, these are indeed hard constraints on policy choices. Adherence to pan-European norms is necessary for countries that wish to 'rejoin Europe' and to be accepted into the EU and NATO. Post-communist countries are subject to intense monitoring and diplomatic pressure to comply with these norms. For example, as the studies in this volume indicate, Slovakia and Estonia have retreated from policies that were judged incompatible with these norms. But the idea of 'international standards' is part of the rhetoric used in all countries to either defend or criticize particular policies.

This means that a legal analysis of the text of international declarations on language rights certainly is of great importance. These international standards are not always clear and have been changing regularly in recent years, so an up-to-date analysis of international law is an important starting-point for understanding policy choices (see, for example, Dunbar, 2001; Henrard, 2000; de Varennes, 1996).

However, in the end, these international standards set only minimal limits on domestic policies. An exception must be made for the Charter, because its emphasis is not on 'rights', but on practical measures that may be adopted under a policy of minority-language protection and promotion.[8] To the extent that they focus on rights, however, the 'other' legal texts mentioned primarily protect certain 'negative' rights—that is, the right of members of linguistic minorities to publish their own magazines, establish their own private schools or form their own cultural organizations, and the right not to be discriminated against on the basis of one's mother tongue. These rights can be seen as part and parcel of traditional individual rights to freedom of speech, freedom of the press, freedom of association and non-discrimination. International declarations are far less clear on the extent of 'positive' rights—for example, the right to public funding of minority-language schools, or of minority-language radio/television, the right to use one's language in dealing with public officials, the right to have judicial proceedings in one's language or to receive government documents in one's language or the right to official language status. Yet it is precisely these 'positive' rights that are at the heart of most language conflicts in Eastern Europe (and around the world).

As a result, existing international norms are clearly inadequate to resolve most of the disputes discussed in this volume. Some commentators have pushed to strengthen these international standards and/or to reinterpret them so as to be more responsive to the demands of linguistic minorities. One version of this movement is the campaign for 'linguistic human rights', associated with some high-profile sociolinguists (on this matter, see, for example, Skutnabb-Kangas and Phillipson, 1994).

It is doubtful, however, that international law (to the extent that it is formulated in terms of 'rights', which, let us repeat, is not the case for the Charter) will ever be able to do more than specify the most minimal of standards. The members of various linguistic groups have different needs, desires and capacities, depending on their size, territorial concentration and historic roots. A set of guidelines that is satisfactory to a small, dispersed immigrant group will not satisfy a large, concentrated historic minority. The right to public funding for mother-tongue university education, for example, might be meaningless for the former, but might be seen as essential to the latter. Any attempt to define a set of rights applying to all linguistic groups, no matter how small and dispersed, is likely to end up focusing on relatively modest claims. For example, the 'linguistic human rights' movement has focused primarily on securing a universal right for publicly-funded mother-tongue primary education. This is not trivial, but it falls far short of what is at stake in many linguistic conflicts around the world, where groups are fighting over the use of languages in public administration, higher education and public media. Both majority and minority groups want much more than is guaranteed in international law.

---

[8]   The European Charter for Regional or Minority Languages attempts to deal with this problem of the variable situations of minority groups by adopting an *à la carte* approach, which offers a menu of 68 measures, from which a minimum of 35 must be adopted. Ideally, the measures chosen from the menu would be tailored to match the situation of different minority groups. However, nothing in the Charter requires states to adopt more robust language rights for more sizeable/concentrated groups, and many states in Eastern Europe have refused to do so, for reasons discussed below.

In short, while international norms may constitute 'hard' constraints on countries in the region, they nonetheless leave much room for domestic policy choices. This is the space for 'language politics' in which the members of various groups stake claims for their own language and contest the claims of other linguistic groups.

In other fields of public policy, this sort of domestic politics can often be explained and predicted through rational-choice models based on people's self-interest and bargaining power. It is clear from the studies in this volume, however, that language politics is considerably more complicated. People's sense of their legitimate entitlements in terms of language, and of the rightful claims of other language groups, is heavily influenced by larger systems of values, beliefs and political ideologies.

The most powerful of these, in the post-communist countries of Central and Eastern Europe and the former Soviet Union, is the ideology of nationalism. This ideology gives many people a sense of what is 'normal' for a state and what is the 'proper place' for minorities. For the titular national group within each state, nationalist ideology defines a 'normal' state as a state with one official language—'one state, one nation, one language'. In this nationalist image, other language groups are (more or less) tolerated if they 'stay in their place'—that is, if they confine their claims to elementary schools, cultural associations and churches, but do not make any claims to share public space or state power.[9]

The power of this nationalist ideology is seen in several of the studies. It defined several governments' initial objectives when adopting language laws during and immediately after the collapse of communism. This was true not only of countries with a high degree of ethnolinguistic homogeneity, like Slovenia, but even in countries where this monolingual objective was radically at odds with existing language use (e.g., in Ukraine, Estonia, Romania, Armenia or Slovakia). In these countries, sizeable minorities (and even some members of the titular group) were accustomed to using another language when dealing with public institutions. Yet even here, the power of nationalist ideology was such that the 'one state, one language' model became the default position, so that linguistic minorities who demanded positive language rights were seen as asking for 'special' treatment or for some sort of privileged deviation from the norm.

The centrality of nationalist ideology is evident not only in the initial policy goals in these countries, but also in the depth of people's emotional response to minority-language claims. For example, it is considered normal and natural that ethnic Hungarians in most parts of Romania have to speak Romanian when interacting with public officials, but it is apparently considered a 'humiliation' for ethnic Romanians to have to speak Hungarian when interacting with public officials in villages where Hungarians form a clear majority. For Romanians to have to speak Hungarian is not just an inconvenience or cost, it is an insult: How is it possible that we have to speak another language in 'our' country?

Much of the 'language politics' described in this volume can be seen as attempts by linguistic minorities to fight against the power of this nationalist ideology, and they have had some success. However, the extent to which titular groups have been willing to accommodate

---

[9]   For an interesting discussion of the idea of 'designated areas' where it is legitimate for minorities to express their identity, see Tsilevich (2001).

linguistic minorities varies. From a nationalist point of view, not all minorities are entitled to the same level of tolerance, since some are perceived as more of a threat to the nation than others. There are 'good' linguistic minorities who have proven their loyalty and 'bad' minorities who have historically collaborated with the enemies of the nation and/or have strong ties with foreign states (particularly those usually described as 'kin-states'). Thus, for example, Slovenia has been more sympathetic to the Hungarian minority than the German minority, since the former was seen as less collaborationist during the Second World War. By contrast, Romania has been more sympathetic to the claims of the German minority, since it is now seen as weak and passive and hence less of a threat than the much larger and potentially irredentist Hungarian minority. Attempts by Romanian authorities to satisfy various smaller linguistic minorities, like the Germans, can be interpreted as a tactic to paint the Hungarians as selfish, extremist and disloyal. Similarly, Estonian authorities have tried to satisfy various smaller linguistic groups as a way of ensuring that they do not side with the powerful Russian minority.

We cannot begin to understand language politics without a sense of how these historical and geopolitical factors are perceived and interpreted through the lens of nationalist ideologies. Nationalism provides not only a picture of the desired goal—the construction of a unitary nation-state—but also a filter for identifying which minorities are a threat to that goal, and hence which minorities are to be generously pampered, which are to be merely tolerated and which are to be actively suppressed.

Of course, it is not just the titular group that is affected by nationalist ideology. Minority groups too may be inspired by the goal of seceding and forming their own unitary nation-state, or of (re)joining a neighbouring state. Alternatively, they may seek some form of confederation, as in Abkhazia or Trans-Dniester, in which they would in effect be a state within a state. In these cases, most members of the minority appear to share the same nationalist commitment to 'one state, one language' as the dominant group, but want to redraw state boundaries so that it will be their language which unifies the state. As one Macedonian leader is alleged to have said: "Why should I be a minority in your country when you can be a minority in mine?"

Even where these particular nationalist aspirations are absent, minorities may insist that they are entitled to a distinctive set of rights, not applicable to other linguistic minorities, in virtue of certain treaties or inherited practices, or, say, as compensation for historic injustice, or as the autochthonous group in a particular territory. They may even argue that their language is superior to the dominant language, and it would therefore be unreasonable to expect them to shift 'downwards' in their language use.[10]

What is striking about all of these claims and counter-claims is that they go beyond what could be considered the rational assertion or calculation of self-interest. They are deeply normative claims: They embody views about what is 'right' and 'proper', about what is 'owed to', or 'deserved by' particular groups. Very little of the debate is conducted in the vocabu-

---

[10]   For an interesting example, see Laitin's discussion of the different attitudes of ethnic Russians in Estonia compared to Kazakhstan. In the former case, the Russians have generally been willing to learn the titular language, which they view as "European" and "advanced", whereas they view the idea of learning Kazakh as "absurd", since it is "Asian" and "backward" (Laitin, 1998).

lary of utilitarian costs and benefits—even if the non-material kind is taken into account. Language policies are contested, not so much on the grounds that they cost too much, either for individual speakers or for society as a whole, but rather that they violate people's mental image of the appropriate status of particular languages and linguistic groups.

While the debate is normative, it is very different from the sort of normative liberal theory discussed in Section 1. In general, neither the titular group nor the linguistic minorities defend their claims by appealing to the basic principles of liberalism. People do not advocate particular language policies by saying that they maximize individual choice, or remedy involuntary inequalities in the distribution of resources, or respect the principle of state impartiality, or that they would be chosen from behind a Rawlsian "veil of ignorance".

This is not to say that the sorts of nationalist and historicist arguments invoked by both majorities and minorities are inherently illiberal or undemocratic. On the contrary, majorities and minorities are both quick to pledge their allegiance to liberal values. Both have learned and adopted the discourse of 'diversity' and 'multiculturalism' that has developed within the liberal West over the last two decades.[11] Yet, it is safe to say that the new discourse of liberal multiculturalism has not displaced the old discourse of national self-determination and historic entitlements. Nor have the two discourses been well-integrated: The former often seems to be simply tacked on to the latter, without any clear explanation of how they relate to each other.

Many transition countries are struggling to appear liberal and pluralistic, yet are unsure of the implications of these new concepts for issues of language policy or for their old 'one state, one language' ideology. This is hardly surprising since, as we have seen in Section 2, liberal political theorists have themselves been quite unclear on the topic. The diffusion of liberal multiculturalist ideas, combined with the emergence of new international norms, has undoubtedly served to soften the homogenizing tendencies of various countries in the region and helped to expand the designated areas where minorities can use their language. Yet it has not yet succeeded in articulating an alternative model of the state, or in displacing existing assumptions about what a 'normal' state looks like. To date, moves towards greater minority-language rights in post-communist Europe are still relatively modest reforms to what remains at its heart a nation-state model.[12]

So 'language politics', as analysed in these chapters, is a complicated mixture of factors, such as international law, history, demography and geopolitics, all of which are interpreted and filtered through a variety of ideological lenses, such as nationalism and liberal pluralism. Given the complexity of the issues and the contested nature of the interests and ideologies, it is not surprising that language politics remain controversial. There is rarely, if ever, full consensus on the appropriate policies.

However, decisions must be made, and policies adopted, even if only provisionally. This leads us to the final element of the analytical toolbox—namely, the field of policy analysis and

---

[11]   On the striking diffusion of this Western discourse of multiculturalism around the globe, see Cowan et al. (2001).

[12]   Put another way, despite the recent codification of international law and the diffusion of liberal multiculturalist ideals, multilingual federations like Switzerland, Belgium or Canada are still seen very much as aberrations or exceptions, not as the new norm to be followed.

the need for careful attention to the actual consequences of the policies adopted. Do language policies achieve the goals that legislators and bureaucrats intend? What are some of the costs and unintended consequences of these policies?

As we noted earlier, this issue has been surprisingly neglected in the literature to date. There has been very little attention to issues of policy implementation, and to ensuring that they meet familiar standards of effectiveness, cost-effectiveness and democratic participation. Governments have adopted policies that require use of the titular language, yet in many cases little attention has been given to the incentives needed for citizens to shift their language use, or indeed whether it is even possible for citizens to do so (e.g., whether language training is actually available to the people who need it). Similarly, there is little attention to the pedagogical evidence about the conditions under which children or adults best learn languages.

A striking example was the insistence of the Romanian government that children in Hungarian-language elementary schools use the same textbooks to learn Romanian as children in Romanian-language schools. From a pedagogical point of view, it might be more effective to use textbooks geared specifically to students who are learning Romanian as a second language. However, the Romanian government simply rejected the idea that Romanian could ever be treated as a foreign language within Romania's own school system because this would have contradicted the nationalist equation between one state and one language. This example again shows the hegemonic power of nationalist ideologies. It was more important that the language policy symbolically reaffirm the nationalist image of the state than that it actually enable students to learn Romanian. The need for the former displaced or pre-empted questions about the latter.

Similarly, the decision to eliminate Russian-language secondary schools in Estonia is said to be motivated by a desire to ensure that Russian-speakers acquire better knowledge of Estonian. Yet, there has been little attempt to determine whether this is a necessary or effective way of encouraging knowledge of the official language. Arguably, the real motivation for the policy is not pedagogical effectiveness, but the desire to eliminate a set of institutions established under Soviet rule that contradict the nationalist image of a state characterized by a single, specific language.

The indifference to professed outcomes is also evident in state policies that attempt to 'purify' the official language of words drawn from foreign languages. Sociolinguists widely view such laws as misguided and ineffective, since the tendency to borrow words from other languages is a natural and normal part of linguistic evolution, and since it is impossible to stop individual speakers from using whatever words they find most convenient or accessible. Yet here again, we misunderstand the real aim of the policy if we suppose that it is intended to somehow improve understanding or communication. The aim, rather, is to reaffirm the national image of the state. If an official language contains too many foreign words, particularly in areas of modern technology and institutions, this might be seen as implying that the titular group is culturally backward and in need of political tutelage. The widespread use of Russian words in Armenian can be seen as implying that Armenia falls within the Russian 'sphere of influence', or simply as a humiliating reminder of the decades of Soviet rule. Even if 'foreign' words cannot be eliminated from people's actual day-to-day conversation, a language purification law can nonetheless symbolically reaffirm that the state belongs solely to the titular group and not to any 'foreign' powers or cultures.

In short, the lack of attention to outcomes is not necessarily an innocent oversight or intellectual failing. Rather, it reflects the fact that the explicit goals of a language policy are not always the only, or even the most important, goals. In countries where nationalist ideology defines the contours of public debate, a central if unstated goal of language policy is to preserve the image of the state as a nation-state. Within such an image, there should be no visible evidence of former colonizers or linguistic minorities—hence, their languages should be 'purified' or privatized. Policies which ostensibly aim to improve language training or language purity may fail to achieve these explicit aims, yet retain popular support because they succeed in achieving their unstated aim of rendering linguistic minorities invisible.

Given the complexity of the issues at hand, it should come as no surprise that overt and covert policy goals may be at variance with each other. This observation supports our conclusion that the study of state intervention in the area of language requires an interdisciplinary, yet integrated perspective, and it is our hope that the set of instruments developed in this chapter can contribute to this very necessary enterprise.

REFERENCES

Anderson, Alan B. (1990) "Comparative Analysis of Language Minorities: A Sociopolitical Framework". *Journal of Multilingual and Multicultural Development*, 11(1–2): 119–136.

Baubock, Rainer (2000) "Why Stay Together? A Pluralist Approach to Secession and Federation". In Will Kymlicka and Wayne Norman (eds.) *Citizenship in Diverse Societies*. Oxford: Oxford University Press, pp.366–394.

Breton, Albert (1978) "Nationalism and Language Policies". *Canadian Journal of Economics*, 11: 656–668.

Calvet, Louis Jean (1974) *Linguistique et Colonialisme*. Paris: Payot.

Cooper, Robert L. (1989) *Language Planning and Social Change*. Cambridge: Cambridge University Press.

Cowan, Jane K., Marie-Benedicte Dembour and Richard A. Wilson (eds.) (2001) *Culture and Rights: Anthropological Perspectives*. Cambridge: Cambridge University Press.

de Swaan, Abram (2001) *Words of the World. The Global Language System*. Cambridge: Polity Press.

de Varennes, Fernand (1996) *Language, Minorities and Human Rights*. The Hague: Martinus Nijhoff.

Dunbar, Robert (2001) "Minority Language Rights in International Law". *International and Comparative Law Quarterly*, 50(Part 1): 90–121.

Edwards, John (1990) "Notes for a Minority-Language Typology: Proce-dures and Justification". *Journal of Multilingual and Multicultural Development*, 11(1–2): 137–51.

Grin, François (ed.) (1996) *Economic Approaches to Language and Language Planning*. Theme issue of the *International Journal of the Sociology of Language*, 121.

Grin, François (1999a) "Language Planning as Diversity Management: Some Analytical Principles". *Plurilingua*, 21: 141–156.

Grin, François (1999b) "Economics". In Joshua Fishman (ed.) *Handbook of Language and Ethnic Identity*. Oxford: Oxford University Press, pp.9–24.

Grin, François (2000) *Evaluating Policy Measures for Minority Languages in Europe: Towards Effective, Cost-Effective and Democratic Implementation*. ECMI Report No. 6. Flensburg: European Centre for Minority Issues.

Grin, François (2003) "Language Planning and Economics". *Current Issues in Language Planning*, forthcoming.

Grin, François, Tom Moring *et al.* (2003) *Support for Minority Languages in Europe*. Report to the European Commission. 2000-1288/001-001 EDU-MLCEV.

Grin, François and François Vaillancourt (1999) *The Cost-Effectiveness Evaluation of Minority Language Policies. Case Studies on Wales, Ireland, and the Basque Country*. ECMI Monograph No. 2. Flensburg: European Centre for Minority Issues.

Guillorel, Hervé and Geneviève Koubi (1999) *Langues et Droits*. Brussels: Bruylant.

Henrard, Kristin (2000) *Devising an Adequate System of Minority Protection*. The Hague: Martinus Nijhoff.

Jernudd, Björn (1971) "Notes on Economic Analysis for Solving Language Problems". In Björn Jernudd and Joan Rubin (eds.) *Can Language Be Planned?* Honolulu: University Press of Hawaii, pp.236–276.

Jernudd, Björn (1983) "Evaluation of Language Planning. What Has the Last Decade Accomplished?" In Juan Cobarrubias and Joshua A. Fishman (eds.) *Progress in Language Planning*. Berlin: Mouton, pp.345–378.

Jernudd, Björn (2001) *Language Planning on the Eve of the 21st Century. Paper presented at the 2n Congrés Europeu sobre Planificació Lingüística*. Andorra, 14–16 November, 2001.

Kaplan, Robert B. and Richard B. Baldauf (1997) *Language Planning from Practice to Theory*. Clevedon: Multilingual Matters.

Kontra, Miklós, Robert Phillipson, Tove Skutnabb-Kangas and Tibor Várady (1999) *Language: A Right and a Resource*. Budapest: Central European University Press.

Kymlicka, Will (1989) *Liberalism, Community, and Culture*. Oxford: Clarendon Press.

Kymlicka, Will (1995a) *Multicultural Citizenship. A Liberal Theory of Minority Rights*. Oxford: Clarendon Press.

Kymlicka, Will (ed.) (1995b) *The Rights of Minority Cultures*. Oxford: Oxford University Press.

Kymlicka, Will and Magda Opalski (eds.) (2001) *Can Liberal Pluralism Be Exported? Western Political Theory and Ethnic Relations in Eastern Europe*. Oxford: Oxford University Press.

Laitin, David D. (1998) *Identity in Formation: The Russian-Speaking Populations in the Near-Abroad*. Ithaca, NY: Cornell University Press.

Mill, John Stuart (1972 [1861]) *Utilitarianism, Liberty, Representative Government*, edited by H. B. Acton. London: J.M. Dent.

Nelde, P., M. Strubell and G. Williams (1996) *Euromosaic: The Production and Reproduction of the Minority Language Groups in the EU*. Brussels: European Commission.

Patten, Alan (2001) "Political Theory and Language Policy". *Political Theory*, 29(5): 683–707.

Pool, Jonathan (1991) "The Official Language Problem". *American Political Science Review*, 85(2): 495–514.

Rawls, John (1971) *A Theory of Justice*. London: Oxford University Press.

Réaume, Denise G. (2000) "Official-Language Rights: Intrinsic Value and the Protection of Difference". In Will Kymlicka and Wayne Norman (eds.) *Citizenship in Diverse Societies*. Oxford: Oxford University Press, pp.245–272.

Ricento, Thomas (2000) "Historical and Theoretical Perspectives in Language Policy and Planning". In Thomas Ricento (ed.) *Ideology, Politics and Language Policies. Focus on English*. Amsterdam: John Benjamins, pp.9–24.

Schiffman, Harold F. (1996) *Linguistic Culture and Language Policy*. London: Routledge.

Skutnabb-Kangas, Tove (2000) *Linguistic Genocide in Education—Or Worldwide Diversity and Human Rights?* Mahwah, N.J.: Lawrence Erlbaum.

Skutnabb-Kangas, Tove and Robert Phillipson (eds.) (1994) *Linguistic Human Rights: Overcoming Linguistic Discrimination*. Berlin: Mouton de Gruyter.

Tsilevich, Boris (2001) "New Democracies in the Old World." In Will Kymlicka and Magda Opalski (eds.) *Can Liberal Pluralism Be Exported? Western Political Theory and Ethnic Relations in Eastern Europe*. Oxford: Oxford University Press, pp.154–170.

Vaillancourt, François (1978) "La Charte de la langue française au Québec: un essai d'analyse". *Canadian Public Policy/Analyse de politiques* (4): 284–308.

van Parijs, Philippe (2000) "Must Europe Be Belgian? On Democratic Citizenship in Multilingual Polities". In Iain Hampsher-Monk and Catriona McKinnon (eds.) *The Demands of Citizenship*. London: Continuum, pp.235–253.

van Parijs, Philippe (2001) "Linguistic Justice". *Politics, Philosophy and Economics*, 1: 59–74.

One State, One Language?

The 1999 Slovak Minority Language Law:
Internal or External Politics?
Farimah Daftary and Kinga Gál

∎

Language Battles in the Baltic States:
From 1989 to 2002
Priit Järve

∎

Identities and Language Politics in Ukraine:
The Challenges of Nation-State Building
Viktor Stepanenko

The 1999 Slovak Minority Language Law: Internal or External Politics?

Farimah Daftary and Kinga Gál

The 1999 Slovak Minority Language Law: Internal or External Politics?[1]

Farimah Daftary and Kinga Gál

INTRODUCTION

The case of independent Slovakia illustrates the political importance of language in the transition period in Central and Eastern Europe and the virulence of the disputes which can arise between majorities and minorities over language issues. Indeed, the recurring tensions between the Slovak leadership and the Hungarian minority—the largest in the country—illustrate the sensitivity of demands for minority rights in general and language rights in particular during the early phases of state-building, especially when accompanied by a belated process of nation-building.

A difficult task faced by Slovakia in the first decade following the fall of the Czechoslovak communist regime (as by many other newly independent post-communist states) was that of restoring the status of the language of the titular nation—Slovak—and ensuring that all inhabitants of the country have a proper knowledge of it, while at the same time respecting the language rights of minorities, in accordance with international commitments. These at times seemingly conflicting imperatives were summarized by the OSCE High Commissioner on National Minorities, Max van der Stoel, in a letter to (then) Slovak Foreign Minister Juraj Schenk as follows:

> [I]n states with national minorities, the question inevitably arises how to find a balance between the right of a state to ensure that the position of the state language is safeguarded and the need to ensure that the languages of the national minorities are protected in accordance with international standards (van der Stoel, 1995).

[1] An earlier version of this paper was presented at a panel organized by the European Centre for Minority Issues (ECMI) at the Fifth Annual Convention of the Association for the Study of Nationalities (ASN) (Columbia University, New York, 13–15 April 2000) and published as ECMI Working Paper No. 8 under the title *The New Slovak Language Law: Internal or External Politics?* (Flensburg: ECMI, 2000); can be found at http://www.ecmi.de/doc/public_papers.html). Kinga Gál contributed with Sections 3.2 and 4. The authors wish to thank Balázs Jarábik of the Center for Legal Analyses/Kalligram Foundation in Bratislava as well as Anna Nogová of the Slovak Helsinki Citizens' Assembly.

After the split of Czechoslovakia in January 1993, Slovakia opted for the 'one state, one language' approach, seeking to establish the primacy of Slovak over the languages of other ethnic groups living in the country, especially of those which had historically been cultural colonizers (Hungarians and Czechs). Language policy served a dual purpose: by attributing to the Slovak language a dominant position in the state, it sought to foster the (ethnic) Slovak national identity; it was at the same time a method for promoting the assimilation of non-ethnic Slovak citizens into a Slovak nation-state. The Slovak leaders especially sought to assert Slovak national identity in opposition to that of the 'old enemy'—the Hungarians—a large group of whom lived in the country. Thus, rather than face the multiethnic and multilingual realities and accept the ethnic Hungarians and other minorities as constituent elements of the state, certain politicians exacerbated interethnic tensions by claiming that the ethnic Hungarians' demands for minority rights were unjustified and that they should be converted into 'loyal citizens' by being made to speak the state language. Ethnic Hungarians and other minorities such as the Roma also played a useful role in the nation-building process by taking on the role of 'others', thereby (unwillingly) assisting efforts to define the identity of the titular group.

A series of legal acts affecting minority-language rights were adopted under the nationalist-populist coalition governments of Prime Minister Vladimír Mečiar (1992–1994, 1994–1998), each increasing confusion and tension. Whilst Slovak leaders attempted to justify restrictive language policies by the imperatives of nation-building and consolidating the identity of the state, the Hungarian minority perceived these policies as specific attacks against minority identities and culture—and against theirs especially. In the context of majority leaders' insecurity about the identity of the new state, Hungarian demands for language rights were perceived as a threat to the integrity of Slovakia. In fact, anti-minority policies (or policies perceived as such) fell within a broader set of anti-opposition policies as the state sought to extend its control not only in the sphere of language but also in the fields of culture, education, the economy, etc. The nationalist policies pursued under Mečiar also served to divert attention from badly-needed economic reform.

Ever since the adoption of the restrictive State Language Law in 1995, pressure had been on Slovakia, both domestically from the Hungarian minority and internationally, to enact a law regulating the use of minority languages. The country as a whole paid the price for the intransigence of the Mečiar governments on the minority issue, and for undemocratic government in general, by being excluded from the first round of negotiations on accession to the EU.[2]

The new coalition government of Prime Minister Mikuláš Dzurinda, formed after the 1998 elections, included ethnic Hungarian parties for the first time since independence and showed an eagerness to integrate Slovakia into European structures. On 10 July 1999, after an intense debate, the Slovak parliament rushed through a Minority Language Law. It was unanimously welcomed by the international community and Slovakia was invited at the European Council Summit in Helsinki in December 1999 to begin accession talks.

---

[2]   The countries invited in July 1997 to begin talks were Cyprus, the Czech Republic, Estonia, Hungary, Poland and Slovenia.

However, this chapter will seek to demonstrate that there were problems both with the process behind the adoption of the 1999 Minority Language Law and with the standards contained in it and policies following this law. In order to understand why such a law was adopted, we must look at both internal and external politics, by placing the law within the broader context of nation-building and state-building and ethnic politics in general, and by also examining Slovakia's international relations. After a short background (Section 1), we shall analyse the role of language and language policy in Slovakia and highlight key legislative initiatives affecting the use of minority languages and interethnic relations during the period 1990–1998 (Section 2). We shall then focus on the 1999 Minority Language Law, presenting the debate behind its adoption and immediate domestic reactions as well as the expectations of the international community regarding this law and the extent to which they were fulfilled (Section 3). In Section 4 we shall analyse the law itself as well as its impact on the actual use of minority languages (implementation). Finally, in the concluding section, we shall offer some thoughts on the impact of the Minority Language Law on the level of language rights and on interethnic relations in Slovakia, as well as on Slovakia's 'return to Europe'.

1. BACKGROUND

1.1 Ethnolinguistic Make-Up of Slovakia

Slovakia is a multiethnic state of 5.3 million inhabitants where about 15 per cent of the population declared an ethnicity other than Slovak (the actual share of non-ethnic Slovaks may be as high as 21–22 per cent).[3] According to the 1991 Czechoslovak census, there were eleven ethnic groups in the Slovak Republic[4] (Table 1.1). Ethnic Hungarians constitute the largest minority (10.6 per cent), followed by the Roma (1.6 per cent), Czechs (1 per cent), and Ruthenians/Rusyns and Ukrainians (0.3 per cent each); other minorities numbered less than 7,000 persons (0.1 per cent or less).[5]

---

[3]   Some sources place the number of ethnic Hungarians closer to 700,000 (Minority Rights Group, 1997: 246). As in other East European countries, it is estimated that the size of the Roma community is much larger, between 350,000 and 520,000 or 6.5–9.7 per cent of the population but that a majority of Roma choose to declare another ethnicity (usually Slovak or Hungarian) (Minority Rights Group, 1997: 246; Liégeois and Gheorghe, 1995: 7).

[4]   There is no legal definition of the term 'national minority' in Slovak legislation nor are they specified. Nevertheless, eleven ethnic groups (Bulgarians, Croatians, Czechs, Germans, Hungarians, Jews, Moravians, Poles, Roma, Ruthenians and Ukrainians) were considered national minorities by Slovakia and covered by the Council of Europe Framework Convention (Slovak Republic, 1999: Article 3).

[5]   The first census conducted in independent Slovakia in May 2001 did not indicate a major change in the order of the three largest ethnic groups ('nationalities') (see Table 1.1) though it confirmed the decline of the Hungarian community. The size of the self-declared Roma community remained under 2% even though, for the first time, bilingual Slovak–Romani (as well as Slovak–Hungarian, Slovak–Ruthenian, and Slovak–Ukrainian) census forms were used in an effort to increase the accuracy of the data on minorities.

Table 1.1
National Minorities in Slovakia by Ethnicity
(Derived from the 1991 Czechoslovak Census and the 2001 Slovak Census)

Ethnicity	1991 Census		2001 Census	
	Total number	Per cent	Total number	Per cent
Slovak	4,590,100	85.69	4,614,854	85.78
Hungarian	568,714	10.62	520,528	9.67
Roma[6]	83,988	1.57	89,920	1.67
Czech	51,293	0.96	44,620	0.83
Ruthenian	17,277	0.32	24,201	0.45
Ukrainian	14,341	0.27	10,814	0.20
German	5,380	0.10	5,405	0.10
Moravian, Silesian[7]	6,361	0.12	2,348	0.044
Other and unknown	18,753	0.35	59,852	1.11
Total	5,356,207	100.00	5,379,455	100.00

About 15.5 per cent of the Slovak population declared a language other than Slovak as their mother tongue (Table 1.2). Hungarian-speakers constitute the largest linguistic minority in Slovakia, with 11.5 per cent.[8] Although the 1991 census showed Czech-speakers to be the second largest linguistic minority (1.1 per cent), it is believed that speakers of Romanes constitute a group of 245,000 to 365,000 persons (i.e., 4.6 to 6.9 per cent).[9] Finally, 0.9 per cent declared a dialect of Rusyn to be their mother tongue.[10]

---

[6] The Roma population is estimated to be 350,000 to 520,000 persons (6.5–9.7 per cent) (Minority Rights Group, 1997: 246; Liégeois and Gheorghe, 1995: 7).

[7] Only the option "Moravian" was provided in the 2001 census.

[8] This number is higher than the number of persons who declared themselves ethnic Hungarians due to persons from mixed Slovak–Hungarian families who listed Hungarian as their mother tongue but also to those Roma whose mother tongue is Hungarian. Some Roma may also have declared Hungarian as both their ethnicity and mother tongue and would have therefore been included in the figures for the Hungarian minority; the size of the latter category is estimated at 150,000 (see US Department of State, 1999). In any case, it is incorrect to state that half of all ethnic Hungarians in Slovakia are actually Roma, as Mečiar has claimed (OMRI, 1996)

[9] It is estimated that roughly 70 per cent of Roma in Slovakia speak Romanes as their mother tongue (European Roma Rights Center, 1997: 26–28). The 2001 census indicated that Romanes-speakers constitute the fourth largest linguistic group in Slovakia, after Slovak-, Hungarian- and Ruthenian-speakers (Table 1.2).

[10] According to one estimate, cca. 120,000 people master the Ruthenian/Rusyn language and have preserved Ruthenian traditions (Slovak Helsinki Committee, 1999).

Table 1.2

National Minorities in Slovakia by Mother Tongue
(Derived from the 1991 Czechoslovak Census and the 2001 Slovak Census)

Mother tongue	1991 Census	2001 Census
	Per cent	Per cent
Slovak	84.3	83.9
Hungarian	11.5	10.7
Czech	1.1	0.9
German	0.1	0.1
Ruthenian	0.9	1.0
Ukrainian	0.2	0.1
Romanes	1.5	1.8
Polish	0.1	0.1
Others	0.1	0.2
Undetermined	0.2	1.2
Total	100.0	100.0

SOURCE: Slovak Statistical Office.

Most of Slovakia's ethnic Hungarians are compactly settled in an almost continuous strip along Slovakia's southern border, in 'ethnically mixed' regions (defined as regions where they make up more than ten per cent of the population) (Bakker, 1997: 40–48). The share of ethnic Hungarians declined from 12.4 per cent in 1961 to 10.7 per cent in 1991.[11] Still, 97 per cent of all ethnic Hungarians live in municipalities where they constitute 20 per cent or more of the local population. In the 'ethnically mixed' districts, language use is flexible, and most persons are bilingual. In these areas only three per cent of ethnic Hungarian respondents claimed to speak Hungarian only; and more than 60 per cent of ethnic Slovaks claimed that they could also speak Hungarian (Bakker, 1997: 85–86). The Ruthenian/Rusyn and Ukrainian minorities are also compactly settled, in the Prešov region of northeastern Slovakia.

1.2 THE LEGACY OF HISTORY

The minorities living on the territory of Slovakia are indigenous and owe their minority situation to the redrawing of borders throughout the centuries. As new rulers have come and gone, some ethnic groups have gained in status while others have lost.

---

[11] This is in part due to drastic declines in the aftermath of the two World Wars but also to successive waves of immigration of ethnic Slovaks and to a lower birth rate of ethnic Hungarians.

With the creation of the Czechoslovak state in October 1918 and the Peace Treaties of Trianon (1919) and Saint-Germain (1920), three million ethnic Germans, one million ethnic Hungarians, as well as smaller groups of Ruthenians, Ukrainians and Poles found themselves within the boundaries of this new state of Czechs and Slovaks. Minority rights were guaranteed by the protection clauses of the two treaties, as well as by the Constitution of the Czechoslovak Republic (1920) and a language law.[12] Although minorities in the inter-war Czechoslovak Republic (1918–1938) claimed discrimination, in comparison with those living in other parts of Central and Eastern Europe they enjoyed unique opportunities to organize politically, economically and culturally.

The most flagrant violations of minority rights occurred during and immediately after the Second World War—a period marked in Czechoslovakia, as in many other parts of Europe, by genocide, deportations and mass population displacements. Both the regimes of Slovak fascist leader Jozef Tiso (established on 14 March 1939) and that of Admiral Horthy in Hungary were characterized by discriminatory practices against minorities in education, language use, government employment and administration; expulsions also took place. Within a short period, an estimated 100,000 ethnic Czechs and Slovaks left the southern region of Slovakia which had been incorporated into Hungary in 1938, followed by Ruthenia in 1939 (Bakker, 1997: 39). After the Second World War, the territories of the first Czechoslovak Republic were reunited, with the exception of Ruthenia (today part of Ukraine). Over 70,000 Jews were deported from Slovakia under the Tiso regime. Slovak Roma, too, suffered severe discrimination; but, fortunately, most avoided extermination and many later settled in the Czech lands.

Through the Beneš Decrees (1945), the post-war Czechoslovak leaders attempted to create a Slavic nation-state through expulsions, as well as forced displacement and population exchanges (Bakker, 1997: 41); German- and Hungarian-language schools were closed and the use of the two languages in public was forbidden. In 1946, a re-Slovakization policy, accompanied by strong incentives,[13] was launched. Although anti-Hungarian policies were gradually discontinued after the 1948 Communist coup, this did not signify a return to the pre-war level of rights.

The legal guarantees established during the 1968 Prague Spring were considered outstanding, even by Western standards;[14] but they were never fully implemented due to the August 1968 Warsaw Pact invasion and the subsequent period of 'normalization'. In 1978, there was even an attempt to abolish education in the Hungarian language.

Unlike the Hungarian and Ukrainian minorities, the Roma, Ruthenian and German minorities had no opportunity for education in their mother tongue under the communist regime.

---

[12] Act No. 121 of 1920, which introduced the Constitutional Law of the Czechoslovak Republic; and Act No. 122 of 1920, based on Article 129 of the 1920 Constitution, which set out the principles of language rights in the Czechoslovak Republic.

[13] Hungarians who declared themselves to be ethnic Slovaks could regain their citizenship and property (Bakker, 1997: 39).

[14] Act No. 144 of 1968 on the Status of National Minorities in the Czechoslovak Socialist Republic recognized the Hungarian, German, Polish and Ukrainian minorities as constituent nations that complemented the Czech and Slovak nations.

Historical grievances continue to play an important role in Slovak–Hungarian relations to this day. It is interesting (though not uncommon) to note that the attitudes of ethnic Slovaks towards ethnic Hungarians are more positive in the 'ethnically mixed' regions (Bakker, 1997: 86–88). Mistrust between the two groups is fomented by politicians on both sides who make frequent reference to periods of history in which one group was oppressed by the other. Furthermore, some argue that the Slovaks' sense of national identity has developed in reaction to Hungarian and Czech culture. It is true that, unlike the Czechs, the Slovaks had very limited opportunities for developing their national identity until after the Second World War. When Slovaks and Czechs were united in the Czechoslovak Republic in 1918, many Slovaks felt that Hungarian rule had merely been exchanged for rule from Prague. Thus, the inter-war period was characterized by Slovak resentment and the rise of Slovak nationalism. The fact that most of the historical figures seen positively by Slovaks are associated with the Slovak national movement, and that, similarly, Hungarians in Slovakia identify with important figures in Hungarian history, also creates a problem in fostering a sense of identity inclusive of members of other ethnic groups (Wolchik, 1997: 202).

1.3   Minority Political Actors and Their Demands

1.3.1 The Hungarian Minority

Because of its size and high degree of organization, the Hungarian minority has been particularly effective in pressing its demands and is therefore the main domestic political actor which the Slovak government has had to contend with on the minority issue. However, following the split of the Czechoslovak Federation on 1 January 1993, the Hungarian minority increasingly turned to the international community for support. Its ability to generate criticism of Slovakia's minority policies has tended to create a backlash as Slovak nationalists blamed ethnic Hungarian politicians for Slovakia's exclusion from the first wave of EU candidates. It also made most Slovak political actors wary (until 1998) of openly cooperating with ethnic Hungarian parties for fear of being labelled 'anti-Slovak'.

A key factor in the relations between the Slovak government and ethnic Hungarians is neighbouring Hungary, a kin-state for whom the rights of fellow Hungarians abroad is a main element of its foreign policy.[15] Disputes over minority issues have at times threatened to seriously disrupt Slovakia's relations with its neighbour. One low point came in the first half of 1993, during the accession discussions of newly independent Slovakia to the Council of Europe, when Hungary threatened to veto Slovakia's membership due to concerns over the situation of Slovakia's Hungarian minority.

Most ethnic Hungarians vote for 'ethnic Hungarian' parties. These parties representing the Hungarian minority formed immediately after the 1989 'Velvet Revolution', drawing both on the official pre-1989 networks of the Hungarian minority as well as on the dissident

---

[15]   In 1989, Hungary set up an "Office for Hungarian Minorities Abroad" to coordinate matters concerning Hungarian minorities (see http://www.htmh.hu/english.htm).

movements. The Hungarian minority in Slovakia was represented by three parties: Coexistence (Együttélés), the Hungarian Christian Democratic Movement (Magyar Kereszténydemokrata Mozgalom, MKM)[16] and the Hungarian Civic Party (Magyar Polgári Párt, MPP).[17] These three parties, supported to varying degrees by their ideological counterparts across the border, held different positions on the adequate protection of ethnic Hungarians and especially on the question of autonomy (Fisher, 1995b: 60; 1995a). On 21 June 1998, they fused to form the Hungarian Coalition Party (Magyar Koalíció Pártja, MKP) (see Section 3).

Parliamentary representation of the Hungarian minority in the Slovak National Council (Národná rada) has ranged from 14 to 17 seats (out of 150). There are no special measures to facilitate minority representation.[18]

Whilst the Slovak government often claimed that the situation of the Hungarian minority was far better than that of other minorities in Europe, the Hungarian minority pointed to various instances of curtailing of minority rights. These complaints came to the surface after the collapse of the communist regime in 1989. Language-related issues in general, and minority-language education in particular,[19] have been a major area of friction, especially after 1994 when the government sought to assert greater control over Hungarian-language schools (Bakker, 1997: 78–80; US Department of State, 1999). Questions related to the use of the minority language in official contacts, the registering of names in the minority language, and the use of topographical signs in the minority language have also been recurrent subjects of dispute.

Because language rights are strongly linked to the share of the minority population in municipalities, municipal boundaries are a particularly sensitive issue. Ethnic Hungarians

---

[16]   The Hungarian Hungarian acronym and name is given in the cases of Hungarian ethnic parties. In other cases, the acronym is based on the Slovak name.

[17]   According to a survey conducted in May 1994, Coexistence (Chairman: Miklós Duray, originally representing not only ethnic Hungarians but also other minorities) was the most popular among ethnic Hungarian respondents (31%), followed by the centre-right MKM (28%), the SDĽ (9%) (there is no leftist ethnic Hungarian party) and the MPP (8%) (Wolchik, 1997: 232). Later opinion polls suggested that the MKM (Chairman: Béla Bugár) had become the largest of the three. The liberal MPP (Chairman: László Nagy) is the oldest and most moderate. There is also a fourth party, the Hungarian People's Party, but it has failed to gain a significant following.

[18]   In fact, the 1992 election law increased the minimum threshold for entering parliament for a single party from 3% to 5%; the threshold for a coalition of two parties is 8%. Coexistence and the MKM were represented in parliament from 1990 to 1998, having joined forces in pre-election coalitions. The MPP (then called Hungarian Civic Initiative, Magyar Polgári Kezdeményezés, MPK) ran on the Public Against Violence (Verejnosť proti násiliu, VPN) ticket in the 1990 elections and thus participated in government from 1990 to 1992. Having failed to reach an agreement with the successor party to the VPN—the Civic Democratic Union (Občianska demokratická únia, ODÚ), the MPP fell short of the new 5% threshold in the 1992 elections. Since 1994, it has been represented as part of the Hungarian Coalition (renamed the Hungarian Coalition Party in 1998).

[19]   While there were many primary and secondary schools with instruction in Hungarian or in both Hungarian and Slovak, there were no opportunities in Slovakia for studying in Hungarian at the university level. Education in the mother tongue is guaranteed by the 'Schools Act' (Act No. 29 of 1984 on the Network of Primary and Secondary Schools) to citizens of Czech, Hungarian, German, Polish and Ukrainian (Ruthenian) ethnicity (see Slovak Republic, 1999: Article 14).

have strongly opposed administrative reforms which would dilute their share, while proposals by the Hungarian minority for increased local autonomy are in turn perceived by Slovak parties as a threat to Slovak sovereignty. In 1993, the government announced plans to reorganize the administrative districts on a north-south basis which would lead to a reduction in the percentage of ethnic Hungarians to less than twenty per cent in all districts. The Hungarian minority reacted by proposing the creation of autonomous administrations.[20] The reforms proposed by the government were eventually carried out in 1996, despite a presidential veto, and in direct violation of Slovakia's international commitments.[21]

1.3.2 Other Minority Actors

Although other minorities share some of the concerns of the Hungarian minority, there has not been the same level of friction with the government on the language issue for the various reasons already touched upon. There have been numerous publications in Romanes since the late 1980s and the Roma community has shown increasing interest in the codification of the Romani language in Slovakia; but instruction in Romanes is almost non-existent, allegedly because the Roma have not asked for it, and opportunities to study the language are limited.[22] It is true that priorities lie with addressing other problems, such as the widespread discrimination in employment and education, and extremely poor social and economic conditions. Political representation of the Roma is fragmented; no Roma party has ever made it to parliament.[23]

There has been a revival of the Ruthenian language and identity since 1989 thanks to organizations such as the Rusyn Renaissance Society (Rusyn'ska Obroda). The language was codified in Slovakia in 1995 and instruction in Ruthenian is provided in a few schools. There is one party representing Ruthenians/Ukrainians.

---

[20] The so-called 'Komárno Proposal' (January 1994) was presented by Slovak politicians and the domestic media as a ploy to reorganize the administrative division of southern Slovakia so that ethnic Slovaks would become a minority. This was compounded by the fact that the proposed map of the 'Hungarian region' resembled that of the territories annexed by Hungary in 1938 (Bakker, 1998: 29; Fisher, 1995b: 59–60).

[21] The 1996 administrative reform recreated eight regions, reducing the number of districts from 83 to 79. Two of the main centres of Hungarian settlement, Komárno and Dunajská Streda, were split between three different regions; other districts with large ethnic Hungarian populations were also divided (Wolchik 1997: 223). For more on the 1996 reform, see Bakker (1997: 88–107, esp. 99–100). The issue of regional autonomy surfaced again in 2000-2001 during the debates over the reform of public administration and local government (see concluding section).

[22] Romanes is used at one secondary art school as well as within the Romani Culture Department at Constantine University in Nitra. It is also used as a supporting language in nursery schools and pre-school preparatory primary school classes with a high concentration of Roma pupils (see Slovak Republic, 1999: 31–32 and European Roma Rights Center, 1997: 26–28).

[23] In an effort to remedy this situation, in September 1999, fourteen out of the fifteen registered Romany associations and parties set up a 'Council of the Coalition of Romany Parties' in preparation for the 2002 general elections (*Newsline*, 1999c).

2. NATION-BUILDING, STATE-BUILDING
AND THE REVIVAL OF SLOVAK NATIONALISM (1990–1998)

In the period immediately following the events of 1989, strong nationalist sentiments, which had been subdued under the communist regime, came to the fore in Slovakia. Under the two nationalist-populist coalition governments led by Vladimír Mečiar (1992–1994, and 1994–1998, with a short interruption in 1994), Slovakia experienced a phase of intense na-tion-building and state-building, accompanied by restrictive policies against minorities and any other form of opposition. By attributing a dominant position in all spheres to the Slovak nation and the Slovak language, it can be argued that the legislation adopted in this period ultimately resulted in the foundation of a basis for the domination of the minorities by the titular nation. At the same time, it served to legitimize the position of the ruling (ethnic Slovak) elite and to maintain their system of privileges by excluding minorities from the sphere of official life as much as possible.

In this section, we shall examine the main initiatives in language legislation and policy in the period 1990–1998 and place them within the general process of Slovak nation-build-ing and state-building.

2.1 The Emergence of Interethnic Tensions over Language Issues (1990–1992)

The democratic elections held in Czechoslovakia in June 1990 brought to power in the Czech and Slovak Republics the dissident movements which had contributed to the fall of the com-munist regime. In Slovakia, Public Against Violence (Verejnost' proti násiliu, VPN)—the Slovak equivalent of the Civic Forum of Václav Havel—united individuals with very different ideas about how to deal with the immediate tasks during the transition to democracy. Mečiar, then a member of VPN, enjoyed his first term as prime minister from June 1990 until his resignation in April 1991.

Because the 'Velvet Revolution' began in Prague, and because of the high degree of cooperation between Czech and Slovak leaders in the period of change, many Slovak intel-lectuals at the forefront were susceptible to criticism of not sufficiently standing up for Slovak interests. The first signs of tension over minority issues, and language in particular, appeared in 1990. At the end of the summer, the Slovak National Party (Slovenská národná strana, SNS)[24] launched a campaign for a language law aimed at depriving the Hungarian minority of the right to use its mother tongue in official matters, as a sort of 'historical justice'. This proposal was supported by the Slovak nationalist cultural organization, Matica Slovenská. Ethnic Hungarians circulated a rival proposal to allow minorities to use their language where they constituted at least ten per cent of the population of a given municipality.

---

[24]   The SNS is a radically nationalist, pan-Slavic and europhobic party, established in 1990, which openly pro-fesses nostalgia for the period of independence under the fascist leader Jozef Tiso. Although it has never enjoyed mass support (apart from a score of almost 14% in 1990, its share has ranged from 6 to 9%), it was a member of the governing coalition until 1998 due to the failure of the HZDS (Hnutie za demokratické Slovensko—Movement for a Democratic Slovakia) to win a comfortable majority; it continues to be a strong presence on the political scene (see also Žitný, 1998).

Slovak National Council Act No. 428 of 1990 on the Official Language of the Slovak Republic, adopted on 25 October 1990 (hereafter, '1990 Official Language Law')[25] was supposedly a compromise. It established Slovak as the official language (Article 2) and "as a means of mutual understanding and communication". It also aimed to "support the development of democracy, the cultures of the Slovak nation and the national minorities in the Slovak Republic, the spirit of understanding and the strengthening of national tolerance . . .".[26] It did not grant official status to any other language, but it did allow for the use of Czech in official contacts and for minorities to use their language in dealing with authorities in municipalities where they constituted at least twenty per cent of the local population. But, even there, employees of state administration and local self-government bodies were not required to know and use the minority language. Furthermore, all official documents were to be issued in Slovak only (Article 6).

Although the 1990 Official Language Law might be viewed as a legitimate step in language policy (primarily status planning, but with elements of corpus planning [see Section 5 of the law, "Care for the Official Language"]), with the aim of clarifying the official language of Slovakia which until then had been "Czechoslovak",[27] it could also be seen as a means of ethnic containment through restriction of the use of minority languages on the territory of the Slovak Republic at the discretion of state authorities and local officials. Furthermore, it did not grant official status to any minority language, even in regions where the minority language was predominantly used.

Rather than establish certain standards concerning language use, the 1990 Official Language Law caused confusion and interethnic tensions (Kontra, 1995/1996: 348; 1996), satisfying neither the nationalists (who claimed it went too far in granting minority-language rights) nor the Hungarian minority (which claimed it did not go far enough). In October 1991, the Ministry of the Interior decided that the bilingual city signs which had been put up by mayors after the collapse of the communist regime were illegal and ordered them to be taken down. However, as the text of the law did not explicitly prohibit such signs, ethnic Hungarians argued that "what is not prohibited is permitted" (Kontra, 1995/1996: 347). In the years following the adoption of the 1990 Official Language Law, fierce disputes erupted over bilingual place name signs, the use of names in the mother tongue, bilingual certificates, etc.

2.2 The First HZDS Government: Building the Slovak Nation-State (1992–1994)

Having been re-elected Prime Minister in 1992 under his own party—the Movement for a Democratic Slovakia (Hnutie za demokratické Slovensko, HZDS), Mečiar moved fast to assert Slovakia's position against Prague, in line with a five-step plan which he had presented

---

[25]   An unofficial English translation of the Act on the Official Language of the Slovak Republic may be found in Šedivý and Maroši (1995: 24–25).

[26]   Act on the Official Language of the Slovak Republic, Section 1 "Introductory Provisions".

[27]   The state language, according to the 1918 Czechoslovak Constitution, was "Czechoslovak" in two versions: Czech and Slovak. Article 1 of Constitutional Law No. 122, adopted on 29 February 1920, asserted that "The Czechoslovak language is the state and official language of the Republic".

during the 1992 election campaign (Butora, 1998: 73). By the end of that year, Slovakia had declared sovereignty (17 July 1992) and adopted a new constitution. Following the failure of negotiations on the future of the Czech and Slovak Federal Republic between the Czech Prime Minister Václav Klaus and Mečiar, the Federal Assembly adopted a law in November 1992 dissolving the Federation. Thus, on 1 January 1993, for the second time in its history, Slovakia became an independent country and the Mečiar government was faced with the task of strengthening the identity of a state whose population, for the most part, had been in favour not of outright independence but rather of some sort of confederation, an option which it was not given.[28] The Slovak Constitution, adopted on 3 September 1992, was a key step in Slovak nation-building, with implications also in the field of language. It also led to Slovakia's 'one nation, one state, one language' policy. The Constitution reflects the ethnic concept of nationhood, stating that the Slovak Republic is the state of the Slovak nation (and not of Slovak citizens). The preamble of the Constitution begins:

> We, the Slovak nation..., proceeding from the natural rights of nations to self-determination, together with members of national minorities and ethnic groups living on the territory of the Slovak Republic..., that is, we, citizens of the Slovak Republic...[29]

The Constitution confirmed Slovak as the official state language (Article 6). Minority relevant provisions are contained in Chapter Four "The Rights of National Minorities and Ethnic Groups" (Articles 33 and 34). In terms of language rights, the Constitution guarantees minority citizens the right to receive and disseminate information in their mother tongue (Article 34[1]), the right to education in the minority language (Article 34[2][a]) and the right to use the minority language in official communications (Article 34[2][b]). However, the use of minority languages in official communications is to be regulated by separate legislation (Article 6). Also, the rights granted in Article 34(2) are coupled with the 'right' to learn the official language.

---

[28]   Although the break-up of the Czech and Slovak Federal Republic may be partially attributed to the revival of nationalist sentiment in Slovakia, a majority of the population (54.8%) did not vote for the HZDS or the SNS. The split was essentially a process which took place at the elite level, without a direct consultation of the Czech and Slovak populations. Another explanation for Mečiar's success in the 1992 elections was his promise to find a road to the free market that would take Slovakia's specific features into account (for a re-examination of the split, see Wolf, 1998; see also Fisher, 1996a).

[29]   In Slovak, the Constitution reads: *"My, národ slovenský ..."*. There was a lengthy debate as to whether the word *národ*—which can be translated both as 'people' and as 'nation'—refers to members of the Slovak nation only or whether it could be interpreted as referring to all citizens of Slovakia. The Hungarian minority believes in the former (and these authors would tend to agree). If the drafters had wanted to make an unambiguous reference to all citizens, then a different phrasing could have been used, for example, *"My, občania Slovenskej republiky"* ("We, citizens of the Slovak Republic"). When, in preparation for joining the EU and NATO, amendments to the Constitution were being discussed, the issue of the preamble was again raised. However, no changes were made to it in the amendments enacted in February 2001, which came into effect on 1 July 2001. The Slovak Constitution, including these latest amendments, may be found, in Slovak and in official English translation, on the website of the Slovak Constitutional Court (http://www.concourt.sk).

Although the Constitution, which guaranteed basic human and minority rights, represented a great step forward, it was criticized by the Hungarian minority (whose objections rested mainly with the preamble) as well as by scholars who noted that the rights guaranteed could be taken away through a simple parliamentary majority, rather than a constitutional amendment which requires 60 per cent approval. Also, the clauses in Article 34 guaranteeing minority rights are immediately followed by a clause stating that the exercise of these rights "may not threaten the sovereignty and territorial integrity of the Slovak Republic or discriminate against other citizens" (Article 34[3]). This clearly meant that there would be no discussion of territorial autonomy; it also addressed the 'fear' of ethnic Slovaks that the granting of minority rights might lead to their assimilation in mixed regions.

The degree of sensitivity with respect to the Slovak language, even on the part of linguists, and the use of language to awaken patriotic feelings, was evident on 7 July 1993 when, in order to fulfil requirements for Council of Europe membership (see Section 3), a 1950 Czechoslovak law on minority names was amended. Slovak nationalists protested along with the Institute of Linguistics of the Slovak Academy of Sciences. The latter argued that the law did not conform to the rules of the Slovak language and that Slovak grammar was not within the Council of Europe's competence (Reisch, 1993). Bowing in to pressure by Mečiar, President Kováč vetoed the law.[30] That same year was also marked by disputes over place-name signs in Hungarian and the first mass demonstrations of ethnic Hungarians in Komárno in favour of autonomy.

2.3   Language Policy under the Interim Moravčík Government (March–October 1994)

Some damage control and progress in the field of minority protection (and also economic reform) were achieved when Mečiar's rule was briefly interrupted in March 1994 and replaced by a broad left-right coalition, under the leadership of (then) Foreign Minister Jozef Moravčík, which governed until autumn 1994, with the tacit support of the ethnic Hungarian deputies.

Under Moravčík, two important laws fulfilling Council of Europe requirements were adopted: one on names in birth registers and marriage certificates, the other on the use of bilingual signs (see Section 3). Still, these acts failed to satisfy the Hungarian minority as common Hungarian names which are not on the approved list of names may not be used; and only the religious part of the marriage ceremony may be conducted in the minority language.

---

[30]   This issue was allegedly settled at the end of 1993 with the adoption of the Act on Names and Surnames (Act No. 300 of 1993). However, there are still reports that the Slovak '-ová' ending is imposed on the surnames of some minority women (Council of Europe, 2000).

2.4 The Second HZDS-Led Government (1994–1998): Consolidating the Slovak Nation-State

The 1994 HZDS and SNS election campaigns were characterized by 'anti-Slovak' finger-pointing at the Hungarian parties especially (Fisher, 1996a).[31] This strategy yielded some results, although the HZDS failed to win a majority of votes in the elections held on 30 September and 1 October. Unable to convince the post-communist Party of the Democratic Left (Strana demokratickej ľavice, SDĽ) to enter the coalition, the new government formed by Mečiar on 13 December consisted of the HZDS, the SNS and the Association of Slovak Workers (Združenie robotníkov Slovenska, ZRS). The HZDS took twelve out of the eighteen portfolios; no one was willing to offer the Hungarian Coalition a position in the government, even though it had obtained ten per cent of the votes.

After the elections, nation-building and state-building intensified, although popular support for the government's nationalist policies seems to have followed an opposite trend. During this period, the state extended its control to all spheres, including education and culture. For example, the system of granting subsidies to minority organizations for cultural activities and publications was modified, and grants to Hungarian organizations were greatly reduced, while over 70 per cent of requests by other minority organizations were satisfied (Fisher, 1996b). At the same time, politicians in power used their privileged position to reap political and other benefits. An aggressive anti-minority campaign was launched, in line with the government programme where, for the first time, it was openly said that the state would be built on the national principle (Fisher, 1995b). This approach was exemplified by the adoption, one year later, of the State Language Law.

The original proposal for such a law was made by the SNS in April 1995 in accordance with the government's policy statement of 12 January 1995, whereby it had announced its intention to "create the conditions for the thorough learning of the state language in the linguistically mixed areas of the Slovak Republic" (van der Stoel, 1995). However, the law had much more ambitious aims and was accompanied by additional efforts to contain minorities and the opposition.[32]

On 15 November 1995, the Slovak National Council adopted Act No. 270 on the State Language of the Slovak Republic (hereafter, '1995 State Language Law') (Harlig, 1997).[33] Before voting began, an HZDS representative clearly stated that "anyone who votes

---

[31]   This was not the first time that such a strategy had been used by Mečiar. Indeed, the foundation of the HZDS in 1991 was justified by Mečiar as a reaction to the supposed 'anti-Slovak' tendencies of the VPN which supported preserving the Federation and the pace of economic reform advocated by Prague (Wolf, 1998: 46–51). In 1992, the Christian Democratic Movement (Kresťanskodemokratické hnutie, KDH) was labelled 'anti-Slovak' for not supporting the declaration of sovereignty and the new constitution.

[32]   As an example, in April 1995 the SNS proposed an amendment to the criminal code stipulating punishments for anyone engaging in actions seeking to subvert Slovakia's territorial integrity or to reduce its autonomy and expanded the definition of criminal activity to include spreading false news and endangering the security of the Republic (Fisher, 1995a). This amendment was rejected by parliament in February 1997.

[33]   The text of the law in Slovak is on the website of the Slovak Ministry of Culture (at http://www.culture.gov.sk), while an unofficial English translation, along with the "Justification" which was attached to the Draft Law on the State Language submitted to the Slovak National Council on 24 October 1995, may be found in Minority Protection Association (1996: 12–17). The contents of this Law will be analysed in Section 4.

against the bill is against the fulfilment of the Slovaks' desires and deserves public contempt" (Fisher, 1996a). Almost all opposition deputies voted for the law for fear of being labelled 'anti-Slovak'. Ethnic Hungarians alone voted against it, while the Christian Democratic Movement (Kresťanskodemokratické hnutie, KDH) abstained (though more because of church-related concerns). It was signed by President Michal Kováč, and entered into force on 1 January 1996, thereby cancelling the 1990 Official Language Law. As of 1 January 1997, very high fines could be imposed. The Ministry of Culture was entrusted with monitoring compliance with the Law and, in February 1996, 'language consultants' were put to work.

The 1995 State Language Law was seen by its drafters as finally giving the Slovak language the position it was due, i.e., that of a 'state language' rather than an official language. It adopted the 'one state, one language' model, and in the justification section, reference is made to (allegedly) comparable policies in other European states and also to the 'English Only' or 'Official English' movement in the United States.[34] It is also stated that the State Language Law seeks to protect the Slovak language against foreign influences, notably 'Americanisms'.

However, the Law was more than a piece of legislation concerning language use. It was clearly designed as a pillar of Slovak nation-building, stating:

> [T]he Slovak language is the most important distinctive feature of the uniqueness of the Slovak nation, the most valuable piece of the cultural heritage and expression of sovereignty of the Slovak Republic and the general means of communication for its citizens, which guarantees them freedom and equality in dignity and rights in the territory of the Slovak Republic.[35]

The 1995 State Language Law aimed to fulfil the requirement of the state to "establish the conditions for every citizen to be able to master the [Slovak] language in which he can make himself understood in the entire territory of the state".[36] At the same time, it was a means of reasserting the position of the Slovak language not only against the Czech language, which had enjoyed a dominant position during the period of joint statehood, but primarily against the languages of Slovakia's minorities, especially Hungarian (in the historical overview of the Slovak language at the beginning of the justification attached to the Law, reference is made to the period of "very consistent Magyarization" from 1938 to 1945).[37]

The 1995 State Language Law undoubtedly represented a key step in the process of building a Slovak nation-state, without the participation of Slovak citizens belonging to ethnic minorities. Part II of the justification of the Law states: "The Slovak language is the national language of the Slovaks, who comprise the only state-forming element of the Slovak Republic".[38] A Slovak political scientist wrote that, since 1 January 1993, "Hungarians and

---

[34] On the 'English Only' movement in the US and how the Slovak language law compares, see Kontra (1995/ 1996) who argues that restrictive legislation for language use seems to be an equally central issue for some politicians in "established democracies" such as the US, as well as in "emerging democracies" such as Slovakia (Kontra, 1995/1996: 345; see also Taras, 1998).

[35] Unofficial translation in Kontra (1995/1996: 351-357).

[36] "Justification," in Minority Protection Association (1996: 13).

[37] "Justification," in Minority Protection Association (1996: 12).

[38] Yet, paradoxically, the following sentence refers to the Slovak language as "the unifying language of all citizens of the Slovak Republic" ("Justification," in Minority Protection Association, 1996: 13).

other minorities have become tenants in the country in which they have lived together with us because the Slovaks turned it into their own nation-state".[39] According to another analysis, "its barely hidden purpose is to remedy the 'historical grievances' that fell upon the Slovak language, to eliminate the linguistic identity of minorities and to use the linguistic superiority of the state-forming nation as a tool of assimilation" (Minority Protection Association, 1996: 6).

The opposition (KDH and MKM) challenged the new Law on legal grounds. The Constitutional Court ruled on 9 September 1997 that its Article 3(5), which stated that written communications intended for public-legal administration matters must be in the state language, was contrary to the Constitution.[40] At the international level, too, the adoption of the State Language Law led to widespread concern and criticism (see Section 3). Domestically, however, practical repercussions were actually marginal, as means of circumventing the law were found in many areas. At this point, many ethnic Slovaks, too, were feeling increasingly alienated by the policies of the Mečiar government, as illustrated by the low turnout for the demonstration held on the day the law was adopted (Fisher, 1996a: 14).

The final symbolic act of the Mečiar government was the adoption, in 1996, of an Act on State Symbols which restricted the playing of foreign anthems and the display of foreign flags. Again, the Hungarian minority felt that it had been targeted.

Despite the ruling by the Constitutional Court and strong international pressure, no steps were taken under the Mečiar government to amend the 1995 State Language Law nor to adopt a law regulating the use of minority languages, disregarding both domestic and international commitments. By the end of 1997, it was clear that the Mečiar government had no intention of adopting a minority language law. Some government representatives claimed that existing legislation gave sufficient protection to minority languages and that they would rather favour acceding to the European Charter for Regional or Minority Languages (*Newsline*, 1997b).

3. THE NEW SLOVAK COALITION GOVERNMENT AND THE ADOPTION OF A MINORITY LANGUAGE LAW (OCTOBER 1998–JULY 1999)

3.1 Internal Politics

3.1.1 Why Was the Adoption of a Minority Language Law Necessary from the Domestic Legal Perspective?

As seen above, already in 1992, the Slovak Constitution (Article 6) called for the further regulation of the use of minority languages in official communications through a separate

---

[39]   Slovak political scientist and activist Miroslav Kusý, translated in Kontra (1995/1996: 348).

[40]   However, the Court did not uphold ten other complaints against the law, stating that a number of mistakes had been made when filing them (*Newsline*, 1997a).

48

law. However, apart from three legislative acts,[41] no comprehensive law regulating the use of minority languages in official contacts had been adopted. Furthermore, with the enactment of the 1995 State Language Law, a "legal vacuum"[42] in the sphere of minority-language use in official contacts was created, as it cancelled the 1990 Official Language Law. In other areas such as education, media, culture, etc., the State Language Law prevailed, except for the few articles from separate laws specifically mentioned in footnotes to the law.[43]

3.1.2 The 1998 Elections and the 1999 Act on the Use of Languages of National Minorities

Although the HZDS obtained the greatest share of votes (27 per cent) in the September 1998 parliamentary elections, it was defeated by four opposition parties which together won a constitutional majority of 93 of the 150 seats in the Slovak National Council.[44] On 30 October, a coalition government was finally formed by these four parties, with Slovak Democratic Coalition (Slovenská demokratická koalícia, SDK) Chairman Mikuláš Dzurinda as prime minister.[45] For the first time in the history of independent Slovakia, ethnic Hungarian parties participated in the government. The Hungarian Coalition Party (MKP) obtained three portfolios, including that of Deputy Prime Minister for Human Rights, National Minorities and Regional Development.[46] The creation of this position, filled by Pál Csáky, and the inclusion of Hungarian parties in the government sent a strong signal, mainly to the international community but also to nationalist forces at home, that the new government was determined to break with the previous nationalist-populist direction. The MKP had made the necessary political concessions by issuing a declaration prior to the elections that it would not "push

---

41   See footnotes 61, 62, 63.

42   According to a letter dated 26 February 1996 by the OSCE High Commissioner to (then) Slovak Foreign Minister Juraj Schenk, "the Law on the State Language . . . states . . . that the usage of languages of national minorities and ethnic groups will be dealt with in separate legislation. On the other hand, however, article 12 of the Law states that Law 428/1990 on the Official Language of the Slovak Republic is null and void. . . . However, the right to use a minority language in official communications has been laid down in article 34 para. 2, sub. b, of the Slovak Constitution 'under provisions fixed by law'. As long as new legislation on this subject is not yet in force, there is, therefore, a legal vacuum . . ." (van der Stoel, 1996).

43   See also Slovak Foreign Ministry (1996). Although the Slovak government claimed that these articles guaranteed minority language rights such as the right to receive education in a minority language or the right to disseminate and receive information in the native language, it can hardly be argued that a few disparate provisions which did not specifically mention minority languages could ensure the full enjoyment of these rights.

44   For election results, see *Newsline* (1998).

45   The parties which formed the government were: the Slovak Democratic Coalition (SDK), the SDĽ, the Hungarian Coalition Party (MKP) and the Party of Civic Understanding (Strana Občianskeho porozumenia, SOP). The SDK itself was a coalition of five parties formed in 1997 with the aim of presenting a united front against the HZDS: three right-wing parties—the Christian Democratic Movement (KDH), the Democratic Party (Demokratická strana, DS), and the Democratic Union (Demokratická únia, DÚ)—as well as two left-of-centre parties—the Social Democratic Party (Sociálnodemokratická strana Slovenska, SDSS) and the Green Party (Strana zelených na Slovensku, SZS).

46   See website of the deputy prime minister at http://www.vlada.gov.sk/csaky/.

for ethnic autonomy either in its political programme or in practice" (*Newsline*, 1997c). The expectations of the Hungarian and other minorities were high concerning Slovakia's minority policies.

Under Section 4(1) ("Democratic Legal State") of its Programme Declarations of 19 November 1998, the new Dzurinda government stated that it would "undertake an analysis of the state of human and minority rights in the Slovak Republic with regard to international documents, and on the basis of its results it [would] decide on entering further international conventions, on the adoption of a Constitutional law or a law on the position of minorities of the Slovak Republic".[47] Section 4(3)(F) ("Culture") mentions, among others, the preparation of an "Act on the Use of Languages of National Minorities and Ethnic Groups".

A draft was expected already in February 1999, but an agreement between the coalition parties was delayed by arguments over the content of the law, namely on its 'scope' and 'percentage' (minimum threshold for its application) (*Slovak Spectator*, 1999b). The MKP was strongly in favour of a wide-ranging law, regulating not only the use of minority languages in official contacts, but also in education, culture and media, in order to match the fields covered by the 1995 State Language Law. Furthermore, it proposed that the minority language be allowed in official contacts in municipalities where the minority constituted at least ten per cent of the population, arguing that a twenty per cent minimum threshold, as proposed in the government draft, was too high for the other minorities and would leave out 158 municipalities representing 100,000 minority members in total. There were also concerns that the main motivation of the government was to quickly draft a law before the summer recess in time for a key meeting of the EU,[48] and that the priority was to satisfy EU accession criteria, with little regard for how the law was to function in practice (*Slovak Spectator*, 1999a).[49] Still, the coalition parties were optimistic that a law could be adopted in time without compromising on quality and stated that the most important consideration was to approve a "well-shaped law that people would benefit from".[50]

On 8 June, the Slovak cabinet finally approved a draft law whose guiding principle was that the Slovak language should play an integrating role in society (*Slovak Spectator*, 1999e). The first version was deemed unacceptable by the MKP. Two weeks later, on 23 June, the gov-

---

[47]   Programme Declarations of the Government of the Slovak Republic, 19 November 1998 (in both Slovak and English on the Slovak government's website, at http://www.vlada.gov.sk/VLADA/VLADA_1998/PROG_VYHL/en_programove_vyhlasenie_1998.shtml).

[48]   The European Commission was due to meet in July 1999 to review Slovakia's petition requesting inclusion in the talks.

[49]   According to another article, the Hungarian and Slovak parties had different reasons for wanting such a law: while the Hungarian Coalition wanted a clear, consistent and wide-ranging bill, the Slovak parties did not care about the niceties of the law and were mainly preoccupied with winning the approval of the EU (*Slovak Spectator*, 1999c).

[50]   Slovak Deputy Prime Minister Pavel Hamzík, quoted in *Slovak Spectator* (1999b). One of the coalition parties, the SDĽ, was especially critical of the MKP, implying that it was using the time pressure and international support to push through "irrational proposals". In the eyes of the controversial SDĽ leader Róbert Fico (later the leader of Smer 'Direction'), it was all a question of dealing with minority languages "in a way that allows us to keep our face and a certain measure of independence from not-always objective international organisations" (*Slovak Spectator*, 1999b).

ernment approved a revised version, taking into account the recommendations of the OSCE High Commissioner who travelled to Slovakia twice in relation to the law during this period (*Central Europe Review*, 1999). Despite the inclusion of these recommendations, the revised draft still failed to win the endorsement of the MKP, which decided to submit its own version.[51] Thus, two drafts—both emanating from the government—were presented to parliament on 28 June. The MKP's proposal was defeated on 6 July, while the proposal submitted by the other three coalition parties remained, along with twenty amendments proposed by the MKP. However, an unchanged draft bill was rushed through and, on 10 July 1999, Act No. 184 on the Use of Languages of National Minorities (hereafter, '1999 Minority Language Law') was adopted by a narrow majority. The MKP voted against it while the opposition (HZDS and SNS) boycotted the vote.[52]

3.1.3 Domestic Reactions

Before the 1999 Minority Language Law was even adopted, the opposition organized demonstrations and also attempted to organize a referendum on the use of the state language in official contacts. But President Schuster decided not to allow such a referendum to take place, having been informed by experts, including the OSCE High Commissioner on National Minorities, that it would infringe upon constitutional provisions prohibiting plebiscites on human rights issues.[53]

According to some analysts in Slovakia, while the government stood to gain minority votes by satisfying (ethnic) Hungarian demands, it risked losing a great deal more among the (ethnic) Slovak electorate. However, given the stability of its electorate, the MKP could only benefit from pressing its demands and adopting an uncompromising stance.[54] According to MKP Chairman Béla Bugár, the long-awaited language law represented a great disappointment and the MKP was even considering leaving the government coalition because of it; but the MKP's official reaction was quite moderate, stating that it was not entirely satisfied with the law because it did not alleviate the negative impact of the 1995 State Language Law (*Slovak Spectator*, 1999e). Furthermore, according to the MKP, the new legislation would result in a situation where ethnic Hungarians and Ruthenians would continue to break the State Language Law by using their mother tongue (the Ruthenians were especially unhappy about the 20 per cent threshold which excluded many of them from the benefit of the new rights) (*Rusyn News*, 1999). As the Roma in Slovakia have not yet codified their language, it was not expected that they would be able to claim application of the law for members of their community. Nevertheless, on 9 March 2000, the Romani Civic Initiative

---

[51]   Even without the votes of the MKP, the other three parties in the government coalition had 78 out of 150 seats in parliament; this was sufficient to pass a law (there is no minority veto mechanism).

[52]   Of the 89 deputies present, 70 voted in favour, 18 were against and one abstained (*Slovak Spectator*, 1999e).

[53]   The question read: "Do you agree that the Slovak language should be used exclusively in official contacts as it was before 1 June 1999?" Enough signatures (over 350,000) were collected for the referendum which was also due to include a second question on privatization (see *Newsline*, 1999a).

[54]   Ľuboš Kubín, political scientist at the Slovak Academy of Sciences, quoted in the *Slovak Spectator* (1999d).

(Rómska občianská iniciatíva, ROI)[55] announced that it was demanding that the Minority Language Law be applied in the 57 municipalities where Roma make up more than twenty per cent of the population (Adam, 2000).[56]

The other three coalition parties considered the new law a success and were optimistic that the final major hurdle to becoming an EU front-runner had been removed. Still, Deputy Prime Minister for European Integration Pavol Hamžík stated that he would have been happier had the law also been approved by the MKP (*Slovak Spectator*, 1999e).

3.2 The 1999 Minority Language Law
from the Perspective of Slovakia's International Relations

This section will focus on the expectations of international organizations from Slovakia in the field of language use of national minorities, as a particular aspect of their overall protection. The enlisting of expectations in this field will help not only to better understand the reactions of international actors but also domestic dynamics in the field of minority policies. Furthermore, we will try to address whether Slovakia fulfilled these expectations through the adoption of the 1999 Minority Language Law and why the reactions to it were so different and contradictory.

3.2.1 Expectations Concerning a Law on the Use of Minority Languages

The November 1998 Programme Declarations of the Dzurinda government addressed international expectations extensively. Also, in a letter to the OSCE High Commissioner on National Minorities, the Slovak Prime Minister stated that: "We regard the rapid solution of the open questions concerning national minorities in our country as our contribution to build an inclusive type of society and thus extend the zone of peace and stability in Central Europe, which is an important element of the European integration process in this part of our continent" (Dzurinda, 1998).

(a)   The European Union

The adoption of a language law was regarded as one important political criterion which Slovakia had to meet in order to be considered for EU membership.[57] As Slovak Foreign Minister Eduard Kukan stated in an interview: "Slovakia cannot rely on EU understanding if it fails to meet this requirement" (*Slovak Spectator*, 1999b).

---

[55]   The Romani Civic Initiative (ROI), established in 1990, is the oldest Roma party in Slovakia; its membership is estimated at about 30,000 (BBC Worldwide Monitoring, 2000).

[56]   ROI stated that this would imply creating 20,000 new jobs in local government and civil service for members of the Roma minority. However, this does not flow from the law which does not require that local officials speak (or even understand) the minority language (see Section 4).

[57]   At the Copenhagen meeting of the European Council in June 1993, the heads of states and governments agreed that the associated countries in Central and Eastern Europe (i.e., those countries with which the EU

The first Report on Slovakia prepared by the European Commission in 1997 expressed serious concerns about the level of democracy and the rule of law in the country in the context of the Copenhagen Political Criteria. The protection of national minorities in general, and the language rights of minorities in particular, were deemed especially important. The absence of minority legislation was a major source of concern.

In its 1998 Regular Report on Slovakia, the Commission concluded, *inter alia*, that "[t]here have been problems in the treatment of minorities and a lack of progress concerning the adoption of legislation on minority languages".[58] Therefore, the adoption of legislative provisions on minority-language use and related implementing measures were enshrined in the short-term political priorities of the March 1998 Accession Partnership Agreement on Slovakia, while the medium-term priorities included "the policies and institutions protecting the rights of the minorities".[59]

(b)   The OSCE High Commissioner on National Minorities

The expectations of the OSCE High Commissioner on National Minorities Max van der Stoel, who had been suggesting the adoption of a law on the use of minority languages ever since the enactment of the 1995 State Language Law, were also high. He had initiated several negotiations in this regard with the Mečiar government but without much success. In his first letter to Prime Minister Dzurinda on 4 November 1998, he again stressed the importance of adopting a law on minority-language use:

> [I]t would be desirable to draft a law on minority languages as a counterpart to the Act on the State Language. I am aware that several existing laws contain provisions regarding minority languages. I therefore suggest that references to these provisions will be included in such a law (van der Stoel, 1998).

He also made specific recommendations and initiated negotiations between the coalition parties aiming at reaching a compromise on its contents.

---

had already concluded or planned to conclude "Europe Agreements") "that so desire shall become members of the Union" and that "accession will take place as soon as an associated country is able to assume the obligations of membership by satisfying the economic and political conditions". These conditions (known as the "Copenhagen Criteria") are that the candidate country: "(1) has achieved stability of institutions guaranteeing democracy, the rule of law, human rights, and respect for and protection of minorities; (2) the existence of a functioning market economy, as well as the capacity to cope with competitive pressure and market forces within the Union; (3) the ability to take on the obligations of membership, including adherence to the aims of political, economic and monetary union." The criteria listed in (1) are known as the 'Copenhagen Political Criteria'.

[58]   At the same time, the Regular Report referred to the lack of stability in the institutions guaranteeing democracy, the rule of law and the protection of human rights, as reflected by the inability to elect a president, the controversial use of the transferred presidential powers, the unsatisfactory functioning of the parliamentary committees and the disregard for Constitutional Court rulings in the period from July 1997 to end September 1998 (European Commission, 1998).

[59]   To the same extent were mentioned "free and fair presidential, national and local elections, effective opposition participation in parliamentary oversight committees and supervisory boards". Slovakia's 1998 Accession Partnership was revised on 13 October 1999 and again in February 2000. The latest Accession Partnership was adopted on 13 November 2001 (European Union, 2001).

(c) The Council of Europe

Slovakia also had several 'debts' in the field of minority-language use to be satisfied in the framework of accession to the Council of Europe since the recommendations adopted by the Parliamentary Assembly of the Council of Europe upon approval of Slovakia's membership had not yet been fulfilled.

Slovakia was invited to become a member of the Council of Europe on 29 June 1993 by the Committee of Ministers in its Resolution (93)33. This Resolution was based on Parliamentary Assembly Opinion No. 175 (1993) on the application by the Slovak Republic for membership in the Council of Europe (Reisch, 1993; Fisher, 1995b: 59).[60] This document asked the Slovak authorities "to base their policy regarding the protection of national minorities on the principles laid down in Parliamentary Assembly Recommendation 1201(1993) on an additional protocol on the rights of national minorities under the European Convention on Human Rights" (Article 8). Article 9 of the Opinion took note of:

> the Slovak authorities' commitment to adopt a legislation granting to every person belonging to a minority the right to use his/her surname and first names in his/her mother tongue and, in the regions in which substantial numbers of a national minority are settled, the right for the persons belonging to this minority to display in their language local names, signs, inscriptions and other similar information, in accordance with the principles contained in Recommendation 1201 (Council of Europe, 1993: Article 9).

It also took note that "whatever administrative divisions may be introduced in the Slovak Republic, of the declaration made by the Slovak authorities that they will respect the rights of national minorities" (Council of Europe, 1993: Article 11).

The 1993 Act on Names and Surnames,[61] as well as the 1994 Act on Registers[62] and the 1994 Act on the Indication of Settlements in the Language of National Minorities[63] settled some of the outstanding debts from accession to the Council of Europe. By becoming a member state of the Council of Europe on 30 June 1993, Slovakia had also undertaken commitments in the field of general human rights as well as minority protection (it ratified the European Convention on Human Rights and the Framework Convention for the Protection of National Minorities).[64] A broad range of

---

[60] The Council of Europe's recommendations were based on the final report by its Rapporteur Tarja Halonen, submitted on 13 January 1993. In this document, she lists the specific requirements that had to be met with regard to minorities. On 12 May, the Political Committee voted to propose Slovakia's admission on the basis of the Halonen report and a ten-point list of conditions that Slovakia had to fulfil; these included abolishing the Beneš Decrees.

[61] Act No. 300 of 1993 on Names and Surnames, Article 2(1).

[62] Act No. 154 of 1994 on Registers, Article 16 and Articles 19(3) and (5).

[63] Act No. 191 of 1994 on the Indication of Settlements in the Language of National Minorities, Article 1.

[64] These and other treaties of the Council of Europe are on the website of the Council of Europe at http://conventions.coe.int.

rights are guaranteed to persons belonging to national minorities by the Framework Convention (entered into force in Slovakia in February 1998), including linguistic rights and freedoms such as, *inter alia*, the freedom to receive and impart information in the minority language (Article 9); the right to freely use the minority language, in private and in public, orally and in writing (Article 10); and the right to use surnames and first names in the minority language, and to display in the minority-language signs, inscriptions and other information of a private nature visible to the public (Article 11).

It is interesting to note that although Slovakia was among the first countries to sign and ratify the Framework Convention in 1995, that same year it adopted a contradictory piece of domestic legislation—the State Language Law.

(d) Slovakia's bilateral treaties

Article 15 of the Treaty on Good Neighbourliness and Friendly Cooperation between the Slovak Republic and the Republic of Hungary[65] established a whole range of language rights in the field of the overall minority protection envisaged in the document. The basic right to use one's mother tongue in private and in public was complemented with a detailed list of linguistic rights.[66] Thus, the bilateral treaty between Slovakia and Hungary also reflected the expectations of international organizations. To the same extent, it was a clear sign that the effective protection of minorities was a major impediment in the development of relations between the two states. According to the treaty, Slovakia would have to take further legislative measures in order to implement the provisions enshrined in the document.

Unfortunately, the treaty could not automatically solve existing disputes between the two states; neither did it directly contribute to the improvement of the situation of the respective minorities. On the contrary, its Article 15 led to further misinterpretations by both the Slovak and the Hungarian sides regarding European norms concerning minority protection.[67] For almost three years, the two governments were unable to

---

[65] The treaty was signed in Paris on 19 March 1995 (ratified in March 1996), in the framework of the Pact on Stability for Europe which aimed at improving neighbourly relations by avoiding the issue of borders and establishing minority rights on the basis of existing international standards, with the prospect of accession to the EU. The desire to be considered a serious candidate for the EU and NATO certainly served as a strong incentive for Slovakia to sign the treaty.

[66] Several provisions dealing with minority rights in the bilateral treaties strongly bear the imprint of international and regional instruments on minority issues (such as the 1990 OSCE Copenhagen Document, Recommendation 1201 (1993), and the 1992 UN Declaration on Minorities). The bilateral treaties give legal force to these documents (Gál, 1999) (see e.g., Articles 2 and 15 of the Slovak–Hungarian Treaty, in de Varennes, 1996: 368–369).

[67] In particular the interpretation of Recommendation 1201 (1993) which includes a reference to special minority arrangements and alludes, according to some interpretations, to different types of autonomies as well as collective rights (Article 11). The Slovak government, obviously wary of incorporating any reference to collective rights or to the special status of national minorities in a bilateral agreement, attached an interpretation of this article to the treaty before its ratification, unilaterally amending the agreed text, insisting that "it has agreed to mention the Recommendation of the Parliamentary Assembly of the Council of Europe 1201 (1993) exclusively with the inclusion of the restricting clause: '. . . respecting individual human and civil rights, including the rights of persons belonging to national minorities'."

agree upon the composition of joint Slovak–Hungarian committees to be established to monitor implementation of the treaty. Only in November 1998 did the Slovak and Hungarian Foreign Ministers sign a protocol on the implementation mechanism. The Joint Commission had its first meeting in January 1999.

3.2.2 International Reactions to the Adoption of the 1999 Minority Language Law

(a)   The European Union

The adoption of the 1999 Minority Language Law was interpreted as very positive by international organizations. The 1999 Regular Report of the Commission on Slovakia's Progress Towards Accession (European Commission, 1999) took into account the developments in Slovakia following the 1998 elections and argued that minority protection was one of the areas where the Slovak authorities had made significant progress over the previous year (European Commission, 1999: B.1.2.). According to one Slovak source: "The report marked a decisive moment for Slovakia, because for the first time a report produced by an international organization was similar to the Slovak government's view of itself ..." (*Slovak Spectator*, 1999g).

Based on the 1999 Regular Report, the European Commission started accession negotiations with Slovakia in February 2000, after the favourable decision taken by the European Council in Helsinki in December 1999. That was the clearest sign that the Commission was in favour of the steps taken regarding minority protection, i.e., of the adopted language law.

(b)   The OSCE

The OSCE High Commissioner on National Minorities, Max van der Stoel, called the language law a considerable step forward (*Slovak Spectator*, 1999f). In a press release in July 1999, he stated that:

> [b]y adopting Article 2 of the new law concerning the use of minority languages in official communications, not only has the Slovak Republic restored an established practice which was eliminated under the previous Government, but it brings Slovakia's law in this matter back into conformity with the Slovak Constitution, applicable international standards and specific recommendations from relevant international institutions, including my own office. With regard to application of the law as a whole, I have received the assurance of the Government that the provisions of the Act on the Use of Minority Languages will prevail, as a matter of subsequent and specific law, when interpreting and applying the law in relation to provisions of the Act on the State Language. I consider solution of the question of the use of minority languages in official communications to be a step forward which follows previous decisions of the Government in the field of inter-ethnic relations ... (van der Stoel, 1999).

(c) The Council of Europe

The Parliamentary Assembly of the Council of Europe terminated the monitoring of Slovakia's fulfilment of its undertakings soon after the Minority Language Law was adopted, putting an end to six years of monitoring since Slovakia's entry.[68] This decision was based also on the fact that "a law was adopted on 10 July 1999 to regulate, in conjunction with other specific laws, the use of minority languages in official communications".[69] The document emphasized that "the law, which restores previous practice—interrupted by the adoption of a law on the state language—and satisfies a constitutional requirement, was adopted following consultations with the OSCE High Commissioner for [sic] National Minorities, the European Union and the Council of Europe and is welcomed".[70]

(d) The kin-state Hungary

The only negative outside reaction was from Hungary which, in a letter dated 21 July (*Newsline*, 1999b) stated that the new law did not satisfy the commitments undertaken by Slovakia in the bilateral treaty with Hungary. It also expressed regret that the proposals set forth by the MKP had been ignored and raised the issue of minority-language use not only at the local level in areas where the minority constitutes twenty per cent but also at higher levels of public administration.

Having stressed the expectations on the international level regarding the adoption of a law on minority-language use and the diverging domestic and international reactions after the adoption of this law, the immediate questions are: why these discrepancies in the interpretation of the law? And why were the reactions so different and contradictory?

---

[68] Parliamentary Assembly Recommendation 1419 (1999) Honouring of Obligations and Commitments by Slovakia, "1.ii.e. regarding minorities: the post of a deputy prime minister responsible for human rights, minorities and regional development, and a parliamentary committee for human rights and minorities has been created; bilingual certificates are used in schools with instruction in a minority language; a law was adopted on 10 July 1999 to regulate, in conjunction with other specific laws, the use of minority languages in official communications: the law, which restores previous practice—interrupted by the adoption of a law on the state language—and satisfies a constitutional requirement, was adopted following consultations with the OSCE High Commissioner for [sic] National Minorities, the European Union and the Council of Europe and is welcomed; other problems, however, resulting from the state language law, with regard to freedom of expression, as well as the use of minority languages in other settings, notably education, still need to be regulated, in conformity with recommendations by the three international organisations; the ratification of the European Charter for Regional or Minority Languages is also strongly recommended" (http://assembly.coe.int/Documents/AdoptedText/TA99/erec1419.htm).

[69] Ibid.

[70] Ibid.

4.   ANALYSIS OF THE 1999 MINORITY LANGUAGE LAW AND ITS IMPACT[71]

In order to understand the different attitudes towards the 1999 Minority Language Law, it must be analysed from two points of view: (1) what this legal text states; and (2) what it means in practice. Furthermore, in order to better understand the situation created by this legal act, two additional acts of national legislation will also be considered: the 1990 Official Language Law and the 1995 State Language Law (see also Section 2). We shall also look at the implementation of the law, or rather, lack thereof.

4.1   What Does the Law State?

There are three main problem areas in the 1999 Minority Language Law:

1.   The Law regulates the language use of national minorities living in Slovakia only in their 'official contacts' with local self-governments: ". . . The purpose of this law is to establish, in harmony with other legislation, the rules of use of minority languages also in official contacts" (Article 1). Although the concept of "official contacts" is not defined here, it is clear from the wording of this article that the law regulates minority-language use in contacts with the local administration (state administration bodies and territorial self-management bodies, referred to as 'public authorities').
      The law guarantees the following rights:
      - The right of members of national minorities to submit written requests to local administration, and to receive an answer, in addition to the state language, also in the minority language (Article 2[3]) "with the exception of public documents".
      - The right of local administrative bodies to distribute official forms in a minority language 'on request' (Article 2[6]), as well as to provide 'on re-quest' information about general legal regulations in a minority language (Article 4[3]).
      - The right of local administrative bodies to conduct meetings in a minority language, 'if all present at the meeting agree' (Article 3[1]); and the right of representatives of local administration to use the minority language at meetings with the assistance of an interpreter provided by the municipality (Article 3[2]).
      - The right of the municipality to keep records/chronicles also in a minority language (Article 3[3]).
      - The right to display important information (warnings, advice and health care notices) in public areas also in the minority language (Article 4[2]).

---

[71]   The Slovak original, *Zákon o používaní jazykov národnostných menšín*, and an official English translation are on the website of the Ministry of Culture at http://www.culture.gov.sk.

The law provides the possibility to designate streets and to display other local geographical signs in a minority language (Article 4[1]). It also enables local administrative bodies and their employees to use a minority language in official contacts (Article 7[1]); however, it leaves the decision up to the municipality or local administration: "The community ... may, in its territory, designate" (Article 4[1]) and "may use the minority language" (Article 7[1]).

Article 5 clearly establishes that the use of minority languages in judicial proceedings, education (pre-school, primary and secondary) and culture is regulated by separate laws. At the same time, it regulates in its Article 2(4) that decisions made in administrative proceedings are issued in both the minority and the state language upon request, although the Slovak version shall prevail in case of doubt.

2. In addition to its most important feature of regulating minority-language use in official contacts only, another condition must be fulfilled: minority-language use in official contacts is restricted to those municipalities where "citizens of the Slovak Republic who are members of national minorities and, by the results of the latest census, represent at least twenty per cent of the total population of the community" (Article 2[1]). As provided by the law, the government establishes by decree those communities (municipalities) that meet this condition (Article 2[2]).

The twenty-per-cent threshold is not a new requirement in the history of Slovak law. As seen in Section 2, this minimum percentage was already established for the use of minority languages in official contacts by the 1990 Official Language Law (Act No. 428 of 1990).

3. Although the 1999 Minority Language Law could be regarded as generous in providing the above-listed rights for persons belonging to national minorities in those municipalities which fit the requirements, the provisions by themselves are quite restrictive. While establishing certain rights, the law immediately restricts them by creating exceptions that are not properly defined. It thereby leads to the possibility of contradictory interpretations (e.g., Article 2[3] "with the exception of public documents"). The best example of the contradictions contained in the text is provided by Article 7. The second paragraph of this article states that "the public authority in the community ... shall establish conditions for use of the minority language under this Law and other legislation" (Article 7[2]). However, the first paragraph declares that "public authorities and their employees shall use the state language in official contacts, and may use the minority language under the conditions established by this Law and other legislation" (i.e., if this complies with the terms set by law). This declaration is immediately restricted by adding that "[p]ublic authorities and their employees are not required to have command of the minority language" (Article 7[1]).

4.2   What Does the Law Mean?

Having briefly analysed the text of the 1999 Minority Language Law, it is crucial to look at the meaning and implementation of these provisions since a legislative act only makes sense if it regulates an existing issue or relationship and if it can be used in practice.

1.   Being formulated in a vague and contradictory way, and containing a number of escape clauses, this is a legislative act full of loopholes. To the same extent, it leads to doubts as to the intention of the legislators as enshrined in the preamble of the law which says that the law was enacted "acting upon the Constitution of the Slovak Republic and international covenants binding the Slovak Republic" and that it is "acknowledging and valuing the importance of mothers [sic] tongues of citizens of the Slovak Republic who are members of national minorities as an expression of the cultural wealth of the country". At the same time, it recognizes that "the Slovak language is the state language". This makes it difficult to ascertain the real intentions of the legislators concerning each article and the law in its totality.

The first deficiency is that it defines neither the term "official contacts" in general (Article 2[1]) nor that of "public documents" in particular (Article 2[3]). The rights enshrined in the provisions are formulated either inconsistently or vaguely in order to avoid effective implementation. As in the case of street signs and other geographical designations, the use of the minority language depends on the goodwill of the given municipality (who "may" use the minority language). This can be regarded as a restrictive interpretation of the provisions enshrined in Article 15(2)(g) of the Slovak–Hungarian Bilateral Treaty[72] as well as in Article 7(3) and 7(4) of the Council of Europe Parliamentary Assembly Recommendation 1201 (1993).[73]

Furthermore, the contradictions in Article 7 (see above) create a confusing legal situation. It is not easy to imagine how this provision can ever be implemented or how its application can be claimed in judicial proceedings. In practice, a citizen speaking a minority language in a municipality that is in conformity with the law (minority population above twenty per cent) has the right to address a question to the employee of the local administration in his/her mother tongue (Article 7[2]). On the other hand, that employee is not obligated to understand the request, as the local administration is not required to hire a minority-language-speaking employee (Article 7[1]). Even if, by mere

---

[72]   Article 15(2)(g) states ". . . They shall also have the right, in conformity with the domestic law and with the international commitments undertaken by the two Contracting Parties, to use their mother tongue in contacts with official authorities, including public administration, and in judicial proceedings, to display in their mother tongue the names of municipalities in which they live, street names and names of other public areas, topographical indications, inscriptions and information in public areas."

[73]   Article 7(3): "In the regions in which substantial numbers of a national minority are settled, the persons belonging to a national minority shall have the right to use their mother tongue in their contacts with the administrative authorities and in proceedings before the courts and legal authorities". Article 7(4): "In the regions in which substantial numbers of a national minority are settled, the persons belonging to that minority shall have the right to display in their language local names, signs, inscriptions and other similar information visible to the public . . .".

coincidence, the employee does understand it, he/she must answer in the state language (Article 7[1]). However, he/she "may" answer in the minority language.

The law provides at the same time certain rights that will not work automatically between the person belonging to the minority and the local administrative bodies. This is the case where the rights are exercised only upon request (Articles 2[4]; 2[6] and 4[3]), presuming that the person belonging to the minority is aware of his/her right to submit a request or speak in the minority language.

The intention of the legislators is even more confusing when one looks at the basic conditions established by the law. There is the requirement of a minimum of 20 per cent of minority members in a municipality in order for it to take effect. But this provision is further restricted by a government decree that gives a list of municipalities satisfying these conditions (as one of the analyses prepared by the Hungarian Human Rights Foundation (HHRF) concluded, Government Decree No. 221 of 1999 failed to include several minority-inhabited communities).[74]

2.   The 1999 Minority Language Law has to be placed and defined in the context of Slovak national legislation. It is a simple legislative act and, as such, does not take precedence over other laws. Its next-to-last article cancels Article 10 of the 1995 State Language Law, which merely refers to the fines that can be levied—and not to the official use of the state language (this is covered in Article 3).[75] As there are no other acts cancelling the 1995 State Language Law, and as the 1999 Minority Language Law does not contain any provisions on its position within overall Slovak legislation, it is *de facto* unclear which act takes precedence, that is, whether any of them could be regarded as *lex specialis* over *lex generalis*.

3.   According to some interpretations, as the last article of the Minority Language Law cancels only Article 10 of the 1995 State Language Law, this highly contested piece of

---

[74]   One of the reasons for the omission was that the list, originally excerpted from Act No. 191 of 1994 on the Designation of Localities in National Minority Languages, did not include municipalities which received their Slovak-language equivalents after 1945. In addition, since 1994, several primarily Hungarian-inhabited suburbs have decided to separate and create their own administrative unit. These changes were not reflected in the government's list either, resulting in the omission of one Czech-inhabited and 66 Roma-inhabited municipalities (see HHRF, 1999).

[75]   Article 3 of the 1995 State Language Law states: "(1) State agencies and entities, organs of the territorial self-governments and public institutions ... are obliged to use the state language in exercising their competencies on the entire territory of the Slovak Republic. Proof of adequate proficiency in speaking and writing the state language is a condition to employment or engagement in other work-like situations, and is a prerequisite to completing specified contractual work for public bodies ... (3) In the state language ... hold all deliberations of public bodies; are recorded all official documents ...; are indicated the official names of communities and their parts, the names of streets and other public places, other geographic terms, as well as data contained in state maps, including cadastre maps; a separate law will regulate the designation of localities in other languages; ... (4) All public bodies, and all organisations established by them, are obliged to use the state language in every informational system and inter-agency contact. (5) Citizens prepare all written submissions to public bodies in state language" (1995 Slovak State Language Law, see Minority Protection Association, 1996: 7–8).

legislation remains in force. The general principle of the 1995 State Language Law (see Section 2) was to position the Slovak language as the exclusive language to be used in almost every aspect of life. The fields addressed included: use of the state language in official contact (Article 3); in education (Article 4); in mass media, cultural events and assembly (Article 5); in the armed forces, armed services and fire departments (Article 6); in court and public administration proceedings (Article 7); and in the economic sector, service industries and health care (Article 8). At the same time, it restricted to a large extent the use and overall status of minority languages since there was no other legislation regulating minority-language use. It could also be used to discriminate against minority members employed in the civil service, or against teachers at Hungarian minority schools. For these reasons, the 1995 State Language Law was considered a major setback for minorities.

Article 3 of the 1995 Law described official contacts in a broader sense, referring to all public bodies, such as state agencies, self-governments, public institutions, transportation and telecommunication, armed forces, armed security services, fire departments. These public bodies were not enlisted in the 1999 Minority Language Law. The uncertainty created by the latter could easily lead to the interpretation that, if it is not clear enough or does not regulate in detailed fashion the language use of minorities in official contacts, then Article 3 of the State Language Law will prevail, except for Article 10 (no taxes will be levied for violating the State Language Law). The assurances of the government that the provisions of the Minority Language Law will prevail, as a matter of subsequent and specific law, when interpreting and applying it in relation to provisions of the State Language Law (Dzurinda, 1998), are not enough.

4.3 Impact of the Minority Language Law

The Minority Language Law came into effect on 1 September 1999. It primarily concerns the Hungarian minority as well as the Roma, Ruthenians, Ukrainians, Croats and Germans in those municipalities where they make up at least twenty per cent (the Ministry of Interior established a list of the 656 municipalities where it applies, as required) (European Commission, 2000). However, as foreseen, it seems to have had little impact on the actual use of minority languages due to the absence of clear instructions for local civil servants as well as the lack of employees with knowledge of the minority languages. This confirms the view that it was adopted mainly to ensure Slovakia's fulfilment of the expectations of the international community, with a view to joining the EU.

In its Opinion on Slovakia, the Council of Europe's Advisory Committee on the Framework Convention for the Protection of National Minorities welcomed the "recent improvements in the legal status of minority languages in official contacts"; however, it also found that "the legislative framework touching upon minority languages still contains shortcomings stemming *inter alia* from the content of the State Language Law and from the lack of detailed provisions on education in minority languages" (Council of Europe, 2000). In order to overcome the "ambiguous legal situation" which could have negative consequences for minorities, it recommended that the degree to which the 1995 State Language Law affects minority languages be ascertained, and that this Law be amended, if necessary. While it also recommended that the Minority Language Law, as *lex specialis*, take precedence over the State Language Law, it suggested that due consideration be given to a wide-ranging law concerning the protection of national minorities. Regarding the 1999 Minority Language Law more specifically, the Advisory Committee concluded that it represented a positive step in the implementation of Article 10 of the Framework Convention (on the use of minority languages in private and in public, orally and in writing) but recommended that the reported problems, such as the lack of language skills, be addressed by allocating adequate resources for training and other measures to ensure full implementation of the law. In its response Slovakia stated that it would handle these recommendations in the context of the European Charter for Regional or Minority Languages (hereafter, 'Charter') without prejudice to the use of the state language (Slovak Republic, 2001: Article 12).

Following a year-long debate within the government coalition about the application of the Charter in public administration, it was finally signed on 20 February 2001 and ratified on 5 September 2001. It entered into force on 1 January 2002 and applies to the Bulgarian, Croatian, Czech, German, Hungarian, Polish, Romani, Ruthenian and Ukrainian languages in municipalities where persons belonging to the respective minorities constitute at least twenty per cent of the population (these are the same as those listed in Decree No. 221 of 1999). This also holds for Article 10 of the Charter on administrative authorities and public services where the Hungarian language benefits from more generous provisions.[76] With the Charter, many outstanding issues such as the regulation of the use of minority languages in other spheres (especially in education, media and culture) are now covered.

CONCLUSION: SLOVAKIA'S 'RETURN TO EUROPE'

The 1999 Minority Language Law was a direct outcome of the Dzurinda government's programme and aimed at fulfilling both domestic commitments, as established mainly by the Constitution, and international commitments, associated with Council of Europe membership. However, one of the first conclusions derived from a pure analysis of the Law is that it mostly follows international requirements. From a strictly legal point of view, it does not contradict the major international, bilateral and national legal documents, such as the Charter, the Framework Convention, Recommendation 1201 (1993), the 1990 OSCE Copenhagen Document, the Slovak–Hungarian Bilateral Treaty or the Slovak Constitution. Nevertheless, the spirit

---

[76]   In the case of Hungarian, Slovakia undertakes to ensure that officials who are in contact with the public use Hungarian in their relations with persons applying to them in Hungarian (Article 10[1][a][ii]). It stops short, however, of committing to ensure that administrative authorities use Hungarian in the provision of public services (Article 10[3][a]), but rather undertakes to allow Hungarian-speakers to submit a request and receive a reply in Hungarian (Article 10[3][b]). For other minority languages, Slovakia undertakes to ensure that users of these languages can submit oral or written applications and receive a reply in these languages (Article 10[1][a][iii–iv]) (although, in an apparent contradiction, it later undertakes only to ensure that a request may be submitted in a minority language without guaranteeing that the reply be made in the minority language (Article 10[3][c]).

of the Minority Language Law is questionable from several aspects: problems lie in content and implementation, as well as with the process behind the adoption of the law.

Due to the vague wording of the text, the loopholes that were built into its various paragraphs and the legal uncertainty it creates, it can hardly be said that the law was formulated with the intention of being used in everyday practice (this would be almost impossible given the contradiction in Article 7 for example).

In order to implement the 1999 Minority Language Law, other laws or decrees were needed to clarify its provisions, fill in the legal gaps and give concrete meaning to the terms used. The recently ratified Charter partially fills in gaps in areas such as education, media and culture. Still, it does not refer to language use at the regional level. Thus, for minority-language use in areas not covered by the two above-mentioned instruments, the 1995 State Language Law still applies. As the latter instrument does not provide for any minority-language rights, one can conclude that no right to use a minority language exists at the level of higher administrative units, i.e., the newly established regions.[77] The State Language Law also still applies to municipalities where the share of minorities is under twenty per cent.

Internally, the 1999 Minority Language Law did not have a significant positive impact; rather, it exposed disagreements between the parties within the coalition government, satisfying neither the Slovak nationalists—who considered the law to be too far-reaching—nor the ethnic Hungarians—whose proposals were not taken into account. It is indeed striking that a law concerning minorities could be adopted without the support of the minority concerned, even though it was represented in government. Still, the law was arguably the best which could have been achieved, given the particular political context and the lingering fear of (ethnic) Slovak parties that it is politically dangerous to be seen as too conciliatory to the Hungarian minority. A stronger version of the law, as proposed by the MKP, might have seriously disrupted interethnic relations.

However, the mere existence of a law on the use of minority languages was a positive fact in itself and represented progress compared to the legal situation in Slovakia after the adoption of the 1995 State Language Law, and even compared to the 1990–1995 period when the 1990 Official Language Law was in force.

One can therefore conclude that the 1999 Minority Language Law served mainly to boost the legitimacy of the Dzurinda government and, seen together with the ratification of the Charter, it represented a milestone in the process of Slovakia's accession to the EU. The weak impact on the actual use of minority languages thus far supports the prediction that the Law will not be invoked by minorities in contacts with local authorities. A continuation of the traditional discrepancy in Slovakia between what is laid down in the law and the actual situation, referred to as 'posturing' (Kontra, 1995/1996: 347) (when legal provisions are curtailed by government decrees or circumvented by local decrees of mayors of predominantly Hungarian municipalities), is therefore to be expected. Thus, while one important point of the government programme was satisfied with the adoption of this law, minorities remained unsatisfied, yet again.

---

[77]   See fn. 80 on the reform of public administration in 2001.

Following the election of a new government in 1998, Slovakia experienced a marked improvement in its international standing and chances of EU (and NATO) membership. Slovakia's relations with Hungary also improved, despite the latter's strong disapproval of the Minority Language Law (*Newsline*, 1999d). Improving the situation of Hungarian and other minorities, especially in the field of mother-tongue education and teacher training, was a stated priority of the Dzurinda government. There have indeed been some positive steps to resolve other outstanding issues in Slovak–Hungarian relations such as the question of Hungarian higher education.[78] But these have been half-steps, never fully meeting the demands of the Hungarian minority. Due to a range of internal and external factors (notably the so-called Hungarian Status Law),[79] friction between the MKP and the other coalition parties steadily increased, with the MKP even temporarily withdrawing from the government in July 2001 in protest against the new Law on Local Public Administration.[80] Another development which cast a shadow on interethnic relations in Slovakia was the election, in March 2002, of a nationalist to the newly-created post of Parliamentary Commissioner for Human Rights (Ombudsman).[81]

On 5 January 2000, Pál Csáky announced that the government had accepted a multi-ethnic model for Slovak society, meaning respect for all minority communities, and not only the Hungarian minority.[82] However, the Slovak nation and language continue to enjoy, at least on paper, a dominant position in all spheres of life. In its Programme Declarations, the government also stated that it would "ensure the protection and development of the state language".[83] Accordingly, a "Concept of Care for the State Language of the Slovak Republic" (Government Resolution No. 131 of 2001 *Koncepcia starostlivosti o štátny jazyk Slovenskej*

---

[78] On 25 January 2001, the government approved the establishment of a Hungarian-language faculty for the training of Hungarian-language teachers and also offering arts-related degrees at Constantine University in Nitra. The MKP, however, wanted an independent university (*Newsline*, 2001a).

[79] The so-called Hungarian Status Law (Hungarian Parliament, 2001), adopted by the Hungarian parliament on 19 June 2001, grants certain benefits to ethnic Hungarians in neighbouring countries. It came into effect in Slovakia at the beginning of 2002 but has been met with the strong opposition of the Slovak government which believes that it infringes upon Slovak sovereignty. While the 'Status Law' has led to a deterioration of relations between Slovakia and Hungary, the tense atmosphere can also be partly attributed to nationalist rhetoric on both sides prior to the 2002 parliamentary elections (April 2002 in Hungary and September 2002 in Slovakia).

[80] The MKP had been calling for a unified ethnic Hungarian administrative region. The final government proposal, supported by the MKP, was for twelve administrative units (i.e., a return to the pre-1996 administrative districts). However, this proposal failed and the current division into eight regions was preserved in the new Act on Local Public Administration adopted by parliament on 4 July 2001, allegedly because coalition members SDĽ and SOP joined the opposition in voting against the government's proposal (*Newsline*, 2001b).

[81] Surprisingly, it was the candidate of the HZDS who was elected rather than the government candidate, a human rights expert who enjoyed the support of about 260 civic organizations. This apparently occurred because two coalition parties—the SDĽ and the SOP—voted for the HZDS candidate (*Transitions Online*, 2002).

[82] Radio Slovakia International, 5 January 2000 (in Hungarian Human Rights Monitor). One of Csáky's stated goals was to neutralize the effect of the so-called Hungarian Card (Csáky, 1999).

[83] Programme Declarations, Section 4(3)(F) on "Culture".

republiky) was adopted on 14 February 2001.[84] The Concept outlines the main principles and aims of language policy in the Slovak Republic and also addresses implementation. While it emphasizes the importance of the Slovak language as an integrating factor in Slovak society and, for example, mentions the need to pay increased attention to the teaching of Slovak in minority schools, most of it is devoted to the issue of corpus planning.

With the adoption of the Act on the Use of Languages of National Minorities and the ratification of the Charter, Slovakia moved several steps closer to EU membership. The EU's decision to invite Slovakia to begin membership negotiations was described by Prime Minister Dzurinda as "the greatest achievement in the history of Slovakia" (*Newsline*, 1999e). At the November 2002 NATO summit in Prague, Slovakia was also formally invited to join NATO. But the international community has stressed that Slovakia's 'return to Europe' would be conditional upon active efforts to improve the situation of minorities and especially that of the Roma (European Union, 2000). Thus, the increased attention paid by the Slovak government to the Roma issue should be interpreted as a direct acknowledgement of the new priorities set by the European Commission regarding Slovakia's fulfilment of the Copenhagen Political Criteria. Improving the situation of its Roma community will be the real test of Slovakia's commitment to multicultural ideals and ethnic diversity and of its preparedness to accept members of ethnic minorities as equal constituent elements of the Slovak state.[85]

In its 2001 Regular Report on Slovakia (European Commission, 2001), the Commission noted that the Charter had been ratified and concurred with the Council of Europe's Advisory Committee on the Framework Convention in highlighting the achievements in improving inter-community relations, notably *vis-à-vis* the Hungarian minority. But it reiterated the impression expressed in its 2000 Regular Report (European Commission, 2000) that, in many areas, minorities were not making use of the rights granted to them due to lack of information, citing, for example, that no Roma had apparently taken advantage of the new possibilities to use the Romani language.

In fact, it was political instability[86] which represented the greatest potential obstacle to Slovakia' integration into Euro-Atlantic structures. Dzurinda's victory in the September 2002 elections was thus met with relief by the international community and paved the way for the historic meeting of the European Council in Copenhagen (December 2002) at which Slovakia was informed that it had qualified to join the EU in 2004.

To conclude, the legal uncertainties related to minority-language use which were created by a confusing piece of domestic legislation mainly catering to the international community—the 1999 Minority Language Law—have been settled, at least on paper, by the

---

[84]   In Slovak, on the website of the Ministry of Culture, at http://www.culture.gov.sk.

[85]   In 1999–2000, the Slovak government adopted a two-staged strategy to improve the situation of the Roma community. It has been welcomed by the European Commission, although its implementation has been quite problematic (EU Accession Monitoring Program, 2001: 480–484)

[86]   There have been a series of defections from the government coalition as well as disturbing voting behaviour of coalition members. In February 2000, Prime Minister Dzurinda left the KDH to launch a new party, the Slovak Democratic and Christian Union (SDKÚ). In November 2000, the government coalition pact had to be amended due to the departure of several MPs of the KDH and the DS. Mečiar has also made various attempts to destabilize the government by calling for early elections.

ratification of the Charter. Still, despite this initiative and the marked improvements in interethnic relations following the 1998 parliamentary elections, the future of Slovak–Hungarian relations remains uncertain so long as nationalist political stratagems and undemocratic behaviour of influential political leaders prevail. It is to be hoped that the process of democratization and stabilization will continue in Slovakia up to and beyond EU accession and that language issues and policies will be resorted to less as populist instruments but rather as genuine means of preserving and fostering diversity.

REFERENCES

Adam, Gejza (2000) "Slovak Roma Want Language Law Implemented". RomNews Network. 9 March 2000. http://romnews.com/community/modules.php?op=modload&name=News&file=article&sid=485.

Bakker, Edwin (1997) *Minority Conflicts in Slovakia and Hungary*. Capelle a/d Ijissel: Labyrint.

Bakker, Edwin (1998) "Growing Isolation: political and ethnic tensions in the Slovak Republic". *Helsinki Monitor*, 9(1): 23–36.

BBC Worldwide Monitoring (2000) "Slovak Romany Party Planning Political Allegiance with Left Parties". RomNews Network. 26 March 2000. http://www.romnews.com/a/109-00.html.

Butora, D. (1998) "Mečiar and the Velvet Divorce". *Transition* 5(8, August): 72–75.

Central Europe Review (1999) "The New Minority Language Law in Slovakia". *Central Europe Review*, 1(2) (5 July).

Council of Europe (1993) "Opinion No. 175 (1993) of the Parliamentary Assembly of the Council of Europe on the application by the Slovak Republic for membership of the Council of Europe". Adopted on 29 June 1993. http://assembly.coe.int/Documents/AdoptedText/ta93/EOPI175.htm.

Council of Europe (2000) "Advisory Committee on the Framework Convention for the Protection of National Minorities, Opinion on Slovakia," adopted on 22 September 2000. http://www.humanrights.coe.int/Minorities/Eng/FrameworkConvention/AdvisoryCommittee/Opinions/Slovakia.htm.

Csáky, Pál (1999) "I Bring More Empathy to Romani Problems". *Slovak Spectator*, 16–22 November 1999.

de Varennes, Fernand (1996) "Language, Minorities and Human Rights". In *International Studies in Human Rights*, 45. The Hague: Martinus Nijhoff.

Dzurinda, Mikuláš (1998) "Letter to the OSCE High Commissioner on National Minorities". OSCE. 12 November 1998. http://www.osce.org/hcnm/documents/recommendations/slovakia/1998/11gal98.html.

European Commission (1998) "Regular Report from the Commission on Slovakia's Progress Towards Accession". http://europa.eu.int/comm/enlargement/ report_11_98/pdf/en/slovakia_en.pdf.

European Commission (1999) "Regular Report from the Commission on Slovakia's Progress Towards Accession". http://europa.eu.int/comm/enlargement/report_10_99/pdf/en/slovakia_en.pdf .

European Commission (2000) "Regular Report from the Commission on Slovakia's Progress Towards Accession", 8 November 2000. http://europa.eu.int/comm/enlargement/report_11_00/pdf/en/slovakia_en.pdf .

European Commission (2001) "2001 Regular Report on Slovakia's Progress Towards Accession", 13 November 2001. http://europa.eu.int/comm/enlargement/report2001/sk_en.pdf.

European Union (2000) "Accession Partnership 1999—Slovakia", 13 October 1999 (revised February 2000). http://europa.eu.int/comm/enlargement/dwn/ap_sk_99.pdf.

European Union (2001) "Accession Partnership with Slovakia", 13 November 2001. http://europa.eu.int/comm/enlargement/report2001/apsk_en.pdf.

EU Accession Monitoring Program (2001) *Monitoring the EU Accession Process: Minority Protection*. 2001. Budapest: Open Society Institute.

European Roma Rights Center (1997) "Time of the Skinheads. Denial and Exclusion of Roma in Slovakia". *Country Reports Series*, No. 3. Budapest: ERRC.

Fisher, Sharon (1995a) "Treaty Fails to End Squabbles over Hungarian Relations". *Transition*, 1(9) (9 June 1995): 2–7.

Fisher, Sharon (1995b) "Ethnic Hungarians Back Themselves Into a Corner". *Transition*, 1(24) (29 December 1995): 58–63.

Fisher, Sharon (1996a) "Making Slovakia More 'Slovak'". *Transition* 2(24) (29 November 1996): 14–17.

Fisher, Sharon (1996b) "Slovak Government Clamps down on Culture". *Transition*, 2(24) (29 November 1996): 57–59.

Gál, Kinga (1999) *Bilateral Agreements in Central and Eastern Europe: A New Inter-State Framework for Minority Protection*. ECMI Working Paper No. 4. Flensburg: European Centre for Minority Issues.

Harlig, Jeffrey (1997) "National Consolidation vs. European Integration: The Language Issue in Slovakia". *Security Dialogue*, 28(4): 479–491.

Hungarian Human Rights Foundation (HHRF) (1999) *Hungarian Minorities Monitor*, 1(1) (July–August 1999) New York: HHRF. http://www.hhrf.org/monitor.

Hungarian Parliament (2001) "Act LXII of 2001 on Hungarians Living in Neighbouring Countries". http://www.htmh.hu/law.htm.

Kontra, Miklós (1995/1996) "English Only's Cousin: Slovak Only". *Acta Linguistica Hungarica*, 43(3-4): 345–372.

Kontra, Miklós (1996) "The War over Names in Slovakia". *Language Problems and Language Planning*, 20(2, summer): 160–167.

Liégeois, Jean-Pierre and Nicolae Gheorghe (1995) *Roma/Gypsies: A European Minority*. London: Minority Rights Group.

Minority Protection Association (1996) *The Slovak State Language Law and the Minorities —Critical Analyses and Remarks*. Minority Protection Series 1. Budapest: Kossuth Publishing.

Minority Rights Group International (1997) "Slovakia". In *World Directory of Minorities*. London: Minority Rights Group International, pp. 245–247.

Newsline (1997a) "Slovak Constitutional Court Rules on Language Law Complaints". *RFE/RL Newsline*, 10 September 1997. http://www.rferl.org/newsline/1997/09/100997.asp.

Newsline (1997b) "Slovak Government Won't Pass New Language Law". *RFE/RL Newsline*, 5 November 1997. http://www.rferl.org/newsline/1997/11/051197.asp.

Newsline (1997c) "Slovak Opposition to Cooperate with Hungarian Ethnic Parties". *RFE/RL Newsline*, 4 December 1997. http://www.rferl.org/newsline/1997/12/041297.asp.

Newsline (1998) "Slovakia Opts for Political Change". *RFE/RL Newsline*, 28 September 1998. http://www.rferl.org/newsline/1998/09/280998.asp.

Newsline (1999a) "Slovak Opposition Completes Referendum Drive". *RFE/RL Newsline*, 7 July 1999. http://www.rferl.org/newsline/1999/07/070799.asp.

Newsline (1999b) "Hungary Files Objection to Slovak Language Law". *RFE/RL Newsline*, 23 July 1999. http://www.rferl.org/newsline/1999/07/230799.asp.

Newsline (1999c) "Slovak Romany Parties Agree on Unification". *RFE/RL Newsline*, 13 September 1999. http://www.rferl.org/newsline/1999/09/130999.asp.

Newsline (1999d) "Hungary Praises Slovakia's Improved Minorities' Policies". *RFE/RL Newsline*, 1 October 1999. http://www.rferl.org/newsline/1999/10/011099.asp.

Newsline (1999e) "Slovak Politicians Welcome EU Summit Decision". *RFE/RL Newsline*, 13 December 1999. http://www.rferl.org/newsline/1999/12/131299.asp.

Newsline (2001a) "Slovak Government Approves Hungarian Language Faculty at Nitra University". *RFE/RL Newsline*, 25 January 2001. http://www.rferl.org/newsline/2001/01/250101.asp.

Newsline (2001b) "Hungarian Party in Slovakia 'Temporarily Withdraws' from Ruling Coalition". *RFE/RL Newsline*, 9 July 2001. http://www.rferl.org/newsline/2001/07/090701.asp.

OMRI (1996) "Slovak Prime Minister on Minorities". *OMRI Daily Digest*, 31 October 1996. http://archive.tol.cz/omri/restricted/article.php3?id=15455.

Reisch, Alred A. (1993) "Slovakia's Minority Policy under International Scrutiny". *RFE/RL Research Report*, 2(49): 35–42.

Rusyn News and Information Service (1999) "Ruthenian Language Rights Takes one Big Step Forward, a Half Step Back in Slovakia, while Slovakia Takes a Big Step Forward". Rusyn News and Information Service, 23 July 1999.

Šedivý, Vladimir and Viktor Maroši (1995) *The Situation of National Minorities and Ethnic Groups in the Slovak Republic*. Bratislava: Minority Rights Group–Slovakia.

Slovak Foreign Ministry (1996) "Letter from the Slovak Foreign Minister to the OSCE High Commissioner". OSCE. 23 April 1996. http://www.osce.org/hcnm/documents/recommendations/slovakia/1996/32hc46.html.

Slovak Helsinki Committee (1999) "Report on the Implementation of the Framework Convention of the Council of Europe on the Protection of Minorities in the Slovak Republic". http://ww.riga.lv/minelres/reports/slovakia/NGO/slovakia_NGO.htm.

Slovak Republic (1999) "Report Submitted by the Slovak Republic pursuant to Article 25(1) of the Framework Convention for the Protection of National Minorities". http://www.riga.lv/minelres/reports/slovakia/slovak.htm.

Slovak Republic (2001) "Comments of the Government of the Slovak Republic to the Opinion of the Advisory Committee on the Report on the Implementation of the Framework Convention on the Protection of National Minorities in the Slovak Republic". http://www.humanrights.coe.int/minorities/Eng/FrameworkConvention/AdvisoryCommittee/Opinions/Slovakia.Comments.htm.

Slovak Spectator (1999a) "Road to EU Paved with Good Intentions, Untried Laws". *Slovak Spectator*, 1–7 February 1999.

Slovak Spectator (1999b) "Language Law Held up by Squabble". *Slovak Spectator*, 7–13 June 1999.

Slovak Spectator (1999c) "If Hungarians Won't Board EU Train, Leave Them at the Station". *Slovak Spectator*, 28 June–4 July 1999.

Slovak Spectator (1999d) "Hungarian Language Bill Defeated". *Slovak Spectator*, 12–18 July 1999.

Slovak Spectator (1999e) "Minority Language Law Passed after Emotional Seven-Day Debate". *Slovak Spectator*, 19–25 July 1999.

Slovak Spectator (1999f) "Van der Stoel Likes Slovakia's Minority Language Law". *Slovak Spectator*, 13–19 September 1999.

Slovak Spectator (1999g) "EC Report Crowning Achievement of 1999". *Slovak Spectator*, 20–26 December 1999.

Taras, Ray (1998) "Nations and Language-Building: Old Theories, Contemporary Cases". *Nationalism and Ethnic Politics*, 4(3): 79–101.

Transitions Online (2002) "Slovak Government Disunity Marks Ombudsman Vote". *Transitions*, 19–25 March 2002.

US Department of State (1999) "Country Reports on Human Rights Practices, Slovak Republic, 25 February 2000". http://www.state.gov/g/drl/rls/hrrpt/1999/359.htm.

van der Stoel, Max (1995) "Letter to Slovak Foreign Minister Juraj Schenk". OSCE High Commissioner on National Minorities. 24 August 1995. http://www.osce.org/hcnm/documents/recommendations/slovakia/1995/26hc95.html.

van der Stoel, Max (1996) ""Letter to Slovak Foreign Minister Juraj Schenk". OSCE High Commissioner on National Minorities. 26 February 1996. http://www.osce.org/hcnm/documents/recommendations/slovakia/1996/32hc46.html.

van der Stoel, Max (1998) "Letter to Slovak Prime Minister Mikuláš Dzurinda". OSCE High Commissioner on National Minorities. 4 November 1998. http://www.osce.org/hcnm/documents/recommendations/slovakia/1998/11gal98.html.

van der Stoel, Max (1999) "OSCE Welcomes Restoration of Minority Languages in Slovakia", *OSCE Press Release*, OSCE. 19 July 1999. http://www.osce.org/news/generate.php3?news_id=825.

Wolchik, Sharon L. (1997) "Democratization and Political Participation in Slovakia". In Karen Dawisha and Bruce Parrott (eds.) *The Consolidation of Democracy in East-Central Europe*. Authoritarianism and Democratization in Postcommunist Societies 1. Cambridge: Cambridge University Press, pp.197–244.

Wolf, Karol (1998) *Podruhé a naposled, aneb mírové dělení Československa* (For the second and the last time, or the peaceful break-up of Czechoslovakia). Prague: G plus G.

Žitný, Milan (1998) "Slovakia: Party of 'Pure Slovak Blood'". *Transitions*, 2(7) (15 July 1998): 37–38.

Language Battles in the Baltic States: 1989 to 2002

Priit Järve

Language Battles in the Baltic States: 1989 to 2002[87]

Priit Järve

INTRODUCTION

Language is one of the most powerful tools that we possess to understand ourselves and control our relations with other people in society. Language as a collective enterprise, public and intimate at the same time, is inseparable from the identity of the people who use it. Frequently, language is the most important pillar of a people's culture and a no less significant marker of its political universe. Therefore, it has not been incidental that in new or restored states of Central and Eastern Europe, including the Commonwealth of Independent States (CIS) and some members of the Russian Federation, the languages of the titular nations have been given the status of 'official' or 'state language' by law. This language legislation has received much publicity, especially in the context of minority-majority relations.

Language legislation establishes a direct link between politics and national identity, because legislation is a core component of a nation's political development and language is essential to national identity. Legislation follows the political development of the national elite and reflects its perceptions, aims and ambitions. But once adopted and enforced, legislative acts have a formative influence on the political process. Therefore, when dealing with changes in rationale of language legislation, we are actually referring to two interrelated processes of change; this legislation is being altered in the course of political development, and a new political reality is being shaped by the enforcement of language legislation.

Language legislation can be part of different political strategies such as nation-building, ethnic containment and the management of linguistic diversity, depending on the ethnic composition of the population, the nature of democratization processes, on country's international ambitions, etc. To be sure, there are no clear-cut dividing lines between nation-building, ethnic containment and the management of linguistic diversity. For example, the very establishment of an official language by law, an important contribution to nation-building and to the nation-state, can display elements of ethnic containment (in which other linguistic groups are automatically disadvantaged), as well as elements of the management of linguistic diversity (languages might be assigned different roles in education, administration,

---

[87] Earlier versions of this chapter under the title "Two Waves of Language Laws in the Baltic States: Changes of Rationale?" were presented at the panel Language Laws: Nation-Building, Ethnic Containment, or Diversity Management? at the 5th Annual Convention of the Association for the Study of Nationalities (ASN), New York, 13–16 April 2000, and published in the *Journal of Baltic Studies*, 2002, 33(1): 78–110.

access to state funds, etc.). These political strategies are different, but they represent interrelated aspects of nation-state building in which language legislation may play an important role. However, their relative importance can change in different phases of political development, depending on the country's progress in democratization and on its international position.

It can be assumed that at the initial stage of development of a newly independent state the rationale of language legislation is nation-building and nation-state building. Thereafter, depending on the nature of minority-majority relations, 'ethnic containment' may become more prominent, and then, as democratization and globalization advance, a more sophisticated management of linguistic diversity might emerge as a principal issue. In the following, I will test this general assumption with regard to the language legislation of the newly independent Baltic states of Estonia, Latvia and Lithuania.

1. BACKGROUND

Throughout the eighteenth and nineteenth centuries, when nation-building together with language rationalization became prominent issues in Western Europe, the peoples of the contemporary Baltic states of Estonia, Latvia and Lithuania were living in the Russian Empire. In Western Europe, many smaller peoples lost their languages after having been assimilated in the processes of nation-building. Estonians, Latvians and Lithuanians escaped this fate. Although quite small (there were less than one million ethnic Estonians, less than two million Latvians and less than three million Lithuanians), these peoples were not assimilated by Russia. Instead, they were able to start cautious nation-building from the second half of the nineteenth century, but not nation-state building. As David D. Laitin (1998: 43) explains, language rationalization happened historically too late in Russia and conflicted with the needs of mass education and economic development. Being a late modernizer, Russia could not be a very efficient assimilator, although some assimilation was naturally taking place. At the end of the nineteenth century, it made the last concerted attempt to promote Russian, but largely failed. This failure was repeated one hundred years later by the Soviet Union, which only shows that empires and multinational states are not as good assimilators as nation-states. When the Russian Empire entered the era of industrialization, its workforce had to be educated fast. There was not enough time for language rationalization, i.e., for teaching Russian. Another important reason was that Russian nationalism (not to be confused with imperial ambitions) has been practically non-existent throughout Russian history, which largely explains the collapse of both Tsarist Russia and the Soviet Union (Rowley, 2000).

As a result, after the First World War, the Baltic peoples escaped the crumbling Russian Empire with their own languages, which then became the official languages of the independent nation-states of Estonia, Latvia and Lithuania between the two World Wars (Loeber, 1993). In 1940, the Baltic states were forcibly annexed to the Soviet Union, and when they regained their independence in 1990–1991, there were, especially in Latvia and Estonia, sizable Russian-speaking minorities (almost 45 per cent and 35 per cent of the total population respectively) with a limited knowledge of the local languages. In Lithuania, Russian-speakers and Poles constituted less than ten per cent of the population each, due to which minority and language issues were less prominent than in Latvia and Estonia. According to new population censuses in Estonia and Latvia (in 2000) and in Lithuania (in 2001), the shares of minorities in the populations had decreased since 1989. The total number of Russians in the Baltic states fell from 1,726,000 in 1989 to 1,273,000 in 2000–2001, or 26 per cent. In Lithuania, the share of Russians diminished by 37 per cent, in Estonia 26 per cent and in Latvia 22 per cent (see Table 1.3).

At the end of the 1980s, Estonia, Latvia and Lithuania undertook legislative efforts to achieve a more independent status within the Soviet Union. In November 1988, Estonia started the so-called 'constitutional war' with Moscow by declaring that only those all-Union legislative acts which Estonia approved would be valid on its territory; otherwise, only the laws adopted by Estonia should apply. During Gorbachev's reforms of the late 1980s, the Baltic states could openly express concerns over their language situation, which had changed considerably during the Soviet era due to the influx of Russian-speakers and the spread of Russian. In this political and legal context, the first wave of language legislation was enacted in the Baltic states. It consisted of declaring Estonian, Latvian and Lithuanian the official languages of the respective republics at the end of the 1980s. But it was only after 1991 that they could resort, as independent countries, to straightforward legislative measures, often perceived as controversial, to change the situation principally to the advantage of the respective titular languages.

Table 1.3
Ethnic Composition of the Baltic States
(Percentage of the Total Population According to the 1989, 2000 and 2001 Censuses)

Ethnic origin	Estonia		Latvia		Lithuania	
	1989	2000	1989	2000	1989	2001
Titular nation	61.5	67.9	52.0	57.7	79.6	83.5
Russians	30.3	25.6	34.0	29.6	9.4	6.3
Ukrainians	3.1	2.1	3.5	2.7	1.2	0.7
Belarussians	1.8	1.3	4.5	4.1	1.7	1.2
Poles	0.2	0.2	2.3	2.5	7.0	6.7
Others	3.1	2.9	3.7	3.4	1.1	1.6
Total	100.0	100.0	100.0	100.0	100.0	100.0

SOURCES: Statistical Office of Estonia (2001); Central Statistical Bureau of Latvia (2002); the preliminary results of the Lithuanian census of 2001 were obtained from: http://www.std.lt/Surasymas/Rezultatai/index_pirm.htm. According to these censuses, the total population of Estonia was 1,370,052, while Latvia's was 2,377,383 and Lithuania's 3,483,972 persons.

2.   PRE-INDEPENDENCE LANGUAGE LEGISLATION IN THE BALTIC STATES

At the end of the 1980s, in the atmosphere of *perestroika* and under the influence of strong popular movements, the constitutions of the Baltic Soviet Socialist Republics were amended by the respective Supreme Soviets to give their titular languages an official status of a 'state language'. This set the scene for the adoption of language laws.

Two periods of language legislation in the Baltic states can be identified. The first period includes the laws, or respective decrees, adopted by the then Soviet Socialist Republics of Estonia, Latvia and Lithuania. The second period started with independence and has produced new language laws and their subsequent amendments.

2.1   The 1989 Estonian Language Act

On 18 January 1989, the Language Act of the Estonian Soviet Socialist Republic, adopted by the Supreme Soviet of the Estonian Soviet Socialist Republic, was promulgated. This law was the first of its kind in the Soviet Union and attracted considerable interest (Raun, 1995). It inaugurated a period of adoption of similar legislative acts throughout the Soviet Union, including Latvia and Lithuania, and was not unnoticed in the rest of the world. For example, Grin evaluated this law as "an important milestone in the development of language legislation worldwide". He compared it with Quebec's Bill 101 (the 'French Language Charter') and found that, in both cases, "a local linguistic majority is trying to keep in check the influence of a minority language that is, in turn, the majority language of a broader federation—respectively English in Canada and Russian in the USSR" (Grin, 1991: 193).

Because of its ground-breaking nature and direct relevance to nation-building, a few typical features of this law deserve attention here. First of all, it is the special attitude towards the Russian language that is characteristic of this law as well as of other language laws of this period. The Preamble of the 1989 Estonian Language Act states that "in its treatment of the Russian language, the present law proceeds from the needs of all-Union communication, as well as from the fact that after Estonian it is the second largest native language spoken in the Estonian SSR" (Kiris, 1991: 7).[88] It could have gone further than that, but it did not. Estonian national communists, who dominated the Supreme Soviet, refused to vote for any official status of Russian (such as 'language of interethnic communication') into the law, which frustrated Russian-speaking members of that legislative body and added to the political confrontation of Estonians and Russian-speakers in Estonia (Pettai, 1996: 20).

Despite the denial of an official status, Russian was given a lot of attention in the law (it is referred to in twelve articles out of thirty-nine). More importantly, individuals were given the right to communicate and conduct their affairs with all bodies of state authority and government, as well as institutions, enterprises and organizations on the territory of Estonia, in Estonian (Article 2) and in Russian (Article 3). The law in fact proclaimed the Estonian SSR to be a bilingual country. Citizens in their relations with authorities, subordinates in their relations with superiors at the workplace, as well as clients in the service sector, were given

---

[88]   The references to the law below follow the text of this edition.

the right to choose either Estonian or Russian as the language of communication. Individuals were guaranteed not only the right to communicate with institutions, enterprises and organizations in Estonian and in Russian, but even the right to receive documents in these two languages according to their wish.

In comparison with the pre-1989 years, the law was a principal step forward because it established equal rights for both Estonian-speakers and Russian-speakers in using their native tongues. As Grin (1991: 199) pointed out, the Language Act would have offered no protection of the Estonian language if the massive immigration of Russian-speakers had continued. However, at the beginning of the 1990s, their immigration changed into emigration and this danger did not materialize.

The Language Act specified different transition periods, during which those local governments, enterprises and organizations that were conducting their business in Russian at that time had to switch to Estonian, and the officials there had to acquire a necessary knowledge of Estonian (Articles 35, 35, 37). However, these transition periods did not yield satisfactory results because, for various reasons, the change of the working language tended to require more time than initially planned.

In education, the Language Act treated Estonian already as more prominent than Russian. While education in Estonian was guaranteed on the whole territory of the country, education in Russian was guaranteed only "in accordance with the distribution of the Russian-speaking population" (Article 19).

Thus, the 1989 Language Act was not only a contribution to nation-building (at this time, rather, to the preservation of the Estonian nation) by establishing the parity of Estonian and Russian. It was also the first legislative move aimed at containing the Russian language and monolingual Russian-speakers in Estonia, while promoting Estonian instead. Many monolingual Russian-speakers were confronted with the choice of learning Estonian or losing their jobs in a few years.

In 1989, the most important direct political objective of ethnic Estonians was the establishment of the equality of Estonian and Russian in public life. In a situation where Russian tended to dominate in many spheres of life, a certain containment of Russian became inevitable. But at the same time, Russian was explicitly recognized as an essential element of the Estonian linguistic environment and the Language Act guaranteed extensive rights for Russian-speakers to use their language practically everywhere.

One more aspect of the Act deserves attention. Article 1 declared: "The present law shall establish the regulations for the use of the official language of the Estonian SSR, Russian and other languages". Therefore, it could be claimed that this law was also an attempt to manage linguistic diversity seen as consisting of at least three elements—Estonian, Russian and other languages. However, ethnic containment and diversity management were not the main objectives of the 1989 Estonian Language Act. At that time, nation-building and nation-state building were much more prominent aims.

The short period of time between the adoption of the 1989 Language Act and the restoration of independence in 1991 did not allow for major practical changes to emerge. Therefore, one can agree with Raun that the most important impact of the law was "psychological: It halted the further erosion of the status of Estonian and began the process of reasserting its position in society, especially in the crucial period 'before' the restoration of independence in August–September 1991" (Raun, 1995: 524).

2.2   The Lithuanian and Latvian Language Acts of 1989

Language legislation in Estonia, Latvia and Lithuania moved in parallel fashion. As in Estonia, Lithuania and Latvia adopted their first legislative acts in 1989. These acts articulated the constitutional status of the state language in more detail for various spheres of life, established a transition period for switching from Russian to the state language in public life and explicitly established rights and guarantees for Russian-speakers.

On 25 January 1989, the Presidium of the Supreme Soviet of the Lithuanian SSR issued a decree on Lithuanian SSR official language usage.[89] The decree proclaimed Lithuanian "the principal means of official communication" for all spheres of life, enterprises, institutions and organizations of the Lithuanian SSR, irrespective of their institutional chain of command (with the exception of the Soviet army). For those enterprises, institutions and organizations whose internal business was conducted in Russian, a two-year transition period to Lithuanian was introduced.

At the same time, the decree prescribed that persons whose native language was other than Lithuanian shall be provided with appropriate facilities for organizing pre-school education, classes, elementary and secondary education, for training teachers and for publishing books and newspapers in their native language. For those persons, adequate means were to be provided to learn Lithuanian in educational institutions where the language of instruction was not Lithuanian, as well as in special courses provided for that purpose. It was decreed that the courts, state notary offices, bodies of procurators and internal affairs, institutions of public health, social security, trade, transportation, communications, finance, housing, as well as other institutions shall provide their services in Lithuanian or in a language acceptable to both parties. The state government bodies were assigned the task to enhance the prestige of the Lithuanian language, preserve Lithuanian personal names and place names, provide assistance to scholarly institutions devoted to the Lithuanian language and create the material bases necessary for the development, research and expansion of the Lithuanian language. At the same time, conditions had to be provided for the development of other languages used in Lithuania.

The Latvian Act on Language of 1989 contained similar provisions; but in contrast to Estonia and Lithuania, it was amended already in 1992 and explicit references to Russian were deleted. However, the 1992 version still assumes that Latvian is not the only language which can be used officially. Article 4 of the law states: "In order to fulfil residents' right to language preference, the employees of all state bodies and governmental institutions, as well as those of institutions, enterprises and organizations should know and should use the official language and other languages to such an extent as it is necessary to perform their professional responsibilities".[90] Thus, explicit reference to Russian was replaced by an implicit one. Under this law, monolingual Russian-speakers could not work in the public sector. To control the sphere of administration, Latvian–Russian bilinguals were needed who were able to speak

---

[89]   In the Soviet legal system, the Decree of the Presidium of the Supreme Soviet was a legislative act of lower rank in comparison with the laws adopted by the Supreme Soviet. The text of the decree is available at http://www.lrs.lt.

[90]   http://www/migrationweb/legislation/countries/la/Latvia_language_eng.html.

Latvian or Russian according to the preferences of lower-ranking officials or clients. Thus, despite the amendments of 1992, the Latvian Language Act could not fully leave behind the rationale of the pre-independence period of Baltic language legislation: the imposition of Russian-titular bilingualism on key job holders in administration and in the public sector. Such a legal arrangement has been evaluated as a contribution "to the maintenance of two linguistic collectivities that were already in existence during the Soviet period" (Druviete, 1999: 270).

3.   POST-INDEPENDENCE CHANGE IN LANGUAGE POLICY

The dissolution of the Soviet Union in 1991 and the re-establishment of independent Baltic states created a totally new situation that was difficult for Russian-speakers to cope with. As Laitin explains: "In 1989 and 1991 the Russian-speaking populations of the Union republics were struck by a double cataclysm that turned their world upside-down. The first blow was the passage of the republican language laws in 1989 ... The second punch was the collapse of the Soviet Union itself ... The Russian-speakers of the 'near abroad' suddenly found their citizenship, their homeland, and their very identity in question" (Laitin, 1998: 85–86).

For Russians living in the Baltic states, the language acts of 1989 were not a bolt from the blue. As early as 1988, confrontation had developed between the Popular Fronts of Estonia, Latvia and Lithuania, and the corresponding 'Interfronts', counter-organizations of those Baltic Russian-speakers, mostly employed by the Soviet military industrial complex, who accused the Popular Fronts of nationalism and advocated the preservation of the Soviet Union.

Yet, the swift collapse of the Soviet Union was something truly unexpected for everybody, even for the Baltic titular nations who suddenly found themselves in charge of their countries. Their start was bold, but the ensuing political pluralism soon degenerated due to friction within and among the ruling elites. The virtual lack of democratic tradition and civil society, non-transparent privatization and arbitrary redistribution of state ownership produced a political and economic reality that was shocking to many when compared with initial expectations. Still looming in the background was a deep-rooted existential fear of the titular nations related to the prospects of their physical and cultural survival. On top of it was a new fear that the much-awaited state independence of the Baltic states might be lost again in an unpredictable international environment.

The re-establishing of state independence could not automatically free the titular nations of their fears concerning the fate of their languages. Moreover, two new factors gradually took shape that seemed even to aggravate these fears. First, the Baltic states were now exposed to a new political philosophy and practice in which the very idea of the nation-state was being challenged by political and economic integration in Europe, global finance, trade and communication. The Baltic states themselves, trying to catch up with the mainstream and pushed by their common Russophobia, developed strong ambitions for joining the EU and NATO as soon as possible. As a result, the Baltic titular languages found themselves in a market where they had to compete with widely spoken languages of international communication, primarily English and Russian.

The second factor followed from the first. The former political majority, i.e., local Russians, could now claim protection for their language, culture and education and appealed to regional and international organizations with references to human and minority rights. The Baltic peoples found themselves between the hammer and the anvil—between Russian and European hegemony, as Ozolins described the situation (1999). The second round of Baltic language legislation and post-1991 language policies can only be understood, if not justified, as an attempt to balance and recognize the presence of large populations of Russian-speakers in the context of the countries' aspirations for future membership in European and transatlantic organizations. To cope with this double-sided situation, Estonia and Latvia have been pursuing, in this author's opinion, two different language-related policy agendas simultaneously (see Table 1.4).

Table 1.4
Language-Related Policy Agendas in Estonia and Latvia

Time period	Official agenda	Additional agenda
1989–1992	Restoring of the status of titular languages and preservation of national culture and identity	Exclusion of monolingual Russian-speakers from top jobs and achieving of political dominance by titular nation
1992–1999	Establishment of naturalization procedures with titular language proficiency tests	Stimulation of remigration of Soviet-era settlers to their former homelands
1999–	Introduction of national integration programmes with an emphasis on the learning/teaching of the state language as the main agent of integration	Continuation of previous citizenship and language policies in order to control the access of non-titular groups to political power

SOURCE: Author's observations.

3.1   The Containment of Russian and Russian-Speakers

Even before new language laws were adopted in the Baltic states (in 1995 in Lithuania and Estonia; in 1999 in Latvia), the notion of state language was included in other laws to shape a policy of containment of Russian-speakers, most notably in citizenship laws. Later, laws on education and elections followed suit. It can be claimed that all these laws contributed to the 'ethnic containment' of non-titular groups even more than the language laws, in particular in Estonia and Latvia where citizenship was not granted automatically to Soviet-era settlers. To become citizens of their countries of residence, those settlers had to take the path of naturalization instead. As naturalization procedures included language tests and as the Russian-speakers' knowledge of the titular language was relatively poor (see Table 1.5), the slow pace of the ensuing naturalization was easily predictable.

In Latvia, where the competence of Russian-speakers in the state language is higher and where the Russian minority is bigger than in Estonia, special age quotas ('naturalization windows') were in force between 1995 and 1998, which excluded older cohorts from applying for citizenship for years. This sought to keep an anticipated massive naturalization under control. As expected, the rate of naturalization in Latvia during that period was much lower than in Estonia. Between 1995 and 1998, only 11,432 persons were naturalized in Latvia. After the naturalization windows were abolished by referendum in 1998, over 27,000 persons were naturalized in 1999–2000. By the end of 2000, the total figure of naturalized citizens stood at 38,759, including 5,132 children below the age of 15 (Baltic Institute of Social Sciences, 2001: 5). At the beginning of December 2002, Latvia reported that the total of naturalized citizens had reached 57,483 persons.[91]

Table 1.5

Language Competence of Titular Nations and Russian Minorities in the Baltic States (According to the 1989 Census)

Country	Population of titular nation	Percentage of which knows Russian	Population of Russian minority	Percentage of which knows titular language
Estonia	963,269	33.6	474,815	13.7
Latvia	1,387,647	65.7	905,515	21.2
Lithuania	2,924,048	37.4	343,597	33.5

SOURCE: Jamestown Foundation, http://www.amber.ucsf.edu/homes/ross/public_html/russia_/ruslang.txt

One commentator claimed Latvian legislative acts on naturalization "were not passed to stimulate the naturalisation but were rather targeted towards stimulating emigration of non-citizens" (Baltic Data House and University of Latvia, 1998: 6). As later admitted, the joint effort of legislators and civil servants in Estonia was "to turn the life of Russians into hell" (Ernits, 2000). Therefore, it was not by accident that, until 1997–1998, the Estonian government, having established the requirements and the system of checking the level of state language competence, took no efficient measures to promote the learning of Estonian (Vihalemm, 1999: 73). All this seems to confirm that the initial aim of citizenship policies in Estonia and Latvia was not so much the naturalization of non-titular Soviet era settlers, as their emigration.

As we know today, only a limited emigration of Russian-speakers took place from the Baltic states. The overwhelming majority of them decided to stay. Estonian and Latvian elites, carefully watched by the West, had to reconsider their attitudes and embark on a different course to meet the expectations of the EU and NATO in the first place. However, anti-Russian feelings were still looming large among the titular populations, and politicians considered it beneficial to continue playing the 'nationalist card'. Therefore, initiation of changes in citizenship and language legislation was regarded as politically suicidal. All international

---

[91]   The News of the Naturalization Board, *Monthly Newsletter*, No. 10, 15 November–15 December 2002, at http://www.np.gov.lv/en/news/November_December.doc.

recommendations towards that end, issued by the OSCE and its High Commissioner on National Minorities, the Council of Europe or the EU, provoked heated debates in the parliaments of Estonia and Latvia, which happened to be more conservative on these matters than the governments. As a result, only a few of these recommendations were implemented (Poleshchuk, 2001b).

Meanwhile, the legislative process of the countries in transition had to move quickly. Lithuania and Estonia adopted their new language laws in 1995. In Latvia, the draft of the law was ready the same year. However, the discussion of this draft took more than three years before the law was finally adopted in 1999 (and came into force on 1 September 2000). As mentioned above, Latvia was the only Baltic state to amend its first language law as early as 1992 in order to delete from it the special rights and role of the Russian language. Lithuania and Estonia did the same in their laws of 1995. There are no explicit references to the Russian language in these new laws, but Russian is implicitly referred to as a 'foreign language'.

However, the word 'Russian' was not dropped for cosmetic reasons only. The 1995 Estonian Language Act (Article 2) states that "for the purposes of this act any language other than Estonian is a foreign language". At the same time, Estonian officials, according to this law, have no obligation to use foreign languages in their official capacity. If the officials do not agree to use a foreign language (for example, Russian) in communication with a person who does not speak Estonian, it is up to that person to provide the translation at his or her own expense (Article 8). This effectively excluded Russian from official business on the national level.

Although there was no need for all-Union communication as in 1989, Russian had remained the second largest native language spoken by more than 30 per cent of the population of Estonia. Yet, the 1995 Act makes no explicit reference to that circumstance. However, it defines a language of a national minority as "a foreign language, which Estonian citizens who belong to a national minority have historically used as their mother tongue in Estonia" (Article 2). Article 10 proclaims: "In local governments where at least half of the permanent residents belong to a national minority, everyone has the right to receive answers from state agencies operating in the territory of the corresponding local government and from the corresponding local government and officials thereof in the language of the national minority as well as in Estonian".[92] In the demographic situation of contemporary Estonia, particularly in the northeastern part of the country, only Russian would correspond to this definition.[93]

According to Article 11, a language of a national minority which constitutes the majority of the permanent residents of the unit of local government may be used alongside Estonian as the internal working language of local government on the proposal of the corresponding local government council and by a decision of the government of the Republic. Several such local governments exist in northeastern Estonia where Russian is used by the majority of permanent residents. As to the practical implementation of this article, it must be noted that as of the beginning of 2003 the Estonian government has rejected all such proposals.

---

[92]   More than 50% can be regarded as a high requirement, especially when compared to 20% in Slovakia and 6–8% in Finland. The reason behind this might be the reluctance to include Tallinn, the capital of Estonia, where Russian-speakers constitute only slightly less that 50% of the population, bilingual.

[93]   In the northeastern county of Ida-Virumaa, the share of ethnic Estonians is below 20%.

Article 14 of the law allows the use of national minority languages in cultural autonomy bodies of national minorities as internal working languages, while all communication with state agencies and local governments where this language is not used as an internal working language is to take place in Estonian. As no minority has constituted itself as a cultural autonomy, this norm has also not yet been implemented.

The Estonian Language Act of 1995, unlike the 1989 Act, does not stipulate the role of languages in education and does not deal with the language of the courts because other laws regulate these issues.[94]

Table 1.6

Viable Language Repertoires of Native Estonian-Speakers and Native Russian-Speakers in Estonia According to Different Periods[95]

Time period	Native Estonian-speakers	Native Russian-speakers
1978–1988[96]	Partial 'Estonian–Russian' bilingualism	Russian monolingualism
1989–1995[97]	Partial 'Estonian–Russian' bilingualism	Partial 'Russian–Estonian' bilingualism
1995–2003[98]	Estonian monolingualism	Partial 'Russian–Estonian' bilingualism
After 2003	Partial 'Estonian–English' bilingualism	Partial 'Russian–Estonian–English' trilingualism

SOURCE: Author's observations.

3.2 Estonia Seeks Compensation

The adoption of the Language Act in 1995 was not the end of the debates on language issues in Estonia. Amid heated political discussions, the law has already been amended several times. At the same time, the concept of state language continued to play a prominent role through other laws.

---

[94] On 4 April 2000, the Estonian parliament approved a package of amendments to the Act on Basic School and Gymnasium to promote integration in schools. Under the new regulation, a secondary school with 60% of its curriculum in Estonian would be considered an Estonian-language school. All secondary schools must start the transition to that status in the 2007–2008 academic year. Schools will have flexibility as regards the language of instruction of the remaining 40% of their curriculum. Instruction in the mother tongues of minorities will remain in force for basic education (up to grade nine) under the amendments (*Newsline*, 2000). In March 2002, a new amendment to the Act on Basic School and Gymnasium was adopted, which gave the boards of trustees of minority schools the right to apply for the postponement of the 2007 deadline.

[95] In this context 'viable language repertoire' refers to the set of languages of which knowledge is required under existing laws and practices and to be able to function in a given society.

[96] In 1988, Estonian was proclaimed the official language by the Constitution of the Estonian SSR and in 1989 the Language Act of the Estonian SSR was adopted by the Supreme Soviet of the Estonian SSR.

[97] In 1995, the new Estonian Language Act was adopted by the *Riigikogu* (parliament of the Republic of Estonia).

[98] By 2003, Estonia intends to be ready for membership of the EU.

The most dramatic developments unfolded in December 1998, shortly after the *Riigikogu* (Estonian parliament) had amended, under mounting international pressure, the Act on Citizenship to grant citizenship on easy terms to children born in Estonia who would otherwise be stateless.[99] In fact, these amendments followed from Estonia's international commitments (Estonia ratified the UN Convention on the Rights of the Child in 1991).

In an orchestrated vote on 15 December 1998, the parliament amended the Language Act, the Riigikogu Election Act and the Local Government Council Election Act, establishing proficiency requirements in the state language for elected officials. This move of the Estonian legislature was popularly understood as a sort of compensation after concessions had to be made to the international demands regarding citizenship legislation.

The new amendments to the election laws were sharply criticized internationally as an unreasonable restriction of a citizen's right to be elected, in accordance neither with the Estonian Constitution nor with Estonia's international obligations and commitments. The OSCE High Commissioner on National Minorities urged the President of Estonia, in his letter of 19 December 1998, not to promulgate the amendments. He explained that "the rationale for the … absolute entitlement to stand for office to be enjoyed by citizens (without unreasonable restriction) is rooted in the essence of the democratic process" (Zaagman, 1999: 70), but failed to convince the president who promulgated the amendments on 31 December 1998.

In February 1999, subsequent amendments to Article 5 of the Language Act were passed, which basically required that employees of private companies, non-profit associations and foundations have proficiency in, and use, the Estonian language while doing business in Estonia. Even foreign experts temporarily working in the country could be subjected to proficiency requirements in Estonian. The minority representatives interpreted these amendments as a deliberate move of the state to tilt the conditions of economic competition on the Estonian market in favour of native speakers of Estonian.

The European Commission addressed the amendments directly in its 1999 Regular Report on Estonia's Progress Towards Accession. In the Commission's opinion, the amendments raised concerns, which "go beyond the non-compliance by Estonia of the political criteria for membership on minorities issues and could conflict between the law and the obligations of Estonia under the Europe Agreement, in particular in the fields of free movement of persons, right of establishment, supply of services, capital movements and award of public contracts". This assessment was followed by a prediction that "the imposition of linguistic knowledge requirements may not only deter Community companies from exercising their right of establishment in Estonia but also force them to reduce the scale of business operations in the country" (European Commission, 1999).

This was a serious warning, which a country on its way to the EU could not ignore. Estonia reacted on 14 June 2000 when the parliament adopted new amendments to the Language Act to bring it into compliance with OSCE recommendations and EU regulations. Language requirements for foreign experts were abolished.

---

[99]   The Latvian Citizenship Act came under similar pressure, and many Latvian legislators put up a staunch resistance. The amendments were finally approved only by a national referendum.

The amendments further stipulated that:

> The use of Estonian by companies, non-profit associations and foundations, by employees thereof and by sole proprietors is regulated if it is in the public interest, which, for the purposes of this Law, means public safety, public order, general government, public health, health protection, consumer protection and occupational safety. The establishment of requirements concerning proficiency in and use of Estonian shall be justified and in proportion to the objective being sought and shall not distort the nature of the rights which are restricted (*Riigi Teataja*, 2000).

The European Commission welcomed these amendments and acknowledged Estonia's considerable progress in its subsequent report of 2000 (European Commission, 2000). In May 2001, following the recommendations of the European Commission, the government adopted new regulations for state language use in the private sector. The Commission's 2001 Regular Report stated: "Estonia should ensure that in the implementation of this regulation the principles of proportionality and justified public interest are properly respected" (European Commission, 2001).

It seems that the European Commission and the Estonian government have reached mutual understanding on language requirements in the private sector, which is based on the notion of "justified public interest". The legal ambiguity of this notion opens it to different interpretations which enable Estonia to regulate the tension between the protection of the state language and its international commitments regarding minorities. In Latvia, a similar notion of "legitimate public interest" has played the same role in the exchanges of the Latvian government and the European Commission on language requirements (Poleshchuk, 2002).

3.3   Latvia Takes Its Time

Latvia took its time in discussing the new draft language law, and was subjected to a great deal of international criticism and even mild threats during the process. For example, Finland announced that if the new Latvian language law, which would deprive the Russian minority from participating on an equal footing with Latvians in public communications, was implemented, Finland would not support Latvia's EU membership bid (Nordic Council of Ministers, 1999).

In July 1999, the President of Latvia vetoed an initial version of the law and sent it back to the parliament where it was revised and brought into harmony with international norms governing freedom of expression and the sanctity of private life. The Latvian parliament finally adopted a new State Language Act on 9 December 1999.[100] This version of the law earned positive evaluation internationally, among others from the OSCE High Commissioner on National Minorities. However, already on 14 December 1999, the Latvian Human Rights Committee issued its bulletin, which pointed out that the most crucial issues

---

[100]   See the text of the law at http://www.riga.lv/minelres/NationalLegislation/Latvia/Latvia_Language_English.htm.

of language use were not addressed by the law itself but left to be decided by the Cabinet of Ministers. Such issues included the language of public events, stamps, seals and letterheads; the language of documents that can be accepted by state and municipal institutions, as well as by enterprises in which the state or local governments own the biggest share; the language of documents from private persons and the language of the answers that these persons are supposed to receive from these institutions and enterprises (Minelres Forum, 1999). The Latvian Centre for Human Rights and Ethnic Studies also expressed the opinion that "the law leaves a large margin of legal uncertainty, as a number of the most important provisions are left for decision by the executive branch" (Muiznieks *et al.*, 2000: 38).[101]

A characteristic of the young legal systems of the Baltic states is that the constitutions in many cases refer to laws, and laws, in turn, often make it the responsibility of the executive branch to work out the necessary details and implementation procedures. As a result, the eventual implementation of laws is largely at the discretion of civil servants, the absolute majority of which are recruited from the titular ethnic group. If they personally feel like putting the perceived interests of the titular nation first, they can easily do so. In that case, an ethnically biased implementation of laws can follow, even if the laws are in no formal contradiction with international human rights standards.

In Latvia, this became obvious during the battle over the draft regulations of the Cabinet of Ministers on the implementation of the State Language Act, which were made public by the Ministry of Justice of Latvia in June 2000. According to the State Language Act, these documents had to be adopted before 1 September 2000. Typically, representatives of national minorities were not included in the governmental working groups in charge of preparing these regulations. Therefore, they were able to express their concerns only after the drafts had been made public.

The first concern was that the new regulations were to provide the right of inspectors of the State Language Centre to visit all public and private institutions, business enterprises and non-governmental organizations (NGOs), to invite all persons for the Latvian language examination to the Centre, and to annul certificates of state language knowledge even if a person had received it in full accordance with the procedure envisaged by law. The second concern was that the highest category of state language knowledge, which would require that a person must know Latvian at the level "equal to mother tongue", was going to be applied to a very broad range of professions and elected posts, including chairpersons of NGOs. In the opinion of minority representatives it meant that all these positions and professions would be reserved for native-speakers of Latvian only, while persons whose mother tongue was not Latvian would not be able to qualify for these professions. The third concern was that if the state language proficiency certificate was lost, it could not be renewed. And finally, they were concerned that all open public and cultural events, including theatre performances, concerts, circus shows, opera and ballet had to be translated into the state language (Minelres Forum, 2000a).

---

[101] At the same time, the involvement of international experts in the preparation of the new Language Act must have deeply annoyed radical ethnic Latvian politicians. On 4 May 2001, at the ceremonial session of the Latvian parliament to commemorate Latvia's declaration of independence in 1990, the Speaker of Parliament criticized Latvian politicians for long and unnecessary discussions with foreign experts during the adoption of the law, referring to the discussions throughout the year 2000 (*Vesti Segodnya*, 5 May 2001).

Before these regulations were adopted in August 2000, the Ministry of Justice had to re-work them after criticism from the OSCE, the Latvian National Human Rights Office and a number of actions of public protest against the Latvian authorities' language policy. Several recommendations of the OSCE High Commissioner on National Minorities, as well as some suggestions of the pro-minority faction in the Latvian parliament were taken into account.

In particular, in the private sphere, an employer now determines the necessary level of state language knowledge for employees in his/her business enterprise. The highest category of state language knowledge no longer requires that a person must speak Latvian at the level "equal to mother tongue".

The final version of the regulations does not provide inspectors of the State Language Centre with the right to annul the state language proficiency certificate. Private persons, enterprises, associations and international institutions, when organizing public events, must translate into the state language only that information which relates to legitimate public interests, as well as information about the event. Thus, theatre performances, concerts, circus shows, opera, ballet and pantomime must not be necessarily translated, contrary to the initial draft version of the regulations. Private institutions, enterprises and NGOs now have the right to publicly display information in other languages alongside the state language (this was prohibited by the draft regulations, and by the previous Language Act, which was in force until 1 September 2000).[102] Moreover, state and municipal institutions can (but are not obliged to) provide information in a foreign language upon request by a private person (Minelres Forum, 2000b).

Regardless of these adjustments, the overwhelming attitude among minorities towards the new regulations remained very critical. On 4 September 2000, the pro-minority coalition of the parliament called a conference and stated that the regulations on implementing the language law had not fully resolved the problem of incompatibility of Latvia's language legislation with international standards of minority rights. It was also pointed out that the process of elimination of state-supported education in minority languages continued; and that the Latvian authorities consistently refused to engage in dialogue with political parties and NGOs representing national minorities. Under these circumstances, the coalition declared a campaign of non-violent civil disobedience. The coalition confirmed that the most important purposes to be achieved with the campaign were: ratification and fair implementation of the Council of Europe Framework Convention for the Protection of National Minorities and state guarantees for the preservation and development of a state-supported education system in minority languages. Furthermore, the state should recognize the multicultural nature of Latvia's society, and respect dignity, rights and interests of everyone, regardless of ethnic origin and mother tongue (Minelres Forum, 2000c).

---

[102] In this aspect, the Latvian Language Act is more liberal than Estonian legislation which prohibits the public display of information in other languages except when this information is registered as a trademark.

3.4 Non-Estonians' Changing Attitudes

One still has to wait to see the consequences of the new Latvian Language Act, while in Estonia the implementation of the language and citizenship laws of 1995 has already contributed to the ethnic containment of Russian-speakers. More specifically, it contributed to the decrease of the rate of naturalization after 1996 and slowed down the growth of the non-Estonian electorate at national elections. In 1996, 16,740 persons passed the citizenship language exam, which followed the old rules and requirements. In 1997, only 2,099 persons passed an upgraded language exam (UNDP, 1999: 42).

There is some sociological evidence that the attitude of non-citizens towards the learning of the state language and to citizenship tests might have started to change before 1996. Already in 1995, 42 per cent of Tallinn Russian-speakers said that "they have not passed the Estonian language exam and have no intention to do so", whereas a year before only nineteen per cent of Tallinn Russian-speakers expressed the same attitude. Among the Russian-speakers of the northeastern towns of Estonia the corresponding shares were 39 per cent and 32 per cent (Tartu University Market Research, 1995). This means that, instead of integration, a growing number of Russian-speakers, willingly or unwillingly, are opting for separation.

While the learning of the Estonian language is most frequently associated with citizenship and naturalization, there are also other important motives at work in practical life. Getting a good job, for example, seems to be far more important for many than acquiring citizenship. In 1997, 61 per cent of respondents both in Tallinn and in the cities of the northeast agreed that "mastering Estonian is necessary to get a good job", while only 26 per cent in Tallinn and 19 per cent in the cities of the northeast agreed that "mastering Estonian is needed first of all to get Estonian citizenship" (Vihalemm, 1997: 146). What deserves special attention is that only two years before, in 1995, as many as 44 per cent of respondents in Tallinn and 45 per cent in the cities of the northeast agreed with the citizenship motive (Vihalemm, 1997: 146).

Due to interaction of different factors, the tempo of naturalization slowed down in Estonia after 1996. The earlier hopes of Russian-speakers to pass the language exam might have died after the new Estonian Citizenship Act enforced more demanding language requirements in January 1995.[103] It may also be that most of those who knew the state language were able to naturalize before these new requirements were imposed. Those who did not know the language well are now confronted with more demanding requirements at the exams. Under the existing legal framework of naturalization and given the possibilities of potential citizenship applicants, the rate of naturalization in Estonia is bound to be low.

---

[103] The Citizenship Act of 1995 added an exam on the Constitution (currently including 165 questions) to be taken for the naturalization also in Estonian. In fact, it is another, even more demanding language exam as the examinees also have to know legal terminology.

3.5 The Lithuanian Way

The Lithuanian Language Act, promulgated on 31 January 1995, is broader and more detailed than the decree of 1989 (the law contains twenty-seven articles as compared to ten articles in the decree).[104] Besides status planning (i.e., specifying the functions of the state language in public life), it also touches upon general issues of corpus planning such as the correctness of the state language (Articles 21, 22 and 23) and the procedures of approving linguistic norms (Article 20). Articles 3, 4, 5, 6 and 7 require that all institutions, enterprises and organizations of Lithuania function and provide services in the state language (Lithuanian) and that the officials who provide services to the population must know the state language. In contrast to the Estonian Language Act which does not regulate the language of the courts, Article 8 stipulates that participants in legal proceedings who do not know the state language shall be provided with the services of an interpreter free of charge. Articles 11 and 12 deal with education, guaranteeing the right of residents to acquire education in the state language on the entire territory of Lithuania and making the teaching of the state language obligatory for all secondary schools. The law also says that place-names and personal names have to use Lithuanian forms (Articles 14 and 15), as do the names of enterprises, offices and organizations (Article 16). Public signs must be in the state language (Article 17); names of ethnic communities may be in other languages along with the state language, while the format of signs in other languages cannot be larger than that of signs in the state language (Article 18). A special chapter is dedicated to the protection and correctness of the state language (Articles 19 to 23). According to Article 27, the enforcement of the law shall be determined by the "Act on the Enforcement of the Act of the Republic of Lithuania on the State Language", while control over enforcement is the responsibility of the Language Inspection of the State Language Commission under the parliament of Lithuania (Article 25).

The Act on the Enforcement was adopted on 6 February 1995. It consists of three articles. Article 1 states that the government has the obligation to adopt, two months after this law has entered into force, the state programme for the usage and development of the state language, as well as the regulations on the requirements for civil servants, teachers, employees of mass media and publishing houses for the correct usage of the state language. Article 2 establishes that the State Language Commission must determine the rules of usage of foreign languages for information purposes in transport, customs, hotels, banks, tourist agencies and advertisements. Unofficial usage of the languages of ethnic communities as well as other languages is not to be regulated. Article 3 states that in the documentation of the Ignalina nuclear power station, all standard languages of the International Atomic Energy Agency (IAEA) can be used. Thus, Lithuania wisely avoided possible dangers that might have been created by forcing the Russian-speaking crew of this power station to operate in Lithuanian, as a state enterprise would normally be required to. The fact that no amendments to either of the laws of 1995 have been made seems to indicate that their implementation has not caused any major problems. It also proves that language issues in Lithuania are much less politicized than in Latvia or Estonia.

---

[104]   The English text of the "Act of the Republic of Lithuania on the State Language" is available at http://www.litlex.lt.

4.   NEW CHALLENGES

4.1   Do Majority Languages Need Protection?

As estimated, there are almost 6,800 languages in 228 countries.[105] Estonian, Latvian and Lithuanian belong to those approximately 200 languages that have more than one million native speakers. They are also endemic languages, i.e., they exist in one country only. Today, they also happen to be the languages of the titular majorities of these countries.

Generally, the vitality of a language is influenced, among other things, by the number of its speakers, and more specifically, by its native speakers (Grin, 1993). In this sense, languages are not equal and, correspondingly, they have different prospects of survival. It is estimated that one hundred years from now the majority of the languages existing today might be extinct (Skutnabb-Kangas, 1999).

The spread of the Russian language in the Soviet Union generated the need for the protection of other titular languages. It should be remembered that Estonian, Latvian and Lithuanian are spoken only by approximately one million, one and a half million and three million people respectively. During the Soviet years, Russian made powerful inroads into the Baltic states while a full set of Russian language educational, cultural and media institutions was established there to serve the needs of Russian-speaking immigrants. Gradually, as the lingua franca of the Soviet Union, Russian became the working language of administration and several branches of economy. Ethnic Estonians, Latvians and Lithuanians were taught Russian at school as a second language, while the teaching of the titular languages in Russian-medium schools was unpopular and largely ignored. The Baltic peoples developed a habit of switching to Russian when speaking with Russians, or in a company which included Russian-speakers.

In the 1970s, the promotion of asymmetric non-Russian/Russian bilingualism became the official Soviet language policy, triggered by the inability of the Soviet armed forces to absorb the growing number of conscripts from the Central Asian republics who spoke almost no Russian. In the Baltic states, this policy was perceived as a step towards linguistic assimilation, so local languages were seen to be at an even greater risk. It was in this atmosphere of endangerment that the first language laws of 1989 were written and adopted.

According to the public debate on language issues in the Baltic states, language laws were adopted in order to reinforce the cultural identity of the titular nations, to secure their cultural domination in the respective countries and, last but not least, to protect the languages in question. As the Preamble of the 1989 Estonian Language Act put it: "In Estonia, the ancient territory of the Estonians, the State shall accord special attention and protection to the Estonian language. Through the institution of Estonian as the official language, a firm foundation has been laid for the preservation and development of the Estonian people and its culture".

---

[105]   See: http://www.sil.org/ethnologue.

A very similar view is reflected in the Preamble of the Latvian Language Act of 1992: "Latvia is the only ethnic territory in the world, which is inhabited by the Latvian nation. One of the main prerequisites for the existence of the Latvian nation and for the preservation and development of its culture is the Latvian language. During the last decades there has been a marked decrease in the use of the Latvian language in state affairs and social life; therefore it is necessary to establish special measures for the protection of the Latvian language".[106] Calls to protect and purify the Estonian language continue to be made (Tomusk, 2000). This raises an intriguing question: Do majority languages really need protection, why and of what kind? Usually, it is understood that only minority or regional languages need protection.

On this question, two different discourses have emerged. Some scholars have claimed that, due to recent history, Estonian and Latvian are not ordinary majority languages but 'minorized majority languages' (majority languages in need of the protection usually necessary only for threatened minority languages), while Russian is a 'majorized minority language' (a minority language in terms of numbers, but with the power of a majority language) (cf. Skutnabb-Kangas quoted in Ozolins, 1999: 23). This is an 'endangered majority language' discourse, which looks at language from a 'geolinguistic' point of view, focusing on the linguistic environment of a particular language rather than on its formal status. This is related to a quite popular victimization discourse in the Baltic states at the end of the 1980s and the beginning of the 1990s. Both are linked to and can be understood in the context of the weak state syndrome, a by-product of the post-communist transition. This discourse is openly pro-Baltic and the Baltic governments have naturally been supporting it.

Ina Druviete explains why and how to protect Latvian: "The Russian language and the other main competitor, English, possess two crucial features: they are very widely spoken and function as languages of international communication. The Latvian language has no such 'carrots' to offer. Under the conditions of the market economy the only compensatory mechanisms for Latvian can be of a legal nature" (Druviete, 1999: 270). This seems to suggest that while Russian and English possess the carrot, Latvian has to resort to the stick.[107] According to Druviete, the present use of Russian in Latvia should be limited and the vicious circle of self-sufficiency of the minority language needs to be broken (Poleshchuk, 2001a: 17–18). This task is complicated by the widespread Latvian-Russian bilingualism among ethnic Latvians. The census of 2000 established that while 52 per cent of Russians in Latvia knew Latvian, 70 per cent of ethnic Latvians knew Russian.[108]

However, the shares of native speakers of state languages and Russian in the respective populations should be considered more important. In Estonia and Latvia, according to the censuses of 2000, the native speakers of state languages constituted 67.3 per cent and 58.2

---

[106] http://www.iom.ch/www/migrationweb/legislation/countries/la/Latvia_language_eng.html.

[107] Naturally, where there is a law, there must be sanctions. Sanctions for violation of the Latvian Language Act have been in place since 1992. On 14 June 2001, the *Saeima* (Latvian parliament) adopted amendments to the Code of Administrative Misdemeanours. As reported by the Latvian Human Rights Committee, twelve different types of misdemeanours in the field of language use are now mentioned in this Code, one of them being a hard to interpret "obvious disrespect towards the state language" which can be fined with up to 400 USD.

[108] Central Statistical Bureau of Latvia (2002: 143, 147).

per cent of the respective populations, whereas native speakers of Russian constituted 29.7 per cent and 37.4 per cent respectively. In both cases the native speakers of state languages are in a clear majority. Table 1.7 shows that the titular nations of the Baltic states as well as Russians in these countries have preserved their native languages quite well. In Latvia, 95.7 per cent of Latvians had Latvian as their mother tongue and 94.5 per cent of Russians had Russian as their mother tongue. While 3.5 per cent of Latvians said that Russian was their mother tongue, as much as 4.4 per cent of Russians indicated Latvian as their mother tongue. According to these data, the Latvian language has a stronger position in Latvia than Russian, and not vice versa as is sometimes claimed.

Table 1.7

Preservation of Native Tongue by Titular Nations and Russians in the Baltic States

Nation or ethnic group	Native language as mother tongue [%]	Russian as mother tongue of members of titular nations and titular language as mother tongue of Russians [%]
Latvians in Latvia	95.7	3.5
Russians in Latvia	94.5	4.4
Estonians in Estonia	98.9	1.0
Russians in Estonia	98.6	1.3
Lithuanians in Lithuania	96.7	n/a
Russians in Lithuania	89.2	6.3

SOURCES: Statistical Office of Estonia (2001); Central Statistical Bureau of Latvia (2002); and http://www.std.lt/Surasymas/Rezultatai/index_pirm.htm

In Estonia, 98.9 per cent of Estonians and 98.6 per cent of Russians indicated their native language as their mother tongue. Only one per cent of Estonians had Russian and 1.3 per cent of Russians had Estonian as their mother tongue. It can be claimed that linguistic assimilation in Estonia and Latvia is very limited as far as the titular nations and local Russians are concerned. Russians in Lithuania seem to have changed their mother tongue slightly more than Russians in the other two countries. However, linguistic assimilation remains a problem for smaller ethnic groups in the Baltic states. For some groups this might mean switching to Russian depending on the choices of parents and availability of schools in their native languages.

Another major language protection discourse is legalistic, based on international legal standards and principles, and promoted by international or regional organizations in which the Russian Federation has often actively tried to protect the rights of Russian speakers beyond Russia. The unit of analysis here is a separate state where the language of the majority should be promoted as a common language of all citizens while minority languages must be protected by the state. Latvia and Estonia do not feel very comfortable with this approach because of their large minority populations. For historical and 'geolinguistic' reasons the Baltic governments tend to pay more attention to the protection of their own titular languages than to those of the minorities. It goes without saying that minority representatives very much participate in and support this discourse.

The second need for protection refers to more recent developments such as the spread of English and the declining number of course-hours for learning the Baltic languages in secondary school.[109] Estonian radio introduced courses in the Estonian language to correct and streamline the Estonian of native-speaking presenters, who were warned that they may be fired if they fail to attend the courses regularly.[110]

Many Baltic language-speakers are concerned that the advance of European integration together with a growing internationalization of the economy might reduce the practical significance of their languages regardless of their present high formal status.

4.2 How to Manage Diversity: The Problem of a Second Official Language

The first problem with linguistic diversity is that it has to be protected and maintained. This is a global problem requiring local solutions. Some scholars even relate linguistic diversity to biological diversity (Skutnabb-Kangas, 1999). The second problem is the extent to which linguistic diversity can be reasonably managed and at what cost. In other words, how many languages can be maintained and promoted by a state that is meanwhile prioritizing its official language. The most crucial form of this question is whether there should be several official languages in a country in which sizeable linguistic or ethnic minorities live. The Republic of South Africa, for example, has introduced eleven official languages in the wake of apartheid.

I will now look at the problem of the second official language as it stands in Estonia. In order to solve the problem of statelessness, it is often suggested that the language requirements at the citizenship exam be lowered. However, these suggestions are usually dismissed as politically unacceptable because too many non-Estonian voters could allegedly change the Estonian political system, introduce Russian as the second official language, take Estonia to the CIS, etc. Public debate on the issue of the official language often takes quite an irrational twist with emotions running high. The debate is customarily inflamed by the demands of Russian politicians (in Estonia or Russia) that Estonia give Russian some sort of official or special status.

A more sober look at the constitutional arrangements and current political realities in Estonia clearly shows that even if all Soviet-era settlers receive citizenship, a second official language cannot be introduced under the present Constitution. Article 6 stipulates that "the official language of Estonia shall be Estonian". To introduce another, or additional official language, Article 6 must be amended. To initiate such an amendment, the approval of at least one fifth of the members of Parliament is needed as stipulated by Article 161. According to Article 162 of the Constitution, Article 6 can be amended only by referendum because it

---

[109] By 2002, the whole curriculum of Estonian-language secondary schools had dropped more than 400 hours from the total of 2,450 devoted to Estonian-language learning in the curriculum of 1985, in order to make room for various new subjects (see *Postimees*, 21 November 2002).

[110] See *Eesti Päevaleht*, 9 February 2000.

belongs to the First Chapter of the Constitution. In order to call for a referendum to amend the Constitution, the approval of a three-fifths majority of the members of Parliament is required.

Therefore, to start the process, at least twenty-one members of Parliament (out of the total of 101) must support the amendment. The next step requires the approval of 61 members of Parliament. And finally, the majority of citizens who participate in the referendum must approve the amendment. Anyone who knows the basics of Estonian politics (since 1992, the share of ethnic Estonians in parliament has not fallen below 95 per cent) understands that there is practically no chance that a referendum would come out in favour of the amendment. It is unlikely that the 61 votes necessary to call the referendum could be garnered.

If all current non-citizens were to obtain Estonian citizenship, non-Estonians would constitute 25–30 per cent of the electorate. Hypothetically, if all non-Estonians were to vote only for non-Estonians, which is not the case even now, it would be possible to elect enough MPs to initiate the amendment process. Still, it is very unlikely that the 61 votes necessary to call the referendum could be secured, let alone that the referendum would decide in favour of Russian as the second official language. Thus, under the current Estonian Constitution and taking into account the present ethnic structure of the population, the introduction of a second official language is an unrealistic option. All warnings that a second official language might be established if all non-Estonians who get citizenship have one aim—to continue the containment of Russian-speakers and to restrict their access to political power.

4.3   The Coming of English

It is no secret that, of all the languages being taught and learned in the Baltic states, the one which is taken most seriously at schools, and is most supported by parents, is English. According to Latvian statistics, in 1996–1997, 57.6 per cent of all school children in Latvia were studying English as a foreign language (Karklins, 1998: 292). According to the data provided by the Estonian Language Strategy Centre, this percentage was 51.8 in Estonia (46.7 per cent in Estonian and 75 per cent in Russian-language schools).

In the survey "Russian youth in multicultural environments", conducted in June 1997 in Estonia, the competencies in English and Estonian among 15–40-year-old urban Russian-speakers were compared based on the respondents' self-evaluation. It revealed that these Russian-speakers know Estonian better than English, which could be generally expected. However, the difference, still quite noticeable, does not look dramatic. While fourteen per cent of the respondents said that they speak Estonian fluently and 69 per cent said that they understand Estonian and speak it a little, the corresponding evaluations for their knowledge of English were five and 52 per cent (Vihalemm, 1997: 145).

Stimulated by the prospects of European integration, consumption of popular culture, access to the Internet, even the knowledge of English among young non-Estonians is improving. As young Estonians already know English much better than Russian, English might emerge as the common language of young people in Estonia (Proos and Pettai, 1999: 9).

Given the pressures of European integration on the language skills of intellectuals, business people, civil servants, military, police, etc., in a longer perspective English may gradually establish itself as a new lingua franca in the whole Baltic region. This phenomenon is already observable, for instance, among politicians, intellectuals, military and students. The population census of 2000 in Estonia showed that the proficiency in English among young Estonians and young Russians depends on age (the younger the age group, the higher the proficiency). The proficiency in Estonian among young Russians follows the same pattern and remains higher than their proficiency in English (59 per cent and 38 per cent among 15–19 year-olds respectively). Among young Estonians proficiency in Russian is diminishing faster than proficiency in English is growing (56 per cent and 71 per cent in the same age group). At the same time, over 99 per cent of young Estonians and Russians have retained proficiency in their national languages (Statistical Office of Estonia, 2001: 222–225). Nevertheless, for the time being, in Estonia, Latvia and Lithuania the respective state languages and Russian have better positions as common languages than English (see Figure 1.1).

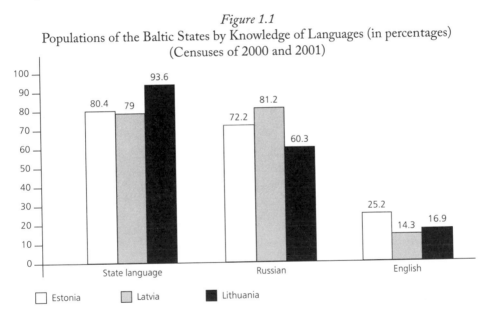

Figure 1.1
Populations of the Baltic States by Knowledge of Languages (in percentages)
(Censuses of 2000 and 2001)

The Baltic states have another common problem: the language of official documentation. Under the present laws, it must be in the state language. As mentioned above, Lithuania has made an exception for the Ignalina nuclear power station, allowing it to use documentation in Russian, which is one of the languages of the IAEA. This has proved useful not only for maintaining the safety of operations at the station, but has also enabled easy inspection of these operations by the IAEA. A nuclear power station can be regarded, of course, as a special case. However, in the course of the internationalization of Baltic economies and continuing foreign investment, the pressures for keeping financial records, for example, in a language that can be understood at the headquarters of a multinational company with a branch in a Baltic state, may mount. Meanwhile, a quiet grumbling of multinationals has started. At the same time, many Baltic firms are already extensively using documentation in English (Tomusk, 2000). Obviously, at some point legislative adjustments have to be made to better manage this problem of growing linguistic diversity.

Some experts see another serious challenge to small and medium-sized languages in new information technologies, particularly in the pending switch to oral communication with computers (Vabar, 2002). In that case, the supremacy of English will prevail already in early childhood, given the interest of children in electronic games and other computer applications.

4.4 NATO: The Ultimate Shaper of Baltic Language Policies

Another field in which Estonia and Latvia have been fighting for the preservation and promotion of their state languages regards language proficiency of elected officials. On 15 December 1998, the Estonian parliament amended the Riigikogu Election Act and the Local Government Council Election Act, establishing proficiency requirements in the state language for elected officials. This immediately triggered international criticism, which reached a climax by the end of 2001 when the international community linked the abolition of these requirements to a long-awaited closure of the OSCE Mission to Estonia.

Meanwhile, NATO joined the critics by sending clear signals that changes in the election laws would be a prerequisite also for NATO membership. Eager to get rid of the Mission, perceived as a stigma, and wishing to enhance its chances regarding NATO, the Estonian parliament gave in and made the required changes on 21 November 2001, securing the closure of the OSCE Mission a month later.

And again, as if seeking compensation and responding to loud warnings in the press against any official status of Russian, the parliament amended the law on local governments on 4 December 2001. The amendment specifies that if a local government unit has been granted the right, in accordance with Article 11 of the Language Act, to use the language of a national minority for internal communication alongside Estonian, the sessions of such local government, which shall be conducted in Estonian, may be fully or partially translated into the language of a national minority. The amendment entered into force after local elections in October 2002. It is no secret that several local governments in northeastern Estonia were using Russian in their official business without formal approval by the Estonian government as required by Article 11 of the Language Act. For some reason, the government preferred neither to grant such approvals nor to see this violation.

While Estonia put an end to the issue of proficiency requirements in the state language for elected officials by amending the law, in Latvia, despite international criticism and pressures, this issue was still very much on the agenda at the beginning of 2002. Meanwhile, in 2001, Latvia had already suffered its first international setback on this issue in the UN Human Rights Committee.[111]

---

[111]   In 1997, a deputy candidate for the Riga city council was removed from the electoral list due to insufficient state language proficiency. Dismissed in Latvia, the case reached the UN Human Rights Committee. On

However, as opposed to Estonia, Latvia was able to close the OSCE Mission at the end of 2001 before the amendments to the Latvian election laws could be discussed, let alone adopted. The President of Latvia, siding with international organizations, played a decisive role by making a proposal in December 2001, unexpected by many, to abolish language requirements for elected officials as non-democratic. Subsequently, the president discussed this proposal at several meetings with Latvian politicians and language experts. As in Estonia, a symptomatic change in the focus of the debate occurred. Democratic discourse was upstaged by discourse on the protection of Latvian. It was decided that before election law can be amended, the positions of the state language must be secured by additional means. The president even stated that Latvia has no language policy and no policy for the protection of Latvian.[112] In January 2002, the president and the prime minister proposed the establishment of a standing Commission on the State Language for elaboration of guidelines of Latvian language policy for the next three years (in Estonia, the Minister of Education established a similar body, a language council, at the end of 2001) (Valge, 2002). However, the reaction of Latvian MPs was not supportive.[113]

In January 2002, when the OSCE Mission to Latvia had just been closed, other powerful actors—the EU and the United States—voiced their strong support for the initiative of the Latvian president to delete language requirements from election law (Baltic News Service, 2002). It became clear that changes in election law were being linked to Latvia's prospects of NATO membership. The visit of the Latvian president to the United States in February only confirmed that viewpoint on the part of the United States. Speaking in the Latvian parliament on 21 February 2002, the Secretary General of NATO stressed that in order to progress on its way to the alliance, Latvia had to abolish the provisions that require candidates to possess the highest degree of proficiency in Latvian. He also mentioned that attitudes towards national minorities are significant in the evaluation of a state's readiness to join NATO. In spite of this direct and clear message, the MPs of the ruling parties did not show any readiness to change the law in the near future (Minelres Forum, 2002a).

Latvia's political elite was facing a difficult dilemma. The international community in general, and the NATO leadership in particular, had linked the country's membership in NATO to the suggested changes in the election law. While membership of NATO was one of the most cherished goals of Latvian politics, so was the promotion of the Latvian language. A partial sacrifice of the latter even for the benefit of the former would have constituted a deviation from the policy of containment of Russian. The situation was further complicated by the upcoming national elections of October 2002.

---

25 July 2001, the Committee decided that a violation of Article 25, in conjunction with Article 2 of the International Covenant on Civil and Political Rights had occurred, and that the state party is obliged to provide the aggrieved person with an effective remedy and to take steps to prevent similar violations from occurring in the future (Minelres Forum, 2001).

112   See http://rus.delfi.lv/archive/index.php?id=2436394.

113   See the Latvian President's proposal and the reactions it elicited in Minelres Forum (2001).

In this situation the Latvian parliament applied the Estonian "model of anticipatory compensation" starting with the amendments to the Constitution to strengthen the status of the Latvian language before it considered changes to election law. On 30 April 2002, the parliament of Latvia adopted 'language amendments' to four articles of the constitution. Article 18 was supplemented with the provision that every MP is obliged to swear or to give a promise "to be loyal to Latvia, strengthen its sovereignty and the Latvian language as the sole state language, defend Latvia as an independent and democratic state, fulfil his/her duties in good faith, observe the constitution and the laws". Article 21 provides that the sole working language of the parliament is Latvian. Article 101 states that "full-fledged citizens of Latvia elect local governments" and that "the working language of local governments is Latvian". Article 104 was supplemented with the provision that "everybody has the right to receive an answer in Latvian" from state or local government institutions (Minelres Forum, 2002b).

In the view of the Latvian Human Rights Committee, these amendments were un- necessary; almost all adopted provisions were already included in other Latvian laws. At the same time, the Committee was concerned that MPs' obligation to swear "to strengthen the Latvian language as the sole state language" may limit the rights of parliamentarians to pro- pose amendments to language legislation (Minelres Forum, 2002b).

Finally, on 9 May 2002, the parliament of Latvia abolished the state language require- ments for deputy candidates in parliamentary and municipal elections. Previously, all Latvian citizens who had received education in other languages than Latvian had to produce a certifi- cate of the highest level of state language proficiency in order to be registered as candidates. Now, such certification is not necessary; deputy candidates are asked to evaluate their level of state language proficiency individually (Minelres Forum, 2002c).

CONCLUSION: OUTCOMES AND PROSPECTS

Soviet language policy since the late 1970s had been aimed at creating bilingualism among non-Russians. Russians themselves could easily survive under this system as monolingual Russian-speakers. By contrast, the first wave of Baltic language legislation, beginning imme- diately prior to independence, created legal conditions in which a respective titular-Russian bilingualism was expected. This wave of language legislation can be generally associated with the restoration of the rights of the Baltic titular languages, policies of nation-building, but also with the beginning of ethnic containment of the non-titular groups.

The second wave of Baltic language legislation, which started after independence and is far from being completed, had to cope with the 'double hegemony' of Russian and English, stemming from large Russian-speaking minorities in Estonia and Latvia and from the drive of European integration. In this situation, the Baltic states have resorted to protecting their state language by legislative means and to promoting them by imposing state language profi- ciency requirements on new categories of professionals in certain private spheres. The need to know Russian has actually disappeared for titulars. In Estonia, for example, there is no formal obligation for anyone in the public or service sector to be able to understand or speak Russian. There is an exception for those public officials who work in the local government units where at least half of the permanent residents belong to a national minority and where the officials have to provide replies in the language of a national minority (Article 10 of the Estonian Language Act). In accordance with the new language laws, the titular peoples should be able to survive and function normally, at least in principal, as monolingual speakers of their mother tongues. True, they would not be able to take specific jobs where the knowledge of foreign languages is required. Needless to say, there are many other jobs available to the speakers of titular languages where such requirements do not exist. At the same time, all Russian-speakers are expected to develop their skills in the state language in order to manage in everyday life, compete on the job market and become citizens.

As a result of the second wave of Baltic language legislation, monolingual non-titulars were effectively contained by a combination of different laws, which introduced requirements of proficiency in the state language. This containment tended to go too far in some cases such as the controversial language requirements for private business and elected officials. In Estonia, in the name of national integration, the state language will also be imposed on the state-financed minority-language secondary schools, which have to start switching their language of instruction to the state language in 2007.[114] In Latvia, the same process has to take place even earlier, in 2004. Many experts regard this as too ambitious a target, particularly because of the lack of qualified teachers. The minority representatives claim that their right to receive education in the mother tongue will be restricted. By contrast, Lithuania has no such plans, leaving matters to be decided by the market and by the parents' choice of the language of education for their children. So far, the Lithuanian experience has demonstrated that the volume of education in the languages of national minorities is slowly shrinking without any administrative pressure, mainly due to the choices made by parents.

Of course, Estonians as well as Latvians and Lithuanians cannot survive as monolingual groups, despite the relaxed conditions created by the respective language laws. In the process of global communication and trade, and especially because of accession to the EU and NATO, citizens must become increasingly proficient in English and in other foreign languages. However, in these conditions Russian-speakers must develop even richer language repertoires than Estonians (see Table 1.6). At the same time, some young Estonian-speakers, according to anecdotal evidence, have recently discovered, to their surprise and dismay, that quite a few promising jobs advertised in Estonia include the knowledge of Russian, a language that they have hardly studied in recent years.

So far, the Baltic states have neither developed nor implemented any comprehensive policies for the management of linguistic diversity. However, the advance of English, the continuing large-scale presence of Russian and the revitalization of languages of other minorities are setting the scene in which the management of linguistic diversity will become a necessity rather than an option. One step in the direction of the management of linguistic diversity could be the signing and ratification of the European Charter for Regional or Minority

---

[114]   In January 2002, the outgoing Prime Minister of Estonia cited the fact that the number of pupils in Russian-language schools had diminished twofold during the last ten years as one of the greatest achievements of Estonian nationality policy (*Eesti Päevaleht*, 2002).

Languages. Among the EU candidate countries, Hungary, Slovakia and Slovenia, together with fourteen other states, have already signed and ratified the Charter.[115]

Pierre Bourdieu (1991: 57) warned that those who seek to defend a threatened language are obliged to wage a total struggle. Observations of language situations in the Baltic states and particularly in Estonia and Latvia seem to indicate that the local majorities as well as the minorities perceive various threats to the future status and functions of their languages. In order not to be engulfed in an unnecessary total struggle over language issues, these perceptions need to be carefully scrutinized in an atmosphere of mutual respect and tolerance, facilitated by internal and international cooperation.

REFERENCES

Baltic Data House and University of Latvia (1998) *The Programme for Studies and Activities "Towards a Civic Society"*. Report: The Results of the 3rd Stage. Riga: Baltic Data House.

Baltic Institute of Social Sciences (2001) *Survey of Newly Naturalized Citizens*. Riga: Baltic Institute of Social Sciences.

Baltic News Service (2002) "USA and EU Are Waiting for Changes in Election Law" (in Russian). http://rus.delfi.lv/archive/index.php?id=2543693.

Bourdieu, Pierre (1991) *Language and Symbolic Power*. Cambridge: Polity Press.

Central Statistical Bureau of Latvia (2002) *Results of the 2000 Population and Housing Census in Latvia*. Collection of Statistical Data. Riga: LR Centrālā Statiskas Pārvalde (Central Statistical Bureau of Latvia).

Druviete, Ina (1999) "Language Policy in a Changing Society: Problematic Issues in the Implementation of International Linguistic Human Rights Standards". In Miklós Kontra, Robert Phillipson, Tove Skutnabb-Kangas et al. (eds.) *Language: A Right and a Resource*. Budapest: Central European University Press, pp.263–272.

Ernits, Peeter (2000) "Kodakondsusameti endine peadirektor Andres Kollist: Nende eesmärk oli venelaste elu põrguks muuta." In *Luup* 3 (112). (An interview in the Estonian bi-weekly *Luup* with Mr. Andres Kollist, former director of the Estonian Citizenship and Migration Board. Translation into Russian at http://www.moles.ee/00/Feb/12/6-1.html.)

---

[115] The European Charter for Regional or Minority Languages was adopted by the Committee of Ministers of the Council of Europe on 2 October 1992 and opened for signature on 5 November 1992. The Charter entered into force on 1 March 1998. As of 18 August 2003, seventeen states (Armenia, Austria, Croatia, Cyprus, Denmark, Finland, Germany, Hungary, Liechtenstein, The Netherlands, Norway, Slovakia, Slovenia, Spain, Sweden, Switzerland and the United Kingdom) had ratified the Charter and twelve others (Azerbaijan, the Czech Republic, France, Iceland, Italy, Luxembourg, Malta, Moldova, Romania, Russia, FYR Macedonia and Ukraine) had signed but not ratified (see also http://www.coe.int/T/E/Legal_Affairs/Local_and_regional_Democracy/Regional_or_Minority_languages/).

European Commission (1999) "1999 Regular Report from the Commission on Estonia's Progress Towards Accession". Brussels: European Commission. http://europa.eu.int/comm/enlargement/report_10_99/pdf/en/estonia_en.pdf.

European Commission (2000) "2000 Regular Report from the Commission on Estonia's Progress Towards Accession". Brussels: European Commission. http://europa.eu.int/comm/enlargement/report_11_00/pdf/en/es_en.pdf.

European Commission (2001) "2001 Regular Report on Estonia's Progress Towards Accession". Brussels: European Commission. http://europa.eu.int/comm/enlargement/report2001/ee_en.pdf.

Grin, François (1991) "The Estonian Language Law: Presentation with Comments". *Language Problems and Language Planning*, 15(2) (summer): 191–201.

Grin, François (1993) "The Relevance of Thresholds in Language Maintenance and Shift: A Theoretical Examination". *Journal of Multilingual and Multicultural Development*, 14(5): 375–392.

Karklins, Rasma (1998) "Ethnic Integration and School Policies in Latvia". *Nationalities Papers*, 26(2): 283–302.

Kiris, Advig (ed.) (1991) *Restoration of the Independence of the Republic of Estonia. Selection of Legal Acts (1988–1991)*. Tallinn: Ministry of Foreign Affairs of the Republic of Estonia, Estonian Institute for Information.

Laitin, David D. (1998) *Identity in Formation. The Russian-Speaking Populations in the Near Abroad*. Ithaca and London: Cornell University Press.

Loeber, Dietrich André (1993) "Language Rights in Independent Estonia, Latvia and Lithuania, 1918–1940". In Sergiy Vilfan (ed., in collaboration with G. Sandvik and L. Wils) *Ethnic Groups and Language Rights* (Comparative Studies on Governments and Non-Dominant Ethnic Groups in Europe, 1850–1940, vol. III). London and Dartmouth: New York University Press, pp.221–249.

Minelres (Minority Electronic Resources) Forum (1999) "Minority Issues in Latvia, No. 11". (14 December 1999) http://racoon.riga.lv/minelres/archive//12141999-22:17:19-20156.html.

Minelres Forum (2000a) "Minority Issues in Latvia, No. 17". (10 July 2000) http://racoon.riga.lv/minelres/archive//07102000-13:57:43-28456.html.

Minelres Forum (2000b) "Minority Issues in Latvia, No. 19". (1 September 2000) http://racoon.riga.lv/minelres/archive//09012000-18:08:59-13484.html.

Minelres Forum (2000c) "Minority Issues in Latvia, No. 20". (8 September 2000) http://racoon.riga.lv/minelres/archive//09092000-10:29:02-8811.html.

Minelres Forum (2001) "Minority Issues in Latvia, No. 40". (9 December 2001) http://racoon.riga.lv/minelres/archive//12102001-09:16:25-11465.html.

Minelres Forum (2002a) "Minority Issues in Latvia, No. 45". (1 March 2002) http://racoon.riga.lv/minelres/archive//03042002-13:58:19-15408.html.

Minelres Forum (2002b) "Minority Issues in Latvia, No. 49". (1 May 2002) http://racoon.riga.lv/minelres/archive//05022002-20:49:44-27893.html.

Minelres Forum (2002c) "Minority Issues in Latvia, No. 50". (15 May 2002) http://lists.delfi.lv/pipermail/minelres/2002-May/001910.html.

Muiznieks, Nils, Angelita Kamenska, Ieva Leimane, and Sandra Garsvane (2000) *Human Rights in Latvia in 1999*. Riga: Latvian Center for Human Rights and Ethnic Studies.

Newsline (2000) "Estonian Parliament Passes Amendments on School Integration". *RFE/RL Newsline*, 5 April 2000. http://www.rferl.org/newsline/2000/04/050400.asp

Nordic Council of Ministers (1999) *Norden, the Top of Europe. Newsletter No. 6*. Copenhagen: Nordic Council of Ministers. http://www.norden.org/top/_forsiderOGkal/9906.htm.

Ozolins, Uldis (1999) "Between Russian and European Hegemony: Current Language Policy in the Baltic States". In Sue Wright (ed.) *Language Policy and Language Issues in the Successor States of the Former USSR*. Clevendon/Buffalo/Toronto/Sidney: Multilingual Matters, pp.6–47.

Pettai, Vello Andres (1996) "Estonia's Controversial Language Policies". *Transition*, 2(24) (29 November 1996): 20–22.

Poleshchuk, Vadim (2001a) "Accession to the European Union and National Integration in Estonia and Latvia." ECMI Baltic Seminar 2000, Tønder, Denmark, 7–10 December 2000. *ECMI Report No. 8*. Flensburg: European Centre for Minority Issues.

Poleshchuk, Vadim (2001b) *Advice Not Welcomed. Recommendations of the OSCE High Commissioner to Estonia and Latvia and the Response*. Münster: LIT Verlag.

Poleshchuk, Vadim (2002) "Estonia, Latvia and the European Commission: Changes in Language Regulation in 1999–2001". Budapest: EU Accession Monitoring Program of the Open Society Institute (EUMAP). http://www.eumap.org/articles/content/40/402.

Proos, Ivi and Iris Pettai (1999) *Venelased ja eesti keel. Kommenteeritud andmebaas*. Tallinn: Eesti Avatud Ühiskonna Instituut.

Raun, Toivo U. (1995) "The Estonian SSR Language Law (1989): Background and Implementation". *Nationalities Papers*, 23(3): 515–534.

Riigi Teataja (2000) "Keeleseaduse muutmise seadus (The Act Amending the Language Act)". *Riigi Teataja*, I. 30.06.2000, 51, 326.

Rowley, David G. (2000) "Imperial versus National Discourse: The Case of Russia". *Nations and Nationalism*, 6(1) (January): 23–42.

Skutnabb-Kangas, Tove (1999) "Language Rights: Problems and Challenges in Recent Human Rights Instruments". Paper presented at the colloquium "Les impérialismes linguistiques – hier et aujourd'hui, à l'est et à l'ouest", organized by Maison Franco-japonaise, l'Université de Hitotsubashi and l'Institut National des Langues et Civilisations Orientales, Tokyo, Japan, 22–24 October 1999.

Statistical Office of Estonia (2001) *2000 Population and Housing Census. Citizenship, Nationality, Mother Tongue and Command of Foreign Languages.* Tallinn: Statiskaamet (Statistical Office of Estonia).

Tartu University Market Research (1995) *The Attitude of Town Residents of North-Eastern Estonia Towards Estonian Reforms and Social Policy.* A Comparative Study of 1993, 1994 and 1995. Conducted by the Tartu University Market Research Team, Financed by the Open Estonia Foundation, November, 1995.

Tomusk, Ilmar (2000) "Eesti keel vajab kaitset ja puhastamist". *Eesti Päevaleht,* 7 February 2000.

UNDP (1999) *Estonian Human Developing Report 1999.* UNDP: Tallinn. http://www.iiss.ee/nhdr/1999/EIA99eng.pdf.

Vabar, Sven (2002) "Infotehnoloogia ja rahvuskultuur kui koit ja hämarik". *Eesti Päevaleht Online.* http://www.epl.ee/uudised/artikkel.asp/G=66/ID=122757.

Valge, Jüri (2002) "Keelteaasta lõppes, keelenõukogu jätkab". *Sirp,* 11 January 2002.

Vesti Segodnya (2001) "Untitled". 5 May 2001.

Vihalemm, Triin (1997) "The Equality of Opportunities Offered by Education". *Eesti haridusfoorum 97. Collection of Materials.* Tallinn: Disantrek.

Vihalemm, Triin (1999) "Estonian Language Competence, Performance, and Beliefs on Acquisition among the Russian-Speaking Inhabitants of Estonia, 1989–1997". *International Journal of the Sociology of Language,* 139: 69–85.

Zaagman, Rob (1999) *Conflict Prevention in the Baltic States: The OSCE High Commissioner on National Minorities in Estonia, Latvia and Lithuania.* ECMI Monographs, No. 1. Flensburg: European Centre for Minority Issues.

Identities and Language Politics in Ukraine: The Challenges of Nation-State Building

Viktor Stepanenko

Identities and Language Politics in Ukraine: The Challenges of Nation-State Building

Viktor Stepanenko

INTRODUCTION

Ukraine appeared as a new geopolitical reality in Eastern Europe with the proclamation of the independent Ukrainian state on 24 August 1991 and the endorsement of this act by a popular referendum on 1 December 1991.

The social transformation taking place in post-communist Ukraine is dramatic. The population's identity is undergoing a complex transformation process on both the personal and macro-societal levels. This is relevant to the political, social, ethnic, psychological, historical, cultural, linguistic and religious spheres. This transformation is characterized by inner features, discontinuities and dilemmas which often do not conform to the logic of conventional conceptualization. This is particularly true of the language issue—one of the most complex and problematic components of Ukraine's transformation. One of the paradoxes of the Ukrainian case is the state policy of 'revitalization' (Grin and Vaillancourt, 1999: 99) of Ukrainian, which is the titular language of the prevailing ethnic majority of the country. What is behind the language issue in Ukraine and which strategies in the sphere of language policy are used in Ukraine? These are the questions that will be discussed. Language policies will be analysed in the context of two main perspectives: that of the close relationship between language and identity, as well as that of the relationship between language issues and the process of nation-state building combined with the post-communist transformation.

In order to present the formation of Ukrainian identities and to analyse language issues in this country, it is important to briefly examine the sociocultural, historical, demographic and sociolinguistic background of Ukraine's nation-state building. The legislative framework of language policy in Ukraine will be explored in Section 2. Section 3 is devoted to a presentation of the positions and principal arguments of the main protagonists in the language debate in the country, followed by an analysis of the state policy of 'language balance'. A detailed account of how the Ukrainian state has actually implemented language policy in the spheres of education and mass media will be presented in Section 4. In conclusion, the prospects for language policy and the possibilities for easing the language issue in Ukraine will be examined.

1. UKRAINE'S NATION-STATE BUILDING: TRANSFORMATION OF IDENTITIES AND LANGUAGE ISSUES

1.1 Sociocultural Characteristics of the Ukrainian Case

The building of the Ukrainian nation-state coincides with the process of post-communist transformation. The transition to democracy and a free market overlap with the complex mutation of post-Soviet identities and with the construction of new civic, ethnic and socio-cultural identities for the peoples living in Ukraine, both non-ethnic and ethnic Ukrainians. The complex fusion and mixtures between social and ethnic identifications of various types ('Soviet people', 'post-Soviet Ukrainians', 'Russians of Ukraine', 'Russian-speaking Ukrainians', 'Russian-speaking ethnic minorities') often create tension, controversy and a so-cio-psychological ambivalence that characterize, according to numerous surveys, post-Soviet consciousness in Ukraine (Golovakha and Panina, 1994: 132–138).

Ukraine is a multiethnic society in which two main languages—Ukrainian and Russian—prevail. Ukrainians, the titular nation, constitute the country's ethnic majority, while the ethnic groups of this former Soviet Republic hold the position of Ukraine's mi-norities. This includes, paradoxically enough, the once dominant ethnic group, Russians—the largest of Ukraine's ethnic minorities. The multiethnic diversity of Ukrainian society was almost irrelevant in the historical project of assimilation of ethnic minorities into the 'great Russian nation' in the former Russian Empire and again later in the formation of a new historical community, the 'Soviet people', in the former Soviet Union. Today, however, it has become one of the most important characteristics of contemporary Ukraine. The need for interethnic peace has emerged as an imperative of the country's socio-political stability and geopolitical security.

1.2 Historical Background to Ukraine's Nation-State Building

Unlike the majority of states in Central Europe as well as Russia and the Baltic states, the independent Ukrainian state does not possess a stable and developed historical tradition of statehood. The Ukrainian nation is therefore still in the process of constructing a nation-state. As Kuzio remarks, "Ukraine has only enjoyed two brief periods of independence in the mod-ern era, for a few years after the Cossack rebellion of 1648 and under a succession of weak governments in 1917–1921" (1992: 7). During its dramatic history, parts of Ukrainian ethnic territory have belonged to a series of different countries, including Tsarist Russia, Austria-Hungary, Poland, Romania and Czechoslovakia. Because of these historical circumstances, the Ukrainian ethnocultural core and, likewise, the meaning of identity, have acquired dif-ferent dimensions—regional, religious and linguistic (Kuzio, 1992; Stepanenko, 1999). The declaration of an independent Ukrainian state in 1991 and the adoption of the Constitution in 1996 have historically and politically solidified the lengthy process of achieving independ-ent statehood for the Ukrainian nation.

In these circumstances, Ukrainian policy-makers face the challenge of forming a new ethnocultural community—a modern Ukrainian nation with not only an ethnic but also a civic component. In 1996, with the adoption of the new Constitution, a political and legal framework for the development of a civic nation ("the Ukrainian people—citizens of Ukraine of all nationalities") was provided. It was assumed that the social and cultural background of this new entity would consist not only of Ukrainians, but also include the approximately one hundred[116] other peoples and ethnic groups residing in Ukraine.

Before we examine in greater detail the legislative framework of language policy in Ukraine, some background data on the demographic and sociolinguistic characteristics of Ukraine shall be provided.

1.3 Demographic and Sociolinguistic Characteristics of Ukraine

1.3.1 Demographic Data

According to the results of the recent 2001 population census,[117] the population of Ukraine is 48.46 million, of which Ukrainians make up about 77.8 per cent (37.7 million). Russians are the second major ethnic group, making up less than one fifth of the Ukrainian population or 17.3 per cent (8.3 million).[118]

After the Russians, the other main ethnic groups in Ukraine (each claiming less than one per cent of the population) are Jews, Belarussians, Moldovans, Crimean Tatars,[119] Bulgarians, Poles, Hungarians, Romanians and other smaller groups. As Ukrainians and Russians are the country's two largest ethnic groups, together comprising nearly 95 per cent of the entire population (Figure 1.2), Ukrainian and Russian are the two main languages used in Ukraine. However, nearly a third of ethnic Ukrainians consider Russian as their native language, as we shall see below.

---

[116]   According to different sources, the total number of ethnic groups in Ukraine varies between 90 and 130.

[117]   A new census was conducted in Ukraine in December 2001. The data were announced by the State Committee of Statistics of Ukraine at the beginning of 2003.

[118]   For comparison: according to the results of the 1989 population census (The Ministry of Statistics of the USSR, 1991: 134–136), the population of Ukraine was 51.4 million, of which (ethnic) Ukrainians made up about 72 per cent (37.4 million). Russians were the second major ethnic group, making up more than one fifth of the Ukrainian population or 22.1 per cent (11.3 million).

[119]   More than 250,000 Crimean Tatars had returned to the Crimea by the beginning of 2000 (Bulletin of the State Committee of Ukraine on Nationalities and Migration 1999: 116).

Figure 1.2
Distribution of the Major Ethnic Groups in Ukraine

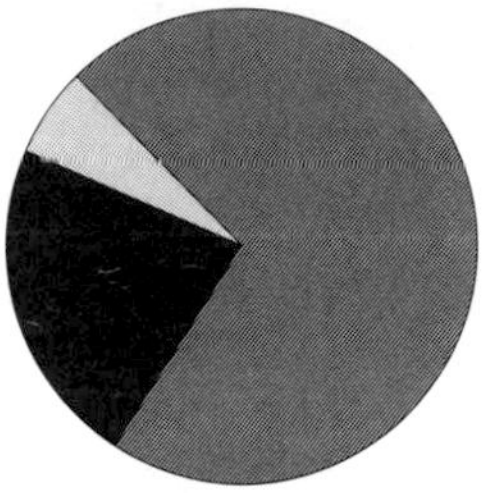

SOURCE: 2001 Census, The State Committee of Statistics of Ukraine, 2003.

These circumstances make the relationship between (ethnic) Ukrainians and the Russian community an issue of strategic significance for the stability of the Ukrainian state and, bearing in mind the active use of the 'ethnolinguistic card' by Russia for the protection of its geopolitical interests in the post-Soviet 'near abroad',[120] for Eastern European regional security as a whole. Because of the historical, religious, and linguistic closeness between Ukrainians and Russians, and the complex historical, political and economic factors in the development of the two nations, the Ukrainian–Russian relationship is the most sensitive issue in current socio-political, cultural and language policies in Ukraine. Ukrainians are the dominant ethnic group, but "one, whose hegemony in their own lands has never been certain, especially in the south and east" (Kuzio, 1992: 8).

1.3.2 Regional and Sociolinguistic Characteristics

Most Russians (about 80 per cent of the total Russian population of Ukraine) live compactly in the southern and eastern industrial regions of the country, bordering Russia and the Black Sea. In these regions and in the Republic of Crimea, Russian is the main language spoken. The highest percentage of Russians in Ukraine live in the Crimea—67 per cent of the Crimean population—which has obtained the special status of administrative-territorial autonomy within Ukraine. The central and, in particular, the western regions of the country are overwhelmingly Ukrainian in terms of ethnic and linguistic composition. Yet, the Russian language still plays a major role in everyday communication in the cities of central Ukraine, including the capital Kyiv. This is not surprising, taking into account that 87 per cent of Russians live in cities. Jews, of whom the majority are Russian-speaking, are even more urban oriented than Russians, with about 91 per cent of them living in cities (UNDP, 1996: 81). Other ethnic groups concentrated in specific parts of Ukraine include

---

[120] Conventional term used in Russian geopolitics to refer to former Soviet countries.

the Crimean Tatars, who mostly live in Crimea; the Hungarians and Slovaks, who are concentrated in Transcarpathia; the Romanians, who are residents of the Chernivtsy oblast (Bukovina) and Odessa *oblast*; and the Bulgarian, Greek, Gagauz and German ethnic communities which reside in the southern regions of the country.

The question of the official status of Russian as the second state language in Ukraine is one of the most problematic and difficult issues of nationality policy (or 'ethno-policy', as it is termed in Ukraine) at the central, regional and local levels. However, despite, or perhaps because of, the 'hot' character of this issue, data on the use of Ukrainian and Russian in the country are rather approximate and vary, sometimes substantially, from one survey to another. It seems that the uncertainty surrounding the issue of language use is problematic for all aspects of Ukrainian political life. This illustrates the complex nature of Ukraine's language context, including widespread bilingualism and the ambivalent ethnolinguistic identity of many people which is the product of the predominant use of the Russian language by a considerable share of ethnic Ukrainians and the difficulties in self-identification of persons from mixed Ukrainian–Russian families.[121] However, in acknowledging the complexity of the language issue, one must also admit that 'linguistic uncertainty' is influenced by some characteristics of language policy in Ukraine, as we will try to demonstrate later (see Section 3.3).

1.3.3 Data on Language Use

While avoiding extreme and politically biased estimates, one must present an approximate snapshot of the situation on the basis of information drawn from different sources and studies about language use in Ukraine. The usual picture painted is that the population of Ukraine is divided almost equally between monolingual Ukrainian-speakers, monolingual Russian-speakers and Ukrainian–Russian bilinguals; furthermore, a small proportion of the population speaks languages other than Ukrainian or Russian. However, statistics often indicate a dominance of Russian over Ukrainian in everyday communication in Ukraine. For example, according to data from a representative country-wide survey conducted during the 1998 parliamentary elections, Ukrainian was the main language of communication for 39–40 per cent of respondents; 45 per cent of respondents preferred to use Russian in their everyday communication; and 15–16 per cent identified themselves as bilingual (Masenko, 1999: 74).

Language rights activists from Ukraine's Russian-speaking population believe that the dominance of the Russian language in the sphere of everyday communication is even stronger. According to their data, the majority, or 45.7 per cent of respondents, use Russian as their main language of communication; 29.8 per cent of respondents use Ukrainian; and 23.5 per cent identified themselves as bilingual (Nestayko, 2000: 4).

---

[121] Khmelko and Wilson discuss "the phenomenon of biethnicity" in Ukraine ("i.e., self-identification of a person as belonging in some respect to two ethnic groups rather than one"). According to the data given by these authors, 25 to 26 per cent of the adult population in Ukraine identify themselves "as somehow both Ukrainian and Russian" (Khmelko and Wilson, 2000: 76).

1.3.4 Ethnolinguistic Self-Identification in Ukraine

Complex research on ethnolinguistic self-identification in Ukraine was conducted in the framework of regular representative surveys by the Institute of Sociology of the National Academy of Sciences. The surveys, conducted during the period 1994–2000, demonstrate a stability of ethnolinguistic identifications (annual indications are nearly the same) (Vorona *et al.*, 1999: 225).

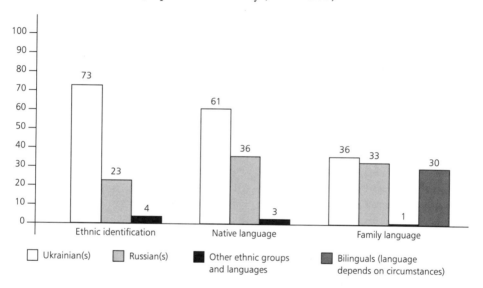

Figure 1.3
Ethnolinguistic Self-Identification in Ukraine
(Representative surveys, 1994–1999)

As Figure 1.3 shows, there are substantial discrepancies between respondents' ethnic and linguistic self-identifications, their concepts of native language and their preferred language of family communication. Those who identify themselves as 'Ukrainians' do not necessarily consider Ukrainian as their native language (though a prevailing majority of them do), and only a half of Ukrainians use Ukrainian only in their family communication (see the columns of "family language" in Figure 1.3). The ethnic and linguistic identities of Russian respondents coincided. Virtually all those calling themselves Russians spoke the Russian language. Moreover, as the surveys show, the number of bilingual and Russian-speaking respondents exceeded the number of Russians in the country.

The surveys also showed that age and gender did not influence the ethnolinguistic self-identification of respondents. The most decisive socio-demographic variables tended to be the respondents' educational level and their region and place of residence. According to the surveys, the higher the respondents' level of education, the more often they identified themselves as Russians and selected Russian both as their native language and as their language of communication. Half of those respondents who failed to complete their secondary education spoke Ukrainian while only sixteen per cent of respondents with a higher education preferred to use this language (Oksamytna, 1999: 151). It has also appeared that the higher the respondent's level of education, the substantially lower the rigidity in the strategy of language use ('Ukrainian only' or 'Russian only'). A higher level of education naturally increases opportunities for a choice between the two main languages, depending on the circumstances.

The very close correspondence between ethnic and linguistic self-identification is characteristic of the rural population of Ukraine. Of the respondents living in villages, 83 per cent identified themselves as Ukrainians, 80 per cent defined Ukrainian as their native language, and 65 per cent stated that they use it in their family communication (Oksamytna, 1999: 152). However, the population of Ukrainian cities, including the capital, showed the most drastic discrepancies between ethnic and linguistic self-identification. Although 77 per cent of Kyiv's respondents considered themselves as Ukrainians and 62 per cent of these respondents defined Ukrainian as their native language, only fourteen per cent of them use Ukrainian in their family communication (Oksamytna, 1999: 152).

Thus, these surveys provide some of the following characteristics of Ukraine's language situation:

   i.   Ukraine is a predominantly bilingual country in which two main languages— Ukrainian and Russian—prevail.

   ii. There are discrepancies between people's ethnic and linguistic identifications on the one hand, and between their concepts of native language and of the language of everyday and of family communication on the other. This is especially true of Russian-speaking ethnic Ukrainians ("Russophones"[122]) and Russian-speaking ethnic minorities.

   iii. Bilingualism is characteristic of Ukraine's language situation, and ethnic Ukrainians, mainly because of different historical, social and cultural factors in the country's development (including historical Russification), are more flexible in their linguistic behaviour than Russians (Figure 1.3).

   iv. In terms of socio-geographic characteristics, the Ukrainian language is predominant in the western part of the country and in rural areas, whereas Russian is prevalent in Ukraine's cities, including the capital Kyiv, and in Ukraine's eastern and southern regions.

   v.   Keeping in mind the high density of the population in the "Russian-speaking" regions and some social, cultural and informational advantages of cities, one can agree with the conclusion that there is a dominance of Russian over Ukrainian in terms of the languages' communicative potential (a spread of usage in different social spheres), despite the nearly equal demographic potentials of the number of speakers of the two main languages of Ukraine (Masenko, 1999: 74–75).

The communicative dominance of the Russian language in Ukraine has led to a contradictory cultural, psychological and ideological framework in the country's language situation. The language issue, transferred to the political and legal contexts, results in complications in

---

[122]   The term used by Arel (1995: 598).

another sphere: that of nation-state building and the significance (real and politically created) of language with respect to this process. National legislation already reflects this.

2.   THE LEGISLATIVE FRAMEWORK OF LANGUAGE POLICY IN UKRAINE

Since its declaration of independence in August 1991, the Ukrainian state has pursued a nationality policy which abides by the main international legal norms and agreements in the sphere of human and minority rights. National legislation in the sphere of minority rights proclaims the equality of the political, economic, social and cultural rights of all peoples and ethnic groups in Ukraine and the right of minorities to national-cultural autonomy.[123]

However, the mechanisms of implementation of laws dealing with minority issues have yet to be clearly defined and the realization of minority rights depends largely on political will at the national and local levels. With the exception of the Act on Languages in Ukraine (adopted in 1989, hereafter, 'Language Act'), the main body of Ukraine's legislation in the sphere of minority rights was adopted at the beginning of the 1990s, during the initial period of state-building. This body of legislation was not developed sufficiently in subsequent legislative norms which regulate the various spheres of social life in Ukraine. This can be witnessed in particular in a legislative provision in the field of language policy in Ukraine.

Current language policy is defined by the Language Act adopted in 1989, before state independence was won, which is still in place. According to this law, Ukrainian alone was granted "state language" status while Russian and other languages were proclaimed as languages of "interethnic communication". Although Russian was not given a distinct status, the free use of Russian and other national languages was guaranteed. According to the law, the studying of Ukrainian and Russian is compulsory in all secondary schools. The legal provisions making Ukrainian the sole state language were passed by the Ukrainian Supreme Soviet in the former USSR during the wave of national-democratic revival in many former Soviet republics. As Ukrainian nationalists admit, claiming a current reverse wave of Russification, a law of that kind could hardly have been adopted by the parliament of an already independent Ukraine (Pohribnyi, 2000: 9), because the communists, their leftist political allies and other pro-Russian political groups in the parliament would have easily managed to block it.

Since independence in 1991, the exclusionary language law adopted in 1989 has become the legal justification for state policies on the historical and sociocultural rehabilitation of the Ukrainian language and for increasing its nation-building role in the newly created Ukrainian state. Practical applications of the law also placed a stronger emphasis on the implementation of Ukrainian in all spheres of public life (the so-called policy of 'Ukrainization'), especially in education (see Section 4.1).

It can be stated that the political emphasis of linguistic Ukrainization was particularly oriented towards the de-Russification of Ukraine's public sphere and it did not have a great impact on those ethnic minorities with a relatively high tradition of cultural and linguistic autonomy, such as the Hungarians, Romanians and Poles. As it has been admitted in the

---

[123]   National-cultural autonomy implies the right of minorities to form associations, receive education in their native language, practice their religion, use their national symbols, commemorate minority holidays and develop their national traditions in any way which does not go against the legislation in force.

particular case of the Hungarians (First Report of the Ethnobarometer Programme, 1999: 95), "the Ukrainian approach can hardly be characterised as a radically nationalising one". However, the introduction of administrative measures on Ukrainization in the public sphere caused criticism and resistance from the members of the ethnocultural communities, in particular of the Russian-speaking communities (above all ethnic Russians, as well as the highly Russified minorities such as the Belarussians, Jews and also the Russian-speaking ethnic Ukrainians) who felt that their linguistic identity was threatened. Although the Language Act guaranteed citizens the right to use their national languages in addition to the state language (this arrangement actually 'works' in regions where ethnic minorities are compactly settled), Russian-speaking communities demanded that the Russian language be placed on an equal footing with Ukrainian as Ukraine's second state or official language. Thus, the legal status of Ukrainian as a state language appeared as a prominent issue in the public and political debates on language policy in Ukraine.

The privileged status of Ukrainian was affirmed in the 1996 Constitution of Ukraine. Article 10 of the Constitution grants the status of state language to Ukrainian; it also "guarantees the free development, use and protection of Russian and of other languages of national minorities of Ukraine". (Thus, according to the Constitution, Russian is nominally one of the minority languages of Ukraine.) Certain aspects of language policy are also regulated by the Act on National Minorities in Ukraine (1992), by laws on local self-government and education and by international legislation in this sphere. The Act on National Minorities guarantees that a minority language can be used equally with the state language in the work of all social institutions and governmental bodies in regions where minority groups constitute the majority of the population. Actual practice shows that this part of the law is implemented mainly at the district (*rayon*)[124] level—in places of traditional minority settlement.

Ukraine ratified the Council of Europe Framework Convention for the Protection of National Minorities in 1997; this legally-binding convention entered into force in Ukraine on 1 May 1998. The complex nature of language issues in Ukraine was evident during the lengthy debates on the ratification of the European Charter for Regional or Minority Languages. The Ukrainian parliament ratified the Charter after three plenary hearings at the end of 1999. However, in summer 2000, the Constitutional Court repealed the law ratifying the Charter. Apparently, the real reason for this decision did not lie in a breach of the procedure of adoption but rather in the 'state logic' of exclusionary language politics (see Section 3.3).

This logic was confirmed by a ruling of the Constitutional Court on the official treatment of Article 10 of the Constitution on the use of the state language in the work of the state and institutions of self-government as well as in the educational process in Ukraine. This case indirectly revealed the ambiguity and contradictions of national legislation on languages and appeared to be a reaction to the decisions on the official status of the Russian language by some local governments in eastern Ukraine. In its ruling of 14 December 1999, the Constitutional Court declared the Ukrainian language the state language and the obligatory means of communication in the work of state and local governmental institutions on the entire territory of Ukraine, although Russian and other minority languages could also be used

---

[124]   Ukraine is composed of the Autonomous Republic of Crimea, 24 *oblasts* (regions), and the cities of Kyiv and Sevastopol, which have a special status. Each oblast is composed of *rayons* (districts).

by regional authorities along with Ukrainian within limits to be defined by law. In this ruling, the Ukrainian language was also defined as the language of instruction in all educational institutions. The languages of ethnic minorities could be studied concurrently with Ukrainian in state and communal educational establishments and in national cultural societies.

At first, the ruling generated concern among representatives of Ukraine's ethnic communities, above all those the Russian community. However, as it later emerged, the ruling did not substantially affect the language situation in the spheres discussed, not even in the sphere of education. In the situation of the general neglect of laws in Ukraine, the ruling appeared to be a ritualistic political act of state support for the Ukrainian language, aiming to satisfy the nationalist public during visible reverse trends of re-Russification. In addition, the ruling did not contain any legislative mechanisms, suggestions for decision-making and assignment of responsibility for implementation of the current legislative regulations on languages. This ruling could also be treated as a kind of test of the public reaction to the hypothetical activation of administrative measures on Ukrainization, though without entailing any political obligation for the authorities (since the ruling did not add anything to existing legislation). Despite its nominally 'explanatory' character on the treatment of the Language Act and of the Constitution, the ruling triggered a diplomatic war between Russia and Ukraine, each accusing the other of violating the linguistic rights of its Russian and Ukrainian minorities respectively.

Thus, the decisions taken by the Constitutional Court have not facilitated the resolution of the complex issues related to the legislative provisions of language policy in Ukraine. As a high-ranking Ukrainian official admitted, language legislation contains many blind spots, particularly in the mechanisms of its implementation and in the realization that state language policies are not clearly elaborated (*Zerkalo Nedeli*, 2000). It appears that all parties in the debate on language policy in Ukraine are united in their understanding that a new legislative provision on language use is needed. However, visions of this new language legislation vary substantially. The principal point of contention is the privileged status of Ukrainian as the sole state language. The dominant 'official party' representing the state approach in language politics not only confirms the exclusionary status of 'titular language' but has also prepared a draft identification. The clash of interests in legislative debates reveals deep and complex cultural and political sentiments that will inform judicial decisions. In order to better understand these issues, it is necessary to present the main parameters of the political context and the protagonists' logic and arguments that inform the language debate and language policy in Ukraine.

3.   THE LANGUAGE DEBATE:
THE CONTEXT AND THE PROTAGONISTS' ARGUMENTS

3.1   Language and Politics of Identity

The language debate between the Ukrainian-speaking and Russian-speaking parts of the population has become one of the most controversial aspects of nation-state building in Ukraine. Some pessimistic commentators even predict a future split of the country into a western (Ukrainian-speaking) and an eastern (Russian-speaking) part (Pieklo *et al.*, 1995: 32). The division of Ukrainian society into Ukrainian- and Russian-speaking parts is revealed by some surveys (not representative, but characteristic) as one of the most difficult obstacles in the formation of the Ukrainian political nation, even more difficult than the political and socio-economic cleavages in contemporary Ukrainian society.

The source of language tensions is the 'one state, one language' ideology combined with actual bilingualism, and possibly the actual dominance of the Russian language over Ukrainian in Ukraine. As a result of the long-term policy of Russification, which was historically undertaken by Tsarist Russia and then actively reproduced in the Soviet politics of ethnic and linguistic convergence, many Ukrainians have linguistically assimilated the Russian language, for centuries the language of political hegemony. The process of historical Russification was facilitated by the linguistic closeness between Ukrainian and Russian, by the common Orthodox religion and by the closeness of the historical development of the two nations.

However, the real source of language tensions in Ukraine also lies in the deep link between language and identity. Because of historical circumstances and current political developments in Ukraine's nation-state building, the Ukrainian language has acquired a special symbolic significance, becoming vital to the ethnic identity of the titular nation. The same could almost be concluded with respect to the symbolic significance of the Russian language for the identity of the ethnic Russians and, to a lesser extent, for the rest of the Russian-speaking population of Ukraine.

In analysing the Ukrainian case, Arel (1995: 597) has argued that "language politics is the politics of threatened identity". As far as the Ukrainian case is concerned, Arel's arguments need correction. Language politics in Ukraine concern not only the politics of 'threatened identity', but also the political logic of nation-state building—the politics of 'constructing identity'. The classic pattern might be expressed through the historical motto of European nation-state formation: 'one nation, one culture, one language'. However, the following questions come to mind: Are the traditional politics of national identity appropriate in contemporary polyethnic and multilingual conditions? How should one characterize the current processes of nation-state building in post-communist countries—this classic project of modernity undertaken in the 'post-modern' age? How are two imperatives of civil society—the right to national self-determination and the civil rights of citizens, particularly those of other ethnic and national groups—to be combined? How are differences, especially linguistic differences, to be accommodated in the framework of civil negotiations?

3.2   The Protagonists' Logic and Arguments

In the Ukrainian case, these questions led to the difficult choice between measures aiming at linguistic assimilation and policies for the accommodation of linguistic differences. The logic and arguments of the principal protagonists in the Ukrainian–Russian language debates, representing mainly public interest groups, are well known. One can summarize the main arguments in the form of a dialogue between two persons who, often, unfortunately, neither understand nor want to understand one another.

Supporters of state status for the Ukrainian language tend to argue that Ukrainian should be the sole state language of Ukraine because:

- Ukrainian is the language of the titular nation which constitutes a prevailing majority in the newly independent Ukrainian state and does not have any other motherland apart from Ukraine.
- The Ukrainian language is the most distinctive identity marker of the Ukrainian nation in the absence of a developed tradition of statehood.
- Ukrainian is in danger of becoming an "endangered" language (Wurm, 1999: 28) because it has been historically and culturally 'oppressed' by the Russian 'metropolitan language'. The status of Ukrainian as the sole state language is the only guarantee of its sociocultural rehabilitation, survival and development.
- Because of the long historical process of Russification and assimilation of Ukrainians into the Russian nation, the measures of active state support for the state language are historically and ethically justified and appropriate for the gradual 'converting' of ethnic Ukrainians to their 'ethnically corresponding' mother tongue.
- Granting official status also to the Russian language is impossible as the unequal possibilities of historical and sociocultural development would lead Russian to inevitably take over Ukrainian as the predominant language in the country (Pohribnyi, 2000: 135).
- The status of Ukrainian as the sole state language confirms the geopolitical, social and cultural identity of Ukraine as an independent, sovereign state. This is particularly significant in the context of geopolitical and cultural pressure by Russia on Ukraine.
- The existing national legislative basis corresponds to the main standards in the field of minority rights and international practice. National legislation provides ethnic minorities, including the Russian minority, with sufficient possibilities to satisfy their cultural and linguistic identity rights. At the same time, national legislation, in particular the Language Act, takes into consideration the specific sociocultural circumstances of Ukraine.

Russian-speaking language rights activists tend to argue that the Russian language should be given a state or official status in Ukraine for the following reasons:

- Due to historical and sociocultural circumstances (which are a contemporary sociocultural 'given', irrespective of ethical or historical arguments), the Russian language is the preferred language of communication for more than half the population of Ukraine. The issue of the realization of the linguistic rights of the Russian-speaking part of Ukraine's population is a confirmation of the real status quo.
- Russians are not really an ethnic minority in Ukraine, at least in comparison with other minorities. Rather, the Russian population is a constituent nation along with Ukrainians in the newly created Ukrainian state due to the historical and cultural closeness between these two related nations and their shared historical genealogies. There should be a common nation-state for Ukrainians and Russians and, hence, the Russian language should enjoy an equal legal footing with the Ukrainian language.

- Language policy should be based on the individual right of ethnolinguistic identification and the rights of Russian-speakers should be affirmed and respected. The policy of 'ethnolinguistic correspondence' is morally and politically inappropriate because it breaches existing national and European legislation on minority and human rights.
- The Ukrainian language is a less developed language in comparison with Russian in terms of informational use and popular communication. For this reason, any legal restrictions on the Russian language cause politically motivated and artificial limitations on cultural, informational and socio-communicative developments in Ukraine, particularly in terms of its inevitable and natural strategic partnership with Russia.

Evidently, the main arguments often lie in separate spheres that do not entirely lend themselves to comparison. The proponents of the supremacy of the Ukrainian language often depend on ethical and historical arguments, mostly operating in terms of the collective nation's right. The proponents of the advancement of official Russian language use base their arguments on the liberal rhetoric of minority and individual human rights. Thus, the question of 'who discriminates against whom?' in the debate on the language issue in Ukraine remains open. The specific compromise between these two positions is represented in the current state policy on languages in Ukraine.

3.3 The State Policy of 'Language Balance'

The linguistic dilemmas presented above make objective policy- and decision-making in the sphere of languages in Ukraine more difficult. Formally, the political ideology of the Ukrainian state is an attempt to reproduce a historical logic for the formation of a nation-state whose language policy is based on the 'one state, one language' principle. The promulgation of a single state language—Ukrainian, the ruling of the Constitutional Court that made Ukrainian the compulsory means of communication for public officials and the language of educational instruction, as well as other legal manifestations reinforce language policy in Ukraine and the traditional strategy of nation-state building.

At the same time, the likelihood of social conflicts and tensions generated because of language issues is great. For example, the ambiguity and contradictions of national legislation on language use leaves room for local governments to declare Russian as a second official language at the local level in eastern Ukraine. Furthermore, there is a substantial gap between legal declarations and the implementation of laws. Russia applies pressure on Ukraine by using political and economic means of influence as well as intensive cultural and informational means to influence language policy. The more developed Russian-oriented informational and cultural infrastructure as well as other 'practical' factors have to be (and are) taken into account in decision-making in the area of language policy.

The state policy of 'speedy Ukrainization' during the first period following Ukrainian independence, from 1991 to 1995, was officially admitted as having been mistaken. Current language policy has been transformed into a policy of balances and counterweights in an attempt to reconcile the existence of two main languages in the country. This policy, however, implies a 'silent' evolutionary transformation in favour of the Ukrainian language from a long-term historical perspective. This, to some extent, equalizes the opportunities of the Ukrainian and Russian languages in their competition and confirms the actual bilingual situation in the country.

In addition, uncertainty about the accuracy of data on language use and other statistics[125] related to language issues prevents any clear language policy and gives the two sides an equally plausible and legitimized opportunity to promote their own position. In this situation, state authorities strive not to interfere in the sensitive Ukrainian–Russian language balance which has been achieved. Having characterized the issues of language and religion as "complex and acute ones", President Kuchma, for example, suggested that "one should not talk too much about these issues, avoiding political turbulence around that, but practically work on resolving them".[126] However, given the lack of practical efforts towards resolving the language issue, exemplified by the absence of a new law on languages during the independence period, the only option remaining is "not talk too much about this", thereby preserving the current shaky balance between the two main languages.

The main parameters of this balance are as follows: Ukrainian is an official language which has been declared "a symbolic integral part of the constitutional order" (according to the Constitutional Court ruling of 14 December 1999), but it is less frequently used in everyday communication than Russian. The Russian language is an unofficial language, but it prevails as the main language of communication in Ukraine. There is also a certain sharing of functions and responsibilities between the two languages, based on the still traditionally strong post-Soviet division of social reality into official and non-official spheres. Ukrainian serves as the official language of government and education, whilst Russian is more actively used in the sphere of everyday, informal and unofficial communication. This type of *laissez-faire* language policy can be demonstrated in the practical application of this language strategy.

4. IMPLEMENTATION OF LANGUAGE POLICY AND LANGUAGE POLITICS

In the historical practice of nation-state building, language policy aiming at linguistic unification was traditionally considered as a policy of cultural and political national homogenization implemented by the state (Guibernau, 1996; Kymlicka, 1999). In the framework of this practice, the state power of the dominant nation imposed its language and extended it through the state agencies such as schools and the media. Does the traditional scheme of national homogenization and language unification work in post-independence Ukraine, and what are the main characteristics of language policy in the spheres of education and media?

---

[125]   The ambiguities of statistical data will be demonstrated in detail in Section 4.1.

[126]   Address of the president to the *Verkhovna Rada* (parliament) at its plenary meeting on 22 February 2000.

4.1   Language Policy in the Sphere of Education

Language policy in the educational sphere is a particularly sensitive issue. As historical examples prove, the implementation of the state language as the dominant language of school instruction and education was an important element of the policy of national homogenization (Guibernau, 1996: 69–71). In our example, the Ukrainization of schools is entirely perceived as a policy favouring the Ukrainian language regime in education. This policy is based on the premise that language is indeed the main marker of national identity. Again, there is a relationship between language politics and the policy of identity construction.

With the establishment of independence in December 1991, the Ukrainian state launched a centralized national policy in the sphere of education according to which state policy and guidelines (embodied in the compulsory "state component" of the national curricula) should be applied to all schools, including minority schools,[127] on the territory of Ukraine. The overwhelming majority of schools for ethnic minorities in Ukraine are state schools. Since the Soviet period, they have been mostly created in regions where Ukraine's ethnic minorities are situated, in accordance with the decision of local administration and the wishes of the local population. Following independence, the network of minority schools was developed (particularly due to the considerable rise of Sunday and private schools of minorities organized by their national societies),[128] but the policy towards national schools has remained centralized.

The representatives of Ukraine's ethnic communities were worried by the trends of strengthening of the centralized 'top-down' approach in educational policy towards minorities. These trends were represented in the Draft of the Concept for Ethnic Minority Education which was elaborated by the Ministry of Education of Ukraine in 1997. As a result of the strong criticism by minority representatives, the concept was not accepted as an official normative document. In the view of these representatives, particularly those of the Hungarian and Romanian minorities, the concept did not take into account the tradition of relative educational autonomy of these ethnic groups. At the same time, many representatives of ethnic communities accepted the need for intensive study of the Ukrainian language in schools alongside national languages, as the concept suggested. However, the lack of textbooks, dictionaries and other learning materials in the Ukrainian language for the minority schools has yet to be resolved (Kuksa, 1999).

The most difficult question related to the subject of language instruction is the issue of the Russian schools. Under Soviet rule, half of the schools in Ukraine operated in the Russian language. Russian schools and, more broadly, Russian-medium education, became the main focus of language policy in Ukraine after 1991, when the Ministry of Education adopted

---

[127]   These are the schools with Russian, Hungarian, Romanian, Crimean Tatar, Moldovan and Polish as the language of instruction for all subjects prescribed by the national curricula. The schools for Ukraine's other ethnic minorities operate on the bilingual principle (Ukrainian or Russian as the language of instruction for all subjects, apart from the teaching of the respective minority language and literature).

[128]   Sunday schools for minorities operate on weekends and are mostly oriented towards teaching the minority language, traditions and culture. According to official statistics, while in 1993 there were 26 Sunday schools for minorities, their number had increased twofold by 1998 (Troszynskyi, 1997: 41).

123

the Plan on the State Programme of Developing Ukrainian and Other National Languages in Ukraine until 2000. The plan's main idea was "to establish the status of Ukrainian in the educational sphere" (Shevchenko, 1991). The ten-year plan presupposed that, by 2000, every citizen of Ukraine would have a good command of Ukrainian and would use it in everyday life. It was also implied that Ukrainian would become a compulsory subject in pre-school educational institutions, schools of different types, and *in vuzy* (institutes and universities). At the same time, the state proclaimed the right of all Ukrainian citizens to have their children taught in their mother tongue. Ten years on, this plan makes visible all of the weaknesses of the administrative approach to language issues in educational policy. This also allows for an analysis of its effects in the realm of politics.

The practical implementation of the plan in the school curriculum has been steadily associated with administrative Ukrainization. The new education policy of Ukraine has also resulted in an increase in the number of schools where Ukrainian is the language of instruction and, respectively, a decrease in the number of Russian schools. According to official statistics from the beginning of the 1998–1999 school year, the distribution of secondary state schools according to the language of instruction was the following: Ukrainian—75.5 per cent of the total number of schools; Russian—12.1 per cent; Romanian—0.5 per cent (108 schools); Hungarian—0.3 per cent (65 schools); Crimean Tatar—3 schools; Polish—3 schools; 2,466 schools (11.6 per cent of the total number) used two languages of instruction[129] (State Committee of Ukraine on Nationalities and Migration, 1999: 110). Official statistics indicating a change in the number of pupils studying in the two main languages are also significant. The dynamics of these changes are represented in Table 1.8.

However, the plans for rapid Ukrainization have failed, mainly because they have not taken into consideration the regional, historical and cultural specificity of the regions and regional disparities in ethnic distribution. Most Ukrainian schools and pupils studying in Ukrainian (83.4 per cent) live in rural Ukraine (Pidgrushnyi, 1995: 64). In terms of regional distribution, Ukrainian schools are predominant in the western and central parts of the country while in the Crimea (where about 25 per cent of ethnic Ukrainians live), 98.1 per cent of pupils study in Russian. A similar situation prevails in the eastern and southern regions of Ukraine (see Table 1.8).

Although the statistics report a formal success in the 'creeping Ukrainization' of the educational system, some reservations should be made. Statistical accounts, as Ukrainian post-Soviet practice shows, are very unreliable. There is much evidence pointing towards the formally administrative character of nationalization reform, which often relies merely on the formal re-naming of Russian schools into Ukrainian ones. The situation where the majority of subjects are taught in Russian in nominally Ukrainian (or bilingual) schools is common practice, particularly in the regions of eastern and southern Ukraine (Pohribnyi, 2000: 221). The discrepancy between two kinds of official statistics can also be found in the above-mentioned data: (1) the distribution of secondary state schools, according to their language of

---

[129]   According to officials of the Ministry of Education of Ukraine, the schools with two languages of instruction are those schools with separate classes for different language of instruction (mostly Russian and Ukrainian) or the so-called 'transitional schools' (often former Russians schools which are in the process of re-organization into Ukrainian-language schools). As we shall demonstrate below, the 'nominal' and 'transitional' statuses of bilingual schools lead to ambiguities for the interpretation of statistical data.

instruction; and (2) the number of pupils in secondary schools, according to the language of instruction (Ukrainian or Russian) (Table 1.8). Official statistics in Table 1.8 do not clearly address the question of how the considerable share of bilingual schools (11.6 per cent) has been 'distributed' in the statistical data on the number of pupils studying in Ukrainian and in Russian as languages of instruction. Statistical accounts might be more reliable if they were based on the number of teachers who actually teach their subjects in Ukrainian or in Russian.

Table 1.8

Number of Pupils in Secondary School According to Language of Instruction
(1991–1996, beginning of the 1998–1999 school year)

Oblasts	Percentage of pupils studying in Ukrainian					
	1991–2	1992–3	1993–4	1994–5	1995–6	1998–9
Ukraine	49.3	51.4	54.0	57.0	58.0	65.0
Crimean Auton. Republic	—	0.0	0.1	0.1	0.1	0.4
Luganska (east)	6.7	7.3	8.0	9.0	9.2	13.2
Lvivska (west)	91.8	93.6	95.0	95.0	96.0	97.6
Odeska (south)	24.5	27.4	29.0	30.0	32.0	37.0
Kyivska (centre)	84.6	86.7	90.0	91.0	92.0	95.1
Kyiv (capital)	30.9	41.7	55.0	64.0	70.0	87.1

Oblasts	Percentage of pupils studying in Russian					
	1991–2	1992–3	1993–4	1994–5	1995–6	1998–9
Ukraine	50.0	47.8	45.0	43.0	41.0	34.1
Crimean Auton. Republic	99.9	99.9	99.7	99.7	99.5	98.1
Luganska (east)	93.3	92.7	92.0	91.0	90.8	86.8
Lvivska (west)	8.1	6.2	5.0	4.0	4.0	2.2
Odeska (south)	73.5	70.7	69.0	68.0	66.0	60.9
Kyivska (centre)	15.4	13.3	10.0	9.0	8.0	4.9
Kyiv (capital)	69.0	58.3	45.0	37.0	30.0	12.9

SOURCES: Prybytkova (1998: 240); State Committee of Ukraine on Nationalities and Migration (1999: 113–114).

The extent of the relative successes of Ukrainization in schools becomes problematic if one takes into account the fact that the Russian language has maintained a rather strong position in the sphere of university education (*vuzy*). This is due to the fact that the pedagogical traditions of the Soviet era are still in practice; it is also due to the fact that the city milieu in the most populated regions of the country is Russian-speaking. Such a language division in the educational sphere into lower (schools) and higher (universities) levels creates ambiguities and psychological difficulties for those pupils who first studied in Ukrainian and then have to switch to Russian at the university level. The widespread practice of the mixing of two main languages (the so-called *surzhik*), which is explained by the attempts at social adaptation of Ukrainian-speakers into the Russian-speaking milieu, appears as a natural way out of this situation.

Even at the pre-university level, the actual effect of Ukrainization could be put in doubt, for it has appeared that many school children who study in Ukrainian schools in central, eastern and southern Ukraine prefer to communicate with each other and with their families in Russian. This is especially true for senior school children in Kyiv (Masenko, 1999: 75). According to a nationwide survey, respondents aged 15 to 19, the majority of whom have studied or are still studying in Ukrainian schools (that is, the pupils who, presumably, should be more oriented towards the Ukrainian language as a result of their education in Ukrainian), show instead the highest level of preference in communicating in Russian compared to other age groups, and the lowest level of communication in Ukrainian (Nestayko, 2000). This can be partly explained by the dominance of the Russian language in youth subculture and mass culture, targeted at that age group. But the possible 'reverse effect' of the forced indoctrination of the Ukrainian language in schools should also not be overlooked.

It is no wonder, then, that the supporters of radical Ukrainization are dissatisfied with the pace and results of language reform. It is assumed that the proportion of school children studying in Ukrainian schools should at least correspond to the proportion of ethnic Ukrainians in the country. However, in the context of the failure of administrative measures on Ukrainization at the beginning of the 1990s and of existing tensions between the centre and the regions on issues of language policy, this nationalist goal seems unattainable. By now, the projections made in 1991 for the new language policies in the eastern regions, which would take "perhaps five to seven years or even more" (Shevchenko, 1991) for their Ukrainization, seem unrealistic. In fact, there are precedents at the level of local self-government in the eastern regions, which are traditionally Russian-speaking, of refusing to follow the decisions of the central authorities on the language issue. For example, Kharkiv, Lugansk and Lisichansk city councils decided to retain the traditional linguistic policy of favouring the Russian language in schools and in official communication.

Moreover, even if one accepts the statistics on the success of administrative Ukrainization, there are clear indications of reverse trends, particularly in the South and East of the country. Ukrainian nationalists consider the recent moves of re-Russification as alarming signals which indicate the need for renewed political and administrative pressure by the authorities. The latter are sharply criticized for a loss of political will and a misunderstanding of the strategic importance of language issues in the sphere of education (Pohribnyi, 2000: 4). The dismissal of the plan of rapid Ukrainization is often explained in nationalist discourse by the change of people in power from 'Ukrainian patriots' to those who are indifferent or even 'Russian chauvinists'. According to this logic, the personal position of a given politician or school director with respect to the language issue is a decisive factor affecting the practical results of the new language policies. It also implies that language and identity might be changed by administrative measures.

However, as the Ukrainian experience shows, this is not true: For language policies to be realistic, they must take into consideration the actual regional, ethnic, social and language distributions in the country and in particular the different identities and cultural affiliations.

4.2   Language Issues and the Mass Media

Information policy and media are among the most important agencies in the implementation of power strategies under any socio-political circumstance. Information policy affects the conditions of social transformation and of nation-state building in Ukraine. In the framework of its ethnopolitical strategy, the Ukrainian state has declared the right of minorities to satisfy their needs in mass media as a part of the policy of cultural autonomy for minorities. However, because of financial constraints at the level of central government, the possibilities of economic support for minority media are limited. Thus, most media projects are financed by their national societies, nongovernmental donors or through other channels.

Regional and local media policy is more flexible with respect to the needs of minorities. There are some statistics from the 'ethnically mixed' regions where ethnic minorities are concentrated. For example, in Transcarpathia, the needs of ethnic minorities are satisfied by two magazines and five newspapers in Hungarian and two newspapers in Russian. The regional radio broadcasts in Hungarian (290 hours a year), Romanian (100.8 hours a year) and Slovak (8.4 hours a year). Regional television has programmes in Hungarian (68.4 hours a year), Romanian (51.6 hours a year), German (24 hours a year) and Slovak (21.6 hours a year) (State Committee of Ukraine on Nationalities and Migration, 1998).

State language policies in the sphere of mass media have their own specifications. Mainly because of the private character of the most influential media companies operating in Ukraine, the state cannot dictate what should be produced and in which language. The possibility of state influence on the information sphere is predominantly related to legislative regulations and control of the functioning of the media. In this respect, languages issues become the focus of state intervention. The reason for the central government's concern during the recent period is the expansion of highly competitive media and information products in Russian. Due to many reasons (including the prevailing Russian-speaking city milieu, traditional positive attitudes of the consumerist majority in favour of the Russian language, the strong information and cultural expansion of Russia's media production in Ukraine's information space, large financial resources used for the support of the Russian media especially in the eastern, southern and central regions), the Russian language has acquired a dominant position in commercial media which substantially exceeds the state-owned publications in circulation.

The media and other cultural-informational products from Russia are also freely distributed and actively supplied on the Ukrainian market. Apart from television transmission of major Russian television channels in the cities of central, southern and eastern Ukraine, there is a Russian-speaking nationwide channel *Inter* (among three main central television channels). Almost half of the periodicals printed in Ukraine (49.7 per cent of the total number of Ukrainian periodicals) are also issued in Russian (Ministry of Foreign Affairs of Ukraine, 2000: 86).

The language situation in Ukraine's information sphere represents one of the traditional, though objective, arguments used by the country's officials against accusations of discrimination against the Russian language and the Russian-speaking population in Ukraine. In particular, this argument has been actively used by the pro-Ukrainian side in the new Ukrainian–Russian inter-state debate over the situation of the Russian language in Ukraine from the end of 1999 to the middle of 2000. Meanwhile, some Ukrainian politicians have expressed their deep concern over the strong position of the Russian language in the domain of national media policy, pointing to the lack (or even absence) of state control and of a rational policy and planning as a matter of concern with implications in the vital sphere of national security. The core of the matter consists of the extent to which Ukrainian patriotism and loyalty towards the independent Ukrainian state can be represented (if at all) in a Russian-language media context.

It seems that, in a paradoxical way, the status of Ukrainian as the sole official language brings additional difficulties for its popularization in the commercial and non-official spheres because the popular media and culture are mainly represented in Russian. Taking into consideration a strong post-Soviet tradition of social alienation of the citizenry from the state and the widespread mistrust of any kind of officialdom, the Russian 'non-official' language has acquired a certain social attractiveness, which is, to some extent, similar to the former status of Ukrainian as the linguistic manifestation of social resistance and democratic revival in Ukraine at the end of the 1980s and the beginning of the 1990s.

The issue of language policy in mass media is particularly subtle and complex. The commercial character of media production often demands from editors and publishers an adherence to the established language attitudes and affiliations of consumers, that is, of potential readers and listeners. The success of Ukraine's most popular newspaper, *Fakty* (Facts), which has the widest circulation in the country and is published in Russian, proves that the Russian language prevails in the media market in Ukraine.

Inevitably, the revitalization of Ukrainian in the media sector (as in other spheres) has to be a long-term and patient process, involving the raising of the attractiveness of the language, the creation of real social motivations for mass use of the language, with the support of non-governmental organizations and activists. The bilingual language publishing policy of popular Ukrainian periodicals and the recent decision of the Russian-speaking nationwide television channel *Inter* to provide a choice between Russian and Ukrainian transmission in western Ukraine are among the real steps in this perspective. At the same time, the administrative measures of the former 'pro-Ukrainian' government can only worsen the situation.[130]

---

[130]   In October 2000, the State Committee of Ukraine on Information Policy demanded fulfilment of the condition of bilingual publishing policy. This condition is obligatory upon registration of the newspaper or periodical. Russian-language periodicals which have analogous versions in Russia were under threat of closure.

4.3   Political Actors Playing the 'Language Card'

Does the traditional scheme of national homogenization and language unification work in Ukraine? The answer is yes and no. The contradictory state language policy is formally oriented to the 'one state, one language' model but, at the same time, the authorities actually conduct a policy of 'language balance' between Ukraine's two main languages, as we have shown in Section 3.3. As it became evident after the failure of 'speedy Ukrainization' at the beginning of the 1990s, the post-communist state appeared to be a weak political actor, rather than an omnipotent administrative centre which is able to reproduce openly and violently the traditional historical scenario of national homogenization and language unification (as, for example, the Soviet totalitarian state had attempted to achieve). In this respect, it is characteristic that the Ukrainian state authorities have demonstratively distanced themselves from the open political promotion of the Ukrainian language in the public sphere, preferring to pass this role on to a formally non-governmental organization *Prosvita* ('Enlightenment') which, however, is subsidized by the state.

The political reasons for the transformation of the state policy of active Ukrainization to the strategy of 'language balance' can also be explained by the fact that the political resources of ethnolinguistic nationalism, used as an effective tool of political mobilization and national consolidation under the slogans of Ukraine's nation-state building at the beginning of the 1990s, are considerably exhausted (Kubicek, 1999: 42). Furthermore, Ukraine's post-communist ruling elite, which actively explored nationalist rhetoric during the period of Kravchuk's presidency, from 1991 to 1994, was (and still is) not actually interested in Ukrainian language purity or the Ukrainian ethnic identity as such. As Schöpflin (2000: 60–61) correctly remarks, post-communist elites elsewhere, but especially in Ukraine, were and are interested in preserving their powerful positions through the political production and reproduction of *étatic* (state-driven) identities and of the patterns of loyalties which usually perfectly fit the politically made 'nationalistic dresses'.

The state's 'balanced' language politics under Kuchma's presidency from 1994 until the present is nothing more than the result of a forced political compromise between opposing political interest groups: above all, between Ukrainian nationalistic parties, on the one hand, and political parties and groups which are culturally, politically and economically oriented towards Russia, on the other. Luckily, thus far, neither of the sides involved in linguistic tensions have advanced convincing political arguments against the opponent; that is to say that there are no arguments convincing enough for a political mobilization of the population of Ukraine, which is already 'used' to being divided according to language affiliation into a Ukrainian-speaking West and a Russian-speaking East and South.

There is the opinion according to which the language issue, at its current stage of 'balanced' status-quo, is not perceived by the majority of Ukraine's population (keeping in mind the Ukrainian ethnic majority) as the most important socio-political issue, at a par with socio-economic problems, personal health and security concerns, etc. (Kubicek, 1999: 42). This view might be indirectly supported by the fact that, according to a representative sociological survey conducted in 2000, the majority of the population (44 per cent of respondents) did not mind official bilingualism and think that the recognition of the Russian language as official is needed (36 per cent of respondents were against and nineteen per cent had no clear answer)

(Vorona *et al.*, 2000: 330). However, as the election campaigns of 1994 (Wilson, 1997), 1998 and 1999 showed, the language issue is easily politicized and its significance cannot be underestimated.

The logic of preserving the sole state status of the Ukrainian language can be explained by a purely political argument. It is implicitly based on the fact that language is the principal symbolic marker of a distinct Ukrainian identity; the privileged status of Ukrainian is therefore the political manifestation of the independent Ukrainian state. Since Russia can be considered as a real external actor in the political debate on language in Ukraine, this argument looks plausible. Again, the official position of the Ukrainian political elite on the language issue has little to do with personal patriotism, but rather with the elite's political interests. As recent Ukrainian history shows, the official status of Ukrainian has thus far proved to be politically 'profitable' for the authorities, because this gives them the possibility to control and, to some extent, manipulate the country's population, whose public opinion is split with respect to official bilingualism. The 1994 presidential elections showed that the pragmatic promise of official status for the Russian language by the Russian-speaking and future president Kuchma won him a victory against his 'nationalist-minded' opponent Kravchuk due to the overwhelming support of the populous, industrial and historically 'Russified' eastern and southern regions of Ukraine. In fact, due to formal (not political) logic, granting official status to the Russian language could have been legally implemented already in 1994 after Kuchma's victory. Why has it not happened? According to the official excuse, which was recently advanced by the president (*Komsomolskaya Pravda*, 2001), political blame for not granting official status to the Russian language should be laid on the parliament. The implicit explanation advanced by the authorities is the threat of territorial disintegration of the country because of the risk of a nationalist political reaction of the population of Ukraine's western regions. But these explanations seem artificial. Public opinion polls demonstrate that nationalist orientations (and political parties representing them) are at the margins of the political sympathies of the Ukrainian population, and it is very unlikely that the nationalists could mobilize a critical 'revolutionary potential' for their political struggle against official status for the Russian language if the majority of the population were to support such a status (Vorona *et al.*, 2000: 323). In addition, in the event of the official legitimization of the Russian language, the whole might of the post-communist ideological state apparatus could be drawn upon for the propaganda of the political usefulness of this step in the perspective of civil peace, the Ukrainian civil nation, Ukraine's adherence to democratic and European values, etc. This step would substantially restrict the arguments for Russia's political and economic pressure on Ukraine, which is politically and morally 'justified' by the Russian authorities on the grounds of protecting the Russian linguistic community in Ukraine.

The deliberate lack of clarity and a policy of 'long silence' by the authorities on the language issue cannot be considered an optimal strategy. Again, it seems that the main reasons for that strategy lie in the logic of the control of power, which is more easily achieved with a divided, politically inert and socially tired population. The political possibility of granting official status to the Russian language is the authorities' last ace in the language game and this ace will be used in due time—most likely during the 2004 presidential campaign by the candidate chosen by the ruling political elite to guarantee its future dominant position in power. However, the language game is very dangerous and unpredictable. The main threat lies in the correlation between regional, linguistic and political cleavages in Ukraine. In terms of political values and orientations, the Ukrainian-speaking West is also the region where the majority of the population is oriented towards democratic values, a free market economy and European integration. The Russian-speaking East and South, on the other hand, are not only strongly affiliated to Russia, politically, culturally and economically, but the population of these regions is also more oriented towards communist and socialist ideas than towards the values and perspectives of 'democratic capitalism' in Ukraine. Thus, the serious problem of unity for the Ukrainian nation, whose democratic consolidation is aggravated by overlapping regional, political and linguistic cleavages, can be stereotypically represented by the 'Russian-speaking Easterner,' mostly from the leftist political spectrum, on one hand, and the 'Ukrainian-speaking Westerner' who sympathizes with national democratic political forces, on the other.

The issue of the Russian language (and implicitly of the linguistic rights of the Russian minority) has already been exploited in election campaigns in Ukraine. In the 1998 parliamentary elections, eight political parties actively used the language issue in their political agenda. The relative success of one of them, the Communist Party, has shown that the issue of minority rights, if unsatisfactorily resolved, may potentially put in doubt not only the prospects for democratic transformation in Ukraine, but also the existence of an independent Ukraine with its present borders. This is due to the fact that calls from the left of the political spectrum (and currently from some representatives of the pragmatic ruling elite) for closer political and economic integration with Russia, for a political union with Russia and Belarus and for dual Ukrainian–Russian citizenship, are usually accompanied and justified by the argument of the cultural, historical and linguistic unity of the Eastern Slavonic peoples. In this political line, demands for a second, co-official status for the Russian language appear inevitable and natural.

One of the biggest challenges in Ukraine's nation-state building is the need for the combination of the nation-state strategy and for a democratic political agenda. The lack of the civic-democratic dimension in the ethno-policy conducted by the political elite, composed mainly of the old communist *nomenklatura*, makes the process of democratic consolidation of the Ukrainian nation problematic. Democratic consolidation in Ukraine implies a national consensus, which in Ukrainian conditions would be hard to achieve without the civic loyalty to the state of both the Ukrainian ethnic majority as well as that of the representatives of Ukraine's ethnic communities, above all Russians. The inclusion of minorities in the democratic process seems problematic without the first and principal political step—granting official status to the Russian language. However, this seems realistic only with the development of democratic self-organizing joint initiatives of the Ukrainian majority and ethnic minorities—a process aiming at applying democratic political pressure 'from below' by democratic public organizations, including those of the minorities. However, the process of self-organization of many ethnic minorities in Ukraine, apart from already mobilized ethnic groups such as the Crimean Tatars, Hungarians, Romanians, Germans and a few others, is still at the beginning of its development. The leaders of the ethnic communities confirm the problem of 'silent minorities', which are not active enough in the elaboration and lobbying of initiatives concerning the state's ethno-policy (*Zerkalo Nedeli*, 1995).

The present highly centralized administrative regulation of ethnolinguistic relations and the irresponsible political manipulation of these relations by the political establishment (particularly during election campaigns) preserve and reproduce the latent divisions of Ukrainian society according to ethnic, regional and linguistic characteristics. As a result, in the absence of coherence and consolidation of the nation, the democratic and economic reforms attempted by the pro-Western government of Viktor Yuschenko in 2000–2001 were mostly supported by the population of the western, Ukrainian-speaking regions of the country. Unfortunately, the inattention of the reformers to the linguistic and cultural differences of the country's regions and some doubtful steps in the activation of linguistic Ukrainization lay the ground for Yuschenko's conservative political opponents to present this policy as 'nationalist' and bring about his dismissal in spring 2001. This proved how subtle ethnocultural and linguistic arguments in the political struggle are, and how much democratic consolidation, based on an ethnocultural and linguistic consensus, is really needed in Ukraine.

CONCLUSION: PROSPECTS FOR LANGUAGE POLICY IN UKRAINE

There are two possible strategic orientations for the nation-state building process in Ukraine. One is linked to a policy of interethnic and linguistic tolerance, aiming at the creation of a 'civic nation' based on the principle of citizenship (implying equality of all citizens of Ukraine before the law, irrespective of their ethnic, cultural and linguistic characteristics). The other orientation is the policy of administrative and forced assimilation of ethnic minorities in the framework of the Ukrainian 'ethnic nation'. As demonstrated by the example of language issues, the actual process of Ukraine's nation-state building still oscillates between these two orientations. However, after more than ten years of independence, there is a clear understanding among Ukrainian policy-makers that the prevailing political orientation towards an 'ethno-centric' model of the nation-state will inevitably generate ethnic and social conflicts, which could even lead to the disintegration of the unitary Ukrainian state.

When discussing the prospects of the formation of a Ukrainian civic nation, one inevitably has to address the question of which language (or languages) should be used by this nation. Is the 'one state, one language' approach appropriate for the country? As has been argued (Majboroda, 2000: 298), there are three options for solving this issue:

i. The development of a new shared linguistic system based on the combination of the two main languages (in this perspective, a widespread everyday linguistic mixture of Ukrainian and Russian, the so-called *surzhik*, could be considered not as a form of linguistic pathology but as a genuine possibility and even the prototype of a new language).

ii. The parallel existence of two languages and two cultures in the framework of one political state—a variant associated with the Belgian or Swedish models, and the Swiss model in the Autonomous Republic of Crimea (Russian, Ukrainian and Crimean Tatar languages).

iii. The absorption of the less developed language by the more developed one (in the Ukrainian case, the prospect of open language competition between Ukrainian and Russian).

It is difficult to forecast future developments or to estimate the adequacy of the extent and limits of state support for Ukrainian. This support is often justified by the implicit idea of ensuring equal starting positions (but who can measure that equality, and by which criteria?) of two languages in their future competition. What is clear now is the potential danger of the policies of administrative enforcement in the sensitive sphere of language attitudes. In the Ukrainian case, this should mean the creation of full possibilities for the satisfaction of the linguistic rights of speakers of the two languages: i.e., satisfaction of the rights of the Russian-speaking population in western Ukraine and of the Ukrainian-speaking population in the eastern and southern regions of the country. The cultural autonomy and minority rights (including linguistic rights) of Ukraine's ethnic communities, in particular of those which reside compactly (Crimean Tatars, Hungarians, Romanians, Bulgarians, Poles, Gagauz, Slovaks and others) should also be preserved and developed.

Optimal solutions to language issues in Ukraine may lie with the fact that the mutual intelligibility of the two main languages can make possible a situation of nationwide dialogue and mutual tolerance in a country which, mostly due to longstanding and developed everyday traditions of multicultural and bilingual coexistence, has thus far managed to avoid acute interethnic conflict.

REFERENCES

Arel, Dominique (1995) "Language Politics in Independent Ukraine: Towards One or Two State Languages?" *Nationalities Papers*, 23(3): 597–622.

Bulletin of the State Committee of Ukraine on Nationalities and Migration 1999: 116

First Report of the Ethnobarometer Programme (1999) *Ethnic Conflict and Migration Europe*. Rome: CSS–CEMES.

Golovakha, Evgenyi and Natalia Panina (1994) *Sotsialnoie bezumiye* (Social Madness). Kyiv: Abris.

Grin, François and François Vaillancourt (1999) *The Cost-Effectiveness Evaluation of Minority Language Policies: Case Studies on Wales, Ireland and the Basque Country*. ECMI Monographs, No. 2. Flensburg: European Centre for Minority Issues.

Guibernau, Monserrat (1996) *Nationalisms. The Nation-State and Nationalism in the Twentieth Century*. Cambridge: Polity Press.

Khmelko, Valeryi and Andrew Wilson (2000) "Regionalism and Ethnic and Linguistic Cleavages in Ukraine". In Evgenyi Golovakha *et al.* (eds.) *Sociology in Ukraine. Selected Works Published during the 90s*. Kyiv: Institute of Sociology, pp.63–80.

Komsomolskaya Pravda (2001) "The President of Ukraine Answers Readers' Questions". *Komsomolskaya Pravda*, 13 July 2001.

Kubicek, Paul (1999) "What Happened to the Nationalists in Ukraine?" *Nationalism and Ethnic Politics*, 5(1): 29–45.

Kuksa, V. (1999) "Menshyny khotily'b vyvchaty Ukrainsku … (Minorities Would Like to Learn Ukrainian …)". *Dan'*, 3 March 1999.

Kuzio, Taras (1992) *Ukraine. The Unfinished Revolution*. London: Alliance Publishers.

Kymlicka, Will (1999) "Minority Nationalism within Liberal Democracies". In Desmond M. Clark and Charles Jones (eds.) *The Rights of Nations. Nations and Nationalism in a Changing World*. New York: St. Martin's Press, pp.100–126.

Majboroda, Oleksandr (2000) "Perspektyvy rozvytku mizhnatsionalnykh vidnosyn v Ukraini (The Perspective of the Development of Inter-ethnic Relations in Ukraine)". In Mylola Golovatyi *et al.* (eds.) *Ukraina na zlami tysiacholit': istorychyi ekskurs, problemy, tendentsii ta perspektyvy* (Ukraine at the Threshold of the Millennium: Historical Excursus, Problems, Tendencies and Prospects). Kyiv: MAUP, pp.286–307.

Masenko, Larysa (1999) *Mova i polityka* (Language and Politics). Kyiv: Soniashnyk.

Ministry of Foreign Affairs of Ukraine (2000) "The Note of the Ministry from 12 February 2000". Moscow, Kyiv: *Russian-Ukrainian Bulletin*, 5: 86.

Ministry of Statistics of the USSR (1991) *Natsional'nyi sostav naseleniya SSSR po rezultatam vsesouznoj perepisi naselenia 1989* (National Composition of the USSR. On the Results of the All-Union 1989 Census). Moscow: Finansy i Statistika.

Nestayko, Vsevolod (2000) "Nashe maibutne chutaye rosiyskoyu (Our Future Reads in Russian)". *Ukraina i svit siogodni*, (4–10 March 2000): 4.

Oksamytna, Svitlana (1999) "Movno-natsionalna identyfikatsia doroslogo naselennia Ukrainy (Linguistic-ethnic Identification of the Adult Population in Ukraine)". In Valeriy Vorona *et al.* (eds.) *Ukrainske suspilstvo: Monitoring socialnykh zmin (1994–1999)* (Ukrainian Society: The Monitoring of Social Changes, 1994–1999). Kyiv: Instytut Sociologii, pp.51–155.

Pidgrushnyi, Georgyi (1995) "Seredni shkoly v Ukraini (Secondary Schools in Ukraine)". *Rozbudova derzhavy*, 7–8: 62–64.

Pieklo, Jan *et al.* (1995) *Conflict or Cooperation. The Media and Minority Problems*. Krakow: Znak Foundation for Christian Culture.

Pohribnyi, Anatolyi (2000) *Rozmovy pro nabolile* (Talks on Burning Issues). Kyiv: Prosvita.

Prybytkova, Iryna (1998) "Movu nam dano … (The Language Was Given to Us …)". *Sociologia: Teoria, metody, marketing*, 1–2: 230–242.

Schöpflin, George (2000) *Nations, Identity, Power. The New Politics of Europe*. London: Hurst.

Shevchenko, Volodymyr (1991) *Zakon pro movy: shliakhy realizatsii* (The Act on Languages: Ways of Implementation). *Osvita*, 9 July 1991.

State Committee of Ukraine on Nationalities and Migration (1998) *Information Letter on Inter-Ethnic Situation in Ukraine*. Kyiv: State Committee of Ukraine on Nationalities and Migration.

State Committee of Ukraine on Nationalities and Migration (1999) *Bulletin*, 3.

Stepanenko, Viktor (1999) *The Construction of Identity and School Policy in Ukraine*. Commack, NY: Nova Science Publishers.

Troszynskyi, Volodymyr (1997) "V poshukakh zgody (The Search for Consent)". *Viche*, 10: 31–44.

United Nations Development Programme (1996) *Ukraine. Human Development Report*, 1996. Kyiv: UNDP.

Vorona, Valeryi *et al.* (eds.) (1999) *Ukrainske suspilstvo: Monitoring socialnykh zmin (1994–1999)* (Ukrainian Society: The Monitoring of Social Changes, 1994–1999). Kyiv: Instytut Sociologii.

Wilson, Andrew (1997) *Ukrainian Nationalism in the 1990s: A Minority Faith*. Cambridge: University Press.

Wurm, Stephen A. (1999) "Languages in Danger. The Life and Death of the World's Languages". *Multiethnica*, 24–25: 28–35.

Zerkalo Nedeli (1995) "Roundtable on Minority Issues". *Zerkalo nedeli*, 16 December 1995.

Zerkalo Nedeli (2000) "Interview with Mykola Zhulinskyi". *Zerkalo nedeli*, 26 February 2000.

PART II

Titular Language Promotion
and Bilingualism

Language Policy in the Republic of Armenia
in the Transition Period
Rouben Karapetyan

■

The Politics of Language Reform
and Bilingualism in Tatarstan
Yagfar Z. Garipov and Helen M. Faller

■

Kalmykia:
Language Promotion Against All Odds
François Grin

Language Policy in the Republic of Armenia in the Transition Period

Rouben Karapetyan

Language Policy in the Republic of Armenia in the Transition Period

Rouben Karapetyan

INTRODUCTION

The present paper is one of the first attempts to comprehend the course of language policy in the Republic of Armenia (RA) over the last ten to twelve years.

After the collapse of the USSR, Armenia, like many countries of the former USSR, came up against the problem of institutional consolidation of state independence. For the new leaders, part of this was the elaboration of a new language policy. Commonalities exist with other CIS countries, but Armenia also had its own peculiarities which influenced the conceptual groundwork of language policy—its revitalization and subsequent clashes stemming from this policy. This paper presents an analysis of these components, distinguishing three main topics.

Section 1 is an attempt to systematize the factors that determined the formation of the chief provisions in Armenian language policy, analyzing the language situation in Armenia before independence and the nature of the polemic surrounding the foundations of the future language policy. Attention is drawn to the integrative combination of historical, social, cultural and political factors that influenced the principles of elaboration of this policy in the initial period.

Section 2 presents the measures adopted. Particular attention is devoted to the formation of its legal base: legislation, governmental resolutions and ordinances on language. The chronological and logical consistency in the realization of language policy is examined on the basis of all the legislative acts and government resolutions.

Section 3 of the paper examines the relationships between language policy and social-cultural processes in Armenia, and the influence language policy had in changing the situation. Legislative provisions that directly affect the languages of national minorities are examined separately. The influence of this policy in language processes among Yezid-Kurds, Russians and Assyrians, the three main groups of national minorities in Armenia, has also been analyzed; the case of speakers of Azeri is not discussed in the paper, since most left Armenia following the war between Armenia and Azerbaijan.

The analysis is based on materials surrounding the legal acts adopted by the National Assembly, resolutions and ordinances of the government on language in RA, census data and three panel sociological studies carried out within the programme and under the guidance of the author of this paper. The paper also takes in interviews with the leading linguists in Armenia, employees with the State Language Inspectorate and members of the National Assembly Commission on Culture, Youth Affairs and Sport, and data of other sociological studies.

1. PRECONDITIONS FOR SHAPING A NEW CONCEPT OF LANGUAGE POLICY

Peculiarities with respect to language at the onset of the Karabakh events[1] and later the logic under which the independence movement developed strongly influenced the redrawing of language policy in the Republic of Armenia.

1.1 Language Situation

Two major circumstances should be mentioned at the outset. The first is the fact that the proportion of national minorities in Armenia was much lower than in other countries in the former Soviet Union, and became even lower after the Karabakh conflict.

As seen from Table 2.1, the share of the titular nation always prevailed and had a tendency to grow. This fact is explained by a constant flow of Armenians from the neighbouring republics and abroad to Armenia, as well as by the reciprocal flows of refugees between Armenia and Azerbaijan from 1988 to 1989. For this reason, the 1989 census does not include Azeris (about 170,000 people, mainly from the countryside) who, after the massacres of Armenians in Sumgait (1988) and Baku (1989), fled Armenia. In turn, Armenia received 350,000 Armenian refugees from cities in Azerbaijan (Pogossyan, 1996: 12), resulting in the comparatively high growth of the proportion of Armenians in 1989. Economic crisis, the devastating Spitak earthquake of 1988, and the blockade of Armenia in the wake of the war with Azerbaijan (Komsomolets, 1989) caused mass emigration from Armenia: Armenians, Russians, Ukrainians and Assyrians went to Russia, the majority of Greeks moved to Greece, Germans to Germany and Jews to Israel (Hratarakchutyun, 2000: 73 ,77, 95).

All this had caused a still greater increase of the share of Armenians in the national composition of Armenia by the time independence was declared in 1991. Thus, the high national homogeneity in Armenia's population determined the specific initial situation in the sphere of language.

The second major circumstance explaining the language situation in Armenia was connected with the fact that the Armenian language has a long and specific history. The Armenian language developed over several stages during 1,500 years of written tradition (the Armenian alphabet was invented in the fifth century). Thus, the development of a uniform literary language can be traced from the fifth to the eighteenth centuries (University of Yerevan, 1980: 224). In the nineteenth and twentieth centuries, Modern Armenian was formed and the historical Armenian territory was divided into two parts: Eastern (part of the Russian Empire and later of the USSR) and Western (part of the Ottoman Empire). Two centres of shaping and developing a literary language were established: Constantinople (Istanbul) became the centre where the Western Armenian literary language developed; the Eastern Armenian literary language developed in the cities of the Russian Empire where

---

[1]   On 20 February 1988, the session of 20th convocation of delegates of the Nagorno-Karabakh autonomous region adopted a resolution seeking transfer of Karabakh from Soviet Azerbaijan to Armenia. This brought on the Armenian-Azerbaijan conflict, which gave rise to a revived nationalist movement in Armenia. These events are described and analysed in Gaume (1993), Suny (1993), Walker, ed. (1991) and Lapidus *et al.* (1992).

the business and cultural elites of the Armenian people were concentrated, in particular Tiflis (Tbilisi), Baku, Nor Nakhichevan, St. Petersburg, Moscow and Yerevan (University of Yerevan, 1980: 224–238).

Table 2.1

Changes in the National Composition of the Armenian SSR
and the Target Rate of Main Nationalities between the Censuses of 1959 and 1989

	Share in total population [%]				Index of population size [%]			
	1959	1970	1979	1989	1959	1970	1979	1989
Armenians	88.0	88.6	89.7	96.4	100	142	123	132
Azeris	6.1	6.0	4.8	—	100	137	109	—
Russians	3.2	2.6	2.3	1.4	100	117	106	73
Kurds[2]	1.5	1.5	1.7	1.5	100	147	136	110
Ukrainians	0.3	0.3	0.3	0.2	100	150	106	90
Assyrians	0.2	0.2	0.2	0.2	100	128	113	97
Greeks	0.3	0.2	0.2	0.1	100	114	100	83
Other nationalities	0.4	0.5	0.3	0.2	100	181	79	84

Source: Data from the 1959, 1970, 1979, 1989 censuses.

After the genocide and deportation of Western Armenians (1915–1920)[3] more than two-thirds of all Armenians were scattered in the diaspora as separate enclaves and dispersed groups in various countries of the world (Khojabekyan, 1979: 27–30). Active centres in national political, scientific-cultural and educational spheres exist in countries with large concentration of Armenians.[4]

The dispersal of national life determined various ethnocultural processes. One such manifestation was the further deepening of the language demarcation between Western Armenians and Eastern Armenians. The fact that these two literary languages had been diverging historically enhanced the gap as various cultural environments where the dispersed groups of Armenians lived influenced the development further. Consequently, the conditions of development of these two forms of Armenian were rather unequal, with the Western in more difficult conditions than the Eastern. Especially in the twentieth century, as the language of Armenians constituting national minorities in many countries, the sphere of its application was severely limited and public functions were restricted.

---

2   The Yezid-Kurds in Armenia were regarded as Kurds in all the censuses, not taking into consideration their sub-ethnic characteristics.

3   See also Bedrossyan (1983), Hovannisian (1992) and Armenian Refugees (1919).

4   There is a large bibliography on the culture of Armenians in the diaspora. For example: Alpoyadjyan (1947; 1951: 235). In the present paper we refer to Gasparyan (1962) and Karapetyan (1992).

Today, with a third generation of Western Armenians born and living in the diaspora, many Armenian linguists find it impossible to imagine a single standard for Armenian.[5] The overwhelming majority of diaspora Armenians are bilingual, and in many cases multilingual. The Armenians of Lebanon, for example, who have mostly moved to the United States, are competent in Western Armenian, Arabic and English. Those living in France are competent in French in addition to Western Armenian and Arabic. It should also be taken into consideration that active processes of changing the language and national identity took place in the diaspora against a background of internal language fragmentation. On one hand, this was conditioned by dialect distinctions, on the other hand by the formation of separate speech groups. For example, Armenian-speaking Lebanese and Syrian Armenians differ from the Armenians of France in their accent and pronunciation. The language of French Armenians differs from that of the Armenians of Greece, Romania and Bulgaria in vocabulary and pronunciation. It should be noted, however, that the uniform Western Armenian literary language, nevertheless, remains the language of national education, mass media and cultural institutions of the Armenians in the diaspora (ICOM, 1979: 6–11).

The Western and Eastern Armenian literary languages differ markedly in spelling and pronunciation (Hambartsumyan, 1993: 28). The formation of an independent Armenian Republic on a part of the Eastern Armenian territory, later included in the USSR as a union republic, determined the development of the Eastern Armenian literary language, which was declared official in the Armenian SSR. The official declaration of that literary language—the language of only one part of the Armenian people—was imposed by Soviet authorities, a policy of which was aimed to isolate "socialist Armenia" from the "hostile" diaspora (Zakaryan, 2000: 4). Hence, the fact that Western Armenians made up quite a large proportion of Armenia's population (as refugees and repatriated persons) was not taken into account. The spelling reform of the Eastern Armenian language carried out in 1924 was also politically determined. In 1920, refugees from Western Armenia made up 25 per cent of the population; suffice it to say that there were 200,000 orphans in the population of 800,000 (Khojabekyan, 1979: 187). During the period from 1920 to 1935, 100,000 Armenians returned to Armenia from the countries of the Mediterranean and Near East, in particular Greece, Turkey and Iran. During the period from 1946 to 1949 the repatriation of 100,000 Armenians from 30 countries of the world (including Turkey, Greece, Iraq, Lebanon, Iran, Syria, Egypt, Romania, France and the United States) was organized (Meliksetyan, 1985: 455–458).

Thus, the establishment of a national state, and later a Soviet Republic, gave rise to another trend in the development of language processes which determined the expansion of social functions and spheres of application of Armenian as the language of state office work, science, education, technology, etc. Under these circumstances, an enrichment of the terminological base (especially borrowing from Russian) took place at the expense of the language's own vocabulary (Old Armenian, Western Armenian and dialects played a special role) (Aghayan, 1987: 224–238, 274–277). The mass repatriation of Western Armenians to Armenia played a significant part in the development of the language, because besides

---

There is also a large bibliography on the problems of Armenians in the diaspora. In the present paper we refer to Leonian (1986: 79–110).

Western Armenian traits, their vocabulary included expressions borrowed from many languages of the world—Arabic, Turkish, French, Greek, etc. (Hakobyan, 1977: 354).

The uniform system of education, the development of mass media and the concentration of large numbers of Armenian people who had migrated from different regions of historical Armenian settlement to the towns of the Armenian SSR contributed to the development and wide propagation of the literary language. In order to present the scale of language processes, it should be pointed out that at the end of the 1950s the population of the capital of Armenia spoke in 36 dialects, and nearly 10 per cent of the inhabitants of Yerevan were competent in Turkish, Arabic, French, English or Farsi (Karapetyan, 1978: 87). In the period following the Second World War, and especially beginning with the 1960s, integration processes among various groups of Armenians, especially in towns, intensified and initial differences faded. The change in the language competence of subsequent generations and their active involvement in the process of developing Armenian–Russian bilingualism was one outcome of these processes.

According to 1976 sociological studies on the population of Yerevan, an essential change in the language competence has taken place over three generations. The language profile usually supposed a good command of another language in addition to Armenian. Armenians of the older generation and living in cities also spoke Turkish, Greek, Arabic, French, Romanian or Farsi. This bilingualism is explained by active contacts with these peoples in their ethnic territories in the past and later in the diaspora. Thirty to forty per cent of Yerevan's citizens above 60 years of age possessed such language skills (interestingly, Soviet censuses did not document this, as they focused on the knowledge of other USSR peoples' languages only). Only one to two per cent of the younger (under 30) inhabitants of Yerevan reported command of the languages mentioned. Along with this, the share of people reporting an effortless command of Russian increased. Thus, while the share of people speaking fluent Russian was ten per cent in the first generation, it was over 50 per cent in the third generation (Karapetyan, 1986: 69–72). According to the materials of three panel sociological studies carried out in Armenia from the1980 to the 1990s, these tendencies were traced both in the speech behaviour and language competence of the respondents.

The data of these censuses point to an increase in the percentage of people who have a fluent command of Armenian among national minorities in Armenia. This tendency was more manifest among the Assyrians, Greeks and Kurds, and weaker among Ukrainians, Russians and less populous nationalities, subsumed under "other nationalities". Moreover, during the period from 1959 to 1989, the portion of Kurds who indicated Kurdish as their native tongue shows a 14.6 per cent drop. An opposite momentum was found among Ukrainians and Assyrians.

Census data shows that the prevalence of the titular nation in the composition of the Republic did not become a factor restraining the spread of Russian among them. Armenia's relations with other republics and with Russia (obviously the pivotal state in the USSR) were decisive. The diversification of industrial development (Armenia was among the republics with a high-level industrial development[6]) abetted the introduction of Russian in the public

---

[6]   This is reflected in the degree of urbanization of Armenia—70 per cent—one of the highest in the former Soviet Union (Hratarakchutiun, 2000).

sphere. This was due to the fact that the overwhelming majority worked for firms and organizations under Soviet authority; their office work and technical documentation was in Russian. In connection with this, the functions of the Russian language in Armenia's public life expanded, while those of the Armenian language (though it was declared an official language) narrowed. The Armenian language was actively excluded from usage as a means of communication and access to information among a significant part of the technical intelligentsia. Materials of sociological studies have shown the inner workings of this process.

Table 2.2

Changes in the Proportion of People Who Consider their Mother Tongue
the Language of their Nationality and Report Fluency in a Second Language,
among the Main Nationalities in Armenia, before 1989

	Percentage who consider their mother tongue the language of their nationality				Percentage with a command of:					
					Russian			Other languages of the USSR [7]		
	1959	1970	1979	1989	1970	1979	1989	1970	1979	1989
Armenians	99.2	99.8	99.4	99.5	23.3	34.2	30.3	1.2	1.1	1.0
Azeris	99.3	99.6	99.3	—	5.1	9.9	—	7.1	10.3	—
Russians	99.6	99.5	99.3	99.1	—	—	—	21.1	29.0	32.0
Kurds	94.6	92.1	84.6	80.0	3.1	5.5	6.5	52.0	59.5	65.0
Ukrainians	49.3	75.3	62.9	65.1	58.6	50.4	48.2	16.9	25.3	28.1
Assyrians	85.6	90.0	56.9	89.6	51.9	40.4	40.0	20.3	37.9	39.0
Greeks	74.4	79.1	64.5	67.7	40.0	39.9	40.0	30.6	32.5	34.2
Other	59.4	77.3	63.3	70.1	34.7	40.4	40.0	22.3	28.1	30.0

SOURCE: Data from the 1959, 1970, 1979, 1989 censuses.

Russian became a major factor in many careers, which stimulated parents' motivation to encourage a language shift in the next generation. Moreover, the sustained immigration of Russian-speaking Armenians to the cities of Armenia gave rise to a greater concentration of Russian-speakers in the top strata of society (Galstyan, 1985: 7–12).

The next factor that strengthened the role of Russian in society was the intensification of migration and exchange with other Soviet republics. Tourism, business trips, private family visits and finally large-scale labour migration (involving five to seven per cent of Armenia's labour potential [Galstyan, 1990: 6–9]) required knowledge of Russian. The share of the Armenian inhabitants of Yerevan with fluency in Russian amounted to 32 per cent in 1976, 34 per cent in 1985, 38 per cent in 1990 and 30 per cent in 2000.

---

[7] For Armenians, these figures do not show the data of having a command of foreign languages, because of the wording of the question. For other nationalities, this wording implies that the knowledge reported refers to the Armenian language.

Table 2.3

Share of the Armenians Reporting Fluency in Russian, by Socio-Economic Status, Selected Age Brackets, 1976–2000

	1976	1985	1992	2000
18–29 years old				
White collar	34	36	40	35
Blue collar	23	24	27	25
50 and older				
White collar	16	18	22	20
Blue collar	6	8	9	8

SOURCE: Archive of the Ethno-Sociological Department, Armenian Academy of Sciences (IAE NAS RA, Volume II, p.10).

Table 2.4

Share of the Armenian People Reporting Fluency in Russian, by Area of Residence (Urban *vs.* Rural), Selected Age Brackets, 1976–2000

	1976	1985	1992	2000
Urban				
18–19 years old	25	28	31	30
50 and older	13	15	18	19
Rural				
18–19 years old	7	8	10	10
50 and older	2	3	5	6

SOURCE: Archive of the Ethno-Sociological Department, Armenian Academy of Sciences (IAE NAS RA, Volume II, p.12).

It is clear from the above tables that a process of bilingual development and language reorientation of the population towards the Russian language took place up to the period when Armenia gained independence. This process was especially intensive in towns, most of all in the capital. Competence in Russian was socially and demographically determined: it was higher in socially advanced groups and younger cohorts. The Armenian-speaking part of the population was more concentrated in the less qualified social group and senior cohorts, consisting chiefly of rural migrants (Karapetyan, 1986: 41, 51).

The latter came up against ethnocultural and socio-economic difficulties. Whereas in other republics similar problems were transferred to a national plane, in Armenia it ran along social-linguistic lines. It is not coincidental that a negative attitude towards the Russian language (particularly as a requirement for the labour market) emerged as part of the nationalist movement, against a background of growing aggravation between Armenia and the Soviet authorities. This underscores the social dimension of the language conflict in Armenia in that period and explains why these issues were put on the agenda by those groups in the population who were not competitive because of the language factor. For the same reasons, the leaders of these layers of the population became the ideologues of language reform.

1.2 Formation of the Language Policy Concept

In the Armenian mass media at the end of the 1980s and beginning of the 1990s, scientists and politicians pursued a heated discussion around the Armenian language and the perspectives for its development. The problematic character of the situation was obvious for all participants in the discussions, but approaches to a solution were seen quite differently. This became the stumbling block that split opponents who were ready to compromise at the beginning. Later, as reform in the sphere of language was carried out and its consequences became appreciable, a polarization of opponents' opinions took place, which split them up into supporters and opponents of radical measures. It is not accidental that disputes around them have not quieted down even now.

To clarify the subject of the polemics, let us examine the arguments of the supporters and opponents of reform. Supporters of the more radical measures sought to evict the Russian language from public life. They put forward several arguments in favour of this language policy; from their perspective, the most important included a political postulate which asserted that "among numerous factors uniting the people and distinguishing them from other peoples, language is the most decisive". Consequently, each state's quest to declare official the native language of the titular nation is natural. "This is a prime objective, because commonality of language in the population ... is a necessary condition, which makes it possible to build common cultural, educational, scientific, informational systems and spiritual independence of the people" (Zakaryan, 1991). Having thus defined the purpose, the radicals point out that in order to achieve these conditions, the state must not only declare its national language as official, but also impart this idea with definite and real contents, such as special language legislation and well-directed language policy (Zakaryan, 1990). Accordingly, the need for the latter is evidenced by the deep language divide in Armenia's population between Russian-speakers and Armenian-speakers, which creates a threat to the integrity of the state. For this purpose, they bring forth several concrete examples, which are worth examining more specifically.

According to the supporters of radical reform, the language divide was most manifest in the sphere of education. Almost 50 per cent of Armenian children attended Russian schools. 20 per cent of the students in higher educational institutions are trained in Russian. Russian-based training continues to be conducted in higher educational institutions considered to be Armenian-based (e.g., the Medical Institute, Conservatory and Institute of Physical Culture), and teaching is Russian-based in high schools oriented toward language and higher educational institutions of foreign languages. As a result, the younger generations have been deprived of the opportunity to be educated in Armenian and estranged from their national culture. Hence, the cultural continuity of the nation has been disrupted and is deteriorating.

The divide occurred in science as well. In research institutions, most scientific works were published in Russian. Soviet authorities required doctoral dissertations to be presented to the SAC (Supreme Attesting Commission) in Russian only. This resulted in the deterioration of the Armenian scientific language and its relegation to the periphery of the social evolution. The same situation was observed in the sphere of industrial production, where Armenian was driven out completely. Most industry was directly subordinated to the Soviet authorities; consequently all documentation was in Russian. A similar situation applied in the sphere of management and services. In all the ministries, most of the documentation was in Russian because of the direct subordination to Soviet ministries. In hospitals, clinics and other medical institutions, all within the structure of the Ministry of Public Health, all documentation was prepared and distributed in Russian. In culture and transport, even tickets and coupons were printed in Russian. All this nurtured a perception and then a conviction that the Armenian language was superfluous. Contrary to those who consider that the official language status, stipulated in all the constitutions of the Armenian SSR (1922, 1936 and 1978), is enough to solve the problem of preserving and developing the Armenian language, the radicals point out that the domains of use of Armenian were gradually narrowing. In the course of many years, the Armenian language did not have the opportunity to develop in the fields of public health, construction, finance, military science, diplomacy or state management.

The radicals' last argument—the existence of a real threat of disappearance of the Armenian language, hence the nation as a whole—is the logical conclusion of all these lines of thought. Taking into account the intensive assimilation of the Armenians in the diaspora, the Armenian people's language cleavage and the threat of displacement of Armenian from Armenia itself, the national state should do the utmost to stop these processes in order to promote the preservation of the Armenian people. The conclusions of the new language policy supporters had one purpose: the principal condition for the survival of the nation is to preserve the purity of the language, to stimulate its further development and overcome the language division among the population of the republic. This will serve as a basis for overcoming the split between Western Armenian and Eastern Armenian. "The Armenian Language Requires Care", "Let Us Become Worthy of Our Language" and other articles with such titles focused on the disastrous situation of the national language, appealed for its protection and offered concrete measures to do this. They specified the necessity of cardinal measures to remedy the situation with the official language, i.e., a serious reform with workable subject-matter was needed. "A pivotal task in language policy is to defend the interests of the national language. Preservation of the national language, moulding the people's consciousness towards honour and dignity of language, love for one's native tongue, preservation of the purity of Armenian"—such were the appeals of reform apologists. Newspaper articles titled "Linguistics and Language Policy", "Language and Language Policy", "Tasks of Unifying the Armenian Language", "Around the Basic Provisions of the Language Policy in the Republic of Armenia", "Language Nationalization and the Language Law" and others[8] actually proposed several main objectives for the language reform that gave grounds for the future conception of language policy.

The opponents of cardinal reform, by and large agreeing with its necessity, emphasized the importance of a gradual and prepared realization of reform provisions. They considered

---

[8]   Published in the newspapers *Hyastani Hanrapetutyun* (1990), *Hayreniki Dzayn* (1991) and others.

the measures proposed by radically biased politicians far from competent. Supporters of a moderate approach to the language problem emphasized the danger of the "revolutionary handling" of the strategically important question of language policy in Armenia. In newspaper articles ("A Dangerous Game with the Native Language", "Language Is Not a Field for Experiments", "Native Language Is Not a Pilot Field", "Modern Spelling Is Not Subject to Reform", "In Defence of Modern Spelling", "Tortures of the Native Language"[9]), the opponents stated that the concept was insufficiently elaborated. They found numerous faults due to a failure to understand regularities in language development and directly showed the unprofessionalism of the authors of the language reform. Attention was drawn to the fact that the situation of the Armenian language was not as dramatic as presented by the radicals. The threat of the Russian language is imaginary; on the contrary, knowledge of Russian allows wide layers of the population to be in touch with Russia and world culture. They stated that the Russian-speaking population in Armenia is the most educated part of society. It could become the nucleus of economic and social transformations. Knowledge of Russian gives access to technical, scientific and other literature—that is, it is a guarantee for Armenia's economic, social and cultural development. In the near future, Armenia cannot afford the 'luxury' of translating all this enormous literature into Armenian.

Without an appropriate preparation, the radical reform would destroy the currently available scientific, industrial-technological and even cultural potential of the Republic. The reform would require colossal financial resources that Armenia does not have today. Moreover, the reform would result in a collapse for a significant portion of the population in legal, economic and professional respects. One should not ignore the interests of refugees from Azerbaijan who comprise ten per cent of the population (more than 350,000 people), most of whom are Russian-speakers (Karapetyan, 1999: 68–70). In all their conclusions, the supporters of a moderate approach to language problems stress that all this is fraught with unpredictable consequences.

Thus, two opposite viewpoints were determined in the formation of language policy. Subsequently, with the development of sociopolitical and economic processes in Armenia, each of these viewpoints influenced the state programme on language and its realization to various degrees.

2. FORMATION OF THE LEGAL BASE FOR A NEW LANGUAGE POLICY

With the beginning of the Karabakh events that later influenced Armenia's independence movement, a radical approach to all the attributes of the existing Soviet socio-political system was claimed in the political context of confrontation with the Soviet authorities. Everything that was connected with Soviet power was rejected. Language also became an aspect of that confrontation. Mashtots[10], a nongovernmental organization which took an active part in the

---

[9]   Published in *Hayastani Hanrapetutyun* (1997), *Aravot* (1997) and *Novoye Vremya* (2000).

[10]   The non-governmental organization Mashtots was established in 1988 by linguist R. Ishkhanyan. The name of the organization—Mesrop Mashtots—comes from the inventor of the Armenian alphabet.

political events of the end of the 1980s and beginning of the 1990s, started a campaign for the purity of the Armenian language and forcing out Russian from public life.

The leaders of the main political force of the country, the All-Armenian National Movement (ANM), put forward the slogan "one nation, one language, one culture".[11] It is clear that such a slogan is the natural consequence of ANM's purpose—the joining of Karabakh and Armenia. The general context of the Karabakh events, a national-liberation struggle that became the basis of the one-nation movement, allowed cardinal reform supporters to play a leading role in the formulation of the future language policy, by peddling the 'language' component of this slogan. It was Mashtots leaders who became the authors of the concept of language reform in RA. They demanded a successive and tough policy in the sphere of language, the basis of which should become legislative and executive authorities. Within the aforementioned slogan, the language component was recognized as primary and three target principles were marked:

1. to correct the existing situation regarding language, exclude the former metropolitan language from public life and state office work and introduce Armenian into these spheres;

2. to ensure the complete volume of attributes of an independent state. The uniform official language should secure the cultural-historical and political-economic unity of the state;

3. to optimize integration of the Armenian people, its constituents settled within the national state and in the diaspora (Mirzoyan, 1996: 13).

Legal consolidation of these principles was of decisive importance for the authors of this concept. Therefore, decrees and resolutions of the executive power adopted under their pressure were later corroborated by legislative acts in an obligatory way.

In 1990, the Ministry of Education of the Armenian SSR (Armenia then was a part of the USSR) adopted a resolution "On Uniform National General Education". In 1991, parliament put forth a resolution about transition to Armenian as a uniform language of teaching for children of Armenian nationality in all general education schools, obligatory for pupils from 1st to 4th grades and optional for the pupils of upper grades (*Armenian SSR*, 1990). The radical nature of this reform is obvious—45 per cent (100,000) of pupils were in Russian-based general education schools in Armenia, and many refugee children did not know Armenian.

Two years later, in 1993, parliament adopted the Language Act (Orenq Lezvi Masin, 1995: 477–479), the articles of which stated the basic principles of language policy, language education, language duties of the citizens, language rights and duties of institutions and execution of state policy in this sphere. The basic principles of language policy in RA were stated in five articles of the Act.

Article One, "Language Policy of RA", enacts that the official language of RA is the Armenian literary language (the Act deliberately did not specify the Eastern or Western literary language). The state likewise promotes the preservation and propagation of the Armenian

---

[11] Members of the Armenian All National Movement comprised 80 per cent of the representatives in parliament during this period.

language among Armenians living outside RA, and comprehensive integration of the spelling in two literary languages. A separate item "guarantees the free functioning of the languages of national minorities in RA".

Article Two, "The Language of Education", enacts an obligatory introduction of the Armenian literary language in general education schools and higher educational institutions of the republic. As for national minorities in the Republic of Armenia, "general education and upbringing may be organized in their mother tongue according to state programmes and sponsorship, with obligatory teaching of Armenian".

Article Three, "On Language Duties of Citizens", obliges all officials and workers in the sphere of service to know Armenian, to keep its purity and to apply it obligatorily in official speeches and negotiations.

Article Four, "Language Rights and Duties of Institutions", resolves obligatory introduction of the Armenian language into office work of all institutions and enterprises (both state and private) on the territory of RA. This article resolves its use at meetings and conferences, in state and public activities, in advertising, names of streets and institutions, and in supplying translation of documents, advertisements and other materials of foreign origin into Armenian. Another point—"Documents, official forms and seals of organizations of national minorities living on the territory of the Republic of Armenia must be presented in the Armenian language along with a translation into their national language"—was added to the paragraph on national minorities in the article.

Article Five, "On the Execution of State Policy in the Sphere of Language", obliges all state institutions and management bodies to strictly adhere to the provisions of the Act and create a special structural department at the government of Armenia to carry out the state policy.

Soon after, in 1994, the government resolutions "On the Abolition of the Committee for Armenian Language Terminology" and the creation of the "State Language Inspectorate" followed (Orenq Lezvi Masin, 1995: 479).

Article 12 of the Constitution of Armenia, adopted in 1995, declared Armenian the official language. It was in effect a new version of the article on language in the previous Constitution of 1978. The paragraph about the Russian language was withdrawn, and the Armenian literary language was declared official, without any specification of Western or Eastern Armenian. Thus, Western Armenians in the diaspora were reserved the right to use their language in the republic, and the uniting of these two languages was given a legislative basis. A paragraph on the "right of national minorities to freely use their language and the necessity of knowing and using Armenian" was added in the Article. Moreover, Article 37 of the Constitution of the Republic of Armenia states that "citizens belonging to national minorities have the right to preserve their traditions and to develop their language and culture". It should be taken into account that along with the adoption of the Language Act, the language component was consolidated in other legislative acts of Armenia, as for instance, the Acts on Mass Media and Education.[12]

---

[12]   For example, Article 5 of the Act on Mass Media: "On the Language of Press and Mass Media" (Orenq Lezvi Masin, 1995: 477–478).

In 1997, the government resolution "On Calling Individuals and Organizations to Account for the Breach of the Language Act" followed (Orenq Lezvi Masin, 1995: 479). The latter may be considered the finale in the creation of a legal base for language reform. In the same year, within the programme of socio-economic development of Armenia, a separate section allocating funds for language policy was singled out that envisaged free teaching of Armenian.

3. IMPLEMENTATION OF LANGUAGE POLICY

3.1 The Activity of Management and Control Bodies in Language Policy

The Language Inspectorate, a management and control body, was formed along with the legislative formulation of the new language policy. It should be noted that the principal staff members of this state institution were recruited from Mashtots members. Two councils—the Supreme Council on Armenian Language and later the Council of Cultural-Linguistic Policy—were established within the Language Inspectorate. The function of the first was to provide the purity of the Armenian language and to develop modern terminology on the basis of available vocabulary resources, also to find ways of uniting the Western Armenian and Eastern Armenian literary languages. In this respect, the Supreme Council on the Armenian Language should closely cooperate with similar councils in the diaspora. One such council, the Terminological Council of the New Armenian Language of Western Armenians (Marseilles, France) actively collaborated with the councils in Armenia.

The Supreme Council of the Armenian Language developed vigorous activities in the following directions:

First, it set out to clear the Armenian language of recently incorporated foreign terms. Words borrowed in the Middle Ages from Greek, Persian and Latin were considered already 'Armenianized'. At its first session, the council discussed the replacement of Russian terms from the Soviet period with Armenian equivalents.

Obviously, terms of Soviet origin such as *kolkhoz* (collective farm), *sovkhoz* (state farm), *sovety* (Soviets), etc., became obsolete without any interference from the Language Inspectorate. Privatization of land and administrative reform themselves radically changed the terminology of management and agriculture.

It turned out to be difficult to reveal and translate terms from various spheres of public life. For over twenty years, the former Terminological Committee employees had worked out a methodological basis to replace Russian terms with Armenian words. Armenia was among the few Soviet Republics where words of key political importance such as *sovety* (Soviets), *respublika* (republic), *revolyutsiya* (revolution) and others were replaced by their Armenian equivalents. However, the work of the former Terminological Committee was considered ineffective. Disregarding accumulated experience, the new council members came up against the same problems that had remained unsolved earlier. Comparatively easily 'Armenianized' were words and terms which—both in Russian and Armenian—were borrowed from Greek. Many Armenian terms and concepts borrowed as far back as the Hellenistic period received a somewhat Russian 'sounding' in the Soviet times. This, for instance, was the case with *ether* and *zephyr*. The Armenians first used the words *yeter* and *zepiur*, then in the Soviet period these words were replaced by Russian *efir* and *zefir* and finally, these words were again replaced by their Armenian forms (Acharyan, 1969: 7).

Armenian linguists applied two approaches when replacing a Russian word—literal translation of meanings (a comparatively easy way on the surface) or finding an Armenian synonym. The first approach, however, usually produced a complex descriptive term, demanding a certain adaptation of consciousness. For example, the word *samokat* (meaning scooter—comprised of the Russian roots 'self' and 'roll'), translated as *inknagnats* (comprised of the Armenian roots 'self' and 'go'), is easy to understand as it consists of similar components. However, the term *inknagnats* expresses the connotation of the Russian word *samokhod* ('self' and 'go') that signifies the general idea of all self-propelled devices, not specifically a scooter, as was intended. Hence, a new word is required to distinguish between the Russian words *samokat* and *samokhod*. So, loan translation does not always provide an easy way of replacing Russian terms, and this often results in great difficulties due to long and bulky terms. The second approach—replacement of international terms borrowed from Russian with Old Armenian equivalents (such as *atom* with the Old Armenian *hyuleh*) is not likely to catch.

So-called 'language building' turned out to be fraught with a whole range of complications. Coinage of new Armenian terms and their introduction into circulation became a rather difficult and long process. The purpose of purifying the Armenian language had to avoid an anti-Russian bias as well. The new terminology must be passed through general education in schools and mass media; only then can it gradually become comprehensible and generally acknowledged. This implied a much longer time-scale than the reformers originally imagined.

The second direction worked out by the council was the introduction of terms for new spheres of state activity: politics, management, international relations, defence, tourism, taxation, etc. With this purpose, new words and terms coined from the vocabulary of the Armenian language (from Old and Western Armenian) were put into circulation. The actions of the council in this sphere were fruitful, as these terms became generally acknowledged as part of the process of forming new institutions.

In politics, such concepts as 'rating', 'populism' and 'presentation' found their Armenian equivalents. Many Armenian terms and words were introduced in the new management system. Thus, after joining the former thirty-seven regions of Armenia into ten new provinces, the Old Armenian *marz* (province) came into use with its derivatives *marzpet* (governor), *marzpetaran* (province management), *marzkentron* (province centre), *marzpetutyun* (governorship). A lot of words, such as 'condominium' and 'police', were given Armenian equivalents as well (*hamatirutyun* and *vostikanutyun*, respectively). The Supreme Council on Armenian Language 'Armenianized' approximately 100 terms and words in the course of one year (Mirzoyan, 1998: 15).

The third direction in the activities of the Supreme Council on Armenian Language was the creation of a general terminological base for the Armenian language. This was problematic due to certain connotative differences for the equivalent terms, as well as by the diversity of words and terms expressing the same concept by the Western and Eastern Armenians. To solve this problem, it will be necessary:

- to clarify and coordinate each word and term with the representatives of similar councils in the diaspora;
- to create new Armenian dictionaries;
- to build up a common system of teaching the native language both in Armenia and in the diaspora.

The next step in this direction should become the unification of spelling, which also requires long and laborious joint work.

The second council, namely the Council on Cultural-Linguistic Policy was to carry out language policy, which meant elaboration of measures that would ensure the observance of the Language Act and prevent its breach. Thus, it was given the function of control over the language of institutions, enterprises and officials. During the first three years of their work, the council published 230 references to language errors in mass media (Mirzoyan, 1998: 13). In particular, when analyzing the level of knowledge of the Armenian language, the council members re-examined a number of students of higher educational institutions and discovered a great divergence in the estimation of their knowledge: out of twenty students only two succeeded in passing the exam (Mirzoyan, 1998: 15).

The council discovered a lot of breaches of the Language Act in street signs and in the offices of enterprises and institutions. At this, fines were envisaged for such beaches. In an interview with the author of the present paper, employees at the State Language Inspectorate complained of the small size of these fines. Owners of shops and offices preferred to pay the fine and leave the signboards without any changes, rather than change the signboard, which would be much more expensive. The requirement was that shop-owners should give priority to the Armenian script, placing it in the upper or left part of the signboard in bigger letters than the translated or transcribed English version.[13]

The council noted that it is a breach of the Language Act when the overwhelming majority of films on TV are shown in Russian translation.

According to the council members, a special situation emerged in general education schools. Evading the Language Act, school principals increased the hours of teaching Russian. To give their children Russian education, parents get certificates about the Russian roots of their children, or about the Russian citizenship of one of the parents. All this is explained by quite pragmatic purposes: the perspective of leaving for Russia. All the facts mentioned bear witness to serious faults in language policy.

For the purpose of realizing language policy completely, the workers of the State Language Inspectorate, together with Mashtots members, prepared the State Programme on Language Policy in RA, which concretized the measures of developing and strengthening the positions of the Armenian language in RA, and determined the financing of these measures.[14]

---

[13]   State Language Inspectorate (2001: 15–17).

[14]   State Language Inspectorate (2001: 15–17).

The programme submitted for government approval in 1997 envisaged the following measures:

- re-testing the language proficiency of state employees, school teachers and professors. In case of failure, they would lose their jobs or be enrolled in courses financed by the government;
- checking the language of state and office materials of state and private enterprises and institutions, with heavy fines for breaches of the Language Act;
- creating computer programmes in Armenian.

The government sent the programme for further elaboration, but it found few supporters. Moreover, the leader of Mashtots, philosopher Valery Mirzoyan, was dismissed from the position of the chief of the State Language Inspectorate. The negative results of the rapid reform of language became obvious. Certain strata of society demanded an easing of the tough provisions of the Language Act. One such attempt reached Parliament. In 2000, a revised version of the Language Act was brought to the National Assembly of Armenia. However, this initiative did not find support among the deputy corps.

It should be noted that the Language Act was carried out in the shortest possible time frame, with a rapid transition to Armenian in education and office work. In this situation, a quick overcoming of the language barrier became problematic for those who did not speak Armenian. Programmes for teaching Armenian were not specified and reasonable time frames for reform were not determined. In fact, quite a serious reform was carried out spontaneously, without any backing programmes. According to the data of recent studies (Hratarakchutyun, 2000), a significant part of the respondents of the titular nationality and an overwhelming majority of respondents among national minority representatives consider that all the citizens of the Republic of Armenia, irrespective of their nationality, must know and use the Armenian language. However, the reform itself, according to respondents' opinion, was carried out without due consideration, and its necessarily step-wise progression was not envisaged. They considered that a preparatory period was needed, followed by programmes of language training for specialists and then only tough requirements of language competence of the population could be put forward.

Taking into account the significant portion of Russian-speaking Armenians, one can imagine the consequences of a sharp transition to the Armenian language; it was observed at once: a great flow of refugees and socially advanced groups (specialists, scientists, etc.) out of Armenia.

3.2 National Minorities and Language Policy

As mentioned earlier, national minorities comprise a bit more than three per cent of the population of Armenia. Armenia signed the European Charter for Regional or Minority Languages (1992), the Declaration of the UN General Assembly on the Rights of Persons Belonging to National or Ethnic, Religious or Linguistic Minorities (1992), the Convention Ensuring the Rights of National Minorities (adopted in Moscow by the countries of the CIS in 1994) and the Council of Europe Framework Convention for the Protection of National Minorities (1995). In 2001, Armenia became a member of the Council of Europe.

These regulations were reflected in Article 37 of the Constitution and Articles 1, 2 and 4 of the Language Act. Special attention was given to the problems of national minorities, to the implementation of legislation to preserve their languages and culture and provide continuity of national values to the new generation.

In Soviet years, in education all over the Soviet republics, the language of the titular nation was not obligatory; it was an optional subject for national minorities. As a matter of fact, members of national minorities had the right not to study and not to know the language of the titular nation. According to the 1989 census, 32 per cent of Russians, 39 per cent of Assyrians, 35 per cent of Greeks and 65 per cent of Yezid-Kurds had a fluent command of the Armenian language (Table 2.2). With the introduction of the Language Act, national minorities faced new problems in education, state business and professional promotion, aggravated under the conditions of socio-economic crisis. During the reforms, most Russian schools changed their profile and were turned into Armenian schools that reduced the number of Russian-speaking specialists (teachers and instructors), on the one hand, and sharply diminished the chances of getting education in a language convenient for certain groups of population, on the other hand. As a result, Russian-speaking Armenians and national minorities found themselves socially disadvantaged. It should be emphasized that the fast pace of reform, not its substance, infringed on the civil rights of Russian-speaking Armenians and refugees (also ethnic Armenians) (Karapetyan, 1999: 3).

In this connection, it is worth taking notice of certain characteristic features in the language processes among national minorities before and after the language reform in Armenia.

Russians, the most numerous national minority group (Dolzhenko, 1998: 171–196), were in the most favourable language situation due to a wide knowledge of Russian in Armenia. Their life in Armenia was socially and culturally comfortable. General and higher education as well as all forms of mass media were available in their mother tongue. When carrying out the language reform, Russians and other national minorities enjoyed a right to Russian-based education according to programmes and textbooks from the Russian Federation. This situation was so favourable that the children of Armenians with Russian citizenship now have the opportunity to receive education in Russian schools in Armenia. There is a Russian university in Yerevan, and there are many popular newspapers and magazines published in Russian in Armenia. Numerous Russian cultural centres contribute to the social and cultural life of this national minority group in Armenia.

Like Armenians, Yezid-Kurds and Assyrians were victims of the genocide in Turkey from 1915 to 1920. The Yezid-Kurds are a subethnic group of Kurds and differ from the latter in religion. Most Kurds in Armenia are Yezid-Kurds. 80 per cent live in rural areas; 17 per cent in mono-ethnic communities and 83 per cent in mixed Yezid-Armenian villages (Aristova, 1961; Guest, 1987: 602–616, 635–636). Such settlements determine the language used locally. In all villages with a majority Yezid-Kurd population, minority-language schools are available. Beginning in the 1920s, curricula were formed, teachers were trained and textbooks published through the efforts of the Armenian and Yezid-Kurd intelligentsia with government financial support. Yezid-Kurd general schools planned to teach Armenian and Russian. Yezid-Kurd schools existed also in those Armenian villages where the number of Yezid-Kurds justified classes in the Kurdish language. After the reform, Yezid-Kurd schools could be opened by any Yezid-Kurd national organization or community. The sole innovation was that obligatory teaching of Armenian was introduced in all Yezid-Kurd schools.

According to census data over 30 years (from 1959 to 1989) the number of Yezid-Kurds considering Armenian their mother tongue increased ten times and their proportion almost five times. Sociological studies in 1999 and 2000 showed a five to six per cent increase in these parameters (Hratarakchutyun, 2000: 101).

Among post-Soviet states, only in Armenia do Yezid-Kurds have state support to develop their culture. Yezid-Kurds have two newspapers published in Kurdish, a department of Kurdish studies at the Institute of Oriental Studies in the Armenian Academy of Sciences, a Chair of Kurdish studies at the university, a number of Kurdish writers in the Armenian Writers' Union and a daily programme in Kurdish on the state radio.

The Assyrians *(Asori)* also occupy a special place among the national minorities in Armenia. The attitude to this small national group is especially emotional, as a result of common historical fates (Yeremyan, 1962: 421–432). Before the reform, most Assyrians (about 6,000) received Russian-based education. After 1972, their native tongue was introduced as optional (Matveyev, 1982: 215–224), and in 1987 it became obligatory in majority Assyrian settlements. This did not affect Assyrians lived dispersed in cities; most attended Russian schools.

It should be mentioned that if the Assyrians learned Russian at school, and they learned Armenian through contact with their colleagues and neighbours. However, Assyrian remained a means of communication within families and in Assyrian neighbourhoods.

In the post-reform period, the problem of training teachers and publishing textbooks in Assyrian became a major issue for this national minority group. The first Assyrian classes were held in Yerevan in 1998 (Hratarakchutyun, 2000: 135).

CONCLUSION

Language policy in Armenia in the transition period was intended to ensure the cultural and informational basis for sovereignty of the newly independent country. The new language policy in Armenia involved expanding essentially the public functions of the Armenian language and giving impetus to its intensive development. New legislation on language stimulated efforts of a significant part of the intellectual potential of Armenia to develop the Armenian language and adapt it to political and economic changes in the country. In this regard, the orientation towards overcoming the language divide between the two large groups of Armenians improved the credibility of the country for the diaspora. Today, state employees, scientists, teachers and representatives of the diaspora have no doubts about the expediency of the policy carried out.

Along with this, the hasty realization of the language policy created many problems for the Russian-speaking population in Armenia. Armenia went through a war and a blockade, took in more than 300,000 refugees, and experienced the consequences of a devastating earthquake and economic crisis. All this resulted in mass emigration, which was stimulated by language reform as well. According to the data of many sociological studies, in addition to social-economic motives for emigration, the language factor was of special importance for refugees, Russian-speaking Armenians and some national minorities.

REFERENCES

Acharyan, Hrachia (1969) *Hajereni armatakan bararan* (Dictionary of Armenian Roots). Yerevan: Yerevani Hamalsarani Hratarakchutyun.

Aghayan, E. (1987) *Lezvabanutjan himunqnere* (The Basis of Linguistics). Yerevan: EPH Hranarakchutyun.

Alpoyadjyan (1947, 1951) *Haj gaghtodjaghneri patmutjune* (The History of Armenian Migration Centres). Cairo: Hratarakchutyun.

Aravot (1997) "Editorials". *Aravot*, 28 April 1997.

Aristova, Tatyana Fedorovna (1961) "Kurdi" (Kurds). In *Narodi Kavkaza*. Moscow: Nauka.

Armenian SSR Ministry of Education (1990) *Hajkakan SSH i lusavorutjan ministrutjan voroshume Miasnakan azgain hanrakrtakan dproci masin* (The Resolution of the Ministry of Education of the Armenian SSR on the Uniform National General Education School). *Hayastani Hanrapetutyun*: N 125.

Armenian Refugees (Lord Mayor's Fund) (1919) *The Plight of Armenian and Assyrian Christians*. London: Spottiswoode, Ballantyne and Co.

Bedrossyan, Mark D. (1983) *The First Genocide of the 20th Century: The Perpetrators and the Victims*. Flushing, NY: Voskedar Publishing.

Dolzhenko, Ivan (1998) *Etnokulturnie procesi sredi ruskogo naselenija Armenii* (Ethno-Cultural Processes among the Russian population of Armenia). Moscow: Nauka.

Frelick, Bill (1994) *Faultlines of National Conflict: Refugees and Displaced Persons from Armenia and Azerbaijan*. Washington, DC: US Committee for Refugees.

Galstyan, Arman (1985) *Jazikovie procesi v stolitchnom gorode* (Language Processes in the Capital City). Yerevan: Izdatelstvo AN Armenian SSR.

Galstyan, M. (1990) *Socialno-kulturnie posledstvija sezonoj migracii* (Social-Cultural Consequences of Seasonal Migration). Yerevan: Izdatelstvo AN Armenian SSR.

Gasparyan, Sergey Tigrani (1962) *Spyurkahay gaghtojaghnern aysor* (The Armenian Diaspora today). Yerevan: Hayastani Petakan Hratarakchutyun.

Gaume, Myriam (1993) *Les invités de la terre: Armenie, Karabakh, 1988–1992*. Paris: Editions du Seuil.

Guest, John S. (1987) *The Yezidis*. London/New York: KPI.

Hakobyan, Tadevos Khachaturi (1977) *Ocherk istoryi Yerevana* (Essays on the History of Yerevan). Yerevan: Yer. P.H. Hratarakchutyun.

Hambartsumyan, V. (1993) *Hajoc lezvi dasakan ughghagrutjun* (The Basis of Classical Spelling of the Armenian Language). Beirut: M. Varandyan.

Hayreniki Dzayn (1991) "Editorials". *Hayreniki Dzayn*, 13 March 1991.

159

Hovannisian, Richard G. (1992) *The Armenian Genocide: History, Politics, Ethics*. New York, NY: St. Martin's Press.

Hratarakchutyun (2000) *Azgain pokramasutjunnern Hajastani Hanrapetutyunum ajsor* (National Minorities in the Republic of Armenia Today). Yerevan: H.H. GAA, Gitutyun Hratarakchutyun.

Hayastani Hanrapetutyun (1997) "Editorials". *Hayastani Hanrapetutyun*, 19 April 1997.

ICOM (1979) *La Struttura Negata: Cultura Armenia nella Diaspora*. Venice: ICOM.

Joseph, John L. (1962) *The Nestorians and Their Neighbours*. Princeton: Princeton University Press.

Karapetyan, Rouben (1978) *Yerevani verabnakitchneri social-demografik parametrere* (Social-Demographic Parameters of Migrants to Yerevan). Yerevan: Hajkakan SSH GALraber.

Karapetyan, Rouben (1986) *Izmenenie socialnoj strukturi naselenija Yerevana* (Changes in the Social Structure of the Population). Yerevan: Naselenie Yerevan.

Karapetyan, Rouben (1992) *Hajeri teghabashkhman dzevere Sphurkum* (Settlements of the Armenian Diaspora). *Hayutyun* (March): 2.

Karapetyan, Rouben (1999) *Problems of Social-Legal and Cultural Welfare of Refugees in Armenia*. Yerevan, Geneva: IOM, UNCR.

Khojabekyan, Vladimir Eghishey (1979) *Hayastani bnaktchutyune ev nra zbaghvactyune, 1828–1978* (The People of Armenia and their Occupation). Yerevan: Haykakan SSH GA Hratarakchutyun.

Komsomolets (1989) "The Demographic Consequences of the Catastrophic Earthquake in Armenia". *Komsomolets Hijastan*, 14 September 1989.

Lapidus, Gail W., Victor Zaslavsky and Philip Goldman (eds.) (1992) *From Union to Commonwealth: Nationalism and Separatism in the Soviet Republics*. Cambridge and New York, NY: Cambridge University Press.

Leonian, René (1986) *Les Arméniens de France: sont-ils assimilés?* Issy-les-Moulineaux: edition of the author.

Matveyev, Konstantin P. (1982) *Assirijci* (The Assyrians). Moscow: Nauka.

Meliksetyan, Hovik Ukhtanesi (1985) *Hayrenik-Spyurk arnchutyunnere ev hayrenadardzutyune, 1920–1980* (Armenian-Diaspora Relations and Repatriation). Yerevan: Yerevani Hamalsarani Hratarakchutyun.

Mirzoyan, Valeriy Armenaki (1996) *Lezvabanutjun ev lezvaqaghakakanutjune* (Language and Language Policy). Beirut: Varandjan, Hratarakchutyun.

Mirzoyan, Valeriy Armenaki (1998) *Lezvabanutjun ev lezvaqaghakakanutjune* (Language and Language Policy). Beirut: Varandjan, Hratarakchutyun.

Novoye Vremya (2000) "Editorials". *Novoye Vremya*, 23 September 2000.

Orenq Lezvi Masin (1995) *HH Geragujn Ghorurdi vorochume* (Act on Language of the Supreme Soviet of RA). State archives, Yerevan.

Pogossyan, Gevorg (1996) *The Conditions of Refugees in Armenia.* Yerevan: GGH Hratarak-chutyun.

State Language Inspectorate (2001) *Project of the State Programme of Language Policy* of RA (Archives of the State Language Inspectorate). pp.15–17.

Suny, Ronald Grigor (1993) *The Revenge of the Past: Nationalism, Revolution, and the Collapse of the Soviet Union.* Stanford, CA: Stanford University Press.

University of Yerevan (1980) *Istoria armianskogo naroda* (History of the Armenian People). Yerevan: Izdatelstvo Yerevanskogo Universiteta.

Walker, Christopher J. (ed.) (1991) *Armenia and Karabakh: The Struggle for Unity.* London, UK: Minority Rights Publications.

Yeremyan, S. (1962) "The Assyrians". In *The Peoples of the Caucasus.* Moscow: Nauka.

Zakaryan, Hovhannes (1990) *Lezvi azgainacume ev lezvi orenqe* (Language Nationalization and the Language Act). *Hyastani Hanrapetutyun*: N124.

Zakaryan, Hovhannes (1991) *Hajoc lezun karot ghnamqi.* (The Armenian Language Requires Care). *Hayreniki Dzayn*, 13 March 1991.

Zakaryan, Hovhannes (2000) "The Task of Unification of the Armenian Language". Report presented at the symposium *Armenia–2000*, Wittenberg, Germany, 2–10 September 2000.

The Politics of Language Reform and Bilingualism in Tatarstan

Yagfar Z. Garipov and Helen M. Faller

The Politics of Language Reform and Bilingualism in Tatarstan

Yagfar Z. Garipov and Helen M. Faller

INTRODUCTION

The democratic social and political changes begun by Gorbachev in the Soviet Union in the late 1980s engendered a powerful growth of national[15] self-consciousness among the peoples inhabiting Russia and, eventually, a transformation in how Russia's inhabitants configure themselves as members of particular communities. This transformation began with a period of ethnic renaissance characterized by changes in nationalities' political mobilization, which commonly manifested itself as changes in language policies. In some regions not automatically accorded independence when the Soviet Union collapsed in 1991, political mobilization continues as a battle to maintain sovereign status under Putin's regime.[16] Among the polities not granted independence arguably the most successful in negotiating sovereignty with Yeltsin's government and consequently under the greatest threat from Putin's re-centralization policies is the Republic of Tatarstan.

The capital of Tatarstan, Kazan, is located some 800 kilometres east of Moscow, while the republic lies to the west of the Ural Mountains on the eastern edge of the European part of the Russian Federation and straddles both the Kama and Volga Rivers. The region was incorporated into Muscovy by Ivan the Terrible in 1552, and its conquest, along with that of the Astrakhan Khanate four years afterwards, provided Ivan IV the legitimization to declare himself tsar of Russia, thereby elevating himself from his previous title as prince of Muscovy (Karamzin, 1969; Pelenski, 1974). Because of this, along with Tatarstan's leading role in sovereignty politics movements among constituent polities of Russia during perestroika, it might be argued that Tatarstan's status as a part of the Russian Federation is symbolically pivotal in terms of the country's continued existence as an authoritative state.

---

[15] In the former Soviet Union the term nationality *(natsional'nost')* was used to refer to what might be considered ethnic differences in other parts of the world. Scholars of socialist states have demonstrated how ethnic difference (Barth, 1969) was imbued with bureaucratic, and hence political, form in daily life, thereby becoming nationalized. This was achieved in part through an internal passport regime according to which each person officially inscribed his or her nationality beginning at the age of 16. See, for example, Brubaker (1996); Lemon (2000); Slezkine (1994); Suny (1997); and Verdery (1996).

[16] Polities that had been accorded the status of union republics during the Soviet period, such as those in Central Asia, the Baltic states and the like, were deemed independent, while those which had lower status, as autonomous republics or *oblasts*, were not.

The population of the Republic of Tatarstan (3,770,000) consists of people of some one hundred different nationalities, over 90 per cent of whom are ethnic Tatars and Russians. It is unclear what the precise percentage of Tatars *vis-à-vis* other nationalities is in Tatarstan. The 1989 Soviet census provides the following figures: 48.5 per cent Tatar and 43.3 per cent Russian, with Chuvash, Mari, Mordva, Bashkir, Ukrainians, Volga Germans, Jews and a number of other Soviet nationalities comprising the remaining 8.2 per cent of the population.[17] More recent Tatarstan data regarding its population asserts that the proportions have shifted so that Tatars make up 51.2 per cent of the population, while Russians are down to 41.11 per cent.[18] This shift is significant for Tatarstan's sovereignty in part because of ethnographer Galina Starovoytova's pronouncements, in her capacity as Yeltsin's Council for Nationalities Affairs, that the republic's political claims should be ignored because they were a minority population in their titular republic (Starovoytova, 1991).

One of the bases for Tatar political claims was the perceived impending death of Tatar language, and over the past ten years the Republic of Tatarstan has made progress in terms of broadening domains of Tatar language use. The first and most important accomplishment has been the introduction of comprehensive schooling in Tatar and other languages spoken in the republic. At present, however, many Tatar intellectuals continue to be apprehensive about the fact that Tatar has not yet become a *de facto* government language. It is still not the working language of legislative activities, official documents, clerical work or management. Although numerous dictionaries for the staffs of different branches of economy have been published, demand for them is low. Concerned intellectuals attribute the existing situation to a lack of attention to Tatar language promotion on the part of local government bureaucrats. However, beyond the realm of policy realization, there are likewise social reasons for the continued absence of Tatar in official domains. The majority of Tatar managers speak only colloquial Tatar, and therefore their level of knowledge is insufficient for producing official documents, while Russian managers do not speak Tatar at all. Moreover, middle-aged and older managers are unlikely to be able to invest the time and energy needed to learn a new language during the current period of social and political upheaval and economic insecurity. This is especially the case since Russian, which they all know, is a government language of equal legal status to Tatar. Despite this, however, government bureaucrats and clerks, as well as other government workers such as tram and trolley bus drivers, are attending free courses in introductory and continuing Tatar funded by the city of Kazan, as well as the Tatarstan government. Although those who start these courses with no knowledge of Tatar have little chance of becoming fluent Tatar-speakers during the two months or less they study the

---

[17]   Data from the 1989 Soviet census.

[18]   Although it is hard to document, this shift is not completely implausible as there has been a wave of Tatars 'returning home' to Tatarstan from Central Asia and other parts of the former Soviet Union. These migrations have been encouraged by local authorities. Meanwhile, there has been some emigration of ethnic Russians, although the latter are likewise moving north to Tatarstan from Central Asia. It is also possible that, since some of the stigma of being Tatar has been lifted since language reforms in Tatarstan began, children of mixed marriages may no longer be automatically recording their nationality as 'Russian' when they receive their internal passports at the age of 16. Faller heard of a couple of such cases during her dissertation research in 1999–2001 (See also Republic of Tatarstan, 2000: 20).

language, this perhaps is not the biggest stumbling block they encounter. Despite the fact that many of them are eager to start employing their newly learned skills at work, there is a certain amount of resistance to this on the part of their Tatar-speaking co-workers who continue to perceive them as Russian-speakers and therefore use the language known by all in order to facilitate communication. The classes, however, seem to be more helpful to persons who already have at least passive knowledge of Tatar, for they help to erode the stigma against using Tatar in the workplace.

Tatarstan authorities attempt to balance policies aimed at reviving the Tatar language and promoting Tatar high culture with those providing equally beneficial conditions to preserve and develop all the languages and cultures of multi-national Tatarstan. Tatarstan's President Shaimiev explains, "Some people think that the government demonstrates too much caution in this matter. But that is the delicate sphere where there can never be too much caution" (Shaimiev, 2000: 2). Reasons for proceeding with caution in introducing language reforms concern not only the need to make urban and frequently monoglot Russian-speaking Tatars[19] feel included in Tatar nation-building efforts, but also to include ethnic Russians and people belonging to other nationalities.

The role of the mass media in the reform of Tatarstan's language policy is significant. Tatarstan has more than 500 mass media outlets, 53 per cent of which are produced in Russian, while the rest are either in Tatar or in both Tatar and Russian. Over the past ten years radio broadcasting in Tatar has increased from 7.5 hours to 47 hours per day, that is, six times; TV broadcasting in Tatar has increased from 17.5 to 41.5 hours per week. The majority of television broadcasting in Tatar takes place on the Tatarstan government station (TRT), while only a few hours per week are shown on one of Tatarstan's independent stations, EFIR. However, plans are afoot to create an independent TV channel which will broadcast in Tatar only. At present, the Tatarstan government radio station broadcasts on short wave for both Tatars living outside Tatarstan in the Russian Federation and for Tatars living abroad.

1. A THUMBNAIL SKETCH OF LANGUAGE IDEOLOGIES AND POLICIES IN TATARSTAN

Vladimir Lenin rejected the idea that Russian language should have a privileged role in the new Soviet state. During the early 1920s efforts were made all across the Soviet Union to educate children in their mother tongue, regardless of whether or not their mother spoke that tongue (Kreindler, 1989; Lewis, 1972). After Lenin's death in 1924, however, Stalin elevated Nikolay Marr to the status of the Soviet Union's foremost linguist. Marr's theories were no more grounded in observed linguistic phenomena than were those of Soviet geneticist Lysenko in observations of genetic mutations (Lysenko, 1948; Soyfer, 1994). For example, Marr proposed that spoken language emerged not as a means of communication, but rather as an instrument of class struggle. Moreover, he asserted that each language emerged at a

---

[19]   The split between monoglot and bilingual speakers tends to be regional, with Russified Tatars living in urban centres and Tatar-speaking ones either living in villages or being first-generation migrants to cities.

particular stage in history corresponding to a change in the mode of production through a process of hybridization with the previously existing language. Eventually, Marr predicted, all world languages would hybridize into a single language (Chikobava, 1951). Stalin modified Marr's theories in 1950, having debunked aspects of them, stating that the major "zonal" languages—probably, Russian, German and English—will "coalesce into one general international language", thereby unequivocally elevating Russian above all other languages spoken in the Soviet Union (Stalin, 1950b: 98).

It was not until Khrushchev came to power, however, that Stalin's Russocentric ideology was translated into official policy (Kreindler, 1989). Until 1958 all Soviet children received education in their mother tongue (Kreindler, 1989: 49). Afterwards, "the use of the mother tongue was actively discouraged in the classroom" and some languages were classified as non-viable (Kreindler, 1989: 50). Although Stalinist glorification of Russian eventually ceased, in practice mastery of Russian became essential to success as 14 to 17 per cent of classroom time came to be spent on teaching Russian and the number of non-Russian languages of instruction in the Russian Republic decreased from 47 in the early 1960s to 16 by 1982 (Kreindler, 1989: 51, 54). As a result, many parents concerned for their children's future did not encourage them to invest their intellectual energies in learning no longer viable languages.

Under Brezhnev the Russocentrism in Soviet language ideology became grotesque as Russian became endowed with high morality and non-Russians were encouraged to abandon their native languages because doing so was touted as progressive, mature and "according to the laws of natural development" (Kreindler, 1989: 56). In practice, this meant that parents were encouraged to speak only Russian at home with their children in order to save them from the stigma of speaking Russian 'with an accent'. Gorbachev did not alter Soviet language policy, although, like Khrushchev, he did not glorify Russian. By 1989, when Tatar-language reform began to get under way in Tatarstan, people there informed Faller that Tatar schools still operated in Tatar villages, but only two schools in which Tatar was the medium of instruction remained in Kazan. One was a Tatar-English school renowned for the poor quality of its teaching and the other was an *internat*, a boarding school, in that case for half-orphaned rural children. Neither of these were institutions to which future-minded parents would wish to send their children.

American linguist anthropologists Gal and Irvine describe a language ideology originating among nineteenth-century intellectuals, most prominently Herder, which equates the identification of a language with that of a nation; that is, the discovery of a linguistically united community is seen to define a nation. Systematizing relations between ideas of nation and language, Gal and Irvine identify three semiotic practices (recursivity, erasure and 'iconicity') through which language ideologies construct difference. Recursivity involves projecting a difference that exists at some level of relationship onto another level. Erasure refers to a simplification of the sociolinguistic field which renders some people or phenomena invisible. Iconicity involves a shift in the sign relationship so that linguistic features which only index social groups come to be perceived as though semiotically, as if a linguistic feature somehow divulged a social group's essence.[20]

---

[20]   These ideas are most carefully laid out in Gal and Irvine (1995), Irvine (1995) and Irvine and Gal (1994).

Soviet language ideologies constructed linguistic, and hence national, difference among speakers of Turkic and other languages[21] using all three of these semiotic practices. For example, recursivity is employed when Russian-speakers assume that their interlocutors whose spoken Russian is influenced by Turkic phonology are uneducated or employed at the bazaar. That is to say, the perception of Turkic-influenced Russian is seen to indicate rural origins, which, in turn, are supposed to reveal low social status. Providing examples of both iconicity and erasure is a phonemic trait of Turkic languages according to which the same phoneme can be pronounced either as [y] or [j]. When Soviet linguists were called upon to help draw national boundaries in the 1920s, they decided that [y] was a Tatar sound, and thus European, while [j] belonged to Bashkirs, a related people whose titular republic is located to the east of Tatarstan and who are considered Asian.[22] In actuality, both Tatars and Bashkirs use both allophones in their speech. However, when Bashkirs say [j] instead of [y], they are seen to be speaking Bashkir, while, when Tatars say [j], listeners do not notice. This is an example of iconicity, for [j] is seen to iconically index Bashkirness and Asianness, while [y] indicates Tatarness and Europeanness. It is likewise an example of erasure because, when Tatars say [j], it is not heard. That is to say, the particularities of their speech is erased and with it the fluidity of the boundaries that divide Tatars from Bashkirs. Because of the need to present a unified language for study, current Tatar language textbooks continue to erase dialect variation and iconically represent nations as linguistically homogenous, thereby serving as vehicles for maintaining the kind of essentialist language ideology demonstrated by this example.

Consequently, in accordance with Soviet ideologies about the relations between nation and language,[23] Tatar perceptions of the relations between ethnicity and language generally continue to be essentialist. Thus, Tatar is considered to be the native language of ethnic Tatars whether or not they speak some version of that language. In addition, a person is usually considered to be 'Tatar' if Tatar is the nationality inscribed in his or her internal passport,[24] regardless of other factors that could influence ethnic self-identification.[25] Indeed, contrary to reality, Tatars generally do not conceive of the categories of people living in Tatarstan as Russian monoglot and at least bilingual in Russian and some other language, but rather as Tatars and everyone else, who, because of the fact that they are predominantly Russian-speakers, then become perceived iconically as ethnic Russians. Thinking about citizens of

---

[21]   Since there are no adequate linguistic criteria for differentiating between languages and dialects (see Hymes, 1967, for example), when we use the term 'language' we will be referring to language variants that are somehow officially recognized as such.

[22]   The same split is perceived to exist between urban-dwelling Uzbeks in Central Asia and their formerly transhumant neighbours, Kazakhs and Kirghiz. Similarly, Tatars are considered settled, while Bashkirs are categorized as nomadic.

[23]   Kerttula (2000) gives a nice summary of how American ethnographer Lewis Henry Morgan's (1995[1887]) model for cultural evolution was adopted by Engels (1993) and then applied to non-Russians in the Soviet Union.

[24]   We should note that the new Russian Federation passports, against the desires of many people from Tatarstan (and Daghestan), no longer contain the *piataia grafika* in which the holder's nationality was recorded.

[25]   These other factors could include such things as linguistic knowledge, religious affiliation, social networks, particularly close kin, or other relations with people of another ascribed nationality.

Tatarstan as either monoglot Russian-speakers or bilinguals provides more analytical salience in regard to the current situation there than an essentialist approach because the former more accurately represents reality. Moreover, it provides a basis for conceiving of the ways in which people negotiate old, as well as create new, social networks as they struggle to navigate shifting structures in an abruptly reconfigured post-Soviet society.

Nonetheless, Tatar nation-builders should not be faulted for subscribing to nineteenth-century ideologies about the relations between ethnicity and language. For, despite earlier assumptions that socialism was a great equalizer which erased ethnic difference, recent scholarship has suggested that differential access to institutional resources served to enhance national consciousness and promote ethnic particularism (Brubaker, 1996; Slezkine, 1994; Verdery, 1991, 1996). For example, Lemon's (1996, 2000) work among Russian Roma reveals that while Roma play with the stereotypes ascribed to them in Soviet ethnographic and other cultural genres, their choice of possible modes for self-presentation is nevertheless constrained by those stereotypes. Faller's own research in Tatarstan demonstrates that linguistic markers in particular, i.e., accent and grammatical calquing from Tatar into Russian, classify Tatar-speakers as non-normative in their quotidian interactions with fellow Kazan residents. In addition to this, one of the effects of the most recent war in Chechnya, especially in Moscow, is that people who look as if they could possibly be from the Caucasus are under constant threat of harassment by the police. Consequently, and despite the demise of official Soviet policies such as nationality quotas for entrance into university, non-Russian inhabitants of Russia continue to be reminded daily that they are indeed not Russian.

2.   LEGISLATIVE FOUNDATIONS OF LANGUAGE REFORMS

Tatarstan's official language policy is formulated in its Declaration on Sovereignty (1990) and its Constitution (1992), in which two languages, Tatar and Russian, are declared to be official (*gosudarstvenniy*). Tatarstan's sovereignty declaration was the first act of language regulation among constituent polities of the Russian Federation. Currently 14 out of 21 of these polities have passed their own laws on languages. Language legislation has been further developed in the 1992 Act on the Languages of the Peoples of the Republic of Tatarstan, which takes as its bases the need for comprehensive development of the languages and cultures ascribed to the peoples of Tatarstan, which the republic pledges to finance; the spiritual growth of a society supported by ethnic customs and traditions; and the realization of equal rights for all nationalities in social, economic, legal and scientific spheres.

Tatarstan legislation particularly emphasizes government guarantees for citizens' rights to use their own languages and to enjoy basic political, economic, social and cultural rights irrespective of their ability to speak either of the two government languages. According to the law, citizens may choose the language of their children's upbringing and education, and it is considered to be parents' civil duty to teach their national language to their children. All citizens of Tatarstan have the right to be schooled in their national language. The republic provides for the creation of a system of educational institutions in the government languages and contributes to the creation of similar institutions in other languages of the peoples of Tatarstan. In their capacity as government languages Tatar and Russian are studied in preschool institutions, secondary schools and professional schools.

The legislation regulates spheres of government languages use, stressing the fact that any discrimination on the basis of language choice or ability is inadmissible. Subject to special regulation is the employment of the government languages in the structures of the republic's administrational units. The work of the Tatarstan parliament, cabinet, executive administration and other government offices, organizations and elected bodies at all levels, including clerical work, is to be done in Tatar or Russian. Legislative bills may be proposed in either of Tatarstan's government languages. According to the law, mass media (newspapers, magazines, television and radio broadcasting) should be disseminated in both official languages, as well as other languages in regions where significant numbers of speakers live.[26] In industry, transport and communications both languages are *de jure* equal, while in operative communications only Russian is supposed to be used.[27] The Language Act stipulates that academic works may be written in either government language, while suggesting that short summaries of a work's contents be included in the other language. Aimed at developing Tatar culture and disseminating Tatar art among different peoples, the Act provides for the financing of translation, the copying and the publishing of written works.

In order to realize Tatarstan's Language Act, the Parliament adopted in 1994 a special government programme on the preservation, study and development of the Languages of the Peoples of Tatarstan. As part of this effort, the following measures are in the process of being implemented: increasing the number of educational institutions, changing the language of study in some schools from Russian to Tatar, providing for better native language teaching, opening new classes specializing in study of Tatar and developing computer software for studying Tatar. The programme consists of thirteen parts which embrace all organizational, as well as administrative, measures for the functional and structural development of Tatarstan's official languages. Its essential function is to undermine the hegemonic role of Russian and to promote the use of Tatar and other non-Russian languages in Tatarstan. The programme promotes the academic study of the government languages by providing for the creation of guidelines for school textbooks, teach-yourself books, dictionaries and other books for learning and receiving instruction in Tatar. Specialized dictionaries for workers in different spheres of the economy, government and public health services are being published; and conferences on Tatar language development are being organized.

Tatarstan's language policy in preschool, secondary and higher educational institutions attempts to provide for conditions to educate children in their native languages. These efforts include supplying literature and visual aids, creating an integral curriculum for Tatar in primary and secondary schools (1st to 11th grade) and establishing Tatar departments in all higher educational institutions of the republic. Contrary to Soviet-period practice, university applicants now have the right to take their oral admission exams in either Russian or Tatar. Measures to introduce lecturing and teaching in Tatar in Tatarstan's higher educational institutions and the opening of a Tatar national university are planned. A special part of the programme provides for implementing information technologies aimed at broadening the functional spheres of Tatar. To do this, it is necessary to create and disseminate Tatar word-

---

26   Chuvash, for example, are the third most populous nationality in Tatarstan, and consequently the official Tatarstan newspaper press finances the printing of a Chuvash newspaper.

27   In actuality, Russian remains hegemonic in most public domains.

processing programmes and an electronic Tatar encyclopaedia. Special editions of dictionaries devoted to various technical terminologies, as well as translation and spelling dictionaries and Tatar–English, Tatar–German and Tatar–French dictionaries, in which Russian is no longer the obligatory mediating language, are planned.

Aimed at encouraging the study of the government languages, above all Tatar, the programme emphasizes the importance of mass media. The government TV channel used to broadcast a weekly television programme entitled "Let's Study Tatar", the purpose of which was to broaden the sphere of formal Tatar use. Later, the situation changed and the TV programme ceased to be vitally important, because nowadays Tatar is being studied in all secondary schools. Pupils in Russian schools have the same amount of hours of study for Russian and Tatar. In big cities (Kazan, N. Chelny) there are private language courses (Western European languages, Turkish, Tatar) available for the adult population. Other crucial steps for broadening Tatar domains of use include plans to increase the broadcasting capacity of radio and TV channels, institute a short-wave Tatar radio station, create educational films and audio resources for those who want to study Tatar and set up cooperative arrangements with TV and radio stations in other parts of the Russian Federation. The programme includes measures providing for the inclusion of both government languages in all spheres, including restoring pre-Soviet names to some villages, cities and streets. A special part of the programme is devoted to government support to the revival, preservation and development of the languages of nationalities with significant diasporas within Tatarstan's territory.[28] In addition to this, since the Tatars living in Tatarstan make up only one-third of those living in Russia, one part of the programme focuses on issues of revival, application and development of the Tatar language beyond the borders of the Republic of Tatarstan.

3.   BILINGUALISM: THE PRESENT SITUATION

Analysis of surveys demonstrates that language identification in Tatarstan continues to be one of the main indicators of ethnic identification (University of Kalmykiya, 2000; Cheshko and Urazmanova, 2001: 511). As noted above, a person's identification with a particular language is frequently iconically grafted onto his or her ethnic identification. Perception of the relationship between language and ethnicity as iconic can result in a readiness to act to preserve and develop one's national language as a form of ethnolinguistic reproduction of one's own people. Often, the foundations of a person's ethnic orientation start with socialization in the family. Because Tatars consider that speaking Tatar is not only a means of communicating, but likewise a sign of respect towards Tatar culture and the people who are seen to embody it, part of being socialized into Tatar cultural values requires being socialized in the Tatar language. Some anthropologists similarly believe that cultural knowledge is embedded in the language in which it is communicated, although they deny the validity of an iconic relation between the two.[29]

---

[28]   In addition to opening Tatar schools, it should be noted that the Tatarstan government has been likewise developing school curricula for other indigenous nationalities, for example, Mari and Chuvash. Moreover, when seeking to renationalize its schools, the neighbouring Mari Republic's Ministry of Education borrowed Mari-language materials from Tatarstan (Uli Schamiloglu, personal communication, July 2000).

[29]   See for example Boas (1911), Sapir (1949) and Whorf (1942) on how grammatical categories affect awareness.

Accepting a particular language as native, however, does not necessarily mean speaking it proficiently. According to the 1994 all-Russia micro-census, 97.8 per cent of Tatars in the republic considered Tatar to be their native language. At the same time, only 81.6 per cent of Tatars report using Tatar with family members, which means that the national language has ceased to be the language of communication, even in the domestic domain, for one-fifth of Tatarstan's Tatars. The number of active Tatar speakers is even lower. In 1999 about 35 per cent of Tatar city-dwellers between 15–30 years of age[30] reported speaking Russian at home exclusively or most of the time (among villagers this proportion is only nine per cent). Approximately one-quarter of young urban Tatars say they speak Tatar at home (in villages it is 60 per cent). Forty-one per cent of urban dwellers and twenty per cent of villagers report speaking Russian and Tatar at home in equal measure. Thus, although ethnic Tatars comprise more than half the population,[31] Russian-speakers, nonetheless, dominate even within the Republic of Tatarstan, which is itself surrounded by the Russian Federation.

More than 90 per cent of ethnic Tatar respondents "speak, read and write fluently in Russian" (Garipov *et al.*, 2000: 41). The Russian language retains a high status not only for monoglot Russian-speakers in Tatarstan, but also for Tatars being educated in Tatar. The stigma attached to not speaking Russian, or even speaking 'with an accent', is such that people speaking marked Russian are considered to be culturally and (consequently) intellectually inferior to people who speak fluent, unaccented Russian.[32] This language ideology can negatively influence a speaker's opportunities for professional and other kinds of advancement. This is the main reason why parents do not want their children to be educated in Tatar schools. Indeed, their children can only have access to a full spectrum of educational possibilities if they can demonstrate functional knowledge of their school subjects in Russian. Although university entrance exams *de jure* may be taken in Tatar, the *de facto* medium of instruction in universities is almost always Russian.

Despite these difficulties, three per cent of young Russians speak Russian and Tatar equally well, up from a reported 1.1 per cent in the 1989 Soviet census (Ravieau, 1992). Beyond this, our research reveals some other details concerning ethnic Russians reported abilities in Tatar not explored in earlier works: those who speak Tatar with some difficulty (7.5 per cent), those who speak it with great difficulty (12.2 per cent) and those who do not speak Tatar, but understand it (21 per cent). Certainly, the shift in attitudes towards the Tatar language must account in part for these changes in reported knowledge. Indeed, it may be

---

[30]   The figures here are based on representative interviews of the 15–30 age group of the Republic conducted by Garipov in 1999. The interviews were held according to stratified multi-staged selection in seven towns and six rural districts. While selecting the units of observation all parameters of sex, age, nationality (ethnic group) and occupation were met. 1,000 workers, clerks, high school, college and university students were interviewed, a high enough number allowing for a selection mistake of five per cent. All Russians and Tatars were asked the following questions: 1. How fluently do you speak Russian? 2. How fluently do you speak Tatar? The interviewees had a choice of answers: A. Fluently speak, read, and write. B. Speak with difficulty. C. Understand, but do not speak. D. Do not know the language (see Garipov, 1999).

[31]   Tatarstan's Tatar population was estimated at 51.4% in 1999.

[32]   For example, one Russian woman in Kazan lamented to Faller that Tatarstan's President Mintimir Shaimiev is so uneducated and speaks with "such an accent".

possible to predict a certain amount of success for Tatarstan's programme to create a nation based upon these figures (Garipov *et al.*, 2000).

Because speaking the language of one's ascribed nationality is seen to index self-identification, it is considered natural that Russians speak Russian. In contrast to this, only 12 per cent of Tatars between ages 15 and 30 replied that their Tatar is better than their Russian, while 42 per cent say they know Russian and Tatar equally well and 45 per cent admit to speaking Russian better than Tatar. In rural areas the picture is completely different, where 46 per cent of ethnic Tatars report speaking Tatar better than Russian. Fourteen per cent of villagers report speaking Russian better, while 41 per cent of peasants speak Tatar and Russian equally well. Two-thirds of young urban Tatars consider Tatar to be their native language, as compared to 85 per cent in rural areas; about 10 per cent of city-dwellers chose Russian as their native language, while in villages the number is 2 per cent. Reflecting the society in which they live, as opposed to an imagined exclusionary nation, 23 per cent of urban Tatars report having both Russian and Tatar as native languages; in rural areas only 13 per cent.[33] These statistics seem to indicate that the chance of language death among young urban Tatars is high. However, survey work conducted by Faller concerning what language speakers use depending on domain and interlocutor suggests that young urban Tatar-speakers usually have close relatives in villages whom they visit on a regular basis (sometimes weekly) and with whom they report speaking Tatar.

4.   ETHNOLINGUISTIC ORIENTATIONS

When asked, "What is your attitude towards the demands of some national leaders to declare Tatar the sole government language?" 18 per cent of urban Tatars and 53 per cent of villagers replied in the affirmative, while the answer was no for 57 per cent of urban versus 19 per cent of rural residents. Despite the relatively successful reintroduction of Tatar language into Tatarstan schools, more than half of Tatars (53 per cent) still prefer to have their children educated in Russian schools, while in raising their children 68 per cent of Tatars are ethnically oriented. Among urban Tatars only two per cent of respondents expressed the wish to get higher or secondary professional education in the Tatar language; the same index among villagers is 11 per cent. However, the percentages of people wishing to be educated in both Tatar and Russian are higher: 35 per cent and 47 per cent among city-dwellers and villagers, respectively. Nonetheless, 60 per cent of young urban Tatars and 37 per cent of villagers responded that education beyond the high school level should be in Russian (Garipov, 1999: 134–154).

Older Tatar speakers rightly note that young Tatars perceive Russian as the medium for higher education because that is indeed the reality of the situation. Thus, the former advocate the creation of a Tatar university, which has been approved by the Tatarstan parliament. Already up and running in Kazan is a similar initiative in a Muslim university (*mädräsä*). Local ethnologist Damir Iskhakov told Faller in a 1997 interview that the reason for opening a Muslim university in Tatarstan was to prevent their young people from receiving religious

---

[33]   See note 27.

education abroad and then returning home Islamic fundamentalists. The fact, however, that only one-third of Tatars live within the Republic of Tatarstan hinders the creation of a unified educational system with significantly large numbers of students pursuing degrees in Tatar language. In response to this, some Tatar scholars consider that Tatar language education would become more popular if Tatar schools were to offer courses taught in English. They draw their example from the Republic of Sakha (Yakutia),[34] where English has been decreed the working language of the republic. As a result of this, a number of schools with classes taught in English have been opened and approximately a thousand students are now studying in Great Britain and the United States.

The results of a survey conducted among young citizens of Tatarstan aimed to evaluate the significance or the value level of their native language. We asked a question which was analogous to the principle of E. Bohardus (Tatarova, 1999: 81–82). Participants were asked: "What is the function of your native language?" They were provided with a choice of answers, as follows: 1) The native language is a means of communication; 2) The native language is part of the cultural life of my nation; 3) The native language is the foundation for the development of the cultural life of my nation; 4) The native language guarantees the continued existence of my ethnic community. (The respondents were to choose only one answer. The variants were enumerated in the order of less significance of the native language). Only fifteen per cent of Tatar and sixteen per cent of Russian youth chose option 4. At the same time, 32.5 per cent of Tatars and 59 per cent of Russians consider their ascribed native languages to be no more than just a means of communication. Survey participants were asked, "Which of the following languages (Tatar, Russian, European languages, Turkish, Arabic) would you like to master? List them in order of preference". Both Tatars and Russians named their ascribed native language first and the other group's language second. This indicates that the young generation appears to be inclined to be linguistically tolerant. These results also testify to signs of healthy pragmatism among young Tatarstan people, as one's neighbour's language can be useful in everyday life. The preferences for foreign languages practically coincide for both Tatarstan's major nationalities: Both Tatars and Russians prefer knowing European languages to Turkish and Arabic, most likely because English has come to function as the language of international communication.

5.   CREATING A SYSTEM OF NATIONAL EDUCATION

The level of education available to Tatars greatly increased during the years of Soviet power, but that education was received at the cost of ethnic assimilation. Soviet schools, in comparison with the religious schools of the pre-revolutionary period, were completely dependant upon the state and served the ideological purposes of 'rapprochement and integration'; that is, they effectively ended up being Russifying institutions. Schooling in the former Soviet Union was supposed to be national only in form, while its content had to be socialist as part of the ideology of proletarian internationalism. By contrast with the past, there are currently real efforts to offer people guarantees of equal treatment irrespective of the linguistic, cultural or

---

[34]   Another Turkic-speaking constituent republic of the Russian Federation.

confessional group to which they belong. For example, every pupil has a choice of at least two languages in which to study, which was hardly imaginable ten years ago.[35]

In a multi-national republic it is very important and difficult to provide all citizens belonging to different ethnic groups with the right to obtain education in their native languages. In 2000, Tatarstan children of different ethnic groups are being educated in their languages as follows: 100 per cent of Russian children, 48 per cent of Tatar children, 55 per cent of Chuvash children, 71 per cent of Udmurt children, 49 per cent of Mari children and eight per cent of Mordva children. Beyond this, nationality cultural centres host 28 extracurricular schools where more than 2,000 children of different ethnic groups are being taught their native languages. In Kazan, which has a population of over one million (40 per cent of which is Tatar), there are 45 music schools, but only three of them hold classes in Tatar; only one out of nine art schools is Tatar. Of the 8,500 children attending music and art schools, 3,010 are ethnic Tatars, but only 18 per cent of these are taught in Tatar language.[36]

Reforms to Tatarstan's educational system are considered essential to the revival of Tatar national culture. Part of this revival is intended to instil Tatar cultural values (respect for elders and temperance regarding alcohol) in Tatar children, teaching them respect for differences and to be trilingual (in Tatar, Russian and a third language). Taking these parameters into account and using both Tatarstan's and Russian Federation's laws on education as a foundation, the History Institute at the Tatarstan Academy of Science has developed an integrated national doctrine for reforming the educational system. The doctrine is aimed at fomenting conditions for the stable development of the Republic of Tatarstan with regard to its readiness to meet the demands and challenges of the twenty-first century, which include devoting resources to re-imbuing Tatar national form with what is perceived as Tatar cultural content, as well as promoting interethnic unity and civil harmony, social and professional mobility, raising the standard of living and public health to an adequate level, and providing universal basic education. The doctrine is based on the principle that the intellectual potential of new generations is Tatarstan's national wealth. It is therefore considered necessary for Tatarstan's national system of education to end its Soviet-period isolation and become integrated into global educational communities.[37] The doctrine's creators emphasize that Tatarstan occupies a special cultural space. It is different from other regions of the Russian Federation in the following ways: the official status of both Tatar and Russian languages, the peaceful co-existence of Islam and Christianity, as well as of a multi-national population. But they also stress that Tatars, whose culture is considered to contain both Muslim and European elements, comprise the main nationality of the republic.

There are two types of national schools in the republic: schools where children study all school subjects in the Tatar language, and Russian-Tatar schools where subjects are supposed to be taught in both languages, but where the primary language of instruction continues to be Russian. In 420 of these schools there are classes made up exclusively of Tatar children.

---

[35] Children living in areas with concentrations of populations neither Tatar nor Russian in nationality have the opportunity to study in the language of the local population.

[36] Current Statistics of the Department of Culture of the Administration of the city of Kazan.

[37] See National Doctrine for Developing Educational Systems in the Republic of Tatarstan.

Currently 63 per cent of Tatar children attend pre-school in Tatar language, while ten years ago only 10.6 per cent of them did so. In 1,220 out of Tatarstan's 2,503 schools teaching is conducted in Tatar. Forty-eight per cent of ethnic Tatar children (34 per cent of urban and 64.9 per cent of rural children) are educated in Tatar. Ten years ago these figures were estimated at twelve per cent (Shaimiev, 2000).

The introduction of Tatar language into the school curriculum for all children at all levels is of fundamental importance. The fact that 98.5 per cent of school pupils of all nationalities currently study Tatar language is an important step on the way to turning *de jure* equality of both government languages into reality. Introducing Tatar language into different educational venues, however, has met with a number of difficulties, including shortages of qualified teachers and textbooks, as well as continuing prejudice against Tatar language speakers. In 1998, for example, due to the sudden jump in demand for teachers of Tatar as the language became an obligatory subject for all school children, Tatarstan suffered from a shortage of 2,000 teachers.[38] This situation, however, has been since ameliorated, in part by paying teachers of Tatar salaries fifteen per cent higher than teachers of other subjects. However, teachers' salaries are so low (now about 30 USD/month) and so irregularly paid by the federal government that working as a teacher is not a terribly attractive profession for the young people benefiting from Tatarstan's blossoming education system. Until quite recently, the majority of Tatar teachers produced to meet the new demand had undergone quick and apparently not thorough 'requalification' courses. Some of these new teachers, many of whom had been teachers of other subjects, possessed enough intellectual agility to become effective teachers, but many of them, previously confined to low-level positions (e.g., cafeteria workers) remain uninspired in their teaching methods.[39] This problem is particularly acute in Russian-language schools. In addition to this, almost all teachers are women and those who are unmarried have little hope of finding husbands at their places of work. An unmarried Tatar-speaking woman may decide that selling clothing at the bazaar or working in a shop is more profitable and perhaps even more pleasant than taking on the burden of being a school teacher.[40] The Soviet-period prestige attached to working as a teacher is evaporating as the development of the market reduces the value of intellectual endeavour and increases the attractiveness of capital.

In response to recent demands to improve Tatar pedagogical methods, Kazan Pedagogical University introduced courses in Tatar language and literature and the history of

---

[38]   Damir Iskhakov, unpublished interview by Faller in 1997.

[39]   Rosalinda Musina (1996) describes the ethnic division of labour in Tatarstan in the late 1980s: more Tatars work in agriculture and unskilled manual labour, while a smaller percentage of Tatars are employed in academic and scientific jobs. For 1987, she cites the following figures: Tatars make up 34.9 per cent of Tatarstan's scholars and researchers (while 56.2 per cent are Russian); however, they represent 48.3 per cent and 42.9 per cent, respectively, of the workforce as a whole (1996: 199).

[40]   Teachers in Tatarstan, like teachers in other parts of the former Soviet Union, are expected to perform all kinds of tasks beyond simply teaching during classroom time and coaching during their office hours. In addition to chaperoning school dances and other events, they are expected to paint their schools' hallways at the end of every summer and to maintain their classrooms, the material support for which (paint, wallpaper, fabric for curtains) often comes from their pupils' parents. The labour, however, is their own.

Tatarstan, as well as in the teaching of English and Arabic languages in Tatar schools. The Department of Tatar Philology, History and Eastern Languages at Kazan State University has continued to train a growing number of Tatar teachers. A Tatar National Institute was founded not long ago.

At present, more than half of ethnic Tatar children still attend Russian-language schools. According to Tatar public opinion, the main disadvantage of Russian-language schools for Tatar children is the socialization of children according to the values of another nationality's culture. This is thought to result in a negative perception of one's native culture and language as inferior, and consequently results in estrangement from them. Only an educational system in which children can be schooled up through university level, and thereafter work in Tatar can produce a generation with an active national self-consciousness. Gellner asserts that a political unit does not possess vital capacity unless it is able to support a system of national education (Gellner, 1991: 86). The acuteness of the situation becomes more apparent if we bear in mind another positive characteristic of the Tatar national school. Tatar children who study in Tatar schools are generally more successful than ethnic Russian children or Tatars who study in Russian-dominant schools. According to Kazan's Department of Education, Tatar school pupils have only very rarely been involved in cases of juvenile delinquency over the past ten years (1989 to 1998), that is, from the time when Tatar schools began to be re-opened in the city. During the same period, one in four boys studying either in Russian or Russian-Tatar schools was involved in at least one criminal incident. A great number of juvenile crimes committed by Tatars could be explained by the marginalization of a significant part of Tatarstan's Tatar population (abandoning their Tatar-speaking social networks, while failing, nonetheless, to integrate into dominant Russophone cultural practices).[41] The percentage of graduates from Tatar high schools successfully enrolled at higher educational institutions in the city of Kazan is higher than the average percentage for all schools in the city (in the 1998–1999 academic year 81.5 per cent of Tatar high school graduates were enrolled at higher educational institutions, while among all graduates of the city this percentage was 78 per cent, and among Tatarstan's high school graduates overall only 50.8 per cent).

The Republic of Tatarstan has a well-developed network of higher educational institutions. In the 1998–1999 academic year, there were eighteen higher educational institutions and seven auxiliary campuses in which 81,800 students were enrolled (25,800 of them were attending night school). Since the 1980s, ethnic Tatar representation among students in higher education institutions has been proportional to their percentage in Tatarstan's population as a whole. While in the 1960s, there were two Russians for every Tatar enrolled in Tatarstan institutions, since 1980 the ratio has evened out. During the 1989–1990 academic year Tatar students made up 45.6 per cent of enrolment, as compared to Russians at 42.9 per cent. Since 1999, enrolment in higher educational institutions has been 51 per cent Tatar and 42.7 per cent Russian, which corresponds to the nationality ratios in the republic. The ethnic division of fields of study is such that the majority of Tatar students are enrolled in Tatarstan's Agriculture and Veterinary Academies and pedagogical universities, while few pursue technical degrees.

---

[41]   For details on how these processes affected people, see Faller (2002).

At present there are no institutions beyond the high school level in which classes are held exclusively in Tatar. However, at Kazan State University and Kazan Pedagogical University courses are taught in Tatar to students preparing to become Tatar teachers and philologists, as well as to Tatar-speakers pursuing law, economics and other degrees, and the students receive supplementary training so as to be able to pursue their professions bilingually. As they do in elementary and high school, Russian monoglot university students continue to be taught the Tatar language at university, usually with Russian as the medium of instruction. University-level study of Tatar is voluntary after the first year; more advanced knowledge of Tatar, however, brings with it the promise of better qualifications and employment possibilities for young people wanting to remain in Tatarstan. Not all university-level institutions have the facilities and infrastructure to offer Tatar to their students, however. In fifteen of Tatarstan's higher educational institutions, 5,600 students (about twenty per cent of Tatar students) are delivered lectures in some courses or tutored in Tatar. The number of students pursuing science majors in Tatar is minute, between 20–50 people.

6.   THE POLITICS OF ALPHABETS

Until 1926, when a Latinized script was adopted, Tatar language was written in non-standardized versions of Arabic script. At that time, there was considerable debate regarding alphabet change for all Turkic languages. Proponents of change, like Lenin, considered Latin script to be technically easier to learn than Arabic (and therefore switching to a new writing system would promote mass literacy), while at least as important an undercurrent was Arabic's perceived unsuitability because of its associations with Islam (Crisp, 1989: 23–26). Opponents denied that there was a difference in difficulty in terms of learning Arabic *vis-à-vis* Latin script. At that time of transformative modernizations, there was even talk of modernizing Russian by Latinizing its alphabet.[42] However, this trend towards opening Soviet society to new possibilities beyond the experiences of Russian imperialism ended under Stalin's rule and all the alphabets of Soviet languages, save Georgian and Armenian, were changed to some form of Cyrillic in the 1930s; this was the case for Tatar in 1936.

Although this factor did not enter into published debates on alphabet change, perhaps the most important difference these reforms made concern the division of various Turkic-speakers living in the Soviet Union into discrete nationalities. Prior to the 1920s alphabet changes which occurred all across the Soviet Union, people who were literate in one Turkic language could read texts written in any other Turkic language, for Arabic script does not mark dialectal vowel differences which constituted the greatest barrier to communication between speakers of different Turkic languages at the turn of the twentieth century. However, the Cyrillic alphabets introduced for Turkic languages provided different spellings—not only for vowel qualities, but also for consonants—for words common to all of them. Thus, one of the implicit changes caused by alphabet changes in the Soviet Union was to create "unique languages" which Stalin considered one of the criteria for being a nation (Stalin, 1950a; 1950b) and simultaneously discouraged pan-Turkic connections across newly formed borders.

---

[42]   In fact, Russian's Cyrillic alphabet was simplified so as to facilitate literacy.

Since the collapse of the Soviet Union, not surprisingly, one of the independence projects of the Turkic republics (Azerbaijan, Kazakhstan, Kyrgyzstan, Turkmenistan, Uzbekistan, as well as Tatarstan) has been to re-introduce Latin scripts for their written languages. To this end, two international congresses have been convened, the first in Ankara in 1990, and a second in Kazan in 1994. The goal of these meetings was to create a common Turkic alphabet so that Turkic speakers of different nationalities would be able to read each other's publications. The model representatives from the former Soviet Union took home from Ankara closely reflected Turkish. However, it was variously modified after the initial congress so as to represent the individual sound variations local scholars wanted to see maintained in writing. Thus, the tensions between pan-Turkic commonalties in self-identification and divisiveness among different Turkic groups continued to exist in the post-Soviet period.

Besides the value of being able to communicate with speakers of similar dialects without having to revert to Russian, Tatar speakers likewise cite as benefits of adopting a Latin script greater access to globalized computer technologies and improved spoken ability by children studying Tatar, who, they believe, will no longer pronounce Tatar texts as if they were reading Russian.[43]

Tatarstan finally adopted by law in 1999 their long-debated Latin script for the Tatar language. There has been a great deal of negative reaction to this from Moscow—it has been treated by Russian journalists as a kind of treachery; other journalists outside Tartastan also reviewed the measure critically.[44] More frighteningly, the Russian Duma passed a measure in 2000 stating that Tatarstan's adoption of Latin script was a threat to Russian national security and banned other constituents of the Russian Federation (such as Bashkortostan, where up to 30 per cent of the population is ethnic Tatar) from using the Latin script to print the Tatar language.[45] Despite these reactions, however, Tatarstan persists in its efforts to Latinize: beginning with the 2000–2001 school year, 60 schools began to teach the Latin script as part of their Tatar lessons. The goal is to completely Latinize Tatar over the course of the next ten years. In response to objections from Moscow concerning Latinization, many Tatar-speakers explain that their cultural integration into Russian linguistic space is too comprehensive to be dismantled by writing their native language in a different alphabet.

CONCLUSION

The Republic of Tatarstan has been developing its own language policy since it became a sovereign republic in 1990. Tatar and Russian are the official languages of Tatarstan. The number of Tatar students and students of other ethnic groups being educated in their native language has greatly increased. The tempo of Tatar mass media growth is high. At the same time, Tatar is still extremely rarely used in management, parliament, government structures, law and

---

[43] Faller's 1999–2000 research in Kazan schools has demonstrated that pronouncing Tatar as if it were Russian is indeed a problem for urban school children.

[44] See, for example, Alimov and Yusin (1999).

[45] *Zvezdi povol'zhiia*, January 2001.

economic production spheres. Russian has retained high prestige and obvious necessity for Tatars. The government of Tatarstan and the peoples of the republic realize that the solution of language problems will take more than one or two decades, but the long-established traditions of mutual understanding and tolerance create favourable conditions for successfully achieving these goals.

REFERENCES

Alimov, Gayaz and Maksim Yusin (1999) "Yazychniki: 'Yazykovaya reforma' zadumannaya vlastyami Kazani, mozhet possorit' russkikh i tatar". *Izvestiya*, 23 September 1999: 1.

Barth, Fredrik (ed.) (1969) *Ethnic Groups and Boundaries*. Boston: Little, Brown and Company.

Boas, Franz (1911) "Introduction". In *The Handbook of American Indian Languages*. Washington: Bureau of American Ethnology.

Brubaker, Rogers (1996) *Nationalism Reframed: Nationhood and the National Question in the New Europe*. New York: Cambridge University Press.

Cheshko, S.V. and R.K. Urazmanova (eds.) (2001) *Tatary*. Moscow: Nauka.

Chikobava, A. (1951) "On Certain Problems of Soviet Linguistics". In John Murra, Robert Hankin, and Fred Holling (eds., trans.) *The Soviet Linguistic Controversy*. New York (Morning Side Heights): King's Crown Press, pp.20–29.

Crisp, Simon (1989) "Soviet Language Planning since 1917–1953." In Michael Kirkwood (ed.) *Language Planning in the Soviet Union*, London: Macmillan in association with the School of Slavonic and East European Studies, University of London, pp.23–46.

Engels, Friedrich (1993) *Origins of the Family, Private Property and the State*. New York: International Publishers.

Faller, Helen (2002) "Repossessing Kazan as a Form of Nation-Building". *Journal of Muslim Minority Affairs*, 22(1): 81–90.

Gal, Susan and Judith Irvine (1995) "The Boundaries of Languages and Disciplines: How Ideologies Construct Difference." *Social Research*, 62(4): 967–1001.

Garipov, Yagfar Z. (1999) *Ethnic Aspects of Education/Urgent Problems in Education*. Moscow: Ministry of Education of the Russian Federation (in Russian).

Garipov, Yagfar Z., Y. R. Zinnurova, *et al.* (2000) *Modern Ethnocultural Processes in the Youth Environment of Tatarstan: Language, Religion, Ethnics*. Kazan: RIC Shkola (In Russian).

Gellner, Ernest (1991) *Nations and Nationalism*. Moscow: Progress (in Russian).

Hymes, Dell (1967) "Linguistic Problems in Defining the Concept of 'Tribe'". In John Baugh and Joel Sherzer (eds.) *Language in Use. Readings in Sociolinguistics*. Engelwood Cliffs: Prentice-Hall, pp.7–27.

Irvine, Judith (1995) "The Family Romance of Colonial Linguistics: Gender and Family in Nineteenth-Century Representations of African Languages". *Pragmatics*, 5(2): 139–153.

Irvine, Judith and Susan Gal (1994) "Language Ideology and Linguistic Difference". Revised version of a paper submitted to the Seminar on Language Ideologies, School of American Research, Sante Fe, NM, April 1994.

Karamzin, Nikolay M. (1969) *Istoriia Gosudarstva Rossijskago.* The Hague, Paris: Mouton.

Kerttula, Anna M. (2000) *Antler on the Sea: The Yup'ik and Chukchi of the Russian Far East.* Ithaca, NY: Cornell University Press.

Kreindler, Isabelle T. (1989) "Soviet Language Planning since 1953". In Michael Kirkwood (ed.) *Language Planning in the Soviet Union*. London: Macmillan in association with the School of Slavonic and East European Studies, University of London, pp.46–63.

Lemon, Alaina (1996) "Hot Blood and Black Pearls: Socialism, Society, and Authenticity at the Moscow Teatr Romen". *Theatre Journal*, 48: 477–492.

Lemon, Alaina (2000) *Between Two Fires: Gypsy Performance and Romani Memory from Pushkin to Postsocialism.* Durham, N.C.: Duke University Press.

Lewis, E. Glyn (1972) *Multilingualism in the Soviet Union: Aspects of Language Policy and its Implementation.* The Hague and Paris: Mouton.

Lysenko, Trofim D. (1948) *The Science of Biology Today.* New York: International Publishers.

Morgan, Lewis Henry (1995[1887]) *Ancient Society.* Tucson: University of Arizona Press.

Musina, Roza (1996) "Contemporary Ethnosocial and Ethnopolitical Processes in Tatarstan". In Leokadia Dobrizheva *et al.* (eds.) *Ethnic Conflict in the Post-Soviet World: Case Studies and Analysis.* Armonk, N.Y.: M.E. Sharpe, pp.195–208.

Pelenski, Jaroslav (1974) *Russia and Kazan: Conquest and Imperial Ideology (1438–1560s).* The Hague and Paris: Mouton.

Ravieau, J.R. (1992) "Tipy natsionalizma, obshchestvo i politika v Tatarstane". *Polis*, 5(6): 42–58.

Republic of Tatarstan (2000) *Statistical Data of the Republic of Tatarstan.* Kazan: Office of Statistics.

Sapir, Edward (1949) *Selected Writings of Edward Sapir.* Berkeley: University of California Press.

Shaimiev, Mintimer S. (2000) "Ten Years of Strengthening Sovereignty". *Republic of Tatarstan* 30 (August) (in Russian).

Slezkine, Yuriy (1994) "The USSR as a Communal Apartment, or How a Socialist State Promoted Ethnic Particularism". *Slavic Review*, 53(2): 414–452.

Soyfer, Valeriy (1994) *Lysenko and the Tragedy of Soviet Science.* New Brunswick: Rutgers.

Stalin, Joseph (1950a) "On Marxism and Linguistics". In *The Soviet Linguistic Controversy*, translated by John Murra, Robert Hankin and Fred Holling, 1951. New York (Morningside Heights): King's Crown Press, pp.70–75.

Stalin, Joseph (1950b) "Replies to Comrades". In *The Soviet Linguistic Controversy*, trans. John Murra, Robert Hankin and Fred Holling, 1951. New York (Morningside Heights): King's Crown Press, pp.96–98.

Starovoytova, Galina (1991) "Bez pobedy demokratii nazionalnyh problem ne reshit". *Komsomolets Tatarstana*, 28, 19 July 1991.

Suny, Ronald Grigor (1997) *The Revenge of the Past: Nationalism, Revolution, and the Collapse of the Soviet Union*. Stanford, CA: Stanford University Press.

Tatarova, G.G. (1999) *Methodology of Data Analyses in Sociology*. Moscow: Nota Bene (in Russian).

Tatar Institute of History (1998) *National Doctrine of Development of Educational Systems in the Republic of Tatarstan*. Kazan: Institut Istorii AN Tatarstan.

University of Kalmykia (2000) "Languages of the Peoples of Russia: Perspectives of Development". Paper presented at the Elista seminar. State University of Kalmykia.

Verdery, Katherine (1991) *National Ideology under Socialism: Identity and Cultural Politics in Ceausescu's Romania*. Berkeley: University of California Press.

Verdery, Katherine (1996) *What Was Socialism, and What Comes Next?* Princeton: Princeton University Press.

Whorf, Benjamin L. (1942) "Language, Mind, and Reality". In John B. Carroll (ed.) *Language, Thought, and Reality*. Cambridge: MIT Press, pp.246–270.

Kalmykia: Language Promotion Against All Odds

François Grin

Kalmykia: Language Promotion Against All Odds

François Grin[46]

INTRODUCTION

Kalmykia may be described as a nation back from the brink. Until a recent past, when the personality of an eccentric leader generated media attention, the Kalmyks were known essentially for one reason: they were one of the peoples deported under Stalin, and permitted to return in the wake of Khrushchev's famous speech at the 20th Congress of the Communist Party in 1956.

However, Kalmykia deserves attention for reasons other than its highly original cultural, religious and linguistic traits. Recent developments in these areas indicate a remarkably modern (some would say post-modern) perspective on identity, bearing witness to the resilience of a people that has been confronted with particularly severe hardship through most of the twentieth century. This chapter provides an account of this process, with particular emphasis on Kalmykia's new language legislation.

In Section 1, I present some general background information about the history and current economic situation of Kalmykia. Section 2 discusses recent political and institutional developments and describes the current position of the Kalmyk language. Section 3 is devoted to key issues addressed in the October 1999 Language Act of the Republic of Kalmykia. Section 4 proposes an assessment of the significance and potential effects of the Kalmyk Language Act.

1. KALMYKIA: ESSENTIAL FACTS AND FIGURES

There is very little published scholarly work on Kalmykia, and it is useful to begin by recalling basic information.

Kalmykia is one of the member republics of the Russian Federation. It is located in a region of dry steppe between the Black and the Caspian seas, south of the Volga and north of

---

[46]   An earlier version of this chapter has been published in the *Journal of Genocide Research* (Grin, 2001). The author thanks Dónall Ó Riagáin, Henry Huttenbach, Farimah Dafatary, Kinga Gál, Priit Järve and Bossia Kornoussova for helpful comments, and William McKinney for research assistance. The usual disclaimer applies.

the Caucasus range; the capital, Elista, is 280 km from Volgograd and 350 km from Grozny. According to the accepted definitions, Kalmykia is still part of Europe, and presents itself as such. The Republic of Kalmykia covers a land area of 76,100 square km, with a maximum north-south span of 640 km, and a maximum east-west span of 480 km. It borders the Republic of Dagestan, the Stavropol *Kray*, the *Oblasts* of Rostov, Volgograd and Astrakhan, and has a stretch of approximately 100 km of Caspian Sea coastline (Figure 2.1).

Figure 2.1
Kalmykia

Recent population figures vary depending on the sources quoted, but range from 317,000 to 330,000; the 1989 census reports a total population of 322,579. For the purposes of this chapter, let us accept 325,000 as an adequate estimate, yielding a population density of a little over four inhabitants per square km. A little less than 40 per cent of the population is considered 'urban' (gorodskoye) mostly in the capital city of Elista, with a population of approximately 95,000.

This population is ethnically diverse, with two groups dominating, namely, Kalmyks and Russians; non-Kalmyks tend to concentrate in urban areas. The breakdown of the resident population by ethnic group is provided in Table 2.5.

Table 2.5
Ethnic Composition of Kalmykia

Ethnic Group	Absolute Number	Percentage
Kalmyks	146,316	45.4
Russians	121,531	37.7
Dargins	12,878	4.8
Chechens	8,329	2.6
Kazakhs	6,277	1.9
Germans	5,586	1.7
Ukrainians	4,069	1.3
Avars	3,871	1.2
Kumyks	1,530	0.5
Belarussians	1,334	0.4
Others	8,067	2.5
TOTAL	319,788	100.0

SOURCE: http://eawarn.tower.ru/most (1999)

The history of the Kalmyks is one of a small nomadic people[47] that has always lived on the fringes of greater powers, and has suffered rather than benefited from any notice those powers took of them.[48]

This 'ethnic' composition, however, tells us little about the 'linguistic' make-up of the country, which shall be discussed later.

The Kalmyks are a western Mongolian people whose language is related to Mongolian; their main religion is Tibetan Buddhism, which makes them one of the three Buddhist peoples of the Russian Federation (along with the somewhat more numerous Buriat and Tuvan peoples) and the only Buddhist people in Europe.[49] This culturally important feature

---

[47]　In this chapter, the Kalmyks will be referred to as a 'people', even though groups comprising more than 30,000 to 35,000 people are often referred to as 'nationalities' by Russian scholars (as distinct from numerically smaller 'ethnic groups'). The use of the term 'people' is, however, in keeping with Kalmyk legal texts, which mention "the peoples of the Republic of Kalmykia", implicitly defining the Kalmyks as one of them (see Hairullin, 1997).

[48]　The information provided by different sources is never quite the same, although sources generally do not contradict each other. The most complete account in English, particularly for recent history, can be found in Tolz (1993), who quotes more detailed Russian sources; much of the information in this section comes from this particular source. See also Mark (1998).

[49]　Some Kalmyks, however, have converted to orthodox Christianity (Tishkov, 1997: 106). The Buryats, who are concentrated in the Buryat Republic east of Lake Baikal in Siberia, also speak (notwithstanding a generalized language shift to Russian) a Mongolian language. The Tuvans, most of whom live in the Tuvan Republic just north of the north western corner of Mongolia, are descendants of Turkified Mongol nomadic groups; they speak a Turkic language, but they are also one of the few peoples of the Russian Federation in which the local language is actually used by a majority of the population, and in which Russian is not in an overwhelmingly dominant position.

is currently gaining increasing legitimacy in Kalmykia, and is used, along with language, to articulate a reawakening sense of identity.

The Kalmyks lived as nomadic herdsmen in Mongolia and Dzungaria, corresponding to (Chinese) Xingjian. They are descendants of the Oirots (or Oyrats), a western Mongolian group.[50] In the seventeenth century, they migrated westwards towards the Caspian Sea,[51] reaching the Volga in 1608. Tsar Peter the Great recognized their organization as a Khanate in 1664, whereby an approximate number of 270,000 became subjects of the Russian empire. However, the arrival of ethnic Russians and Germans invited by Catherine the Great resulted in competition for Kalmyk lands in the course of the eighteenth century. In 1771, the Kalmyk Khan, along with most of the Kalmyk population that had settled east of the Volga (a total estimated at 125,000 people), decided to migrate back to the pastures left by their ancestors 150 years before; sources differ as to the reason for this return migration, as well as to the fate met by those who joined it.[52]

The Kalmyk Khanate was dissolved, and the remaining Kalmyk population in the region, mostly west of the Volga, found itself incorporated into Astrakhan Province, and Kalmykia progressively became a colony on the outer fringes of the Russian Empire; serfdom was abolished there only in 1892. By 1897, when the first general census was taken, the population of the sparsely populated Kalmyk steppes comprised 95.3 per cent Kalmyks, 3.3 per cent Russians and 1.3 per cent other communities.

The 1917 revolution split the Kalmyks into opposite camps; whereas some sided with the Bolsheviks, others, particularly Don (western) Kalmyks, many of whom belonged to Cossack units, joined the White Army and emigrated to the West after its defeat.[53] In 1919, the Council of People's Commissars recognized the inviolability of Kalmyk lands, and the Kalmyk Autonomous *Oblast* was created in the lower Volga region in 1920; it was upgraded to an autonomous republic in 1936 and adopted its own constitution in 1937.

The setting up of these political structures was, on the one hand, accompanied by alphabetization (with the share of illiterate residents moving from 98 per cent before the revolution to nine per cent just before the Second World War, according to Soviet sources quoted by Nekritch [1982: 66]), and by rapid collectivization; by 1937, 95 per cent of families

---

[50]   The name 'Kalmyk' probably comes from a Turkic term for Oirots who had not converted to Islam; in Russian documents, the name appears at the end of the 16th century (see http://www.nupi.no/PubEng/pub-set-en.htm).

[51]   According to some sources, this migration took over 30 years and was the Kalmyks' response to their progressive eviction by Han Chinese from their traditional pastures (*The Economist*, 20 December 1997); other sources indicate that the westward migration was a much longer process that started in the 16th century, with some Kalmyk groups settling near the Irtysh, Om and Ishim rivers, and moving further westwards towards the Volga basin owing to tensions with Siberian Tatars (see http://www.nupi.no/PubEng/pub-set-en.htm).

[52]   Reasons given include in particular the desire to escape increasing encroachments by new settlers backed by Russia, or the need to help Oirots in Xingjian against the Chinese. Some of these eastward migrants were ultimately resettled along the Ural, Telek and Kuma rivers as well as further east in Siberia.

[53]   This is the foundation of the Kalmyk diaspora, who mostly settled in France and the United States. There also are modest concentrations of ethnic Kalmyks in other parts of the Russian Federation (including a little over 9,000 in North Ossetia, and about 8,000 in the Astrakhan *Oblast*, according to 1989 census figures).

were integrated in the kolkhoz structure. This, however, did not protect the Kalmyks from particularly severe cultural persecution, which started soon after the 1918 uprising of some Kalmyks against the Bolsheviks. Buddhist temples, monasteries, cult objects and Tibetan religious books were systematically destroyed in the late 1920s and in the 1930s. Yet worse was still to come.[54]

By August 1942, Nazi forces had invaded Kalmykia; about 25 per cent of the population fled eastwards across the Volga, but some Kalmyks enrolled in the Red Army deserted in increasing numbers, sometimes forming armed groups who collaborated with the Germans, taking advantage of latent antagonisms between Kalmyks and Russians. The extent of this collaboration is, unsurprisingly, a matter for debate. This point is analysed in detail by Nekritch (1982: 70 ff.), who quotes various sources reporting widely diverging degrees of collaboration, from 1 per cent to about half the population. This upper-bound estimate, however, seems implausible, if only because of the fact that a considerable part of the population had fled or was enrolled in the Red Army; furthermore, the number of Kalmyks enrolled in the Kalmyk military units set up by the Germans in late 1942 (with numbers reportedly ranging from a few hundred to about 5,000 by the end of the war) is small by comparison with the total Kalmyk population living on Soviet soil—about 134,000 in 1939. By January 1943, however, Nazi armies were in retreat, and the Soviet authorities proceeded to reassert their power on Kalmykia. In the course of the purges carried out locally, some Russian-born party dignitaries expressed doubts about the political loyalty of the Kalmyks, fuelling existing misgivings which collaboration had revived. As Nekritch (1982: 80) indicates, such representations, which found their way into reports sent to Moscow, constituted the basis for the accusations of the Central Committee of the Party against the Kalmyk people as a whole. The notification of deportation of the entire population was made on 27 December 1943.

The Kalmyks are therefore one of the 'eight deported nations' under Stalin, along with the Volga Germans, the Karachai, the Chechens, the Ingush, the Balkars, the Crimean Tatars and the Meskhetians.[55] In the course of a few days of late December 1943, 93,139 Kalmyks[56] were herded off and sent away aboard some 46 trains, in inhuman conditions, to scattered locations (mostly in southern-central Siberia[57]). The number of those deported is fairly stable, although Tishkov (1997: 38) reports a figure of 81,000 deportees (stressing, however, that this number does not include those imprisoned or shot), while the UNHCR website mentions a figure of 92,000 deportees. The number of deaths, however, seems to vary more considerably depending on sources, all of whom (for lack of any precise knowledge of the full demographic consequences of deportation) provide percentages rather than absolute numbers. For exam-

---

[54]   In this chapter, I do not discuss the destruction caused by the war in Kalmykia; see Nekritch (1982) for a detailed account.

[55]   In addition to these 'eight nations', some twelve ethnic groups were also deported under Stalinism (see UNHCR, 1996).

[56]   This is the precise figure entered in Beria's report to Stalin.

[57]   Altai and Krasnoyarsk *Krays*, and Omsk and Novosibirsk *Oblasts*; smaller numbers, particularly women and children, were separated from the men and sent to special settlements in the Central Asian republics and to Sakhalin. Deportation also affected the 23,000 Kalmyk men serving in the Red Army.

ple, the *World Directory of Minorities* (MRG, 1997: 299) reports that "a third of the population is thought to have perished during and immediately after deportation". The website of the *Norwegian Institute for International Affairs* (NUPI) indicates that "more than a third" of the population died. *The Economist*, in its issue of 20 December 1997, states that "as many as half" of the Kalmyks died. The lowest estimate is that of the National Committee of Domestic Affairs (NKVD), at nineteen per cent, reported by Tolz (1993). Clearly, such discrepancies reflect the fact that it is almost impossible to fully assess the consequences of interrelated factors directly and indirectly resulting from deportation, or to evaluate the number of deaths that would have occurred 'in the absence' of deportation—among other reasons because Kalmykia, which marks the easternmost advance of the German armies, was directly affected by war and the ensuing casualties. In any event, the scale of the demographic disaster that befell the Kalmyk people can hardly be overstated, and given the extent of social and cultural disruption which can be viewed as caused by deportation, upper-bound estimates should be seen as more relevant.

Putting the finishing touch on Stalin's enterprise of annihilation, the Kalmyk Autonomous Republic was abolished in the same month of December 1943, and its territory split between Dagestan and neighbouring regions.

The Kalmyks were one of the peoples rehabilitated in Khrushchev's speech at the 20th Congress of the Communist Party of the Soviet Union (CPSU) in February 1956; the return to Kalmyk lands was permitted in 1957, with the reinstatement of a Kalmyk Autonomous *Oblast*, restored in 1958 to its former status of autonomous republic.[58] By that time, some fifteen years after deportation, the Kalmyks were barely over 100,000 people. If only because of the fact that the Kalmyks were dispersed over various locations, deportation had further weakened the Kalmyk language and culture.[59]

At the time of the collapse of the USSR, Kalmykia was a particularly poor region of the Union, with an agricultural (mostly livestock-based) economy producing wool and dairy products in addition to oil.

Over the last ten years, the economy has been slowing down considerably. The decline has affected all the mainstays of Kalmykia's essentially rural economy, in particular grain, sunflower oil, potatoes and fruit. Livestock figures have also gone down over the same period, particularly sheep and goat (with a reported 1,177,000 head in 1997, down from over 1,400,000 one year before). This is reflected in a sharp decline in the production of meat and milk; typically, in the second half of the nineties, production was barely at two thirds of the levels of the first half the decade.[60] Published figures suggest that industrial production is

---

[58]   However, two *rayons* of the Astrakhan *Oblast* and some 215,000 hectares in Dagestan were not returned to the Autonomous Republic.

[59]   Khrushchev's speech condemned Stalinism, but formal rehabilitation of the Kalmyks had to wait until the 1991 Act on the Rehabilitation of the Repressed Peoples, and then a speech by Yeltsin on 28 December 1993. Since 1990, 28 December is observed as a memorial day for the victims of deportation. None of the deported peoples were offered any compensation for the hardship suffered during thirteen years of deportation, and three of the "eight nations" (Crimean Tatars, Meskhets and Volga Germans) were denied the right to return.

[60]   See "Sel'skoe khozyaynstvo i prishchevaya promyshlennost'—Respublika Kalmykia", at http://www.society.ru/bibl/polros/Kalmyk/. (Last accessed August 2001).

negligible and stagnant, but according to information directly collected in Kalmykia, industrial production may well have declined further over the last three years. Income per capita is estimated at 38 per cent and living costs at 86 per cent of the Russian Federation average.

The decline in livestock figures is a particularly serious evolution. Sheep historically have an important place in Kalmyk material culture and economy, providing a link to the nomadic tradition as well as valuable milk, meat and high-quality wool. To a large extent, this decline can be traced back to catastrophic ecological damage caused by at least three reasons. This first cause of the damage comes from inappropriate irrigation projects which upset the delicate ecosystem of the region, on which an excessive number of sheep were set grazing[61] since the 1950s. Although attempts are being made at replacing these sheep by camels in some parts of the country, much of the damage is beyond repair. Second, careless uranium mining has resulted in some radio-active contamination. Third, fluctuations in the level of the Caspian Sea expose over 90,000 hectares to floods, while some 3,000 hectares had already been lost in the late 1990s. These floods also destroy property, roads and power lines.

2.   RECENT DEVELOPMENTS: POLITICS, CULTURE AND LANGUAGE

Against this backdrop of deportation, cultural and linguistic persecution, economic pauperization and ecological disaster, recent developments in Kalmykia are surprisingly lively, giving the country a media visibility it had never had enjoyed before. In this section, I briefly review political developments, before moving on to the language aspects.

Perestroika made it possible to question and debate issues such as deportation and ecological problems and opened a space for the reassertion of Kalmyk culture. It also allowed for the expression of nationalist tendencies (exemplified by the 'Kalmyk Popular Front'), which, however, remain confined to a small minority of the Kalmyk population.

In 1990, the Republic of Kalmykia adopted a declaration of sovereignty—yet it ruled out breaking away from the Federation. The creation of the post of president was decided in 1991, but owing to scandals that blemished the reputation of the two top contestants for the job, it was not until 11 April 1993 that a president could be elected in the person of Kirsan Nikolaevich Ilyumzhinov, with some 65 per cent of the vote. Much has been written about the political career, business acumen, personal wealth, often quixotic projects and passion for chess of the young president (born in 1962) (Mark, 1998). Suffice it to say that the presidential campaign in 1992–1993 was characterized by promises to harness the forces of the market and put them at the service of political and economic achievement, to run Kalmykia like a business corporation, to turn it into a second Kuwait and to ensure generalized prosperity. Although these prospects have not materialized, Ilyumzhinov (often simply called "Kirsan" by his compatriots) was re-elected in October 1995. While this presumably reflects a degree of genuine popularity, it would be wrong to suppose (as the magazine *The Economist* did, in December 1997, in a rather patronizing tone) that voters uncritically embrace all his policy choices.

---

[61]   Furthermore, these sheep, imported from the mountainous Caucasus region, had sharp hooves well-suited to rocky terrain but highly damaging for flat grasslands, and they contributed to desertification.

The policies carried out over the past ten years set significant store by heightening the linguistic and cultural profile of the republic, which from 1992 to 1996 bore the Kalmyk name of *Khalmg Tangch*, before taking its current name of the Republic of Kalmykia.

In conjunction with these political events, important developments were taking place in the spheres of culture and language.

First, Tibetan Buddhist religious practice is on the rise, relegitimizing in its wake the associated culture. By 1995, there were some 21 Buddhist temples (including the newly-built *Syakusn-Syume*, reportedly the holiest shrine in the country), seventeen places of worship for Christian denominations and one mosque in Kalmykia. Much is made of the visits of the 14th Dalai Lama in 1991 and 1992; Buddhist teachers have been sent in from abroad to help this revival.

Second, the revitalization of the Kalmyk language is seen as a key element in this renaissance.

Kalmyk is, as noted before, a western Mongolian language—the only one of that family that can be considered indigenous to Europe.[62] In 1648, the (vertically written) Mongolian script was adapted for use in Kalmyk by a monk, Zaya Pandita Namka-Djamtso, whose memory is still the object of deep respect among the Kalmyks. This alphabet, referred to as *Todo Bichig* (meaning 'clear writing') was used until 1924, when it was replaced by the Cyrillic alphabet.[63] Cyrillic was then replaced by the Latin alphabet, but was later reintroduced and has been in use to this day. Despite the attention devoted to the choice of a writing system, Kalmyk only has a limited written language and literary tradition (Tishkov, 1997: 96).

Deportation was a further and major blow to the Kalmyk language, and the scattering of speakers across Siberia and Central Asia was an aggravating factor. Even after the Kalmyks were permitted to return in 1957, the Soviet state applied decidedly assimilationist policies. Khrushchev himself believed that communism would be embraced faster and more enthusiastically by Russian-speaking populations, implying that other languages eventually were a hindrance, and Russification was actively pursued under Brezhnev. In the 1960s and 1970s, drastic cuts were made in native-language education; in the late 1970s, the language of instruction in all schools was Russian. By 1985, according to official statistics, 93 per cent of urban Kalmyks and 87.2 per cent of rural Kalmyks could speak, read and write Russian, but only 27.3 per cent of the former and 45.8 per cent of the latter reportedly had a similar level of competence in Kalmyk (Tishkov, 1997: 96), although 97 per cent of the ethnic Kalmyk reported 'knowledge' of their language.

The striking discrepancy between these figures may be traced back to the ambiguity of language-related questions (and their succession) in Soviet censuses, where the question on 'native language' immediately followed that on 'nationality', inducing respondents to indicate a 'native' mother tongue simply because they had just indicated their national identity, even

---

[62]   Kalmyk is part of the "Oyrat" branch, and therefore one of the Mongolian languages that until recently developed under the influence of classical Mongolian; it is accordingly closer to modern Mongolian (Weinreich, 1981).

[63]   According to the MRG's *World Directory*, this change took place in 1938 only. Somewhat confusingly, the *Directory* writes that "the Kalmyk literary *language* was changed into the Cyrillic *script*" (MRG, 1997: 299; my emphasis).

though "in most cases, at least within Russia, their mother tongue and everyday spoken language was in fact Russian" (Tishkov, 1997: 87). This confusion explains why even scholarly sources are liable to grossly overestimate the number of speakers, for example Comrie (1981: 56), who states that "at present Kalmyk is spoken by 91.7 per cent of the 137,194 ethnic Kalmyk in the USSR"—a figure that, even if correct, would actually apply not to the "ethnic Kalmyk", but only to those living in the erstwhile ASSR—or Price (1998: 279), who indicates that "estimates of the present number of speakers range from 125,000 to 150,000"—which also implies that just about all the Kalmyks actually speak their language.

Unfortunately, the reality is much bleaker. Recent estimates carried out by the recently established institute for the revival of the Kalmyk language suggest that the proportion of fluent speakers does not exceed six per cent among the young, and that in only six settlements (villages) in the country, Kalmyk is used as the main language of communication. According to Kornoussova (1999), 98 per cent of Kalmyk pupils entering school do not speak their 'mother tongue'. To all intents and purposes, despite some recently built Buddhist religious monuments, Elista is now a Russian town where the visible presence of the Kalmyk language is, at best, negligible. Kalmyk is a low-prestige code that can legitimately be categorized as a 'threatened' language, justifying the introduction of the language bill passed by the *Khural* (parliament) and signed into law by the president on 27 October 1999.

3.   LANGUAGE LEGISLATION

The cornerstone of Kalmyk language legislation is the Language Act,[64] which contains 27 articles arranged in a preamble and seven chapters.

The preamble states general goals and principles, stressing in particular the right of the peoples "living on the territory of the Republic of Kalmykia" (hereafter: 'RK') "to freely enjoy their mother tongues in various spheres of public life". The act is intended to provide the conditions "to guarantee the revival, preservation and development of languages as a most important element of the spiritual heritage of the peoples living in the Republic", placing these tasks under the responsibility of the authorities of the RK. The preamble further states that "enmity" and "denigration" are inadmissible, and language-based discrimination forbidden.

Chapter 1 is devoted to general provisions on the legal status of the act (Article 1); language freedom (Article 2); official languages (Article 3); the language rights of all citizens of the Russian Federation (Article 4); guarantees for the "languages of the peoples of the RK" (Article 5)—that is, in addition to official languages; the areas of competence of the government in language policy (Article 6); and the programmes to be designed to implement the Act (Article 7).

Chapter 2 focuses on citizens' language rights in the choice of a language of communication (Article 8), language of education (Article 9) and authorities' involvement in language teaching (Article 10).

---

[64]   On the Languages of the Peoples of the Republic of Kalmykia, signed on 27 October 1999.

Chapter 3 addresses language use by political structures and authorities in parliament, by the government and the administration (Article 11), in the publication of legal texts (Article 12), in referenda and elections (Article 13), in authorities at all levels including "enterprises, offices and organisations" (Article 14), in record-keeping (Article 15), official correspondence (Article 16), courts and other legal procedures (Article 17), "production, communication, transportation, power industry and agriculture" (Article 18), post and telegraph (Article 19), mass media (Article 20) and "public services and commercial activities" (Article 21).

Chapter 4 contains two articles (Articles 22 and 23), both on toponymy.

Chapter 5 contains one article (Article 24) on language use in (external) relations between Kalmykia and "foreign states and international organisations".

The only article (Article 25) of Chapter 6 stipulates that non-observance of the Act makes juridical and physical persons liable for prosecution.

Chapter 7 contains two articles (Articles 26 and 27) indicating the date of entry into force of the act (the date of its publication in the newspapers *Khalmg Unen* and *Izvestiya Kalmykii*—which occurred on 17 November 1999) and the repeal of the previous Act of 30 January 1991.

My goal here is not to engage in a detailed legal analysis of the Act, which would not only exceed the scope of this chapter, but would also require familiarity with the legal tradition of the Soviet Union and its successor states. Rather, I shall attempt to provide elements for a basic assessment of the act from a language policy perspective.

I will therefore proceed by discussing a selection of domains addressed by various provisions in the act—hence, the rest of this presentation is organized with respect to issues rather than individual Articles in the Act—on the basis of which a tentative assessment will be made.

3.1. The 'Languages of the Peoples of the Republic of Kalmykia'

The "languages of the peoples of Kalmykia" constitute a set distinct from the "state languages" (introduced later), and one which remains undefined throughout. Presumably, these languages include all the mother tongues of permanent residents on the territory of the RK, whose ten main ethnic groups already make up 97.5 per cent of the population (leaving room for additional "peoples of Kalmykia"—using the wording of the Act—with their respective languages).

The recognition of an open set of languages reflects not just the objective micro-level diversity encountered throughout the Russian Federation, but also the subjective weakness of historically legitimized grounds on which to exclude certain languages. By 'subjective weakness', I mean to refer to perceptions, and the resulting balance of political views on the matter, without passing judgement, at this stage, on whether there may be, or not, objective reasons for prioritising one language or another implicitly favoured set of languages.

This is, of course, in sharp contrast with the Western European experience, in which the process of linguistic homogenization that typically accompanies nation-building was initiated (ideologically if not demolinguistically) in the Renaissance (Lapierre, 1987), as well as with the Central and Eastern European experience, where this process was carried by intellectual and political elites, with notable single-mindedness, in the nineteenth century (Schöpflin, 1996).[65]

The acknowledgement of a large number of languages in Kalmykia, however, may also serve, through a professed equalization of their respective status, to dilute the role of the larger languages, of which there is essentially one—Russian. The absence of any mention of languages other than Kalmyk and Russian in the Language Act would have defined a legal and ideological space in which Kalmyk would have been on its own in a losing competition with Russian; bringing additional languages into the fray deflects some of the pressure.

It should be noted that the "languages of the people of the Republic of Kalmykia" (or simply "of the peoples of Kalmykia") enjoy, if only formally, more than a nod. Not only is the expression to be found in the very name of the act, but it also occurs in Articles 1, 5, 6, 7, 10, and 25.[66] The notion can be likened to that of 'national languages' (as distinct from 'official languages' sometimes encountered in other cases).

3.2   State Languages

Article 3 declares Kalmyk and Russian to be the state languages of the RK. This is arguably one of the few fully clear provisions in the act; the implications of this status are developed throughout the provisions in Chapter 3; it corresponds to the notion of 'official languages' commonly found in Western language legislation.[67]

The status of state languages carries one potentially important consequence, namely, an assurance of "equality of functioning" (*obespechniye ravnopravnovo funktsionirovaniya*) of Kalmyk and Russian. This, of course, must be seen as an intention, since it would be all but impossible to achieve this aim. The important point here is the insistence on symmetry between Kalmyk and Russian, whereas in most successor states of the USSR, the language of the titular nation is given formal precedence.

3.3   General Language Rights

Article 2 of the Kalmyk Language Act explicitly recognizes the usual principle of language freedom; the first paragraph of Article 4 states that the RK guarantees "the enjoyment of fundamental political, economic, social and cultural rights regardless of their knowledge of

---

[65]   The special case in Europe is that of Switzerland, where the ideological nation-building throughout the 19th century rested precisely on the identification of the nation with the coexistence of many languages (Grin, 2000).

[66]   Interestingly, the title of Chapter 3, which includes Article 11, uses the hybrid notion of "state languages of the peoples of the Republic of Kalmykia", whereas "state languages" would have been quite enough—since the chapter is concerned, precisely, only with state languages.

[67]   In the previous Act of the Republic of Kalmykia No. 137-IX of 30 January 1991 on the Languages in the Autonomous Soviet Socialist Republic, Russian and Kalmyk were declared "national" languages.

languages to the citizens of the Russian Federation living on the territory of the RK". The second paragraph of the same article forbids any language-based discrimination. To the extent that 'fundamental rights' cannot, as a matter of principle, not be respected, the import of the provision may simply be to suggest that those rights are not 'equal'; this, however, leaves open the question of whether access to certain jobs, for example, could be made dependent on an applicant's language skills—without being considered a form of discrimination.

The reference to "economic protection" for the languages of the peoples of the RK (Article 5) gives further substance to these 'general' language rights. It implies that provision must be made for facilities to enable or help along the learning and use of the languages concerned.

Along with rights come duties, and Article 8 states that "knowledge of the Kalmyk language is a duty of every citizen living on the territory of the Republic of Kalmykia". Given that only a small proportion of ethnic Kalmyks actually know the language, and that virtually no ethnic Russians do, this provision is, at best, 'aspirational'.[68]

Although communications and media might deserve a special heading given their high profile in language policies, they can be addressed here. As regards the media, Article 20 states that their existence in Kalmyk and Russian must be maintained; however, who must guarantee this, and how, is not specified. As regards communications, Article 19 stipulates that the "post and telegraph correspondence of citizens, administrative authorities and public bodies on the territory of the RK is received and sent in the state languages of the RK". This provision is unusual, since it infringes on the right to privacy in correspondence and thereby contradicts the principle of language freedom put forward in Article 2 of the Act. Yet the right to privacy in correspondence is not absolute (Packer and Siemienski, 1999); nonetheless, restrictions to this right (justified by the state's right to protect itself from, say, acts of terrorism, and the ensuing right to gather intelligence for this purpose) would normally be derived from other jurisprudence without restrictions bearing upon the language of private correspondence being explicitly formulated. In any case, the article covers only two forms of communications, but not electronic mail, whose role is growing even in Kalmykia. It also disregards the case of a resident of Kalmykia sending letters to or getting letters from a correspondent abroad; the latter may not know either Russian or Kalmyk, voiding the law of any applicability—or opening the door to pure arbitrariness.

3.4 Education

As in many language acts, educational matters constitute a major item. In the Kalmyk law, most of Chapter 2 (Articles 8 through 10) is devoted to them. Citizens of the Russian Federation are granted the right to choose any language of education and instruction, provided they receive instruction in the state languages—presumably as subjects rather than languages of instruction. The state provides education in the state languages and "lends its support in organizing education and instruction in other languages".

---

[68]   To use a term suggested by D. Ó Riagáin in personal communication.

The states' involvement in favour of languages other than Kalmyk and Russian is defined by the rather non-committal expression of "providing conditions" for the study and teaching of the "mother tongues and other languages of the RK".

One symbolically important point is that schools must provide for the study of *Todo Bichig*. Further, this 'old Kalmyk script' must be used in teacher training and in the publication of textbooks and teaching materials—although the extent of this requirement is not clear.

In practice, the import of these articles is to confirm the right of individuals and communities to take education into their own hands and proceed as they please, provided some effort is made at learning Kalmyk. It gives a stronger legal basis for the teaching of Kalmyk, and also to pupils enrolled in schools providing Russian-medium education, but now officially required to learn Kalmyk as a subject. This amounts to a reversal of earlier practices. In the eighties, Kalmyk was an optional subject in schools, offered only to ethnic Kalmyk children.[69]

The new law therefore aims, at least in principle, at creating a fully bilingual society, with a pervasive equality of status between Kalmyk and Russian. Even modest achievements in this direction would constitute major gains for Kalmyk, given its current perilous position. This bilingual orientation may reflect not just an ideological preference but objective sociolinguistic and geopolitical constraints. At any rate, it reflects a spirit quite different from that of other early acts, such as the 1989 Estonian Language Act, whose Article 20 insisted that children are entitled to monolingual (Estonian-medium) education, while expressly noting that Russian-medium education would be provided only if the number of Russian speakers in a district justifies it.

3.5   Language in Official Use

Most of Chapter 3 of the act is devoted to the use of the language by authorities, including courts. The provisions contained in this chapter generally specify that Kalmyk and Russian are equally legitimate. The third paragraph of Article 11 goes as far as allowing members of the *Khural*, in case they speak neither of the two state languages, to use "any" other language, if they give prior notice. It is hard to imagine, however, to whom and under what circumstances this provision could apply. A very hypothetical case would be that of a citizen (possibly from one of the smaller ethnic groups in Kalmykia—see Table 2.5) who would have managed to get himself or herself elected to the *Khural* without speaking Kalmyk or Russian, and could give evidence that he or she actually speaks neither language.

Provisions regarding the publication of legal texts (Article 12), matters pertaining to all elections (Article 13), official and judicial records (Articles 15 and 17) and correspondence (Article 16) are straightforward (stipulating that the state languages—that is, both of them—are used) and require no further commentary, apart from noting the very general, even vague character of this provision; Article 16, however, mentions the right for people involved

---

[69]   Which means that Kalmyk children following these courses had to sit in class for longer hours, while Russian children were playing in the courtyard—clearly unfavourable conditions for language maintenance, let alone revitalization.

in a court case, if they do not speak the language used in court proceedings, "to read all materials in detail, participate in the procedure with the help of an interpreter and speak in their mother tongue"; in the case of judicial procedure, the right (e.g., of the accused) to understand the charges brought against him or her should logically imply that the restriction of the set of eligible languages to those "of the peoples of the RK" no longer applies.

Language use in administration is more interesting. The general rule is that the state languages are used, but that citizens of the Russian Federation living on the territory of the RK but who do not speak Kalmyk or Russian have the right to use their language "at meetings, sessions and assemblies of the administrative authorities, local government bodies, enterprises and organisations". Again, given the overwhelming knowledge of Russian by most of the population, it is hard to imagine cases where a resident citizen could actually avail himself or herself of this right—and harder still to assume that the authorities would have the wherewithal, particularly the staff, to handle such situations.

The condition of ignorance of both state languages does not seem to apply in other situations (that is, other than meetings or similar circumstances). By way of consequence, citizens are free to use the language of their choice (these provisions being part of Chapter 3, the eligible languages are those of the "peoples of the RK"). The authorities are also beholden to respond to applications, proposals and appeals made by citizens of the Russian Federation in the language in which they have been addressed. But Article 14 concludes by stating that "[i]n case this is impossible, one of the state languages of the RK is used". Patchy as it is, the available sociolinguistic information clearly indicates that with at least nine interlocutors out of ten, this will indeed be impossible. Hence, the provisions on the official use of languages give citizens the right to speak whatever they want, but not the right to be understood, let alone be given an answer in the same language. The general pro-bilingualism orientation of the law is therefore also illustrated by provisions pertaining to the official use of the language.

3.6   Language in Economic and Related Activities

The provisions of the Kalmyk law pertaining to "enterprises" are interesting, in that they reflect clearly (post-)Soviet conditions. Most probably, the "enterprises" referred to here are state enterprises (they are implicitly defined as such in Article 14[5]).

There is essentially no regulation of the private exchange of goods and services, in which, according to Article 21, unrestricted language freedom applies (without it being explicitly called so). The only related restriction, presented in the same paragraph, is that language-based discrimination in the provision of public services is forbidden.

As regards consumption, "the products made by the enterprises of Kalmykia are supplied with labels, specifications and tags in the Kalmyk and the Russian language"—a worthy aspiration, but one which it will be difficult to fulfil.

No provision of the law explicitly applies to the production, by the private sector, of goods and services, although one paragraph of Article 18 in theory opens the way for regulation in this area. It is more likely, however, that Article 18 represents yet another reflection of the Soviet past, which has left a particularly strong mark on economic activity. The first paragraph of Article 18 stipulates that "in the spheres of production, communication, transport, power industry and agriculture on the territory of the RK, Kalmyk and/or Russian are used". Large-scale operations, such as power generation, are still state-run and/or state-owned; but this no longer applies to small-scale farming, and it is unclear whether this provision is actually expected to apply to purely private sector firms. In the same way, it is likely that the law would not lend itself to an interpretation in terms of the language rights and duties of workers, in contrast with the provisions of the language acts adopted, for example, by the Baltic states.

Finally, presumably to reassure the authorities of the Federation that the act is unlikely to have any noticeable effect on the Russian-speaking community, Article 18 states that in the "operational communication in railway, aerial, river and pipe-line transport and in the power industry, Russian is used as the state language of the Russian Federation". In short, the act does not intend to redress the situation in a particularly important sector, and one in which reassertion of Kalmyk would have a very visible impact.

3.7 Toponymy and Other Provisions

Toponymy is a traditional pet area of language legislation, and it is unsurprising for this issue to be taken up in the Kalmyk Language Act. However, its effects may be limited. The first paragraph of Article 22 does state that "place names, inscriptions and road signs are given in the Kalmyk and Russian languages, if necessary in foreign languages too". However, it is unclear how extensive such a measure is likely to be, given that in the next paragraph, the government is given the responsibility for drafting a "list of territories and objects where place-names and inscriptions and road signs should be given in the state languages of the RK". This provision therefore remains a rather general one: The 'list' can be more or less long and precise; and even if a place-name is on the list as one that should have both a Russian and a Kalmyk name, it does not mean that it necessarily will be given them. By contrast, the 1989 Estonian law provided that 'all' geographical points had to be recorded under an Estonian name, with exceptions for places of special historical or cultural significance; as regards personal names, all of Estonia's citizens were required to use a standard form in the Latin (not Cyrillic) alphabet; it is hard to imagine Kalmykia imposing a symmetrical requirement in which its Russian-speaking residents and citizens of the Federation would be required to record their name in *Todo Bichig*.

This somewhat desultory approach to toponymy may reflect the fact that toponymy matters objectively less in a sparsely populated country, with a nomadic tradition, and in which built settlements may simply have relatively less importance in people's relationship to their environment.

Before closing this quick overview of the provisions in the act, special mention must be made of Article 7, which rather than setting legal standards, outlines the general areas in which programmes must be deployed "for the preservation, study and development of the languages of the peoples of the Republic". These programmes must promote research, education, publishing, literature, the arts and the media, as well as "solving other problems of promotion of the Kalmyk language". This provision squares with the aim, put forward in Article 5, of supporting "scientific programmes for the preservation, study and promotion of the languages of the peoples of the Republic".

Several other provisions in the law could lend themselves to commentary, in particular the chapter on "external" relations, which, however, tends not to have major importance in language acts (since the languages of the parties involved, in addition to whatever language is being promoted, may always be used); in the Kalmyk state, which is not a subject in international law, the matter is of accordingly lesser relevance. Similar provisions apply to contacts of the government of the RK with international organizations.

One may finally note that the law makes no mention of timelines for its implementation, nor of any transitory dispositions for a step-wise implementation, whereas such dispositions existed in the Estonian Language Act.

4.　A PROVISIONAL ASSESSMENT

In the concluding part of this chapter, I shall attempt to look at the Kalmyk Language Act by addressing two questions: First, does it matter? Second, will it change anything?

Contrary to what one could be tempted to assume, the recent developments exemplified by the Kalmyk Language Act certainly matter, for two reasons. The first is that it constitutes, in itself, an interesting case from a scholarly point of view, which deserves to be further documented and analysed. As one of the member republics of the Russian Federation, Kalmykia replicates, at some levels, processes that can be observed in other republics[70] (although in a much less manifest manner than, say, in Tatarstan), and which resemble, *mutatis mutandis*, processes that have taken place in the republics of the former USSR. A local elite, banking on the understandable need for identity, recognition and respect felt in their ethnic constituency, uses language as a tool to reshape the ideological space and carve out a political space in which they can increase their own influence—for better or for worse. Language and identity therefore legitimize new elites; they can also serve to create niche jobs in which speakers of the language being promoted to enjoy oligopsony power (that is, they are among the few possible 'sellers' of a production factor, namely, workforce endowed with specific language skills).

Yet I submit that the nation-building process in Kalmykia takes place against a very specific and little-explored backdrop; as pointed out by Kalmyks themselves, "the Kalmyk language has been practically understudied as a system within the framework of its linguistic-culturological correlations" (Goryaev and Omakayeva, 1999: 1). The determining features of this backdrop are the following: First, the Kalmyks' historically nomadic, non-urban culture, in which the relationship to space, as well as the perception that holding jurisdiction over a particular area may not need to be mediated, to the same extent as in historically sedentary cultures, by the rational-legal state apparatus. This is certainly reinforced by the relative absence of a literary tradition in Kalmyk (Tishkov, 1997). The second key feature is the memory of deportation, with the cultural destruction and the untold suffering it has caused. Finally, the third of these particular features is, venturing on a limb, Tibetan Buddhist religion and

---

[70]　According to Neroznak (1999), fourteen out of twenty-one national republics in the Russian Federation have issued decrees on languages. Yet the Federation numbers some 175 minority groups with as many languages, suggesting that language-related law-making in Russia still has ample scope for future development.

culture. Much is made nowadays, both in Kalmykia and by outside observers, of the renaissance of Buddhism in the country, but the ways in which it influences the political process has, to my knowledge, never been the object of scholarly analysis.[71]

The second reason why the Kalmyk experience matters is because of Kalmykia's position close to the powder keg of the Northern Caucasus. Apart from the successive wars in Chechnya, it is common knowledge that to a varying degree, inter-group tensions are rife in the six other republics of the region, namely Adygea, Karachai-Cherkessia, Kabardino-Balkaria, North Ossetia, Ingushetia and, though apparently less so, Dagestan. These republics are characterized by a lesser discrepancy than in Kalmykia between the percentage of people who self-identify as 'ethnics' from the titular republic in which they live on the one hand, and the percentage of speakers of the titular language on the other hand. This implies a closer link between ethnicity and language, which reinforces potential rifts in the population; it also means that whatever measures are taken in favour of the local languages can be perceived as considerably more threatening by members of the Russian-speaking communities. By contrast, Kalmykia, apart from being characterized by generally conflict-free interethnic relations, is also a non-threatening case from the standpoint of ethnic Russians (or those who self-identify as such). The low titular language fluency figures reported by Tishkov (1997), and the even lower ones reported by local observers (Kornoussova, 1999) indicate that Kalmyk is a severely threatened language, and that it is far from challenging Russian in any sphere of daily life.

Kalmykia can therefore become a useful laboratory of language revitalization for the entire region: If the measures aiming at the peaceful promotion of the titular, yet threatened language prove successful, at least in part, the specific contents of these measures, the specific ways in which they have been implemented and the identification of the conditions that make success possible (or lie at the root of failure) can be highly relevant for the implementation of language revitalization policies in the North Caucasus republics.

Turning now to the question of whether the Kalmyk Language Act is likely to change anything, let us first remember that its adoption is so recent that any assessment can only be conjectural.

One first general observation is that the Kalmyk Language Act actually contains two elements of legislation: One is on the state languages, and guarantees the official position of Kalmyk alongside Russian; the other is on minority languages in general. However, if only because the act does not list them, this dimension can be seen as mainly declarative. In what follows, I shall focus on the effects that the act may have with respect to the promotion of Kalmyk.

As noted by Baklanova (1999: 1), "the ethnolinguistic situation in the RK is characterized by the Russian language functioning in all vital spheres of activities, as well as in the educational field where ... Russian is the language of instruction". With very low percentages

---

[71]   One commonly made, if anecdotal, observation is that the Kalmyk people show remarkable meekness when recounting their history. Foreign observers are frequently struck by the complete absence of ill-feelings towards members of the Russian-speaking community, despite the fact that it was essentially Russian power that was responsible for the deportation, and Russian settlers who took up the space from which the Kalmyks had been expelled.

of competent speakers, the Kalmyks have to start at ground level. Furthermore, the constant changes of alphabets between *Todo Bichig* and the Latin and Cyrillic alphabets implies that a whole generation of Kalmyks has grown up without a clear reference for the written language.[72] Education clearly is a precondition for effective language revitalization and must structurally (though not always chronologically) precede other types of measures in policy plans (Grin and Vaillancourt, 1999), and the Kalmyk government has correctly identified education as a priority area; it is also the only one in which members of the Russian-speaking community are likely to be confronted with any changes as a result of the new act.

Language teaching presupposes some *corpus* development (where "corpus" is opposed to "status", according to the classical distinction proposed by Kloss [1969]), that is, some work that may variously include the choice of an alphabet, spelling reform, terminological development, etc. Presidential decrees adopted on 7 May 1998 (No. 87) and 5 November 1998 (No. 203) addressed these points and paved the way for a clearer definition of the language that is to be promoted. Other measures, including education planning, are part of status planning.

Given the severe motivation problems typically associated with the revitalization of low-prestige varieties, much of the future success of Kalmyk language policy lies with pilot experiments in multilingual education, in which novel and stimulating approaches are applied. Many a revitalization effort has floundered because of the *passé*, punitive or boring character of language instruction.

The Altn Gasn School in Elista is implementing a programme which sets great store by a communicative approach to language teaching, in which attention to learners' motives for language acquisition and their personal development are given a central role. Children at Altn Gasn simultaneously start learning Russian, Kalmyk, English and German at the age of five (Kornoussova, 1999). In third grade, Tibetan is added, and it is a compulsory subject until the seventh grade. The study of the Kalmyk language does not take place in a vacuum, but is supported by courses in Kalmyk culture and history.

The development of teaching materials is an equally crucial condition for the success of the plan; it is being carried out at the Kalmyk Centre for Intensive Language Teaching, which has developed the method *Uinr* for non-speakers, which is being used at Altn Gasn. The results achieved so far are described as good (Baklanova, 1999).

In short, an encouraging sign for the future of the Kalmyk language is that those engaged in its revitalization are not putting the cart before the horse, and that the Language Act gives them the legal basis on which to implement their plans in the crucial area of school.[73] However, it is clear that schools cannot suffice. In what remains one of the most penetrating analyses of reverse language shift, Fishman (1991) insists that while schools are an indispensable pillar of revitalization, they cannot replace what he calls the "home–neighbourhood–community complex"; therefore, creating conditions for (minority) language use to be normal in this complex must become, at an appropriate time and as resources allow, a key objective of language revitalization policy. At this time, Kalmyk has not been restored to this state of normality, and given the prudent, or even restrained tone of the act, it is unclear

---

[72]   I am indebted to Bossia Kornoussova for drawing my attention to this point.

[73]   Article 7 of the law stresses the role of research as a guide to language policy.

whether it will prove sufficient to achieve this; quite probably, decrees to flesh out its general guidelines will, in due course, be required.

Beyond its worthy intentions, much of the law cannot be implemented, because Kalmykia simply does not have the resources to do so, and is unlikely to have them for a long time to come. It follows that its direct effects will remain negligible, and that most people will see no difference. Whatever effects the law can have can only be in the long term. First, despite the extremely constrained material situation of Kalmykia, measures and projects in language instruction, if they succeed in developing motivation, can have some genuine long-term effects. Second, the chief virtue of the law is to provide the legal side of a much broader political and cultural project, which can benefit from a generally favourable context; the act also displays a remarkable 'modernity'.[74]

Whereas the development of language legislation preserving or promoting the position of the language of the titular nation can be assigned to classical nation-building or to defensive ethnic containment, more modern language policy developments, particularly in Western Europe, can be interpreted as forms of diversity management. The notion of nation-building is fairly well-known and does not require further commentary; the expression ethnic containment is self-explanatory; as to diversity management, it refers to the notion that given the fact that linguistic, ethnic and cultural diversity exists, some policy arrangements responding to this diversity are better than others in terms of the welfare (or any other indicator) that they generate (see, for example, Grin, 1996).[75]

We can certainly rule out 'ethnic containment'—the very notion is not relevant in the context of present-day Kalmykia, where ethnic Kalmyks no longer represent an absolute majority, and where inter-community relations are remarkably peaceful. We have seen that there probably are, in the rationale underpinning Kalmyk legislation, some elements of nation-building: Language is used to reassert Kalmyk culture and identity, as well as, possibly, to carve out a political and even economic market for a new elite. However, it would be too restrictive to see nothing else in it. To a large extent, Kalmyk identity rests on a unique historical experience and on its Buddhist culture; the very preliminary overview presented here suggests that the study of the Kalmyk sense of nationhood is not easily shoehorned into the categories developed for the study of less unusual cases in less peripheral parts of Europe.

The Kalmyk Language Act, however, contains circumstantial evidence of a 'diversity management' perspective. We have already noted that many provisions acknowledge not just the two state languages, but the "languages of the peoples of the Republic of Kalmykia". The preamble of the law, as well as its general spirit, is one in which the notion of harmonious diversity, though not expressed as such, is never very far away. It does not only mention "human rights" as one of the benefits from proper consideration for the languages of the peoples of the RK, but also stresses the "full development of the peoples of RK, their culture and their

---

[74] 'Modernity', in this context, refers to the increasingly complex nature of contemporary societies, as shown by Morin; these are characterized not by some kind of 'post-modernity' (a term which is deliberately avoided here), but by the deepening of the inner logic of modernity (Grin and Rossiaud, 1999).

[75] For example, policy choices regarding the integration of immigrants can be more or less favourable to the expression of a given diversity, and range from assimilationist to fully 'multiculturalist' perspectives, yielding different outcomes in terms of overall welfare.

language", and aims at enhancing the "creative potential, customs and traditions of every people", before adding that the Kalmyk language deserves special care and attention, and that the authorities of the RK have a particular responsibility towards this language, because the RK "is the sole national and state structure of the Kalmyk people".

All this is perfectly in keeping with an approach that recognizes diversity as a valuable feature of modern societies. Even the measures aimed at promoting Kalmyk (which also take great care never to downgrade the position of Russian, which is nowhere questioned) cannot be portrayed as a defensive or exclusionary ideology: the preservation of diversity itself requires special measures for threatened languages, and hence the implementation of at least the measures contained in the law.

The effectiveness of the Kalmyk Language Act, in the long term, rests not only with the motivation of the Kalmyks themselves, but also, in large part, with its acceptability to Russian-speakers; the 'diversity management' perspective it embodies, as well as the 'modernity' that can be associated with it, make this positive outcome more likely.

REFERENCES

Baklanova, Galina B. (1999) "The Development of Modern Technologies for the Native Language Teaching as One of the Means for the Implementation of the Kalmyk Language Revival Program". Paper presented at the International Seminar "Minority Languages in Russia: Perspectives for Development", Elista, 10–16 May 1999.

Comrie, Bernard (1981) *The Languages of the Soviet Union*. Cambridge: Cambridge University Press.

Fishman, Joshua A. (1991) *Reversing Language Shift. Theoretical and Empirical Foundations of Assistance to Threatened Languages*. Clevedon: Multilingual Matters.

Goryaev, Andrey and E. Omakayeva (1999) "On Problems of Studying Minority Languages in Russia. Case Study of the Kalmyk Language". Paper presented at the International Seminar "Minority Languages in Russia: Perspectives for Development", Elista, 10–16 May 1999.

Grin, François (1996) "Conflit ethnique et politique linguistique". *Relations internationales*, 88: 381–396.

Grin, François (2000) "Language Policy in Multilingual Switzerland: Overview and Recent Developments". In Kas Deprez (ed.) *Multilingualism and Government*. Pretoria: Van Schaik Publishers, pp.71–81.

Grin, François (2001) "Kalmykia, Victim of Stalinist Genocide: From Oblivion to Reassertion", *Journal of Genocide Research*, 3(1): 97–116.

Grin, François and Jean Rossiaud (1999) "Mondialisation, processus marchands et dynamique des langues". In Sélim Abou and Katia Haddad (eds.) *Universalisation et différenciation des modèles culturels*. Beirut: Presses de l'Université Saint-Joseph, pp.113–142.

Grin, François and François Vaillancourt (1999) *The Cost-Effectiveness Evaluation of Minority Language Policies*. ECMI Monographs, No. 2. Flensburg: European Centre for Minority Issues.

Hairullin, Ruslan (1997) "Rediscovering Culture: Educational Issues for Ethnic Minorities in Russia". *IREX*, 2 (http://www.irex.org/alumni/journal).

Kloss, Heinz (1969) *Research Possibilities on Group Bilingualism: A Report*. Québec: Centre international de recherche sur le bilinguisme.

Kornoussova, Bossia (1999) "Building Multilingual Systems of Education to Motivate Schoolchildren to Study [their] Mother Tongue". Paper presented at the International Seminar "Minority Languages in Russia: Perspectives for Development", Elista, 10–16 May 1999.

Lapierre, Jean-William (1987) *Le pouvoir politique et les langues*. Paris: Presses Universitaires de France.

Mark, Rudolph (1998) "Die Republik Kalmükien (Chalmg Tangch). Das 'Unternehmen Iljumžinov'", *Berichte des Bundesinstituts für ostwissenschaftliche und internationale Studien*, Cologne, No. 35–188.

Minority Rights Group (MRG) (1997) *World Directory of Minorities*. London: MRG, pp.299–300.

Nekritch, Aleksandr (1982) *Les peuples punis*. Paris: Maspéro.

Neroznak, Vladimir (1999) "Language Laws of the Peoples of the Russian Federation and Programming the Language Development". Paper presented at the International Seminar "Minority Languages in Russia: Perspectives for Development", Elista, 10–16 May 1999.

Packer, John and Guillaume Siemienski (1999) "The Language of Equity: The Origin and Development of the Oslo Recommendations Regarding the Linguistic Rights of National Minorities". *Journal of Minority and Group Rights*, 6: 329–350.

Price, Granville (1998) *Encyclopaedia of the Languages of Europe*. Oxford: Blackwell Publishers.

Schöpflin, George (1996) "Aspects of Language and Ethnicity in Central and Eastern Europe". *Transition*, 2(24): 6–9, 64.

Tishkov, Valeriy (1997) *Ethnicity, Nationalism and Conflict in and After the Soviet Union*. Oslo: International Peace Research Institute.

Tolz, Vera (1993) "Russia's Kalmyk Republic Follows Its Own Course". *RFE/RL Research Report*, 2(23): 38–43.

UNHCR (1996) Punished Peoples: The Mass Deportations of the 1940s". *Refugees Magazine*, 1 May 1996. Geneva: United Nations High Commissioner for Refugees. See http://www.unhcr.ch/cgi-bin/texis/vtx/print?tbl=MEDIA&id=3b5555124.

PART III

Identity, Differentiation and Unification

Language Issues in the Context of 'Slovenian Smallness'

Petra Roter

■

Ethnicity, Language and Transition Politics in Romania:
The Hungarian Minority in Context

Carmen Kettley

■

Language Corpus and Language Politics:
The Case of the Standardization of Romani

Ian F. Hancock

Language Issues in the Context of 'Slovenian Smallness'

Petra Roter

Language Issues in the Context of 'Slovenian Smallness'[1]

Petra Roter

INTRODUCTION

With less than two million inhabitants and a territory of just over 20,000 square kilometres, Slovenia undoubtedly falls into the category of small states, and the Slovenian nation into the category of small European nations. Ethnic Slovenians represent almost ninety per cent of Slovenia's population.[2] Based on their right to self-determination, the Slovenians formed their own nation-state only in the beginning of the 1990s.[3] However, the process of building the Slovenian nation and preserving Slovenian national identity are a much older phenomenon.[4] Indeed, the history of the Slovenian nation popularly dates back to at least the tenth century. But in Europe, where a nation's survival tends to be most certain within its own nation-state, the Slovenians, curiously enough, never had their own nation-state. Given the lack of traditional group-binding factors, such as a state, the Slovene[5] language[6] has played a crucial role in the processes of both nation-building and state-formation. The present chapter examines the role of the Slovene language in these processes.

Language is "a fundamental marker of ethnic identity, a highly visible component of group solidarity" (King, 1997: 493–494). It tends to be perceived "as the central if not indeed the only boundary marker" (Schöpflin, 1996: 7). There seems to be a widespread assumption, although it has been described as a misperception, "that a nation, in order that it can call itself

---

[1]   The author would like to thank Farimah Daftary, Miran Komac and Zlatko Šabič and ECMI librarian William McKinney for their helpful comments. This article was originally written in 2001.

[2]   According to the 1991 national census, the total population of Slovenia is 1,965,986. The ethnic breakdown is as follows: 1,727,018 (87.84%) Slovenians; 54,212 (2.76%) Croats; 47,911 (2.44%) Serbs; 26,842 (1.37%) Muslims; 12,307 (0.63%) 'Yugoslavs' (as a non-ethnic category); 8,503 (0.43%) Hungarians; 4,432 (0.23%) Macedonians; 4,396 (0.22%) Montenegrins; 3,629 (0.18%) Albanians; 3,064 (0.16%) Italians; 2,293 (0.12%) Roma (Gypsies); 546 (0.03%) Germans; 199 (0.01%) Austrians; 37 Jews; and 67,810 (3.45%) inhabitants whose ethnic origin is undetermined or who have declared a regional affiliation (Klopčič *et al.*, 1994: 8).

[3]   According to Article 3 of the 1991 Constitution of the Republic of Slovenia, Slovenia is "a state of all its citizens". The English translation of the 1991 Constitution is available at http://www.us-rs.si/en/basisfr.html.

[4]   In a way, state-formation has been a culmination of nation-building. The case of Slovenia is typical of what is commonly known as the Eastern approach towards nation-building and state-formation (see Roter, 2001).

[5]   The adjective 'Slovene' will be used for the language whereas in all other cases the adjective 'Slovenian' will be employed, with exceptions in direct quotations and in cases of certain well-known historical names (e.g., the Kingdom of Serbs, Croats and Slovenes).

[6]   Slovene is a distinct South Slavic language, written in the Latin script.

a nation, should have its own language" (Schöpflin, 1996: 7). Schöpflin might be right in call-ing it a misperception, but the existence of a distinct language has been broadly perceived by the Slovenians as the basis for their self-awareness as a nation.[7] The Slovenians' claim for both the right to self-determination and an independent state has ultimately been rooted in the existence of a distinct Slovenian culture in general, and the Slovene language in particular.[8]

Language policies play a very important role in the process of nation-building, but also in the preservation of a nation. This partially stems from the fact that, unlike religious practices (which tend to be confined to the private domain), the use of language cannot be separated from the state (de Varennes, 1996: 220). Language policies are thus almost necessarily "more than purely symbolic", for, by privileging certain languages, they can have a significant impact on different groups, both the majority and minorities (King, 1997: 494). In a situation where language is perceived as the central group-binding marker, society tends to display a greater sensitivity towards language issues. Not surprisingly, therefore, language and language policies have always been a sensitive issue in Slovenia. However, this sensitivity is not derived solely from the role the Slovenians attach to their language (i.e., as a central ethnic marker). Instead, the present chapter will contend that the attitudes towards language issues and the con-tents of language policies need to be seen in a broader context of what will be coined here 'Slovenian smallness'.

Political, social, cultural and economic factors that have had an impact on the Slovenian nation and its historical development have led to the self-perception by (ethnic) Slovenians as a particularly vulnerable nation.[9] The perception of Slovenian smallness has been predomi-nantly constructed, on the one hand, on the basis of the actual small size of the population

---

[7]   An interesting, though not conclusive, indicator may be the comparison between national or ethnic origin and mother tongue as declared for the purposes of the 1991 national census. Such a comparison shows that there is virtually no difference between the number of Slovenia's inhabitants who declared themselves as (ethnic) Slovenians (1,727,018) and the number of people who listed Slovene as their mother tongue (1,727,360). Although there are no major discrepancies in absolute numbers for other ethnic groups either, such differences are more significant in relative terms (when expressed as a proportion of the ethnic group). Whereas the increase in the number of Slovene mother-tongue speakers represents less than 0.02 per cent of ethnic Slovenians, a similar comparison shows a much higher proportion for other ethnic groups. However, it is virtually impossible to assess this factor of discrepancy between ethnic origin and mother-tongue speakers for ethnic groups from the former Yugoslav republics of Croatia, Bosnia-Herzegovina, Serbia and Montenegro. This is because in addition to Croatian and Serbian, respondents also listed Serbo–Croatian and Croato–Serbian as their mother tongue. Additionally, speakers of several languages can be identified within the category of 'Yugoslavs', which is usually used by people from mixed marriages (all data on ethnic origin and mother tongue are from the 1991 national census; Klopčič et al., 1994: 8).

[8]   Nećak (1997: 20) typically observes that the Slovenian nation and its national identity have been constructed on the basis of the Slovene language and Slovenian culture, rather than a state, dynasty or religion.

[9]   This resembles the social constructivist perspective of defining small states in general, according to which the smallness of an individual state is determined by the views/perceptions of its members and others who relate to that state (Hindmarsh, 1996). Of course, the perceptions of Slovenian smallness both within Slovenia and elsewhere tend to spur reactions at the domestic level (within Slovenia), as well as in Slovenia's relations with other states (e.g., the pursuing of Slovenia's national interests might be influenced by the construction of Slovenian smallness by Slovenians and by the neighbouring states/nations). This chapter predominantly analyses the domestic level and does not aim to explain any actions from abroad as a direct consequence of the perception by neighbouring nations of Slovenian smallness (although such perceptions might have indeed played a certain role in the foreign policies of neighbouring states).

and the territory (when compared with neighbouring nations and states) and, on the other hand, on the basis of Slovenia's geopolitical position—under Habsburg rule, then within the first Yugoslavia (after the First World War), the second Yugoslavia (formed in 1943) and, finally, as an independent state. This changing geopolitical position has been influential in determining the 'significant other' ethnic groups for the Slovenians. Moreover, the experience the Slovenians had in individual periods with those significant other nations (and their nation-states) provided the context in which the actual threats to Slovenian national identity were experienced, but also the context in which the Slovenians constructed the perception of their vulnerability as a small nation. In other words, the changing geopolitical context (political entities and most influential ethnic groups in those entities) provides crucial clues as to the dynamics of the construction of Slovenian smallness.

It was to be expected that this perception of their vulnerability would change at the end of the Cold War when the break-up of the Yugoslav Federation and the formation of an independent state significantly changed Slovenia's geopolitical position. However, such an expectation proved somewhat misplaced. The post-Cold War changes have only shifted, rather than removed, the perceived sources of potential threats to Slovenian national identity, as well as redefined the political system that is to combat such potential threats. The context of Slovenian smallness, in which the Slovenians have developed their attitudes towards their language and formed their language policies, seems to endure. Because the factors influencing that perception have changed over time, it is essential to analyse the role of language in the processes of Slovenian nation-building and state-formation in historical context.

1. THE ROLE OF LANGUAGE IN SLOVENIAN NATION-BUILDING AND THE HISTORICAL CONSTRUCTION OF 'SLOVENIAN SMALLNESS'

Language as the principal cultural marker—which both binds people[10] and separates them from other (languistic or ethnic) groups (Sugar, 1980: 434–435)—is widely perceived as having played a very important role in the process of Slovenian nation-building. In specific historical circumstances, language has been instrumental to Slovenian national awareness. Due to the absence of other mechanisms (e.g., a nation-state) that would enable and provide for the cultural and national homogenization of Slovenians, their language—or what Banac (1994: 112) describes as "a history of cultivating their separate linguistic medium"—has filled that void.[11] By the same token, ethnic differentiation of the Slovenians, especially from neighbouring ethnic groups, has been ultimately based upon speaking Slovene.[12]

---

[10]   This is achieved because language enables communication, and thus the expression of feelings of identity (Sugar, 1980: 434).

[11]   Perhaps the only notable exception to this general rule came in the form of Illyrianism in the first half of the nineteenth century, and in the form of Neoillyrianism at the beginning of the twentieth century, when some Slovenian intellectuals, despite the fierce reaction of many, advocated giving up the Slovene language with a view to becoming part of a greater Illyrian nation that would later speak a form of Serbo-Croatian (see Nećak Lük, 1997: 121; Prunk, 1997: 54–55).

[12]   Religion has never been given any particular attention as a marker of national uniqueness as it did not separate Slovenians from the neighbouring nations (Banac, 1994: 112). Like Slovenians, Italians, Austrians, Hungarians and Croats are all predominantly Catholic.

The historical claim of the Slovene language as the gist of Slovenian national identity dates back to the eleventh century, when three religious texts known as *Brižinski spomeniki* were written in Slovene.[13] It reaches a crucial moment in the second half of the sixteenth century when protestant writers produced and published the first book in Slovene and a Slovene translation of the Bible. However, it was not until the nineteenth century, during the Springtime of Nations (1848), that the language issue openly assumed political importance. Aware of their weaknesses and fearing a strong Germany and an independent Hungary, Slovenians drafted their first political programme, known as *Zedinjena Slovenija* ('United Slovenia'), in 1848. In order to achieve its goal of a united Slovenia, the programme called for Slovene to become the language of education and public administration (Vodopivec, 1993: 159).[14] The language thus became the reference point for the political mobilization of Slovenians, as well as the source of such a mobilization, for it was out of the perceived or actual threats from the nationalism of neighbouring nations to Slovenian national identity (based upon the Slovene language) that Slovenians entered the process of state-formation.

The programme *Zedinjena Slovenija* did not materialize, predominantly due to Slovenian political weakness[15] and fierce resistance by the state authorities in Vienna. Given that Slovenians had no state of their own,[16] their linguistic nationalism was necessarily seen as a highly controversial political issue (Hobsbawm, 1992: 96). Indeed, separate linguistic traditions "were at the root of Slovene nationalism" (Banac, 1994: 113). It should come as no surprise that the language of instruction remained carefully controlled by the state authorities,[17] although the 1848 Revolution did result in a greater emphasis on the equality of nations within the Habsburg state. This also brought about certain linguistic rights for Slovenians: for example, the 1849 reform concerning secondary education made Slovene an obligatory subject for Slovenian pupils; and the official national gazette was to be published, alongside nine other languages, also in Slovene. These measures were of great importance since the Habsburg state thereby effectively adopted Slovene as the name of both the language and the nation (Melik, 1997: 45–46).[18]

---

[13]   *Brižinski spomeniki*, or the Freising manuscripts, date from about AD 1000 and are said to be the "earliest extant examples of the Slovene—and perhaps of any Slavic—language", although "the language was not generally written until the Reformation" (*The New Encyclopaedia Britannica*, Vol. 10, 1997: 884).

[14]   The Slovenian cultural elite also requested Vienna to abolish internal historical borders between the Slovenian-populated lands (Kranjska, Štajerska, Primorska and Koroška) so as to constitute one polity with its *zbor* (assembly).

[15]   Political weakness was related to the relatively poor economic and social situation. The situation was made worse by internal disagreements among Slovenians (see Vodopivec, 1993: 160).

[16]   Karantanija, which is considered the first Slovenian 'state', only lasted from the seventh to the eleventh century. After that and until the break-up of the SFRY in the early 1990s, the Slovenians never had a state of their own. In such circumstances, Karantanija has acquired almost a mythical position in Slovenian national memory. Already in the eighteenth century, and especially in the following century, Karantanija began to be seen as particularly important in the process of unification of the Slovenian nation (Komac, 1998a: 130).

[17]   As a general rule, the higher the level of education, the less Slovene was used in the educational process. Similarly, history, as the subject with the greatest impact on building national awareness, was mainly taught in German. Also, the language of official administration and courts was predominantly German.

[18]   This is particularly important because Slovenians, as latecomers in the process of nation-building, had been internally divided (partly due to territorial divisions). Although it had occasionally been used before, the

In such circumstances, the Slovene language found itself as the central pillar of Slovenian national identity as well as the most important factor distinguishing Slovenians from neighbouring nations. This is what Slovenians have been socialized (and educated) to believe. In this respect, it is not important whether or not the reality might have been that the majority population did not perceive the language as an ethnic marker, binding its speakers into what Anderson (1983) calls an "imagined community". In Slovenia, it was never easy for such a bond to occur. The difficulty was mainly rooted in divisions along class lines rather than ethnic ones, for the upper classes were predominantly of German(-speaking) origin.[19] This meant that language as the basis for a common culture, which should, in principle, define a nation and bind its members into a (more or less) coherent group, had also been a class determinant, and hence increasingly an issue of social promotion. Social promotion was thus subject to Germanization (Bučar, 1993: 37), but as soon as the popular national awakening began to take place, the German language began to lose its momentum. More importantly, the historical experience with the use of German and with Germanization (which was perhaps most obvious in the rejection of the requests from the South Slavic ethnic groups for equality within the Austro–Hungarian state, especially their demands for being equal to Austrians[20]) provided the basis for the perception of Slovenian smallness. This, in turn, made Slovenians increasingly suspicious of German(-speaking) ethnic groups.

The perception of Slovenian smallness was further constructed in relations with Italy and Italians. The 1920 annexation to Italy of a significant part of the Slovenian-populated territory in the West,[21] and the experience of Italian irredentist nationalism, served as crucial determinants in the Slovenian state tradition (i.e., pointing to a decision to join Yugoslavia), but also in its nation-building undertakings.[22]

The geographical position at the intersection of the nationalism of Austrians, Italians and Hungarians[23] thus provided a negative reference point for Slovenian nation-building.

---

word Slovenia—as the name for different geographical units inhabited by the Slovenians—only entered the popular discourse in 1844 (Melik, 1997: 44).

[19] This situation can be traced back for centuries when as "politically subjugated people in the framework of the feudal medieval system", Slovenians "could not develop their own bourgeoisie without political emancipation, so they remained a nation of farmers" (Bučar, 1993: 37).

[20] Slovenia remained under Austrian rule even within Austria–Hungary (formed in 1867).

[21] See Komac (1998a: 130).

[22] Slovenians are still very sensitive to any influence Italians may (wish to) exercise, especially over the western territory of Slovenia (i.e., the territory that used to be under Italian jurisdiction). Such sensitivity seems to be maintained also by Italian nostalgia attitude towards its eastern borders, which are still popularly seen as a great Italian concession to Yugoslavia (Hočevar, 2000).

[23] Due to the fact that the Hungarian nation is numerically much bigger than the Slovenian nation and for certain historical reasons (e.g., the privileged position of the Hungarian nation in the dual state of Austria-Hungary, the ethnic heterogeneity of the bordering regions between what is today Slovenia and Hungary, and Hungary's occupation of the eastern part of Slovenia during the Second World War), Slovenia feared Hungarian irredentist claims in the past. However, the passive standpoint during the Second World War of the Hungarian minority, living in the territory which had been annexed to Slovenia (i.e., the Kingdom of Serbs, Croats and Slovenes) under the 1920 Trianon Treaty, has been described as the decisive factor contributing to Slovenian tolerance towards its Hungarian minority (Komac, 2001: 119). This was in sharp contrast to attitudes towards ethnic Germans, whose fate was similar to their experience elsewhere in Europe.

Historically, Slovenians distinguished themselves, first and foremost, from those three nations. Experience with the expansionist nationalism of neighbouring nations also created an
urgent need to resist various nationalist pressures, and to do so differently and more successfully. Too small a nation to obtain (or even openly demand) a nation-state, Slovenians thus
had to choose between another political haven and national annihilation (Bučar, 1993: 37).
The option chosen was that of a political union with other South Slavs (*Yugo*-Slavs). The union was first known as the State of Slovenes, Croats and Serbs (proclaimed in October 1918,
and encompassing the former Austro–Hungarian lands).[24] In December 1918, the Kingdom
of Serbs, Croats and Slovenes was formed (as a union between the State of Slovenes, Croats
and Serbs and the Kingdom of Serbia, together with Vojvodina and Montenegro, which had
united with Serbia in November 1918). From 1929, the state was known as the Kingdom of
Yugoslavia (Udovički, 1995: 283–285).[25]

Slovenians joined Yugoslavia to be in a better position to resist Germanization and to
safeguard their distinct national identity and hence their language and culture (Prunk, 1997:
53). However, such expectations accounted for difficulties already during the very formation
of post-First World War (or the first) Yugoslavia. With the exception of the territory in the
East (where the region of Prekmurje, populated by Hungarians and Slovenians, was attached
to Slovenia), the drafting of borders was not at all favourable to Slovenians. Over a quarter
of all Slovenians were left outside the new state:[26] a small group found itself in Hungary; the
coastal territory in the West was "lost to Italy as a reward for changing alliance during the
First World War"[27] and the population of Carinthia in the North decided, in the 1921 plebiscite,[28] to remain within Austria (Milanovich, 1996: 28). Although the western border was to
change after the Second World War, it was this post-First World War discrepancy between
the ethnic and political frontiers, creating national minorities on both sides of the border,
that has ever since defined Slovenia's attitudes towards other ethnic groups in general, and its
language policies in particular. Even internally, the battle for promoting a national identity
was not won with the formation of Yugoslavia.

---

[24]   The proclamation is reprinted in Trifunovska (1994: 147–148).

[25]   See also Trifunovska (1994: 157–160).

[26]   See Part I, Article 1 of the *Report submitted by the Republic of Slovenia pursuant to Article 25, Paragraph 1
of the Framework Convention for the Protection of National Minorities* (submitted on 29 November 2000),
at   http://www.humanrights.coe.int/Minorities/Eng/FrameworkConvention/StateReports/2000/slovenia/
slovenia.html (hereafter referred to as 'Slovenia's 2000 Report under the Framework Convention'). Cf. Melik
(1997: 50) who argues that no less than a third of the Slovenian population remained beyond the borders
of the new state after the First World War. Similarly, Komac (1998a: 127) points out that the political programme of *Zedinjena Slovenija* (United Slovenia) was realized after the First World War only in the proportion of 67 per cent.

[27]   This was a particularly painful experience due to the large numbers of Slovenians left under Italian sovereignty (see Melik, 1997: 50).

[28]   For more on this plebiscite, see Suppan (1991).

2. SLOVENIAN NATION-BUILDING IN THE CONTEXT OF YUGOSLAV STATE-FORMATION: THE DEVELOPMENT OF LANGUAGE POLICIES

For Slovenians, Yugoslavia was seen as the only political entity that could (territorially) unite most of the Slovenian-populated lands, thereby constructing a modern Slovenian nation.[29] At the same time, the Yugoslav idea also encompassed the suggestion that different ethnic groups should unite in speaking one language and in using one alphabet. This was fiercely rejected by the Slovenian cultural elite (and the majority of the population). In the end, the first Yugoslavia was multiethnic and multilingual, but decision-making and state administration were controlled by Belgrade (Milanovich, 1996: 29). Thus, pre-war German unification attempts were replaced by 'Serbianism' (Bučar, 1993: 38).[30] It has to be added, however, that Slovene became the official language in public administration and education in Slovenia, and that the first Slovenian university was established in Ljubljana in 1919 (Prunk, 1997: 56). All this provided for an environment favourable to the preservation and development of Slovene (Nečak Lük, 1997: 122–123).

National development was, however, significantly impaired by the 1929 proclamation of absolute monarchy by King Alexander who renamed the Kingdom of Serbs, Croats and Slovenes as the Kingdom of Yugoslavia to wipe out any reference to different ethnic groups (Udovički, 1995: 285–286) and to establish the primacy of the Serbian nation which "unambiguously felt superior to the others" (*Ibid*, 1995: 284). In this context, the perception of Slovenian smallness was to acquire a different momentum; it was to be redefined *vis-à-vis* the big ethnic groups within Yugoslavia itself, especially Serbs. However, it was hoped and expected that this was to change in the post-Second World War Yugoslavia. The common Partisan struggle during the Second World War reduced the distance between different Yugoslav nations, and Tito's successful efforts to gain back a great share of the Slovenian-populated territories previously seized by Italy helped the Slovenians to (re)develop trust in the Yugoslav political union (Moritsch, 1997: 38). They therefore joined the Socialist Federal Republic of Yugoslavia (SFRY) in an effort to achieve cultural and political autonomy and to preserve their national identity (Bučar, 1993).

The SFRY was to be composed of nations, all equal and independent in preserving their distinct ethnic identities.[31] But after the Second World War, communist domination replaced what the majority of Slovenians had hoped for: national and political independence. Unification on the basis of a collective Yugoslav nation was thus replaced by "unification on

---

[29] Slovenian territories within Austria–Hungary did not have the status of a regional entity. The process of intensive nation-building (especially since the mid-nineteenth century) had to combat the regional organization which had been in place since a time when the ethnic identification of people was of secondary importance (Mlinar, 1995: 102).

[30] This again made the Slovenians fight for their national identity and for equality between different nations (Nečak, 1997: 22–23).

[31] However, the state attempted to address the national question that had surfaced not only in the first Yugoslavia but also during the Second World War (especially between the Croats and the Serbs) through the process of national unification. To this end, the slogan 'Brotherhood and Unity' was created (Udovički, 1995: 289).

the basis of a collective unitary Yugoslav working class" (Bučar, 1993: 38). Eventually, this communist centralism and domination began to incite a struggle for national independence. Fuel was added to the fire by the belief that the federal authorities and the Yugoslav (federal) army, under the pressure of Serbian nationalist communism, were striving for a classical national state that would be "led by the Serbian nation, with Serbian as the only official language", and where other languages, including Slovene, would gradually be doomed to extinction (Hribar, 1993: 46). Therefore, although the existence of Slovenia within the SFRY helped to diminish the historically well-established perception of Slovenian smallness *vis-à-vis* neighbouring nations/states,[32] it also led to newly created national fears, and to the re-emergence of the perception of Slovenian smallness *vis-à-vis* other Yugoslav nations, especially bigger ones.[33] The factors influencing this perception remained related to language, culture and national identity, although the economic disparities between the more developed North and the less developed South were also a factor in the national rifts that finally led to the break-up of the SFRY at the beginning of the 1990s.

Due to the central role that has been historically attached to Slovene, language policies may be one of the most significant indicators of Slovenian nation-building and state-formation processes. The question of language policies in Slovenia, while still a part of the SFRY, encompasses two related yet very different issues, both of which are significant for the understanding of Slovenian nation-building in the late twentieth century. On a broader scale (within Yugoslav society), it is important to examine the attitudes towards, and regulation of, different languages within the federal state. From the point of view of Slovenian nation-building (and state-formation) processes, the question to be addressed here is the position of Slovene *vis-à-vis* other Yugoslav languages (especially Serbo-Croatian in its variants), and its use in federal bodies. On a smaller scale (within Slovenian society), the important issue for the present analysis is the regulation of the use of different languages in Slovenia itself. Given that individual Yugoslav republics were accorded (especially in the 1974 constitutional order) considerable autonomy in the area of language policies, it is particularly interesting to study Slovenia's approach towards the use of languages within its republican borders.

2.1   Language Policies in the Federal Context

The central Yugoslav idea of brotherhood and unity of different nations and nationalities manifested itself in the notion of equality of their languages and scripts (Nećak Lük, 1983). Slovene was one of those languages. There was no single official language in the Yugoslav Federation, and yet, soon after its creation, Serbo-Croatian assumed an almost exclusive position as a means of communication in the federal public administration and in the Yugoslav People's Army (Devetak, 1989: 554–555). To a certain extent, this was a natural development as

---

[32]   In this respect, the SFRY was instrumental in overcoming the threat of Germanization.

[33]   A sociological survey of Slovenian public opinion has shown that within the SFRY (especially in the decade prior to independence), the threat to the Slovenian nation—and hence the origin of Slovenian smallness—was "coming not from the North but from the South" (Toš, 1993: 67). This perception in turn influenced the process of Slovenian nation-building.

a great majority of Yugoslavs were native speakers of one of the forms of Serbo-Croatian, and since most of the federal institutions and organs were located in Belgrade (Serbia). However, the use of Serbo-Croatian also extended into individual republics, including Slovenia, where the majority population spoke a mother tongue other than Serbo-Croatian.[34]

For all Slovenian pupils Serbo-Croatian was an obligatory subject (in the fifth grade, two hours weekly),[35] but reciprocal practice was never established elsewhere in the SFRY (with the exception of a few twin towns). This was seen as yet another proof that the equality of Yugoslav languages was actually never achieved (Nećak Lük, 1997: 123). Slovenians were becoming "alarmed by the fact that more and more frequently they had to abandon their own language for Serbo-Croat" (Pirjevec, 1993: 116). The perceived threat to Slovenian national identity was thus constructed, although not exclusively,[36] through the dominance of Serbo-Croatian culture that was most obviously displayed in terms of the use of Serbo-Croatian at the expense of Slovene.[37] It should therefore come as no surprise that Slovenian unease within Yugoslavia in the 1960s was manifested, amongst others, in the form of an influential popular movement for the increased use of the Slovene language (Nećak Lük, 1997: 124). The movement was centred on the question of the use of Slovene in public life, in mass media and in the army. Slovenia soon saw its first national television news broadcast in Slovene (in 1965).

In 1969, the Yugoslav Federal Assembly finally adopted a resolution on the use of languages and scripts as a means of implementing the constitutional guarantees of equality among nations and nationalities (Devetak, 1986: 27–29). Equality in the use of languages (and scripts) at the federal level was then further strengthened in the 1974 Federal Constitution. Since the Constitution left the question of the official languages of Yugoslav nations open, and as it was up to individual republics to determine such language(s),[38] it enabled the federal

---

[34] In Slovenia, instructions for certain products were issued in Serbo-Croatian, movies were subtitled in Serbo–Croatian and the Yugoslav army functioned in Serbo-Croatian.

[35] Except in bilingual schools in the ethnically mixed area of Prekmurje (where the Hungarian minority resides) and in Italian schools in the ethnically mixed area where the Italian minority resides. Pupils in Slovenian schools in the ethnically mixed area where the Italian minority resides learned Serbo-Croatian for only one hour a week. These exceptions were made most likely because all pupils in both ethnically mixed areas already had to learn one additional language (Novak Lukanovič, 1986: 90–91).

[36] A very strong source of Slovenian unhappiness in the former Yugoslav state that is not the subject of the present analysis was generated by the economic situation and differences in the economic development of individual republics whereby the developed North (Slovenia and Croatia) stood in sharp contrast to the undeveloped South (especially Kosovo, but also Serbia proper, Macedonia, Montenegro and Bosnia-Herzegovina). The redistribution of resources according to the principle of 'Brotherhood and Unity' aggravated the situation. On the one hand, the North was increasingly dissatisfied with its greater share in the redistribution process but a limited control over how the money was being spent, whereas the South still felt exploited by the North given that the North benefited from the supply of (cheap) raw materials from the South (Udovički, 1995: 293–294).

[37] It is fair to add that the use of Serbo-Croatian was often voluntarily chosen by Slovenians themselves (e.g., in the federal bodies in Belgrade). However, in the 1980s, it seemed that ever more Slovenians were speaking their language in the federal assembly. This was met with both great interest and approval back in Slovenia.

[38] Under Slovenia's new 1974 republican Constitution, Slovene was defined as the official language in Slovenia.

organs to function, in principle, in five languages and two scripts (Latin and Cyrillic).[39] In practice, however, Serbo-Croatian retained its dominant position and not much effort was made to overcome its disproportional use in federal institutions (Devetak, 1986: 29–30; 41).

Slovenia's increased dissatisfaction with the use of languages in the SFRY was one of the important indicators, as well as causes, of Slovenian dissatisfaction with the Federation itself. At this point, the processes of nation-building and state-formation seemed to have become intertwined, albeit still at a very abstract level. The fate of the Slovene language was described (and popularly perceived) as "a metaphor for the fate of the Slovene nation", and the only solution for ensuring the existence of the nation and its language was identified in the form of an independent Slovenian nation equal to other European nations (Hribar, 1993: 46). Of course, communist dominance allowed for no such ideas to be carried out in practice. Still, Tito and his close collaborators, responsible for drafting the party's doctrine, were not only aware of the Slovenian dissatisfaction with the state of interethnic relations,[40] but also deemed that it was necessary to react to it. The federal communist regime therefore began to exercise tougher control through national curricula.[41] Demands for the unification of all national curricula culminated in the late 1970s and early 1980s when the federal government seemed more determined than ever to carry out educational reform by introducing unified core curricula[42] for individual subjects, with a view to making them the same throughout the state.[43] The public debates in Slovenia in the 1980s revealed fierce resistance to such proposals. They were rejected (especially by education experts) because of certain (technical) aspects of the Slovenian educational system.[44] Perhaps the most open dissatisfaction was, however, due to what was seen as a violation of the principle of the autonomy and equality of nations for, according to the Federation's proposals, the contents of literature, language, arts and history teaching were to be based on the proportional contribution of each nation. Such a proposal was, of course, particularly unfavourable to the smaller nations, while granting a prominent position to Serbian history and literature in all republics (Plut-Pregelj, 2000).

---

[39] Thus, in state institutions at the federal level, one could use Serbo-Croatian (in the Cyrillic script), Croatian (Latin), Serbo–Croatian or Croato–Serbian of the *ijekavski* dialect (in use in Bosnia; in both the Cyrillic and Latin scripts), Macedonian (Cyrillic) and Slovene (Latin).

[40] Slovenians were of course not alone in expressing such feelings.

[41] Until then these had been under communist control for ideological content but had been otherwise determined by individual republics rather than by the federal government.

[42] For a detailed study on the issue of common curricula, see Plut-Pregelj (2000).

[43] Plut-Pregelj (2000: 63) lists two major reasons for the Federation's drive towards unification of the national curricula: the first was to resolve the mounting economic problems by providing for the mobility of the work force, whereas the second one was to reverse developments in Kosovo after it had become clear that in elementary schools in Kosovo, Albanian and Serbian children were using literature, history and geography textbooks which had been directly translated from those used in Albania.

[44] For example, the Slovene language and Slovenian literature, history and geography were taught with a national emphasis; Serbo–Croatian was obligatory in the fifth grade and elective in the sixth and the seventh grades; Slovenian pupils took geography and history as two separate subjects in the sixth grade whereas the proposals advocated such a specialization already in the fifth grade.

The prolonged and fierce resistance (especially) in Slovenia to the proposals for common core curricula proved yet again that Slovenians were particularly sensitive to the questions of their language and national identity, and that the preservation of Slovenian national identity was being threatened even within Yugoslavia. Slovenian resistance in this matter also showed that significant departures from the Yugoslav Communist Party discipline could occur when it came to questions of language or education. Indeed, Slovenian rejection of the proposals from Belgrade was supported throughout by the League of Communists of Slovenia (LCS). They may have voiced their disagreement with the federal proposals in a subtler manner than the Association of Slovenian Writers for example, but the LCS never withdrew its support for the Slovenian educational system.[45] Eventually, core curricula were introduced in all the Yugoslav republics except Slovenia. Slovenians thus succeeded, with the support of the LCS, in resisting Serbian nationalism and preserved autonomy in an area that has always been perceived as crucial for their existence as a distinct nation.

2.2 Language Policies in the Republican Context

The fact that a very significant proportion of Slovenians were left in neighbouring states after the First World War, and again after the Second World War, has been a significant determinant in Slovenia's attitudes towards its own minorities and towards language policies. The existence of Slovenian minorities abroad began to craft Slovenia's minority attitudes (if not yet policies) soon after the formation of the SFRY. In addition to implementing certain aspects of minority protection in the republic (e.g., radio programmes in minority languages were broadcast already in 1949 in Italian, and in 1958 in Hungarian), Slovenia began to advocate the enactment of more specific minority policies at the federal level (which would apply, among other minorities, to the Italian and Hungarian minorities in Slovenia). An adequate minority protection system at home was seen as a way for Yugoslavia to put pressure on Austria and Italy, both of which had relatively large Slovenian minorities. It took quite some time, however, before the Federation decided for minority protection: the predominant homogenizing tendencies in Yugoslavia with a commitment to one Yugoslav socialist culture made it very difficult to address any special minority needs in the 1950s (Čurin Radovič, 2000: 13–14).

Slovenians had been pushing for a new law on minority schooling in Yugoslavia ever since the 1954 London agreement.[46] They drafted a bill providing for "bilingual schooling in

---

[45] The president of the Central Committee of the LCS, Andrej Marinc, spoke on Belgrade television in 1983 about the Slovenian criticism of the core curriculum and he defended "the right of each republic to make its own decisions on education, especially as regards the native language and the nation's history" (Plut-Pregelj, 2000: 75).

[46] Memorandum of Understanding between the Governments of Italy, the United Kingdom, the United States and Yugoslavia Regarding the Free Territory of Trieste. The Memorandum addressed the issue of the border between Yugoslavia and Italy by annexing Zone B of the Free Territory of Trieste to Yugoslavia. This was a territory with "a strong Slovene majority on the one hand and a small (approximately 3,000 members), socially weak Italian minority, on the other" (Komac, 2001: 114).

Zone B of the former Free Territory of Trieste and in Prekmurje" (i.e., for Italians, now a minority in Slovenia [and Croatia] and for Slovenia's Hungarian community, respectively), but Serbian and Croatian representatives in the Central Committee of the League of Communists of Yugoslavia (LCY), which discussed the draft bill in 1957, were against the Slovenian proposal. The explanation offered was that "conditions in their territories were not ready for dealing with the problem of bilingual schooling because of the sizeable Hungarian minority in Croatia and Vojvodina and the Albanians in Kosovo" (Plut-Pregelj, 2000: 60–61). The bill was never enacted, but the Slovenian reasoning for minority protection soon took on a new dimension.

When the Slovenian minority in Austria was stripped of the right to bilingual education in 1959, Austria's explanation included a reference to the unregulated minority situation in Yugoslavia: Why would some 50,000 Slovenians in Austria have something that was denied to some half a million Hungarians in Yugoslavia? The Slovenians again pressed Belgrade for bilingual schooling—this time more successfully (due to additional pressure from another Yugoslav republic, Macedonia); bilingualism was finally introduced in Slovenia in 1962 (Gabrič, quoted in Plut-Pregelj, 2000: 61, fn. 9). The beginnings of the constitutional protection of national minorities that was to remain in place to this date originate in Slovenia's 1963 Constitution which guaranteed the Italian and the Hungarian ethnic groups "the right to equality and the right to the possibility of universal development" (Article 77), whereas members of the other nations of Yugoslavia living in Slovenia were, under Article 75, accorded "the right to education in their own language" (Čurin Radovič, 2000: 14).

At the federal level, ethnic minorities became constitutionally equal with the nation(s) of Yugoslavia only under the 1974 constitutional order; those federal provisions in turn broadened the range of minority provisions in Slovenia's 1974 republican Constitution. Most importantly, the Italian and Hungarian national communities became, according to Article 1 of the new constitution, "constitutive elements" of Slovenia (Komac, 2001: 115). Soon afterwards, specific minority legislation was adopted by the Slovenian National Assembly.[47] The minority protection system applied to the Italian and the Hungarian ethnic groups alone. They were, and continue to be (see below), entitled to schooling (primary and secondary) in their mother tongue; ethnically mixed areas became officially bilingual; and special linguistic provisions were introduced to extend the right of members of the two minorities to use their mother tongue in various situations (e.g., in courts, for street names and topographical signs).

The situation was different with respect to other non-territorial or immigrant ethnic minorities in Slovenia. The most numerous were minorities consisting of members of other Yugoslav nations whose migration to Slovenia intensified at the beginning of the 1970s when Slovenia underwent extensive economic development based on labour-intensive technology (Svetlik and Novak, quoted in Komac, 1997: 75). Although no minority protection system was established for immigrants from other Yugoslav republics, the Slovenian educational system addressed this issue under the 1980 Act on Primary Schools,[48] which established the right for members of other Yugoslav nations and nationalities to be educated in their mother tongue (Article 23). For such persons, supplementary instruction of their mother tongue will

---

[47] Some of these legal acts remain in effect today, whereas the legislation that has been replaced by new legal acts effectively establishes the same minority rights.

[48] *Official Gazette of the Socialist Republic of Slovenia* (SRS), No. 5/80.

to be organized, free of charge, in primary schools (Article 53). But the realization of these rights was rather modest.[49] In the school year 1983–1984, there was only one primary school in Ljubljana with separate Serbo-Croatian classes (i.e., where Serbo–Croatian was a language of instruction, with Slovene as an obligatory subject). Several schools throughout Slovenia organized supplementary lessons of Serbo-Croatian (Novak Lukanovič, 1986: 90).[50]

Whereas Slovenia's language policies with regard to the Italian and the Hungarian national minorities were defined within a broader international context,[51] language policies with respect to the members of other Yugoslav nations and nationalities seem to have been related to, if not dependent on, the general mood in Slovenia concerning its position within Yugoslavia. Specifically, language policies were largely defined by the fact that the great majority of the members of other Yugoslav nations and nationalities in Slovenia were originally economic immigrants. Consequently, overall Slovenian attitudes towards these ethnic groups were dependent on the economic situation in Slovenia (and in Yugoslavia) as displayed in the opinion polls in Slovenia carried out by the Faculty of Social Sciences at the University of Ljubljana.[52] Public opinion in general may not have a direct impact on the regulation of language, but it is certainly a good indication of a society's attitudes towards language issues, for example. As Čurin Radovič (2000: 28) points out: "The quality of the actual coexistence of different cultures is also dependent on public opinion".

The results of the surveys of Slovenia's public opinion throughout the 1980s would seem to suggest that the less favourable the economic situation in Slovenia, the less keen Slovenians were concerning Yugoslav immigrant ethnic groups in Slovenia. This was manifested in the perception of a growing threat posed by the presence of these communities to Slovenian national identity in general, and to the Slovene language in particular.[53] Consequently, the

---

[49]   It is difficult to establish the reasons for this. It is probably fair to say that it was both the state and the immigrant population itself that contributed to such a state of affairs. Whereas the state did not promote the teaching of other Yugoslav languages more actively, most of the children of immigrants were born in Slovenia and grew up speaking either both languages or Slovene only (especially in mixed marriages). Speaking Slovene was also a matter of social promotion, especially with the growing crisis in the Yugoslav state.

[50]   At the time, only Serbo–Croatian was the language of instruction as well as a subject in primary schools in Slovenia because the majority of Slovenia's population that originated from the rest of the SFRY came from the Serbo–Croatian speaking area. Speakers of (different variants of) Serbo–Croatian accounted for no less than 90% of the total population of the SFRY (Novak Lukanovič, 1986: 89–90).

[51]   That is, by playing the game of learning by example, and hoping for positive reciprocal measures in the neighbouring states—though it is fair to add that this strategy, including the granting of special minority rights to Slovenia's minorities, persisted regardless of how (badly) the Slovenian minorities were protected in neighbouring states.

[52]   The results of opinion polls between 1968 and 1990 are published in Toš (1997), and between 1990 and 1998 in Toš (1999). All translations related to the opinion polls in Slovenia are by the author.

[53]   A question was asked repeatedly in the Slovenian opinion polls as to whether immigration from other Yugoslav republics endangered Slovenians, and if it did, what was endangered most. In the 1981–1982 opinion poll, one third of respondents stated that the employment of Slovenians was most endangered by immigrants, and 28% thought that Slovene was being most affected. However, in 1986 when it was becoming more and more apparent that the crisis in Yugoslavia was not only economic but also political, the Slovene language was declared as most endangered by immigrants (39% of respondents thought so), whereas employment was notably in second place (34%). To a somewhat different question ("Do you think that the Slovene language is, or is not, endangered?"), over 65% of respondents answered affirmatively in 1987.

respondents deemed it increasingly necessary to protect the Slovene language when they expressed their belief that immigrants should learn (and speak) Slovene.[54] This is clearly indicative of the nation-building process that began in the late 1970s and flourished at the turn of the 1980s. Nation-building was yet again rather significantly centred around the issue of language. Once it became clear that Slovenia was on its way to independence, the debates about the new constitutional order and its eventual provisions were, as far as the society's and the new state's attitudes towards language issues were concerned, perhaps surprising in several respects but very predictable in others.

3. LANGUAGE POLICIES IN THE INDEPENDENT REPUBLIC OF SLOVENIA

3.1 Language Policies Concerning the Italian and Hungarian National Minorities

The newly independent Republic of Slovenia (RS) adopted the same approach towards protecting its two small autochthonous national minorities—Italians and Hungarians—as before.[55] In its Article 11, the 1991 Constitution specifies that the "official language in Slovenia is Slovene. In those municipalities where Italian or Hungarian national communities reside, Italian or Hungarian shall also be official languages". The Constitution further establishes the right of every person to use his/her language and script, in a manner determined by law, in all dealings with the state and official bodies (Article 62). There is no general law on the use of languages in Slovenia. In line with the pre-independence tradition, the use of languages is instead regulated in numerous laws.[56] With respect to the two traditional autochthonous

---

[54]   In the 1983 opinion poll, 71% of respondents thought that workers from other Yugoslav republics and provinces "should retain their language and habits, and adjust to the Slovenian circumstances", 9% were of the opinion that the workers "should learn the Slovene language and habits, and give up their own language and habits", whereas 10% wanted them "to work and live in Slovenia for a shorter time and then they should go back home". But in the 1986 opinion poll (when Slovene was generally seen as the issue most under threat by the immigrants), 63% of respondents thought that workers from other republics who had lived in Slovenia for a longer period of time "should learn the Slovene language and adjust to the circumstances in Slovenia, but between themselves, they should use their language and enjoy their culture". In 1990, however, when Slovenia was bracing itself for independence, the percentage rose to 69, and an additional 7% were of the opinion that workers from other republics "should abandon their own culture and language and accept Slovene".

[55]   The Constitution (Article 65) also recognizes the Roma community as an ethnic group that requires special protection. Due to their low levels of education, high unemployment rates and poverty, the state has first and foremost concentrated on improving their economic and social situation, thereby also improving the conditions for the preservation of their identity. Much attention has been devoted to their education, with the purpose of integrating Roma children into the broader society while preserving their culture and identity. The issue of the Romani language has been addressed, but adopting any specific measures that would provide for instruction in the Romani language has been hindered by the lack of qualified teachers with a command of the language. The state has offered scholarships to this effect to Roma students, but in the school year 1996–1997 only one student of art (who was also the only candidate) received a scholarship (Slovenia's 2000 Report under the Framework Convention, Part I, Article 12; Part II, Articles 17, 82, fn. 62).

[56]   For a comprehensive overview of Slovenia's legislation on minority protection, see Slovenia's 2000 Report under the Framework Convention (especially Annex II), and Komac (1999). On the linguistic rights of persons

national minorities, the principle followed in various legal acts on different matters (e.g., on education,[57] legal procedures,[58] the use of personal names,[59] street names and other topographic signs,[60] or mass media[61]) is that state bodies, judicial authorities and administration operate in Slovene, except in the two ethnically mixed areas where the use of either Italian or Hungarian is put on an equal footing with the use of Slovene; this also applies to other situations of public interest.[62]

The system for minority protection—which also encompasses the right of minorities to representation at the local and state levels (with the right to veto decisions on minority issues), the right to form self-governing national communities (as a form of autonomy), and many other provisions—led the Council of Europe rapporteur to conclude that, although improvements may always be made, "both communities are rather privileged. They are, *grosso modo*, satisfied with their situation".[63]

---

belonging to national minorities in Slovenia, see also Slovenia's reply to the questionnaire of the OSCE High Commissioner on National Minorities; both the questionnaire and the reply are published in the OSCE Report on the linguistic rights of persons belonging to national minorities in the OSCE area and Annex: Replies from OSCE participating states, Organization for Security and Co-operation in Europe, High Commissioner on National Minorities. For full texts of individual laws in Slovene, see http://www.dz-rs.si.

[57] Slovenian legislation establishes the right of minorities to education in their mother tongue in the form of compulsory bilingual education for pupils from both the Hungarian and Slovenian ethnic group in the ethnically mixed area where the Hungarian minority resides, and in the form of monolingual education in the ethnically mixed area where the Italian minority resides. In the latter case, Italian pupils also learn Slovene as a subject, and the Italian language is a compulsory subject for all Slovenian pupils. Members of national communities are guaranteed education in their mother tongue in ethnically mixed areas from pre-school education to the completion of secondary education (see Slovenia's 2000 Report under the Framework Convention, Part II, Article 34).

[58] All legal proceedings in courts in ethnically mixed areas are conducted in a minority language if a party from such an area uses either Hungarian or Italian (Act on Courts, *Official Gazette RS*, No. 19/94, Article 5). On the guarantee of equality of the Italian/Hungarian language in court proceedings, see Court Rules (*Official Gazette RS*, No. 17/95, Articles 60–69).

[59] The Act on Personal Names (*Official Gazette SRS*, No. 2/87, Article 3) guarantees that the personal name of a minority member be written in the Italian/Hungarian script and form, unless the minority member determines differently.

[60] According to the Act on the Naming and Registering of Settlements, Streets and Buildings (*Official Gazette SRS*, No. 5/80, Article 8), national minorities participate in the decision-making process on the (re)naming, or merging, dividing or abolishing of settlements and streets. In ethnically mixed areas, the names of settlements and streets are written in both Slovene and a minority language (Regulations on Determining the Names of Settlements and Streets and the Marking of Settlements, Streets and Buildings, *Official Gazette SRS*, No. 11/80, Article 25).

[61] Both national minorities are guaranteed the right to be informed in their own minority language (see Act on Mass Media, *Official Gazette RS*, No. 35/01; see also Act on Radio and Television Slovenia, *Official Gazette RS*, No. 18/94; and Statute of the Public Institution RTV Slovenia, *Official Gazette RS*, No. 66/95).

[62] See, for example, Public Administration Act (*Official Gazette RS*, No. 67/94, Article 4), Act on the Register of Births, Deaths and Marriages (*Official Gazette SRS*, No. 2/87, Article 30[2]), Act on Personal Identity Cards (*Official Gazette RS*, No. 75/97, Article 6), Act on Passports (*Official Gazette RS*, No. 65/00, Article 13), Notary Act (*Official Gazette RS*, No. 13/94 and No. 48/94, Article 13) and Act on the Office of the State Prosecutor (*Official Gazette RS*, No. 63/94, Article 6).

[63] Opinion on the Application of the Republic of Slovenia for Membership of the Council of Europe (Rapporteur: Mr. Hörcsik, Hungary, Democratic Forum), Parliamentary Assembly Doc. 6823, 5 May 1993.

It is important to note that the debates on the new constitution[64] and Slovenian opinion polls in the period leading towards independence reveal that there was a very broad agreement that in the new political system the same level of minority protection as under the SFRY should be granted to the Italian and Hungarian ethnic communities.[65] The fact that politicians and a number of intellectuals agreed on such an approach may be a sign of a certain level of political culture, or an indication of certain interests behind it (although reciprocity in minority protection has never been the official position of the RS). The fact that Slovenian public opinion was, during that particular period of state-formation, favourable to adopting a system of positive discrimination for the ethnic Italian and Hungarian minorities (including what could have been perceived as a rather significant leniency with regard to the use of minority languages) is certainly a sign of decades-long education and promotion of Slovenia's system for the protection of its autochthonous minorities.[66] No such system had existed with regard to other ethnic groups in Slovenia.

It has to be added, however, that in the new geopolitical context (i.e., independence), Slovenia's minority protection system was put under some strain. This was largely caused by difficulties in bilateral relations, especially between Slovenia and Italy. More specifically, the process of Slovenia's state-formation in the early 1990s was accompanied by Italian pressure on Slovenia to address certain issues (in return for Italy's recognition of Slovenian independence). That pressure was not centred on minority protection for the Italians in Slovenia or language issues *per se*. Nevertheless, before Slovenia's independence, Italy pushed for the respect of the rights of the Italian minority in both Slovenia and Croatia.[67] In 1990, Slovenia expressed its willingness to agree with Croatia on the international protection of the Italian communities in both states, including the unity of the Italian community in both republics.[68] As an independent state, Slovenia, however, later rejected the Italian proposals on account of not being able to influence minority protection in Croatia (Pucer, 1994–1995: 28).[69]

---

[64]   See, for example, a special issue of *Razprave in gradivo/Treatises and Documents* (Issue 24, 1990).

[65]   However, the constitutional status of the two ethnic communities changed significantly: from being Slovenia's constitutive elements under the 1974 republican constitution, they were downgraded to traditional territorial national minorities in the RS.

[66]   Of course, this is not to say that no opposite opinion has ever been expressed. On the contrary, a group of citizens from Prekmurje (where the Hungarian minority resides) complained to the Constitutional Court that bilingual education was in disagreement with the 1991 Constitution. The Constitutional Court, however, decided that compulsory bilingual education was not contrary to the Constitution (*Official Gazette RS*, No. 77/98).

[67]   See Unity and Respect for the Rights of the Italian Minority in Slovenia and Croatia, Motion for a Resolution Presented by Mr Foschi and others, Council of Europe, Parliamentary Assembly Doc. 6795, 18 March 1993.

[68]   See *Sklep* (Conclusion) of the Assembly of the Republic of Slovenia, No. 009/02/90, *ESA* 217, 13 December 1990.

[69]   In 1993, the Committee on Legal Affairs and Human Rights of the Council of Europe considered that Slovenia, *grosso modo*, already met the requirements listed in the motion for a resolution on the unity and respect for the rights of the Italian minority in Croatia and Slovenia, and that "the motion did not require any further action" (quoted from the Opinion on the Application of the Republic of Slovenia for Membership of the Council of Europe, Doc. 6823, 5 May 1993).

More noteworthy, though not unrelated, was Italy's pressure for the establishment of the right of foreigners to purchase property in Slovenia, with a view to enabling the Italians that left Yugoslavia/Slovenia or were expelled from the SFRY after the Second World War to get their property back. By amending the Constitution, Slovenia eventually allowed for foreigners to acquire property (this had been forbidden under Article 68 of the 1991 Constitution). This was perceived as a great concession made by a small state, as a result of the pressure exerted by a 'big' neighbour which strengthened its case by blocking the beginning of Slovenia's negotiations on accession to the EU. What was really important was that, as a result of this episode in Italian–Slovenian relations, "pressure has increased on minorities on both sides of the border" (Pucer, 1994–1995: 28). Certainly in Slovenia it seemed to have made Slovenian nationalist voices louder, especially those coming from the ethnically mixed area where the Italian minority resides. If not directly causing them, the process of settling the property issues at the bilateral level certainly culminated in a number of cases being sent to the Constitutional Court by members of the majority about certain aspects of Slovenia's minority protection system. The Constitutional Court did not, however, find the provisions on minority protection contrary to the Constitution.[70]

By contrast, Slovenia and Hungary have not had any major disagreements over minority issues. During the sensitive period of Slovenia's efforts to gain independence (and international recognition), Hungary was itself in the process of transition, aiming to establish itself as a democratic state. One can possibly speculate that this required a firm commitment to minority protection (to recall, membership of both the Council of Europe and the EU was made conditional upon minority protection); nationalist pressures with respect to minorities on either side of the border were thus clearly neither in Hungary's nor in Slovenia's interest. Indeed, a bilateral agreement was concluded in 1992 on the protection of the Hungarian minority in Slovenia and the Slovenian minority in Hungary. The agreement (in force since 1994) has been welcomed by Slovenia's ethnic Hungarians.[71]

In the circumstances of the changed geopolitical situation of Slovenia being a small— yet independent—state, two additional issues seem to be particularly important with respect to ethnic issues in general and language policies in particular: the status of Slovenia's largest non-autochthonous populations which ethnically belong to other former Yugoslav nations and nationalities, and the question of the German-speaking population of Slovenia.

---

[70] In addition to the above-mentioned compulsory bilingual education, the Constitutional Court was also asked to establish whether the regulations on the use of minority symbols, and the dual voting right of persons belonging to minorities (according to which one vote is equal to the vote enjoyed by every Slovenian citizen with the right to vote, whereas the other vote is cast to elect a deputy to the National Assembly representing the Italian or the Hungarian minority, respectively) were contrary to the Constitution. In essence, the Constitutional Court found all of the minority rights under examination in agreement with the Constitution; the Court only required that the criteria for obtaining the special dual voting right be specified. For more detail on these rulings, see Slovenia's 2000 Report under the Framework Convention, Part II, Articles 25–27.

[71] Personal communication with the Hungarian representative in the National Assembly.

3.2 Immigrant Populations Originating in the Former Yugoslav Republics

European history seems to be rich in examples where state-formation and nation-building go hand in hand. State-formation and nation-building were carried out simultaneously in post-Cold War Central and Eastern Europe, although with varying intensity. In Slovenia, nation-building seems to have been a somewhat selective process. It applied predominantly to the process of the Slovenians differentiating themselves from other Yugoslav nations. As the old state was falling apart, the Slovenians (as well as other Yugoslav nations) were once again in a situation where they were redefining the so-called 'us-them' relationship, which was simultaneously shifting the basis of Slovenian smallness. Other Yugoslav nations, now no longer members of the same polity, became 'significant others' for the Slovenians. This ethnic differentiation process seemed ever more intense the longer the international community nourished the idea of the preservation of the Yugoslav state. Later, the differentiation became driven by attempts to dissociate Slovenia from the instability and violence that reigned in some parts of the former common state. With the wars on the territory of the former SFRY and the world media coverage of what was referred to as yet another Balkanization, Slovenians persistently emphasized throughout the 1990s that Slovenia was a Central European rather than a Balkan state. In practical terms, this was reflected in several policies, including those on language. Language policies thus displayed a clear effort by Slovenians to dissociate themselves from the former state and its constitutive nations. For example, Slovenia decided already in 1992 (with effect in the 1993–1994 academic year) that Serbo-Croatian would no longer be an obligatory subject in its educational system.

Nowadays, the children of all migrants in Slovenia have the right to supplementary lessons in their mother tongue. Such courses are offered on a voluntary basis, but the state participates in financing them. The initiative to launch such courses was taken by Macedonian and Albanian associations, the embassies of Croatia and Macedonia, the Association of Albanian Societies in Slovenia and the Croatian Ministry of Culture.[72] Macedonian courses are organized on a reciprocal basis (Slovenian children in Macedonia learn Slovene), and a similar programme will be organized with Croatia. While it is true that the state is willing to financially support voluntary language courses for 'children of migrants', it needs to be added that—according to Slovenia's 2000 Report under the Framework Convention—no such courses are organized for the Serbo–Croatian language group.[73] With courses in Croatian to be organized soon, the situation will improve, but this will still leave out the teaching of Serbian.

The state seems to be aware of the unsatisfactory state of affairs with respect to its immigrants. One of the means of addressing this issue has been the provision of financial support since 1993 by the Ministry of Culture to the preservation and development of the culture and identity of the non-autochthonous ethnic groups in Slovenia.[74] It is probably fair

---

[72] In the 1999–2000 academic year, 62 children studied Macedonian and 12 studied Albanian. Similarly, following the interest expressed by Arab associations, 15 children studied Arabic in the 1999–2000 school year.

[73] Slovenia's 2000 Report under the Framework Convention, Part II, Articles 41–43.

[74] Slovenia's 2000 Report under the Framework Convention, Part II, Article 30 and fn. 26.

to say that such programmes are a positive step towards state recognition of a multiethnic reality in Slovenia, but they may be too little to genuinely help the immigrant communities preserve and develop their ethnic identity, culture, language and script—a right accorded to each person under the 1991 Constitution (Article 61).

The situation is worsened by several other factors. Based on Komac's (1997) analysis of the Serbian community in Slovenia (which is by and large representative of the situation of other larger ethnic communities originating in the former Yugoslav republics), such factors include the communities' territorial dispersal and their relatively low level of education, which is directly related to their areas of employment (mainly in labour intensive industries that have experienced severe difficulties during Slovenia's transition from a socialist to a market economy). In such circumstances, the abandonment of their mother tongue may also be perceived as a means for social promotion. As Komac (1997: 76) points out with respect to Serbs, their situation effectively reduces the possibilities for strengthening their ethnic group identity *vis-à-vis* the majority nation. Family thus remains the most important environment for fostering a distinct identity and for developing the mother tongue.

Slovenia was, however, relatively successful in resolving the issue of the citizenship of persons from other Yugoslav republics. Under its Article 40 of the 1991 Citizenship Act,[75] the inhabitants of the RS from other Yugoslav republics and provinces could obtain Slovenian citizenship almost automatically by applying within six months of the entry into force of the Citizenship Act—with no language requirements attached.[76] Some 171,000 persons became Slovenian citizens under Article 40.[77] Because Slovenia accepts dual citizenship, most of these citizens are holders of another passport. In contrast to some other newly independent states (e.g. the Baltic states), such a liberal citizenship regime[78] was mainly the result of Slovenia's desire to carry out its independence plan in a manner acceptable (or as acceptable as possible) to other Yugoslav republics (Mlinar, 1994: 77).[79] But soon after the independence euphoria was over, the Slovenian public became highly critical of the Citizenship Act, especially of Article 40. The criticism was heavily concentrated upon the issue of language. When asked, in a 1990 Slovenian opinion poll, about the criteria that workers from other Yugoslav republics and provinces should meet to obtain Slovenian citizenship, 57 per cent of

---

[75]   *Official Gazette RS*, No. 1/91-I.

[76]   The only condition was a recorded permanent residence in Slovenia on the day of the plebiscite (i.e., 23 December 1990) and that they actually lived in Slovenia (Article 40). In December 1991, Article 40 was amended so that individuals who had committed a criminal act against the RS could not become Slovenian citizens (*Official Gazette RS*, No. 30/91-I).

[77]   Slovenia's 2000 Report under the Framework Convention, Part II, Article 47.

[78]   It has to be added that this liberal regime only applied to persons from the former Yugoslav republics—i.e., persons that were to become Slovenian citizens under Article 40 of the 1991 Citizenship Act. The granting of citizenship by naturalization to other applicants was conditional upon, among others, knowledge of the Slovene language to the extent that it enabled the applicant to communicate with his/her environment (1991 Citizenship Act, Article 10[6]).

[79]   The Citizenship Act was adopted on 5 June 1991, just twenty days before Slovenia declared independence (25 June 1991).

respondents believed that speaking Slovene should be a condition.[80] By 1994, no less than 91 per cent of respondents were convinced that knowledge of Slovene should be a condition for obtaining citizenship, and a further 71 per cent agreed with the option (in the opinion poll) that the knowledge of Slovenian culture should also be a condition.

The Citizenship Act was eventually amended in 1994 to include a much stricter language requirement as a condition for obtaining citizenship. The original law determined that an individual applying for citizenship by naturalization[81] "shall have a command of Slovene to the extent that (s)he is capable of communicating with his/her environment".[82] The 1994 amended text[83] required that an individual applying for citizenship "shall have an active command of the Slovene language in written and spoken form, which (s)he shall prove with a compulsory test" (Article 2).[84]

3.3   The German-Speaking Population

The question of the German-speaking population of Slovenia also needs to be put in a post-independence context. If the existence of Slovenia within the Yugoslav Federation provided an environment in which Slovenian smallness was mostly an intra-state issue and to a lesser extent *vis-à-vis* Slovenia's neighbouring states, then the post-Cold War redrawing of borders significantly modified this perception. Now a small state, Slovenia needed to rely on its own capabilities and resources to defend its newly acquired sovereignty, and to act as a responsible kin-state for Slovenian minorities abroad. In the post-Yugoslav environment, there seem to have been sufficient signs to assume that a similar perception of Slovenian smallness had also developed in Slovenia's neighbouring states. Outside pressure on Slovenia to define its ethnic minority policies, including language policies, began to mount in the early 1990s. Not only Italy but also Austria became increasingly interested in certain issues, including Slovenia's interethnic relations.

The question of the German-speaking population[85] of Slovenia surfaced soon after Slovenia declared independence. It was Austria that wanted Slovenia to recognize the

---

[80]   Two other conditions were recognized as equally important in the 1990 opinion polls: permanent residence in Slovenia and employment.

[81]   The obtaining of citizenship under Article 40 was not considered as naturalization under the 1991 Citizenship Act.

[82]   1991 (original) Citizenship Act, Article 10(5).

[83]   *Official Gazette RS*, No. 13/94.

[84]   Article 2 further specifies that an expert commission, appointed by the government of the RS, shall be responsible for carrying out the compulsory language test. The commission "shall also determine the criteria for the written and oral test of the Slovene language"; the Slovene original is unclear as to the contents of the criteria that are to be determined by the expert commission.

[85]   According to the 1991 national census, 546 inhabitants of Slovenia declared themselves Germans under the category 'ethnicity' (*narodnost*), and 199 as Austrians, while 1,543 people listed German as their mother tongue (Slovenia's 2000 Report under the Framework Convention, Annex I; see also Klopčič *et al.*, 1994: 8).

German ethnic group as a minority with the same status, and hence the same rights, as enjoyed by ethnic Italians and Hungarians. Diplomatic action began in 1991–1992, when the Austrian government commenced expressing its entitlement to protect (and to represent) the interests of the German-speaking minority in Slovenia (Nećak, 1998b: 8). To this effect, a memorandum[86] was drafted by the Austrian government and handed to the Slovenian government in June 1992. According to this memorandum, the 'Germans'[87] should be recognized by Slovenia as a national minority (*Volksgruppe*) and accorded minority rights; German-language classes should be promoted; and Slovenia should financially and otherwise support the cultural activities of its German-speaking ethnic group.

It soon became clear—especially with the increasing popularity of the Freedom Party of Jörg Haider, the governor of Carinthia where most of Austria's Slovenians reside and constitute a national minority—that Austria was up for reciprocity: The 'Germans' should be granted similar rights if the Slovenians of Austria were to enjoy their minority rights.[88] International action followed suit. The issue of the German-speaking population of Slovenia was the subject of a motion for a resolution of the Parliamentary Assembly of the Council of Europe (Doc. 6693, 5 October 1992), and later of a question by the European Parliament to the Commission (No. E-1773/96, 3 July 1996). The Council of Europe rapporteur was of the opinion that "the real German-speaking minority in Slovenia comprises not more that 1,500 persons who are scattered all over the country" and claim "special recognition under the Constitution like the Italians and Hungarians,[89] but, given their numbers and geographical situation, this claim seems to be doubtful".[90] In its answer to Written Question No. E-1773/96, the Commission took the same view as the Council of Europe.[91]

It has to be added that in Slovenia, minority protection has never been conditional upon sufficient representation. With regard to the German-speaking population, other factors seem to be more influential in the state's non-recognition of this ethnic group as a national minority. In particular, only a smaller part of this population—that is, the so-called Kočevje

---

[86]   The German original is reprinted in Nećak (1998b: 9).

[87]   The 1992 Memorandum of the Austrian government refers to the *"österreichischen bzw. deutschsprachigen Volksgruppe"* (i.e., Austrian- and German-speaking ethnic groups).

[88]   However, it has been argued, on the basis of statements by prominent Austrian politicians, that the increased Austrian interest in Slovenia's German-speakers has been in fact a cover-up for Austria's interest in property that belonged to Germans but was confiscated by the SFRY after the Second World War (Nećak, 1998b: 11).

[89]   However, this does not seem to be a common position amongst the 'Germans' of Slovenia. In an interview for *Dnevnik*, Stefan Karner (an Austrian professor who has authored a study on the German-speaking ethnic group in Slovenia, titled *Die deutschsprachige Volksgruppe in Slowenien, Aspekte ihrer Entwicklung, 1939–1997*, commissioned by the Austrian government) has pointed out that, during his interviews with German-speaking Slovenian citizens, it became clear that they wished to preserve their culture and ethnic heritage, rather than press for recognition at the constitutional level (Varga-Novljan, 1998).

[90]   Opinion on the Application of the Republic of Slovenia for Membership of the Council of Europe, Doc. 6823, 5 May 1993.

[91]   Both the question and the Commission's answer are published in the *Official Journal*, No. C 305, 15/10/1996, p.0121.

Germans from the southeastern part of the country—is considered to be autochthonous (as a group resident in a more or less defined territory for a longer period of time).[92] Also, the population is internally heterogeneous.[93] Such heterogeneity encompasses also the issue of language, whereby the Kočevje Germans aim at reviving and preserving their native German dialect, which is virtually incomprehensible to speakers of standard German.[94]

The German-speaking population or ethnic group (to the extent that the German-speakers feel they belong to a common ethnic group) enjoys the constitutional guarantee under Article 61 like any other ethnic group in Slovenia. Slovenia recognizes German cultural associations and supports them financially. For example, the Ministry of Culture has since 1993 provided funds to the "autochthonous Kočevje Germans" for the preservation and development of their culture and identity.[95] Such support may be considered a *de facto* recognition of the minority (Komac, 2000). But this did not appear to convince Austria's Haider as he began to threaten to veto EU expansion (Leidig and Helm, 2000). Eventually, the issue seems to have been dealt with to the satisfaction of both states in the form of a bilateral cultural agreement, signed by Austria and Slovenia on 30 April 2001 in Ljubljana. The agreement on bilateral cooperation in the areas of culture, education and science had initially been drafted by Austria. The negotiating procedure lasted more than three years, predominantly due to disagreements over Article 15, which guaranteed certain cultural rights to the German-speaking population in Slovenia. More precisely, the two states could not agree on how to name that population. In Slovenia's opinion, the use of the term *Volksgruppe* by Austria could mean that the German-speakers would be entitled to the same level of protection as enjoyed by the Italian and Hungarian national minorities (Kalčič, 2001; Brstovšek, 2001a). As explained by the Slovenian Foreign Minister, the final version of the agreement refers to the members of the German-speaking ethnic group in Slovenia, warranting protection in the sense of Article 61 of Slovenia's 1991 Constitution (this is also written in an interpretative statement attached to the agreement) (Brstovšek, 2001b). It has to be added that, whilst the agreement seems to have satisfied both parties, it is unlikely that it will significantly change the situation of the German-speaking population of Slovenia.

3.4 State-Formation in the Context of External Pressure and National Homogenization

It is somewhat unfortunate that the issues related to certain ethnic minorities in Slovenia only became a matter of intensive political and public debate due to pressure from abroad

---

[92] The autochthonous (or indigenous) status (in Slovene *avtohtonost*) has been the officially-declared central concept in Slovenia's system for minority protection since its creation in the post-Second World War decades.

[93] For more details on the origins of Slovenia's Germans, other than those from the Kočevje region, see Nećak (1998a).

[94] Personal correspondence with Assoc. Prof. Dr Miran Komac, Institute for Ethnic Studies, Ljubljana, Slovenia.

[95] Slovenia's 2000 Report under the Framework Convention, Part II, Article 30 and fn. 26.

when they could have been addressed within the context of Article 61 of the Constitution (i.e., the fostering of each person's culture and allowing for the use of his/her language), and by adopting a more relaxed attitude towards ethnic minorities other than Italians and Hungarians. Slovenian parliamentarians missed an opportunity to address the question of the German-speaking population as well as that of other ethnic groups (especially those that ethnically belonged to other Yugoslav nations/nationalities) when a new constitutional order was being discussed. Although civil society was not preoccupied with this issue, there were distinct calls for more attention to be devoted in the new political system to different ethnic groups. Thus, the Ljubljana-based Institute for Ethnic Studies was very active during the process of drafting the new constitution. In 1990, it organized a prominent public debate (with the participation of politicians, lawyers, academics and minority representatives) during which its proposals regarding the constitutional provisions on the regulation of interethnic relations in Slovenia were presented. The participants agreed that the new constitution should not establish lesser rights than already enjoyed by the Italian and Hungarian communities. The institute additionally pointed out that such a minority protection system should be enhanced, and that other ethnic groups might also warrant certain special measures (provided for by the constitution or a separate constitutional law). These ethnic groups were the Roma ethnic community and the autochthonous Serbian and Croatian populations living alongside the border with Croatia;[96] it was pointed out that the existence of the German ethnic group might also raise questions.[97]

The fact that nothing was done to accommodate various aspects of the heterogeneous ethnic reality of Slovenia seems to be predominantly related to the emphasis of the new state to protect the Slovenian nation (especially because of its smallness). Nation-building was intensive. It seemed obvious that the particular approach to Slovenian national identity, centred on the Slovene language and culture, was the government's choice. To enable their development and protection was, in turn, the government's great responsibility. The use of other languages, especially Serbo-Croatian, was reduced to the private domain.[98] It was within the family, rather than at school, that Serbo-Croatian (as well as other minority languages except Italian and Hungarian) was to be used. What needs to be added is that the approach Slovenia has chosen to protect its autochthonous minorities and the decision to deal with its population of immigrant origin in a different manner have been very much in line with the general European practice of helping territorial, non-immigrant national minorities to preserve their identity on the one hand, and not knowing (or not wanting to know) how to address the

---

[96]   Mekina thus argues that "Slovenia should have protected at least" the Croats and Serbs alongside the Croatian border, and the Kočevje Germans "if it wanted consistency in its implementation of the 'indigenousness' factor" (Mekina, 2001).

[97]   The public debate and the institute's proposals, which were neither specifically discussed nor subject to confirmation by the participants, are published in a special issue of *Razprave in gradivo/Treatises and Documents* (Issue 14, 1990). The above summary of the institute's contribution to the public debate is from p.133.

[98]   This, however, only reinforced the previous trend of Serbo-Croatian being mainly used in the private domain (see Komac, 1997).

growing numbers of ethnic minorities that do not fit into the carefully crafted concept of national minority.[99]

CONCLUSION

The Slovene language has played a crucial role in the long process of Slovenian nation-building as well as in state-formation. As Slovenians now popularly believe, it was their distinct language that helped them become a nation and preserve their distinct national identity. Consequently, any threat to their language was, and still is, perceived as a threat to the nation itself. Slovenia became an independent state only in the early 1990s, and Slovenians had previously lived within several polities. In each and every one of them, Slovenians were a (numerical) minority. More importantly, throughout the centuries, Slovenians were surrounded by big nations whose control of the Slovenian-populated territories (providing for access to the Adriatic Sea) included plans for the extinction of the Slovenian nation. In such circumstances, Slovenians have developed the perception of Slovenian smallness—a sense of being threatened as a nation. This 'collective memory' as the basis for Slovenian smallness has made Slovenians somewhat suspicious of neighbouring groups in general, and sensitive to language issues in particular. It is in such a historical context of Slovenian smallness that language policies in Slovenia have been defined and in which these policies seem comprehensible nowadays.

The concerns for Slovene (alongside Slovenian culture) as the central marker of Slovenian national identity (i.e., as the centre of the nation-building process) gradually became one of the driving forces in the Slovenian nation's state-formation efforts. Due to the historical experience under the Habsburg rule, the prospects of mitigating Slovenian smallness more successfully led them to join both the first and the second Yugoslav state. Whereas Serbian dominance within the first Yugoslavia soon buried the hopes of different nations to express and develop their national characteristics freely, Slovenian expectations seemed fulfilled for some time after the Second World War within the second Yugoslavia. Slovenian smallness was certainly redefined. It would have been an almost ideal situation had relatively significant numbers of Slovenians not been left outside the SFRY. In their sensitivity to their culture and language, and all too well aware of the expansionist nationalism of neighbouring nations, Slovenians had a bigger state, Yugoslavia, to 'look after' Slovenian minorities abroad. But this calculation was a battle to be won by not only aiming to establish a number of minority rights for the ethnic Italians and Hungarians in Slovenia, but also by convincing the communist elite of Yugoslavia to accept such proposals, in the spirit of brotherhood and unity. Simultaneously, another battle loomed on the horizon: to provide for the conditions in which Slovenian identity and the Slovene language would be expressed and developed without any obstacles. This other battle is particularly significant for two reasons.

---

[99]   In a personal interview with a governmental official in 1997, it appeared that Slovenia was going to adopt the provisions of the Framework Convention in the same manner as Germany had done: to guarantee the rights contained in the Convention to specifically-mentioned traditional national minorities alone, and to extend certain of these rights to the Roma.

First, the ethnic composition, federal structures and the functioning of Yugoslavia as a whole led to the reconstruction of Slovenian smallness. This time, the potential threats to Slovene were identified as coming from within the state. Second, Slovenian communists were united with civil society in Slovenia (writers, academics) in combating those threats. Especially as far as threats to the Slovene language or to the educational system were concerned, the Slovenian communist leaders stood cautiously, yet firmly, for the Slovenian (rather than Yugoslav) national cause (since the latter was used as a pretext for centralization and unification). Slovenian nation-building was thus carried out in the context of interethnic relations in the SFRY, which appears to contradict commonly held views that, under communism, class identities replaced national adherence (Gilberg, 1980: 194).

Language policies in Slovenia had begun to play a crucial role in the process of nation-building decades before the desire to form an independent state was expressed. It was in that context (especially from the 1960s to the 1980s) that the regulation of the use of national minority languages in Slovenia was set up and the issue of the use of different languages (including Serbo-Croatian) deemed resolved. However, the changed geopolitical situation following the break-up of the SFRY again reinforced the perception of Slovenian smallness and the need to safeguard Slovenian national identity and therefore the Slovene language. Given that Slovenians had now formed their own state, equal to other sovereign states, it was to be expected that the end of the successful state-formation process would put an end to the feelings of being constantly threatened by surrounding nations. But instead of opting for a multinational state structure, Slovenians underwent a process of homogenization with Slovene playing a central role yet again. This was most evident with regard to the use of the languages of the former Yugoslav nations (in particular in the case of Serbo–Croatian). It seemed that in the early 1990s, for the sake of differentiation from the rest of the Balkans, Slovenian politicians and the general public (with probably the only exception of Slovenian entrepreneurs) were willing to disregard Slovenia's economic interests in that part of the Balkans where Slovenia seemed set to display comparative advantages given its Yugoslav experience and knowledge about the markets and their functioning. It would seem that Slovenians have never really managed to completely abolish the feeling of Slovenian smallness. In a changed geopolitical situation, such a perception was only redefined. Furthermore, the pressure exerted upon Slovenia by two neighbouring states—Austria and Italy—to regulate the question of the German-speaking population and the issue of the Italians who had fled Slovenia/Yugoslavia after the Second World War seem to have only strengthened the feeling of Slovenian smallness. In this respect, one may begin to wonder if democratic changes in the rest of the former Yugoslav republics may also permeate bilateral relations between Slovenia and those republics (now independent states) with ethnic issues. For the time being, and based upon the experience with Italy and Austria in the 1990s as well as upon the lack of European (legal) standards on the protection of immigrant minorities, the answer would lean towards the negative. The experience with Italy and Austria bears one resemblance. Both Italian and Austrian threats (and actual efforts by Italy) to block the EU enlargement process until an appropriate settlement of the outstanding issues in Slovenia was reached seemed to have guaranteed some 'progress' in bilateral talks.

However, those pressures have not been a positive contribution to a better regulation of interethnic issues within Slovenia itself. To the contrary: although to a limited extent the public seems to have become more intolerant towards non-Slovenians in general, and less prepared to automatically accept all the positive measures enjoyed by the two national minorities in Slovenia. Not surprisingly, intolerance has been displayed in terms of language. Compulsory bilingual (Slovene-Hungarian) schooling had to be assessed by the Constitutional Court and Slovenian citizenship was made conditional upon fluency in Slovene. Similarly, the Slovenian public has gradually begun to believe that the population of Slovenia that originates in the former Yugoslav republics should speak Slovene, adjust to Slovenian culture and habits and use their native languages within their families alone—this in order to try and prevent any future pressure at the bilateral level similar to that exerted by Italy and Austria.

In sum, because of Slovenian smallness, language has been widely perceived as the only permanent asset in Slovenian claims for nationhood and nation-preservation—both within the multinational Yugoslav Federation as well as within independent Slovenia. But a great challenge seems to lie ahead for the Slovenians: membership in the EU is set to cause concerns about the use of the Slovene language. The use of Slovene might become guaranteed under law but will certainly be limited due to several other (non-ethnic) factors, such as economic interest as a guiding principle for using other languages (especially English). Paradoxically, however, instead of thinking of addressing this challenge, Slovenians seemed to have been more concerned with the traditional processes of national homogenization in the old Yugoslav context of Slovenian smallness.

REFERENCES

Anderson, Benedict (1983) *Imagined Communities: Reflections on the Origin and Spread of Nationalism*. London and New York: Verso.

Banac, Ivo (1994) *The National Question in Yugoslavia: Origins, History, Politics*. Ithaca and London: Cornell University Press.

Brstovšek, Andrej (2001a) "Kulturni sporazum čaka na dejanja". *Dnevnik*, 3 May 2001.

Brstovšek, Andrej (2001b) "Kulturni sporazum med Slovenijo in Avstrijo podpisan". *Dnevnik*, 30 April 2001.

Bučar, France (1993) "Slovenia in Europe". *Nationalities Papers*, 21(1): 33–41.

Čurin Radovič, Suzana (2000) "Presentation of the Ministry of Culture's Programme for the Protection of the Cultural Rights of Ethnic Minorities in Slovenia". Translated by Hugh Brown. Ljubljana (unpublished manuscript).

de Varennes, Fernand (1996) "Autonomy, Human Rights and Protection of Minorities in Central and Eastern Europe". In Local Self-Government, Territorial Integrity and Protection of Minorities. Proceedings of the UniDem Seminar organised in Lausanne on 25–27 April 1996 in co-operation with the Swiss Institute of Comparative Law. Strasbourg: European Commission for Democracy through Law, Council of Europe, pp.217–248.

Devetak, Silvo (1986) "Enakopravnost jezikov in pisav pri poslovanju organov jugoslovanske federacije". *Razprave in gradivo/Treatises and Documents*, 19: 25–43.

Devetak, Silvo (1989) "Jezik: sredstvo za povezovanje (ali ločevanje) večnacionalne družbe". *Teorija in praksa*, 26(5): 552–557.

Gilberg, Trond (1980) "State Policy, Ethnic Persistence and Nationality Formation in Eastern Europe". In Peter F. Sugar (ed.) *Ethnic Diversity and Conflict in Eastern Europe*. Santa Barbara and Oxford: ABC-Clio, pp.185–235.

Hindmarsh, Jennie Harre (1996) "How Do We Define *Small* States and Islands? A Critical Analysis of Alternative Conceptualizations". *Convergence*, 29(2), available at EBSCOhost/Academic Search Elite, http://ebhostweb15.global.epnet.com.

Hobsbawm, Eric J. (1992) *Nations and Nationalism since 1780: Programme, Myth, Reality.* Second edition. Cambridge: Cambridge University Press.

Hočevar, Tone (2000) "Italija 25 let po Osimu". *Delo-fax*, 10 November 2000, p.6. See http://www.delo.si/cgi-perl/delofax.pl/2000-11-10.pdf.

Hribar, Valentin (1993) "Slovene Statehood". *Nationalities Papers*, 21(1): 43–49.

Kalčič, Vesna (2001) "Topli veter z Dunaja". *Dnevnik*, 8 March 2001.

King, Charles (1997) "Policing Language: Linguistic Security and the Sources of Ethnic Conflict". *Security Dialogue*, 28(4): 493–496.

Klopčič, Vera, Jancz Stergar, Boris Jesih, Vladimir Klemenčič, *et al.* (1994) *Ethnic Minorities in Slovenia*. Second edition. Ljubljana: Institute for Ethnic Studies and Information Bureau, Government of the Republic of Slovenia.

Komac, Miran (1997) "Srbska skupnost v Sloveniji (statistična slika)". *Razprave in gradivo/ Treatises and Documents*, 32: 73–115.

Komac, Miran (1998a) "Narodne manjšine v Sloveniji (elementi destrukcije ali varnosti nacionalne države)". In Miran Mitar and Andrej Sotlar (eds.) *Nacionalna varnost in medetnični konflikti v Republiki Sloveniji. Zbornik raziskovalnega projekta*. Ljubljana: Visoka policijsko-varnostna šola, pp.125–171.

Komac, Miran (1999) *Protection of Ethnic Communities in the Republic of Slovenia: Vademecum.* Translated by Mile and Maja Bilbija. Ljubljana: Institute for Ethnic Studies.

Komac, Miran (2000) "Evropska listina o regionalnih ali manjšinskih jezikih v luči ohranjanja manjšinskih jezikov v Sloveniji". In Inka Štrukelj (ed.) *Kultura, identiteta in jezik v procesih evropske integracije*. Ljubljana: Društvo za uporabno jezikoslovje, pp.50–77.

Komac, Miran (2001) "Lesser-Used Language Groups in Slovenia". In *Lesser-Used Languages in States Applying for EU Membership (Cyprus, Czech Republic, Estonia, Hungary, Poland and Slovenia)*. Working Paper in the Education and Culture Series, EDUC 106 EN Rev. 1, 10–2001. Brussels: European Parliament, Directorate-General for Research, pp.113–124.

Leidig, Michael and Toby Helm (2000) "Austria Threatens EU Enlargement in Sanctions Row". *Telegraph.co.uk*, 5 July 2000. http://www.telegraph.co.uk/news/main.jhtml?xml=/news/2000/07/05/waus05.xml.

Mekina, Igor (2001) "Slovenia and Minorities: Some are More Equal than Others". *AIM*, 30 March 2001. http://www.aimpress.org/dyn/trae/archive/data/200103/10330-002-trac lju.htm.

Melik, Vasilij (1997) "Problemi v razvoju slovenske narodne identitete (do 1941)". In Dušan Nećak (ed.) *Avstrija. Jugoslavija. Slovenija. Slovenska narodna identiteta skozi čas: zbornik, Lipica, 29. maj–1. junij 1996*. Translated by Igor Grdina and Vesna Kalčič. Ljubljana: Oddelek za zgodovino Filozofske fakultete, pp.41–52.

Milanovich, Natasha (1996) "Slovenia in the New Geopolitical Context". In Francis W. Carter and Harold T. Norris (ed.) *The Changing Shape of the Balkans*. London: UCL Press, pp.25–49.

Mlinar, Zdravko (1994) "Kdo danes še potrebuje državne meje? Državna zaščita in odpiranje Slovenije v svet". In Niko Toš (ed.) *Slovenski izziv II. Rezultati raziskav javnega mnenja 1992–1993*. Ljubljana: Fakulteta za družbene vede–IDV, pp.73–89.

Mlinar, Zdravko (1995) "Nacionalno in regionalno osamosvajanje in (raz-) druževanje". In Zdravko Mlinar (ed.) *Osamosvajanje in povezovanje v evropskem prostoru*. Ljubljana: Znanstvena knjižnica, Fakulteta za družbene vede, pp.97–123.

Moritsch, Andreas (1997) "Narodna identiteta—nujnost ali anahronizem?" In Dušan Nećak (ed.) *Avstrija. Jugoslavija. Slovenija. Slovenska narodna identiteta skozi čas: zbornik, Lipica, 29. maj–1. junij 1996*. Translated by Igor Grdina and Vesna Kalčič. Ljubljana: Oddelek za zgodovino Filozofske fakultete, pp.33–40.

Nećak, Dušan (1997) "Avstrija. Jugoslavija. Slovenija. Slovenska narodna identiteta skozi čas". In Dušan Nećak (ed.) *Avstrija. Jugoslavija. Slovenija. Slovenska narodna identiteta skozi čas: zbornik, Lipica, 29. maj–1. junij 1996*. Translated by Igor Grdina and Vesna Kalčič. Ljubljana: Oddelek za zgodovino Filozofske fakultete, pp.19–24.

Nećak, Dušan (ed.) (1998a) *"Nemci" na Slovenskem 1941–1955: Izsledki projekta*. Ljubljana: Znanstveni inštitut Filozofske fakultete.

Nećak, Dušan (1998b) "Uvod". In Dušan Nećak (ed.) *"Nemci" na Slovenskem 1941–1955: Izsledki projekta*. Ljubljana: Znanstveni inštitut Filozofske fakultete, pp.7–21.

Nećak Lük, Albina (1983) "Enakopravnost jezikov kot element enakopravnosti narodov in narodnosti SFRJ". *Razprave in gradivo/Treatises and Documents*, 16: 127–135.

Nećak Lük, Albina (1997) "Jezikovna identiteta in jezikovno načrtovanje pri Slovencih". In Dušan Nećak (ed.) *Avstrija. Jugoslavija. Slovenija. Slovenska narodna identiteta skozi čas: zbornik, Lipica, 29. maj–1. junij 1996*. Translated by Igor Grdina and Vesna Kalčič. Ljubljana: Oddelek za zgodovino Filozofske fakultete, pp.117–132.

Encyclopaedia Britannica (1997) *The New Encyclopaedia Britannica. Micropaedia*, Volume 10, 15th edition. Chicago: Encyclopaedia Britannica, Inc.

Novak Lukanovič, Sonja (1986) "Jeziki in izobraževalni sistem v SR Slovenij". *Razprave in gradivo/Treatises and Documents*, 19: 87–96.

Pirjevec, Joze (1993) "Slovenes and Yugoslavia 1918–1991". *Nationalities Papers*, 21(1): 109–118.

Plut-Pregelj, Leopoldina (2000) "Slovenia's Concerns about the Proposed Yugoslav Core Curriculum in the 1980s". In Plut-Pregelj, Leopoldina, Aleš Gabrič and Božo Repe (eds.) *The Repluralization of Slovenia in the 1980s: New Revelations from Archival Records*. The Donald W. Treadgold Papers in Russian, East European, and Central Asian Studies, No. 24. Seattle: The Henry M. Jackson School of International Studies, University of Washington, pp.58–78.

Prunk, Janko (1997) "Razvoj slovenske narodne identitete v prvi Jugoslaviji". In Dušan Nećak (ed.) *Avstrija. Jugoslavija. Slovenija. Slovenska narodna identiteta skozi čas: zbornik, Lipica, 29. maj–1. junij 1996*. Translated by Igor Grdina and Vesna Kalčič. Ljubljana: Oddelek za zgodovino Filozofske fakultete, pp.53–61.

Pucer, E. (1994–1995) "Hardly a Few Houses". *War Report*, 30: 27–28.

Roter, Petra (2001) "Locating the 'Minority Problem' in Europe: A Historical Perspective". *Journal of International Relations and Development*, 4(3): 221–249.

Schöpflin, George (1996) "Aspects of Language and Ethnicity in Central and Eastern Europe". *Transition*, 2(24): 6–9, 64.

Sugar, Peter F. (1980) "Ethnicity in Eastern Europe". In Peter F. Sugar (ed.) *Ethnic Diversity and Conflict in Eastern Europe*. Santa Barbara and Oxford: ABC-Clio, pp.419–444.

Suppan, Arnold (1991) "According to the Principle of Reciprocity: The Minorities in Yugoslav–Austrian Relations, 1918–1938". In Paul Smith (ed.) *Ethnic Groups in International Relations*. New York: New York University Press, pp.235–273.

Toš, Niko (1993) "Social Change and Shift of Values: Democratization Processes in Slovenia, 1980–1990". *Nationalities Papers*, 21(1): 61–69.

Toš, Niko (ed.) (1997) *Vrednote v prehodu I.: Slovensko javno mnenje 1968–1990*. Ljubljana: Fakulteta za družbene vede–IDV–CJMMK.

Toš, Niko (ed.) (1999) *Vrednote v prehodu II.: Slovensko javno mnenje 1990–1998*. Ljubljana: Fakulteta za družbene vede–IDV–CJMMK.

Trifunovska, Snežana (ed.) (1994) *Yugoslavia through Documents: From Its Creation to Its Dissolution*. Dordrecht, Boston and London: Martinus Nijhoff Publishers.

Udovički, Jasminka (1995) "Nationalism, Ethnic Conflict, and Self-Determination in the Former Yugoslavia". In Berch Berberoglu (ed.) *The National Question: Nationalism, Ethnic Conflict, and Self-determination in the 20th Century*. Philadelphia: Temple University Press, pp.280–314.

Varga-Novljan, Zdenka (1998) "Kulturni sporazum? Dobra rešitev". *Dnevnik*, 8 April 1998.

Vodopivec, Peter (1993) "The Slovenes in the Habsburg Empire or Monarchy". *Nationalities Papers*, 21(1): 159–170.

Ethnicity, Language
and Transition Politics in Romania:
The Hungarian Minority in Context

Carmen Kettley

Ethnicity, Language and Transition Politics in Romania: The Hungarian Minority in Context

Carmen Kettley

INTRODUCTION

The end of the Cold War has transformed the ethnic issue in Romania into an 'ethnic panic' that has captured the attention and energies of politicians, voters, the media and the academic community. In a post-communist environment of deep economic recession, political instability and ideological confusion, the resurgence of nationalism and of ethnic disputes in post-communist Romania developed at an unpredictable speed and became internationalized by involving the kin-state, regional institutions and the international community as a whole.

At the centre of the re-emergent interethnic disputes were the restoration of language rights and the return of the formerly Hungarian educational institutions to the Hungarian minority. The focus on the claims of the Hungarian minority is not surprising for three important reasons. First, Hungarians represent the largest, best organized and most vocal minority group in Romania. Further, the Hungarian minority enjoys the support of its equally vocal kin-state, Hungary. Finally, the immediate proximity of the kin-state and the troubled history of shifting boundaries between Romania and Hungary have generated a chronic sense of insecurity and mutual mistrust from both the Romanian majority and the Hungarian minority in Romania.

The disputes that arose between the Hungarian and the Romanian political elites in Romania over language rights have transformed the ethnic issue in Romania into 'the Hungarian question'. Consequently, the relationship between the Hungarian minority and the Romanian majority has had a dramatic influence upon the dynamics of ethnic policies in Romania as minority policies and laws which, while concerning all 'persons belonging to national minorities', were drafted with the Hungarian minority in mind. Hence, the dynamics of the relationship between the ethnic Hungarian and the Romanian political elites have set the tone of the ethnic discourse, defined the nature of interethnic relations and determined the development of the legal framework for the protection of minority rights in Romania.

In the first post-communist decade, Romania experienced a series of swift changes in ethnic politics. These changes varied from early enthusiastic attempts at the restoration of minority rights to a rampant nationalist discourse and restrictive regulations, then again to minority-friendly policies and laws. Finally, following the general elections in 2000, ethnic politics were reshaped by an unexpectedly cooperative relationship between Romanian and

Hungarian political elites in Romania, albeit established in a different political and institutional environment.

This fluctuating picture may seem most confusing to many Western scholars and policy-makers, for Romania, like most of Eastern Europe in the transition period, often appears to escape the classic theoretical explanations of ethnic politics. Indeed, the outbreak of ethnic conflict in Central and Eastern Europe has generated a literature boom of varied quality seeking to explain the ills of a new type of social and political environment which was not experienced before by any Western state: post-communist transition (Rothschild, 1993: 264; Schöpflin, 2000). Tsukimura's (1998) description of Eastern Europe summarizes, perhaps, the popular wisdom regarding the causes of political instability in this region. Building on Stein Rokkan's (1983) concept of Western periphery, Tsukimura describes Eastern European societies as "backward societies", characterized by loss of control over one's own territory, an underdeveloped economy and cultural marginality. Among the 'anomalies' of transition, ethnic disputes are considered a critical obstacle to the establishment of liberal democracy. The underlying causes of ethnic conflict are often explained by pointing at historical legacy, an allegedly innate nationalism and a chronic inability of dominant groups to adapt to the Western understanding of democratic quality and cultural diversity (Burgess, 1997; Jowitt, 1992).

For much of the 1990s, Romania was seen as the embodiment of all of these evils. Such explanations can only provide a narrow understanding of the dynamics of ethnic relations during the first decade of transition in this country. Rather, the twists and turns in interethnic relations in Romania since 1989 have revealed that the quest for political legitimacy and the political skills of the new elites, along with the challenge of transition, have become some of the most important markers of interethnic dialogue.

Romania's shift, within a single decade, from nationalist discourse and discriminatory policies to a power-sharing arrangement and, recently, to a novel type of political cooperation, demonstrates that ethnicity has become part of the wider political engineering of the transition process. I therefore argue that research into ethnicity and language in post-communist countries should not be separated from the specific social, political and economic environments that determine their dynamics. This chapter will therefore address the impact of broader political processes on ethnic politics and on the regulation of minority and language rights in Romania.

1. BACKGROUND

With the collapse of the Ceaușescu regime in December 1989 the new political elites in Romania were faced with the overwhelming task of reconstructing an accountable state and, at the same time, with the challenge of performing radical economic reforms and the democratization of a totalitarian society. In addition to these priorities, which by themselves would place a tremendous strain on any state (Dahrendorf, 2000), the post-communist regime was confronted with the challenge of reforming the status of its seventeen ethnic minorities [100]

---

[100] According to the 1992 census, the ethnic make-up of the population of Romania consists of the following ethnic groups: Romanian (89.4%), Hungarian (7.1%), Roma (1.8%), German (0.5%), Ukrainian (0.3%), Russian (0.2%), Turkish (0.1%), Serbian (0.1%), Tatar (0.1%), Slovak (0.1%), Other (0.3%) (Council of Europe, 1999).

From 1990 to 1996, the dilemma of the new regime was how to contain the demands of the Hungarian minority for language rights while ensuring Romania's successful integration into Western European institutions.

Warned by the disastrous dissolution of Yugoslavia and urged by the potential for social unrest and ethnic violence at home, and under significant international pressure, the first post-communist government proceeded to hastily draft new minority policies and, consequently, new laws. It was hoped that this would be sufficient to resolve deep-rooted ethnic disputes and contain the conflict, whatever this reduction implied for the post-communist elites of the day.

The first Romanian government, which initially included some representatives of the newly established Democratic Alliance of Hungarians in Romania (Romániai Magyarok Demokratikus Szövetsége, RMDSZ),[101] was confronted with an overwhelming task which required foresight, moderation and negotiation skills from the elites on both sides. However, foresight, moderation and adequate negotiation skills were anything but characteristic of the new regime. Consequently, the hasty implementation of early minority policies, including the restoration of education in the Hungarian language, collapsed due to the fierce resistance of Romanian teachers and students who were not consulted on this issue. This failure contributed to a rapid resurgence of nationalism and to a sharp polarization of the positions of the two ethnic groups.

By the end of 1996, the Romanian political establishment was dominated by nationalist elements and no genuine progress had been made on the legislative level. The outcome was a cosmetic reform of minority rights policies, which consisted of including standard minority guarantees in the 1991 Constitution, and in enthusiastically signing the international and regional human rights documents necessary for Romania's accession to the Council of Europe and NATO.

The parliamentary and presidential elections in 1996 brought about dramatic changes in interethnic relations in Romania. The Democratic Convention of Romania (Convenția Democrată Română, CDR) won both the parliamentary and the presidential elections and the RMDSZ was invited to join the new ruling coalition together with the Democratic Party (Partidul Democrat, PD) and the National Liberal Party (Partidul Național Liberal, PNL). This new government represented the first multiethnic political alliance in the history of Romania and the focus shifted towards a more cooperative approach. The result was the emergence of a power-sharing experiment that surprised both the domestic political establishment and international observers.

The direct participation of the Hungarian minority in the central decision-making process, and an unprecedented elite cooperation, indicated that a new era appeared to have begun for ethnic minorities in Romania. The dilemma, then, was how to establish a workable balance between ensuring that all ethnic groups have a reasonable knowledge of the official language while providing them with some degree of control over education in their mother tongue. Thus, from 1996, the Romanian leadership appeared to acknowledge that cultural diversity and minority rights required policies and laws that went beyond mere tolerance and non-discrimination (de Varennes, 1997; Hannum, 1996). Consequently, interethnic nego-

---

[101]   The RMDSZ (the acronym is UDMR in Romanian) was established on 25 December 1989.

tiations encompassed both debates over international standards and debates on how to implement these standards in order to respond to the needs of specific minorities.

The central demand of the Hungarian minority was the legal right to establish a state-funded Hungarian-language university. However, the government's initiative to include this right in an amendment to the Education Act was rejected by parliament and generated fierce protests from the opposition, the majority coalition and the media. A major cause of this crisis was, again, the government's failure to consult with and ensure the support of its own allies, let alone public opinion, on an issue known for being extremely sensitive to both ethnic groups.

Faced with the RMDSZ's threat to withdraw its political support for the CDR, the parliament eventually agreed to negotiate a solution that would accommodate the interests of both parties. The outcome was a dramatic legislative process, extended over two years of negotiations, which eventually led to a compromise. This consisted of establishing the right of linguistic minorities to set up their own private institutions of higher education as well as opening departments and faculties with tuition in the mother tongue in state-funded universities. Thus, by the end of the 1990s, Romania had significantly improved its human rights record and had become an active member of regional human rights institutions.

Yet, a decade after the end of the Cold War, Romania remains ethnically fragile and politically divided, despite having introduced national laws which meet international legal standards. Significantly, the language issue is still perceived as the main obstacle to interethnic accommodation. In spite of the significant progress in the legal field, the debate on language policies remains open as elite cooperation was not followed by genuine inter-group reconciliation. In addition, the Hungarian minority is still not satisfied that the existing legal framework sufficiently guarantees the preservation of its linguistic identity. On the other hand, the Romanian leadership argues that Romania has met the international standards on minority rights and that the present legislation does guarantee adequate protection and ensures a dignified status of its ethnic minorities. Moreover, it is feared that the fragile interethnic reconciliation achieved at the end of the 1990s will not survive future political processes, as the 2000 elections ended the power-sharing experiment with the return to power of President Ion Iliescu and the Party of Social Democracy (Partidul Democrației Sociale din România, PDSR).

However, Romania's considerable achievements in promoting minority rights and interethnic cooperation cannot be underestimated. Furthermore, these achievements need to be analysed and assessed so that both the obstacles to and incentives for interethnic accord can be identified.

2. LANGUAGE RIGHTS IN POST-COMMUNIST ROMANIA: THE POLITICS OF CONTAINMENT (1990–1996)

2.1 The Resurgence of Romanian Nationalism and the Emergence of the Hungarian Political Opposition (1990–1991)

The collapse of the communist regime in Romania found the Romanian majority and the Hungarian minority alike in a celebratory mood. Hopes were high that democracy, economic prosperity and interethnic harmony would be attained overnight. Following the overthrow of the Ceauşescu regime on 22 December 1989, an eclectic group of communist reformists, army officers and former dissidents formed the National Salvation Front (Frontul Salvării Naţionale, FSN). Romania's new leader was Ion Iliescu, a former high-ranking communist official, whose initial ambitions were to promote a reformed socialism.

The early commitment by the FSN on 22 December to the rule of law and to the protection of ethnic minorities gave reason for optimism regarding the future of interethnic relations in Romania. Most importantly, the FSN's stance on the ethnic issue enjoyed the support and the full cooperation of the newly created RMDSZ. This support led to the inclusion of important personalities from the Hungarian minority in the FSN's provisional governing bodies. Significantly, the position of the new regime on the minority issue was embraced by Hungary, Romania's most sensitive neighbour. Hungary was to become the first country to recognize the new Romanian government. Such early and unexpected support from Budapest did much to strengthen the legitimacy of the new regime and bring confidence to the Hungarian minority that its rights and status would be improved (Gallagher, 1995: 75).

Hopes for a new era in interethnic relations in Romania were further enhanced by the adoption of a decree-law on local government,[102] which represented the first attempt of the Iliescu regime to restore language rights. This decree-law was followed by a surprisingly liberal declaration on the status of national minorities released by the FSN on 6 January 1990. The declaration expressed, in unambiguous terms, the commitment of the new regime to provide a new constitutional and institutional framework for the protection of the "individual and collective rights and liberties of all the national minorities" (Nastase, 1998: 627).

However, the first test of the ability of the new regime to change minority policies was to reveal a lack of consensus on ethnic issues within the Romanian majority. At the time the new minority policies were announced, the political landscape of Romania was, at best, confusing. New political parties began to take shape in January 1990 and the nationalist movements were not yet organized. While being initially responsive to Hungarian requests to include guarantees on minority rights in its policy statements, the FSN failed to foresee that other political groups would not be willing to approve such concessions.

In addition, neither Iliescu nor his close allies had an understanding at the time of the controversial aspects of concepts such as collective rights or autonomy, nor were they aware of the potential impact of their implementation. Most importantly, the first steps taken to implement a new direction in ethnic policies were flawed by misjudgements by both the FSN officials and the Hungarian minority's leadership. Thus, the restoration of educational establishments to the Hungarian minority involved removing Romanian pupils from mixed schools and the prospect of breaking-up the Babes–Bolyai University in Cluj before the beginning of the new academic year. As prior consultation at the local level was not considered before taking action, Romanian pupils and teachers, as well as the newly formed Student League, took to the streets and used the media to state their opposition (Gallagher, 1995).

Similarly, the attempt of the new government to restore language rights for ethnic Hungarian pupils in Târgu Mureş was to become another failure, representing the beginning of a bitter division between the RMDSZ and the post-1989 governments. The disputes over

---

[102] Decree-Law No. 8 of 1990, published in *Monitorul Oficial*, No. 4, 8 January 1990.

teaching in Hungarian provided the perfect momentum for the retaliation of those nostalgic for communist nationalism, who found their most effective ally in the media. The retaliation of the Romanian nationalists led to the establishment, in February 1990, of the Romanian Hearth Union (Uniunea Vatra Românească, UVR) and of its political arm, the Party of National Unity (Partidul Unității Naționale Române, PUNR). This was followed, in 1991, by the establishment of the Greater Romania Party (Partidul România Mare, PRM), an extremist party promoting a neo-fascist discourse against the Hungarian, Roma and Jewish minorities.

Following the failure of the hastily implemented new language policies, the FSN leadership was to be faced, towards the end of January 1990, with the choice of securing the political support of nationalist groups or keeping its political commitments towards the Hungarian minority. As Iliescu's main goal was to retain his newly-gained control of the state, he saw his political agenda being jeopardized by supporting ethnic Hungarians' language claims (Gallagher, 1995). Furthermore, the FSN decided to shift from all-inclusive political caretaker to political contender and run for elections later that year. It then became obvious that supporting Hungarian claims for language rights would estrange important nationalist elements whose influence on public opinion was growing. Following these developments, Iliescu (and the FSN) decided to embrace the nationalist agenda of the various political groups formed after December 1989 in exchange for their support in the forthcoming elections.

The failure of the FSN to keep its normative promises, and its reluctance to negotiate a compromise with the Hungarian minority over education in Hungarian, contributed to a sudden and sharp polarization of both ethnic groups at the local level. Consequently, the relationship between the FSN and the RMDSZ worsened and eventually collapsed following the outbreak of street violence in Târgu Mureș on 18–19 March 1990. Although a parliamentary inquiry into the causes of the incident was conducted, no agreement was reached as to who was responsible. The direct involvement of the UVR in mobilizing Romanian villagers to come to Târgu Mureș and fight the ethnic Hungarian protesters represented for many an indication that the street riots were initiated and orchestrated by the UVR, with the assistance of the secret services and the tacit blessing of the FSN leadership.

The street fights in Târgu Mureș were the first act of ethnic violence involving casualties in a series of disastrous ethnic conflicts that have shattered Eastern Europe over the past decade. They had lasting consequences for interethnic relations in Romania, leading to a difficult relationship between the RMDSZ and subsequent Romanian governments. The break-up between the Romanian and the ethnic Hungarian elites was to have far-reaching consequences that would affect the entire Romanian society. Indeed, it has shaped the attitudes of the media, the legislative process and Romania's foreign policy endeavours.

However, the position of the Hungarian minority could not be ignored by the new regime. Demonstrating a remarkable ability to organize itself, the RMDSZ soon became the sole representative of the largest minority group in the country and an important contender in the electoral process. Following the first post-communist elections, in May 1990, the RMDSZ gained 7.2 per cent of the total number of seats in parliament. However, the overwhelming victory of the FSN and of Ion Iliescu in the 1990 elections gave little reason to believe that ethnic relations would improve. Indeed, the relationship between the FSN and the RMDSZ would be one of troublesome coexistence for the entire duration of the Iliescu regime during 1990–1996. As the FSN eventually embraced the nationalist discourse of its political allies, the Hungarian position, too, became increasingly radicalized, leaving little room for compromise in the negotiations with Romanian authorities during the drafting of the new Constitution and of subsequent legislation.

2.2   The 1991 Constitution and the Reaffirmation of Official Monolingualism

Like other constitutions in transition countries, the Romanian Constitution was drafted in a climate of political instability, ideological turmoil and the resurgence of nationalism. Perhaps more than other legal documents, the Romanian Constitution reflects the state of mind of the dominant group regarding ethnicity at a particular moment of its history.

The new Constitution was adopted on 21 November 1991,[103] following consultations with international constitutional experts, and was endorsed by a referendum on 8 December 1991. Admittedly a democratic document (Gallagher, 1995), the Constitution of 1991 represented significant progress in Romania's transition from a totalitarian regime to a democratic state. However, the provisions related to the type of state, the official language and the protection of minority rights fell short of minorities' expectations. Thus, the new Constitution constructed a framework for the protection of ethnic minorities which has been characterized as ethnocentric and "drawing on a Jacobin tradition" (Schöpflin, 1993; Liebich, 1998), as it formally established the dominant position of the ethnic Romanian majority and language.

Indeed, having been drafted without the participation of ethnic minorities, the text of the new Constitution generated fierce political disputes and protests by the political elites of the Hungarian minority over the framework within which the minorities' status was enshrined in the new Basic Law. The main points of discontent have been, and remain, the proclamation of the Romanian state as a nation-state (Article 1[1]), the reference to the "Romanian people" (Article 4[1]) and the official monolingualism enshrined in Article 13. Thus, Article 1(1) proclaims that "Romania is a sovereign, independent, unitary and indivisible National State", while Article 13 declares that "In Romania, the official language is Romanian". Nevertheless, Article 4(2) establishes that Romania is the common land "of all its citizens". Does the term "national state" suggest that the state's foundation is drawn from ethnic values rather than civic ones? What does this contradictory statement imply for minorities? Indeed, Article 4(1) reads: "The state foundation is laid on the unity of the Romanian people", whilst failing to indicate whether the term "people" refers to all citizens of Romania or to ethnic Romanians only.

The interpretations provided by Romanian lawmakers and scholars remain contradictory and confused. The Constitutional Court ruled that the term "official language" does not establish the superiority of the Romanian language over minority languages; rather, it indicates the language to be used in official communications with state authorities.[104] How, then,

---

[103]   Published in *Monitorul Oficial*, No. 233, 21 November 1991 (see website at http://diasan.vsat.ro/pls/dic/act_show?ida=1&tit=&idl=2).

[104]   See Constitutional Court Decision No. 40 of 11 April 1996, *Monitorul Oficial*, No. 76, 13 April 1996.

would this functional definition of the official language relate to the concept of national state enshrined in Article 1?

There is little doubt about the position of the drafters of the Constitution on the meaning of the concept of nation as they state, in unequivocal terms, that the term 'nation' designates "a community of ethnic origin" (Constantinescu *et al.*, 1992: 6–7). Furthermore, the attempts made by the Romanian academic community to explain the terminology used in constitutional texts did little to resolve this conceptual controversy. Thus, Deleanu (1996: 14), whilst maintaining that the concept of nation is based on the "community of ethnic origin, language, culture and religion", acknowledges that a nation is not an exclusively ethnic or biological phenomenon but rather a complex reality. It includes the will of a heterogeneous community, which shares the same territory and history, to live together. Finally, it has been suggested that the term "national" should be given a civic meaning as the Constitution also refers to Romania as the common land "of all its citizens".[105] At the same time, the theoretical position of the RMDSZ on the concept of nation developed towards a similar ethnic stand, albeit from a different perspective. As its proposal to eliminate the term "national state" from the text of Article 1 was rejected by the Constitutional Commission, the RMDSZ suggested a change of wording from "national state" to "multinational state" and the introduction of the term "collective identity" in Article 6. Predictably, the RMDSZ's proposals were rejected as the peculiar provisions regarding the revision of the Constitution reveal the near mythical importance that the drafters of the Constitution attached to the concepts of nation-state and language (Hockenos, 1993). Indeed, Article 148.1 establishes that the constitutional provisions regarding "the national, unitary and indivisible character of the Romanian State ..., and the official language, shall not be subject to revision".

Within such a contradictory conceptual scheme, the Constitution provides minority-specific guarantees. Thus, it establishes "the right of persons belonging to national minorities to the preservation, development and the expression of their ethnic, cultural, linguistic and religious identity" (Article 6[1]), but in conformity with "the principles of equality and non-discrimination in relation to the other Romanian citizens" (Article 6[2]). Furthermore, having set the norm on the official language, Article 32 guarantees the right of national minorities to learn and receive instruction in their mother tongue, whilst leaving the concrete regulation of this right to ordinary laws.

As Liebich (1998) has correctly noted, "[c]onstitutions are not necessarily the best guide to state practice because of their general and exhortative functions". Indeed, the ways in which constitutional principles are implemented, through ordinary laws and specific institutions, can spell the difference between a genuine protection of minority rights and ethnic discrimination. In the end, what matters is the purposes that specific laws serve and how they are implemented. The fact that the wording of the Romanian Constitution remains subject to interpretation may allow less ethnocentric governments to develop a more flexible approach to the concepts of nation and language. More specifically, declaring Romanian the official language of the state does not necessarily prevent the establishment of bilingual or multilingual arrangements that could meet the needs of specific minorities.

---

[105] Interview with Alexandru A. Farcas, former Director of the Human Rights Division, Romanian Ministry of Foreign Affairs, 1994, quoted in Farkas (1996).

Two important consequences follow from the wording of the constitutional principles discussed here. First, the provisions regarding the type of state, the official language and the procedure of revision indicate that it was indeed the intention of the drafters of the Constitution to secure the control of the state by the ethnic Romanian majority. Second, by proclaiming the Romanian language the sole official language, the Constitution may be used to rule out any further debate on official bilingualism, collective rights and on the recognition of autonomy based on ethnic criteria. Thus, the debate over these issues remains important as the wording of the constitutional provisions reveals the limits within which language rights can develop within the Romanian monolingual system. However, the subsequent practice of the post-communist governments in Romania showed that the interpretation of the Constitution is a matter of political will and that constitutional principles can be used both in favour and against minorities.

2.3 Language Politics and the Legal Framework between 1991–1996

The political environment that emerged after the adoption of the new Constitution in 1991 was characterized by a strengthening of the political influence of nationalist forces and their accession to the parliament and local councils in their own right. The local and parliamentary elections held in 1992 confirmed the strong position of the RMDSZ in the parliament and at the local level, but did little to contribute to the improvement of relations between the Hungarian and Romanian elites. In fact, the relationship between the RMDSZ and the FSN further worsened as the FSN split, with Iliescu and his conservative allies forming the National Democratic Salvation Front (Frontul Democrat al Salvării Naţionale, FDSN), later renamed as the Party of Social Democracy of Romania (Partidul Democraţiei Sociale din România, PDSR). In this new format, Iliescu and the PDSR won the 1992 elections and retained control over central state institutions, this time with the support of nationalist and right-wing political groupings: the PUNR, the Socialist Labour Party (Partidul Socialist al Muncii, PSM) and the PRM.

The political partnership between the PDSR and the Romanian nationalist parties led to a widening of the gap between the RMDSZ and the Iliescu regime. The RMDSZ consequently expanded its claims to include territorial and regional autonomy (Andreescu et al., 1994). The establishment, in 1993, of the Council of National Minorities (Consiliul Minorităţilor Naţionale, CMN) did little to improve the protection of ethnic minorities or the political dialogue between the RMDSZ and the government as this new institution was firmly controlled by the Romanian leadership (Oprescu, 2000: 73–74).

Within such a troubled political environment, and despite intense international pressure, only three significant minority-related laws were passed by the end of the first six years of Iliescu's rule: the Constitution (1991), the Act on Local Public Administration (hereafter, 'Local Administration Act') (1991) and the Act on Education (1995). These laws were intended as a response to the increasing political pressure on Romania by the Council of Europe, the OSCE and NATO to improve its human rights record.[106] Nevertheless, the

---

[106]   See van der Stoel (1993).

restrictive provisions on the use of minority languages contained in these laws revealed that the Romanian leadership was not willing to provide more than cosmetic measures in order to meet the formal requirements for accession to the Council of Europe and NATO. Such restrictive provisions were strongly opposed by the RMDSZ and questioned by international observers.[107]

The 1991 Local Administration Act[108] established the Romanian language as the official language of local council meetings, even if all council members spoke a different native language (Article 25). However, Article 23 allowed for council meeting decisions to be published both in Romanian and a minority language if the minority concerned was of "significant numerical importance". Finally, the law established that national minorities could use their native language in communications with local authorities but only if formal requests were accompanied by an official translation. For oral communications, an interpreter was to be provided, although the law did not indicate whether this was the responsibility of the local authorities or of the petitioner.

More than any other regulations, the 1995 Act on Education[109] best expressed the position of the Iliescu regime on the access of minorities to education in their mother tongue. Thus, the law provided for education in minority languages at the primary and secondary levels. However, a disturbing element of this law was the provision for the history "of Romanians" and the geography of Romania to be taught in Romanian at the secondary level (Article 123). Further, the law restricted higher education in minority languages to teacher training and arts subjects although the RMDSZ argued (1995) that there are other important subject areas that require education in the mother tongue such as economics, law or engineering. The law also established that admission and graduation exams were to be taken in Romanian, with the exception of schools where instruction is provided in the mother tongue (Article 124). An important setback, generated by the 1995 Education Act, was Article 122, which established that vocational education should be conducted in Romanian, thus encouraging the liquidation of existing native-language vocational education and the transfer of minority students to Romanian-language schools.

Building on a narrow interpretation of the Constitution, the Education Act generated much debate and fierce protests by the Hungarian minority; it was also sharply criticized by the European Parliament.[110] Both domestic and international pressure forced the Romanian government to amend the law a few months later, although a genuine change to this law was only made in 1997 by Emergency Ordinance No. 36 (see Section 3).

3.   THE POWER-SHARING EXPERIMENT (1996–2000)

The 1996 elections resulted in an unprecedented shift in the political engineering of ethnic relations in Romania. The victory of the CDR in both presidential and parliamentary elections, and the appointment of a minority-friendly prime minister, ended the political isolation of

---

107   Seo on Śj, 1991 and Śeani (1991)

108   Published in *Monitorul Oficial*, No. 238, 28 November 1991.

109   Published in *Monitorul Oficial*, No. 167, 31 July 1995.

110   Resolution No. B4-1025/95 on the protection of minority rights and human rights in Romania, passed by the European Parliament on 13 July 1995 (see website at http://www.europarl.eu.int).

the RMDSZ. Thus, the Hungarian minority joined the Romanian government, together with the CDR, the PNL and the PD, and became part of the majority coalition in parliament, on the condition that the new government would secure adequate legislation on minority rights. Accordingly, the government prioritized the protection of minorities and the implementation of relevant international standards in its Programme of Governance.[111] This new political setting was of special significance for both the RMDSZ and its Romanian partners. First, the participation of the RMDSZ in the central decision-making process represented a remarkable boost to Romania's foreign policy efforts towards accession to the Euro-Atlantic institutions. In addition, by inviting the RMDSZ to join the government, the CDR was able to secure a majority in parliament and an ally in the government that proved to be more loyal than other Romanian parties. Second, this arrangement allowed the RMDSZ to influence minority policies from the very core of the Romanian political establishment. Although this power-sharing deal was based on a coalition of convenience (Horowitz, 1985: 365–78), it proved to be a promising form of political engineering of divisive ethnic interests.

With both parties gaining from such a partnership, Romania embarked on a power-sharing experiment that would have been unthinkable even shortly before the elections. The power-sharing arrangement between the RMDSZ and its Romanian counterparts, albeit escaping Lijphart's traditional prescriptions (1977: 25–44), involved ministerial positions to be held by Hungarian officials, an informal minority veto and the prospect of the establishment of a greater degree of control by the Hungarian minority over Hungarian-language educational institutions. Significantly, the adoption by the government of an emergency ordinance amending the Education Act led the OSCE to declare that "[m]inority rights can be regarded as the most important success of the new political leadership" (OSCE, 1997). However, the legislative process that resulted from this alliance revealed that the political will of the government was not sufficient to meet the RMDSZ's requests for establishing an adequate framework for minority rights. The troubled process of the adoption of the amendments to the 1995 Education Act revealed that Romanian political elites remained sharply divided over the language issue. This division was further compounded by the government's failure to secure the parliamentary support, even of its own allies, to pass these amendments (Gallagher, 1997).

3.1 The Amendments to the 1995 Act on Education: Reconsideration of the Role of the Official Language

Government Emergency Ordinance No. 36 of 1997 (hereafter, 'Ordinance 36')[112] amended the 1995 Education Act. Due to the debates generated by its provisions on access to higher education, Ordinance 36 was subsequently amended and eventually incorporated in the 1999

---

[111]   "The Framework Programme for the Macro-Stabilisation and Development of Romania until the Year 2000. The Government Programme 1997–2000". Chapter VI, Article 2, published in *Monitorul Oficial*, No. 342, 12 December 1996.

[112]   Published in *Monitorul Oficial*, No. 152, 14 July 1997, rejected by the Constitutional Court, renegotiated and finally approved by Act No.151 of 1999.

revised version of the Education Act[113] (which will be discussed below). This regulation retains special importance as it represents significant progress in ensuring minorities' access to education in their mother tongue. Most importantly, it was accepted by the Hungarian minority as a reasonable compromise as it aimed to establish a balance between the official language and the language rights of minorities, rather than focusing on the dominant role of the Romanian language in minority education.

While the amended law restates the constitutional principle regarding the official language ("education at all levels shall be provided in the Romanian language"), it provides the conditions for the exercise of the right of persons belonging to national minorities to learn and receive instruction in their mother tongue (Article 8). A varying degree of instruction in Romanian, and of Romanian, is retained in all minority-language schools and higher education institutions. Thus, in primary schools, Romanian language and literature are taught according to textbooks and curricula especially prepared for the needs of the minority concerned. In secondary, vocational and high schools, Romanian language and literature are taught according to textbooks and curricula that are identical to those used for Romanian-language classes.

One of the most sensitive issues related to the curricula was the teaching of Romanian history and geography. The law provides a level-differentiated solution (Article 120). Thus, in primary schools, these disciplines are taught in the minority languages according to the textbooks and curricula used for Romanian-language classes. For all other levels of instruction, Romanian history and geography are taught in Romanian using standard Romanian textbooks and curricula. Finally, vocational and technical training is provided in the mother tongue, at all levels, with the technical terminology being taught in both languages.

3.2 Access to Higher Education in Minority Languages and the Hungarian University Issue

The government's agenda for education in minority languages included amendments to the Education Act and the Local Administration Act and the adoption of a comprehensive Minority Act. However, faced with a divided parliament and a hostile media, and with strong opposition from within, the government eventually only achieved the revision of the Education Act. Revising the Education Act became a difficult endeavour due to the great challenge posed by the RMDSZ to its Romanian allies: the demand for a Hungarian-language, state-funded university in Transylvania. The status of Babes–Bolyai University in Cluj lay at the centre of the debate.

Traditionally a Hungarian-language university, the Bolyai University was merged in 1959 with the Romanian-language Babes University. Under communist rule, the Hungarian sections of the newly formed Babes–Bolyai University were gradually subordinated and the

---

[113]   The 1999 revised version of the 1995 Education Act was published in *Monitorul Oficial*, No. 606, 12 December 1999 under the title "The Education Act of 1995, Amended and Republished".

Hungarian teaching staff eventually lost any meaningful power in the university's governing body (PER, 1997). Since 1989, the restoration of the Bolyai University has become, along with the more general debate over autonomy, the issue that has maintained the dividing line between Romanians and Hungarians in Romania. The re-establishment of a Hungarian-language university has acquired a symbolic significance to both communities. To the Hungarian community, autonomous control over a higher education institution of its own is more than an issue of rights. Rather, it is a matter of cultural survival and of recognition of the intellectual worth of the Hungarian community in Romania. To the Romanian majority, such an arrangement is seen as the first step towards ethnic separation and ultimately a threat to the territorial integrity of the Romanian state (Nastase, 1998).

A legal solution to this problem was offered in the amendments to the 1995 Education Act. The text was the result of a compromise between the positions of the two parties and attempted to resolve the issue within the state/private education scheme. Thus, the law "acknowledges" the right of persons belonging to national minorities to establish and manage their own 'private' universities (Article 123[2]). The most controversial issue remained, however, minorities' access to education in their mother tongue at state universities, which is a long-standing demand of the Hungarian minority. The law therefore also grants minorities the right to "request" the establishment of groups, sections, faculties and departments with instruction in minority languages "within" the existing state universities (Article 123[1]) or the establishment of "multicultural", that is multilingual, state universities.

Finally, entrance and final examinations can be taken in a minority language at educational institutions where tuition is offered in that language. However, the establishment of monolingual higher education institutions in languages other than Romanian remains an unresolved problem for the Hungarian minority. This is because many Hungarians see the multicultural university compromise as a temporary solution to their wider need to preserve their language and culture.

4. THE HUNGARIAN QUESTION AT THE BEGINNING OF THE TWENTY-FIRST CENTURY: THE ROAD TO NORMALITY?

4.1 Political Engineering of Interethnic Relations after the 2000 Elections: In Opposition but still in Control?

Despite the relative success of the power-sharing arrangement between the RMDSZ and its Romanian political partners, towards the end of the 1990s political life in Romania was developing in a direction that made uncertain the prospects for further progress in minority rights reforms. The eclectic nature of the political leadership, combined with poor political skills and bitter internal divisions, generated a chronic immobility in the decision-making process, and hence further economic and social decline.

Ion Iliescu and the PDSR became the clear favourites for the November 2000 parliamentary and presidential elections, as the government coalition was disintegrating amid fierce disputes among its members. Moreover, the inability of the government to deliver on its promises regarding economic reform, eradicating corruption and improving living standards gave leeway to extremist forces to regain a large part of the electorate. Despite the RMDSZ's repeated warnings, its Romanian allies failed to acknowledge the fact the PRM's rating in opinion polls rose from nine per cent to twenty per cent in the five months preceding the elections.[114]

The November 2000 elections have generated a new political configuration that raised concerns not only about the future of interethnic accommodation but also about the future of democracy in Romania. With Ion Iliescu and the PDSR returning to power, the multiethnic government ended and the prospects for the participation of the RMDSZ in future political arrangements became uncertain as RMDSZ returned to the opposition benches in the parliament. In addition, by becoming the second largest party in the new parliament, with a total of 121 seats out of 467 (CEB, 2000), the PRM represents a most disturbing return of the extreme right to central political decision-making.

However, the past decade has shown that political arrangements in Romania remain fluid and that both the PDSR's own political survival and foreign policy interests would dictate that the PRM will be excluded from any influence in the decision-making process. Thus, it was not entirely surprising that the PDSR and the RMDSZ, albeit old enemies, have brokered a political deal aiming to reassure the Hungarian minority that progress in minority rights reforms will continue.

Indeed, the protocol[115] between the PDSR and the RMDSZ provided for the adoption of a new local administration law that would allow for the use of minority languages in official communication and the display of bilingual or multilingual inscriptions in areas where minorities represent at least twenty per cent of the population. In addition, the PDSR pledged to continue the implementation of the Act on Education by ensuring an adequate framework and financing for the access of minorities to higher education institutions in minority languages. However, the significance of the protocol goes beyond legislative progress. First, it represents a compromise on minority and language policies that accommodate the interests of both parties. Based on a negotiated agreement, such policies have a greater chance to be implemented than a unilateral decision taken by the numerically dominant group. Second, the protocol sets out a novel formula of cooperation between the RMDSZ and the Romanian political leadership. Despite being back in opposition, the RMDSZ retains a certain degree of influence both on the PDSR's minority policies and on its general social and economic reform strategy. Thus, the protocol provides for prior consultations with the RMDSZ in the design and implementation of both minority laws and Romania's domestic and foreign policy agenda. In turn, the RMDSZ pledged to provide the PDSR with parliamentary support and to refrain from initiating or supporting a censorship motion against the government. Finally, the protocol provides a framework for the continuation of the confidence-building process between the Hungarian and Romanian political elites.

---

[114] According to the Institute for Marketing and Polls (IMAS) (see website at http://domino.kappa.ro/imas/home.nsf/Polls).

[115] Signed on 27 December 2000 (see website at http://www.rmdsz.ro/roman/index.htm).

At the time of writing (November 2001) a new law on local administration had been adopted,[116] allowing for the use of bilingual inscriptions and minority languages in official communication, as well as bilingual inscriptions in areas where minorities represent more than twenty per cent of the population.[117] In addition, the implementation of the 1999 revised Education Act made further progress as the first private university with tuition exclusively in Hungarian was established in Cluj.[118]

In the meantime, the Romanian political environment has continued its own process of transition. The PDSR has strengthened its membership and changed its name to the Social Democratic Party (Partidul Social Democrat, PSD), following its merger with the Social Democratic Party of Romania (Partidul Social Democrat Român, PSDR) in June 2001. However, the PSD's membership remains divided over the language rights issue, despite sustained efforts by its leader, Adrian Nastase, to maintain a unified position of his party on ethnic policies. On the opposition side, the RMDSZ's former coalition partners, PNL and PD, have renewed their nationalist rhetoric in the hope of regaining the electorate lost during the four years of power-sharing government. However, the recent revival of nationalism in the discourse of the political elites has had no significant impact on the population, and this time it lacks the support of much of the media. Despite this new wave of nationalism, the cooperation between the RMDSZ and the PSD has been generally good. Yet, implementation remains a difficult task (Andreescu, 1999). The lack of cooperation of many local elites and inadequate funding remain constant pitfalls in the implementation of the language provisions of the Local Administration Act. For example, the effectiveness of the process of posting bilingual inscriptions varies from one district to another. The responsiveness of local leaders often depends on their political affiliation and, in some cases, on the degree of cooperation between local PSD and RMDSZ elites and their central leaderships. In addition, insufficient financial resources and bureaucratic procedures continue to cause delays in the expansion of the infrastructure for higher education in the Hungarian language.

4.2 The Challenge of Transition, the Societal Response and Electoral Games

Much of the analysis of ethnic relations in Romania has been centred on nationalism as the main cause of ethnic conflict.

While some degree of dormant nationalism remains present throughout Romanian society, the nationalist discourse has emerged as a weak determinant of voters' preferences. Perhaps with the exception of the 1992 elections, it would be naïve to contend that elections in Romania were won or lost due to the presence or the lack of nationalist discourse in the main contenders' electoral programmes.

For example, the PDSR lost the 1996 elections despite its anti-Hungarian rhetoric and despite its claims to be the only party capable of safeguarding the territorial integrity of the

---

[116]   Act No. 215 on Local Administration, published in the *Monitorul Oficial*, No. 204, 23 April 2001.

[117]   Articles 17, 38(1)(u), 40(7), 43(3), 90 and 106(8).

[118]   The Sapientia University opened its doors to Hungarian students on 3 October 2001.

state. Similarly, the victory of the CDR in the same elections was the result of the PDSR's failure to reform the economy, improve living standards and eradicate corruption rather than due to the CDR's relative openness towards ethnic issues. The CDR's moderation regarding ethnic issues had no significant contribution to the outcome of the 1996 electoral process, but the new political configuration facilitated the participation of the RMDSZ in the central decision-making.

Finally, the sudden growth in popularity of the PRM in 1999, and its success in the 2000 elections, was largely due to the PRM's populist pledge to eradicate corruption and 're-store order', rather than its traditional extremist discourse on ethnic minorities. That nation-alist rhetoric lost much of its direct electoral appeal is, perhaps, best emphasized by peculiar voter behaviour at the 2000 elections: Five per cent of the Hungarian voters gave their votes to the PRM's presidential candidate, Corneliu Vadim Tudor, despite his pledge to destroy the Hungarian minority.[119] Essentially, both the PDSR and the CDR lost the elections in 1996 and 2000 respectively because they lost the battle with the fundamental challenges of transi-tion, most notably economic reform and corruption.

Perhaps one of the most important determinants of the climate of interethnic coopera-tion has been the political performance of the RMDSZ itself. Despite internal friction and occasional radical positions, the RMDSZ has shown a constant commitment to resolving minority rights issues through democratic institutions and political negotiations. In addition, the RMDSZ's balanced approach to the frequent government crises during 1996–2000 has certainly contributed to an increase in confidence among Romanian political actors. While retaining its traditional ethnic objectives on the agenda, the RMDSZ has clearly demonstrat-ed its commitment to contribute to all the other areas of Romanian public life. It is therefore not surprising that the Romanian political establishment sees the RMDSZ more as a regular political contender rather than an inward-looking, ethnic party (PER, 2001).[120]

Thus, nationalism remains a feature of Romanian society and politics. But nationalism is activated when political elites choose to use ethnicity as an excuse for failing to resolve equally salient issues in other areas of political, economic and social life. Moreover, elite nationalism by itself tends not to generate mass mobilization in the absence of any specific and dramatic evidence of abuse of minority status. Elite nationalism, however, retains a sig-nificant influence upon the design and the implementation of minority policies and laws.

4.3   The Renewal of the Kin-State Controversy

Together with the domestic political arrangements, the attitude of the kin-state continues to have a significant influence upon the dynamics of political engineering of the status of the Hungarian minority in Romania. Hungary and Romania share a troubled history of shifting boundaries and mutual oppression. The presence of large Romanian and Hungarian populations in Transylvania and the frequent shift of sovereignty over this province during

---

[119]   Also according to IMAS, see fn. 114.

[120]   For an overview of the evolution of the political debates on ethnic relations in Romania, see PER (1997).

the twentieth century have generated constant minority rights disputes between the two countries, especially since the end of the Second World War.

The overthrow of Ceaușescu and the collapse of the communist regime represented a time of great promise for the relations between the two countries. The immediate and unequivocal commitment by the new leadership in Bucharest to democracy and the protection of ethnic minorities prompted Hungary to deploy unprecedented support for the post-communist government in Bucharest. However, the post-revolutionary optimism was short-lived. Both Romania's attitude towards its minorities and Hungary's attitude towards its neighbours were put to a test.

The return of the nationalist discourse in the political arena and the failure of the post-communist leadership to deliver on their normative promise of minority rights reform prompted Budapest to renew its long-standing complaints about the status of the Hungarian minority in Romania. This revived the pattern of frequent diplomatic clashes between Bucharest and Budapest, this time regardless of the dynamics of interethnic processes in Romania. Romania's improvement of its minority rights record did not succeed in changing Hungary's stand towards its kin-minorities. The fact that the relationship between the kin-state and the host-state does not necessarily mirror the internal dynamics of majority-minority relations is, perhaps, best emphasized by the recent controversies generated by the Hungarian 'Status Law' (2001).[121] This law was drafted at a time when language rights reform, the process of confidence-building and the consolidation of the RMDSZ's prestige were given a significant boost by the PSD government.

The adoption by the Hungarian parliament of the Hungarian Status Law has revived old and bitter debates regarding Hungary's attitude towards its neighbours. The main points of contention are the preferential access of ethnic Hungarians living in neighbouring countries to the Hungarian employment market and the extraterritorial aspects of its implementation procedures. Thus, the law allows kin-minorities to receive an annual three-month work permit in Hungary (Article 15). In addition, the law provides for the issuance, by the Hungarian government, of special identification cards. The identification procedures are to be carried out by ethnic Hungarian organizations in neighbouring countries on behalf of the Hungarian government (Article 20).

The Romanian government argues that both provisions are discriminatory against other Romanian citizens who may seek employment in Hungary. In addition, Bucharest argues that adequate consultations with, and the consent of, the host-states concerned should have preceded such a unilateral measure with extraterritorial application. Hence, Hungary has failed to observe its international obligations assumed under multilateral and bilateral treaties, in particular those of non-interference, friendly relations among states and *pacta sunt servanda*. In addition, the removal of Austria from the list of countries relevant to the 'Status Law' prompted further complaints by Romania regarding the 'non-European character' of the law, following Austria's refusal to accept the application of the law on its territory. Austria, the only EU member bordering Hungary, rejected the application of the law on its

---

[121] Act LXII of 2001 on Hungarians Living Abroad, adopted by the Hungarian parliament on 19 June 2001 (see website at http://www.htmh.hu/law.htm).

territory, arguing that the law violates EU rules against ethnic discrimination among its citizens. As Hungary is among the front-runners for EU membership, Hungary could not ignore Austria's protest and removed the Hungarian minority in Austria from the list of beneficiaries of the Hungarian 'Status Law'.

Following these developments, Romania requested the European Commission for Democracy through Law (hereafter, 'Venice Commission') to examine the compatibility of the Hungarian 'Status Law' with European standards and with contemporary principles of international law. In response, Hungary requested the Venice Commission to carry out a comparative study on other European laws regulating preferential treatment of kin-minorities. In its report, the Venice Commission (2001) established that preferential treatment of ethnic minorities by kin-states is compatible with contemporary norms of international law while indicating that unilateral acts of this nature should be adopted and implemented with the consent of the relevant host-states. As expected, the report was given diverging interpretations by the two states, each government claiming that its position was 'European', therefore moral.

CONCLUSION

Language and ethnicity do not become salient problems by themselves. As Schöpflin notes, "it is not ethnicity that is the problem, but the absence of other processes that dilute its impact on power" (Schöpflin, 2000: 6). What Romania is attempting to achieve is a political system that acknowledges the importance of ethnicity and of a negotiated minority rights system based on recognized standards and that, at the same time, integrates ethnic interests with other areas of public life within the framework of a liberal democracy, albeit not in its classic form.

The political option chosen by Romania demonstrates that, even in a state that accepts only one official language, ensuring a reasonable degree of protection of minority languages and the participation of minorities in public life is possible. Thus, finding the balance between the state's need for some degree of linguistic uniformity and the needs of minorities to safeguard their identity is an attainable objective, provided that policies and laws are agreed upon by all the parties involved (Hannum, 1990). Once a certain stage of consensus between minorities and majorities has been reached, the issue is not anymore which groups are to contribute to the processes of transition and which are not, but rather the degree to which each group is to contribute to these processes. Monolingual or bilingual models neither promote nor prevent linguistic discrimination or interethnic accommodation by themselves. What is important is the ways in which these models are designed and implemented, the degrees to which they respond to the needs of the parties involved, and the purposes they serve. It is, ultimately, a matter of political will, of an adequate legal framework and of careful and sustained political engineering of ethnic differences.

It is also worth emphasizing here that one of the main obstacles to interethnic harmony between the Hungarian minority and the Romanian majority are deep-rooted security fears on both sides, which are often compounded by the actions of the kin-state. The "bickering over the wording and interpretation" (Liebich, 1998) of the constitutional provisions concerning the type of state and the official language is directly related to such security fears.

It is not cultural and linguistic differences themselves that maintain a tense relationship between Romanians and Hungarians. Ethnic Hungarians in Romania are not seen as an inferior ethnic group. Rather, they are perceived as a threat to the territorial integrity of the state. Therefore, promoting good bilateral relations between Romania and Hungary represents a critical issue to be addressed in any conflict management project involving the Hungarian minority in Romania. As Isakovic (2000) correctly argues, a major determinant of political stability is the degree to which the security fears of both minorities and majorities are resolved.

Finally, language and ethnicity cannot be discussed in isolation from the context in which the broader society develops. The above analysis has attempted to demonstrate that some of the most important factors that influenced minority policies in Romania during the transition period were often related to non-ethnic, more general transition issues, such as economic development, democratic values and the political skills and will of the leaderships of both ethnic groups. Given the impact of such factors, it becomes evident that sustained political engineering of interethnic relations and an adequate legal framework, combined with economic development and the promotion of democratic values, are factors conducive to political stability and sustainable interethnic accommodation.

Romania's progress in the political engineering of ethnic relations and in the legal protection of ethnic minorities represents an interesting example of how the broader political, social and economic contexts influence the dynamics of interethnic accommodation. Moreover, the evolution of interethnic relations in Romania during the 1990s as well as recent developments reveals both the incentives for, and the pitfalls of, sustainable ethnic accommodation. However, democracy in Romania, like in other post-communist states, remains work in progress. It is therefore expected that future political developments will determine whether current improvements in language policies and interethnic cooperation are sustainable and, possibly, replicable in other multiethnic societies that share similar structural and historical features.

REFERENCES

Andreescu, Gabriel, Valentin Stan and Renate Weber (1994) *A Study on the Conception of the UDMR on Minority Rights*. Bucharest: APADOR-CH.

Andreescu, Gabriel (1999) "Shadow Report: October 1999". http://www.riga.lv/minelres/reports/romania/romaniaNGO.htm.

Burgess, Adam (1997) *Divided Europe: the New Domination of the East*. London: Pluto Press.

CEB (2000) "Official Results". *Central Electoral Bureau*. http://domino.kappa.ro/election/election2000.nsf/RezultateFinale?OpenView.

Constantinescu, Mihai *et al.* (eds.) (1992) *The Constitution of Romania. Commented and Annotated* (trans.). Bucharest: Regia Autonoma Monitorul Oficial.

Council of Europe (1999) "Report submitted by Romania Pursuant to article 25 Paragraph 1 of the Framework Convention for the Protection of National Minorities". *Council of Europe*. http://www.humanrights.coe.int/Minorities/Eng/FrameworkConvention/StateReports/1999/romania/Romanianstatereport.htm.

Dahrendorf, Ralf (2000) *Reflections on the Revolution in Europe*. New York: Time Books.

Deleanu, Ion (1996) *Constitutional Law and Political Institutions*, Vol. II, Bucharest: Europa Nova.

Democratic Alliance of Hungarians in Romania (RMDSZ) (ed.) (1995) *Main Objections of the Democratic Alliance of Hungarians in Romania to the New Education Law*. Bucharest: DAHR.

de Varennes, Fernand (1997) "To Speak or Not to Speak: The Rights of Persons Belonging to Linguistic Minorities". Working Paper prepared for the UN Sub-Committee on the rights of minorities. See website at http://www.unesco.org/most/ln2pol3.htm.

Farkas, Evelyn N. (1996) "Circumventing the State: Securing Cultural and Educational Rights for Hungarian Minorities". *Journal of Public International Affairs*, July 1996. http://www.wws.princeton.edu/~jpia/July96/farkas.html.

Gallagher, Tom (1995) *Romania after Ceausescu. The Politics of Intolerance*. Edinburgh: Edinburgh University Press.

Gallagher, Tom (1997) "Danube Détente: Romania's Reconciliation with Hungary after 1996". *Balkanologie* I. http://www.chez.com/balkanologie/voli206.htm.

Hannum, Hurst (1996) *Autonomy, Sovereignty and Self-Determination: The Accommodation of Conflicting Rights*. Revised edition. Philadelphia: University of Pennsylvania Press.

Hockenos, Paul (1993) *Free to Hate: The Rise of the Right in Post-Communist Eastern Europe*. London: Routledge.

Horowitz, Donald (1985) *Ethnic Groups in Conflict*. Berkeley and Los Angeles: University of California Press.

Isakovic, Zlatko (2000) "Democratisation, Democracy and Ethnic Conflict in the Balkans". *Southeast European Politics*, 1(1): 1–14.

Jowitt, Ken (1992) *New World Disorder: The Leninist Extinction*. Berkeley, CA: University of California Press.

Liebich, Andre (1998) *Ethnic Minorities and Long-Term Implications of EU Enlargement*. Working Paper RSC No. 98/49. Florence: The European University Institute.

Lijphart, Arend (1977) *Democracy in Plural Societies*. New Haven, Connecticut: Yale University Press.

Nastase, Adrian (1998) *The Rights of Persons Belonging to National Minorities, Vol. I, Romanian Regulations (1989–1998)*. Bucharest: Regia Autonoma Monitorul Oficial.

Oprescu, Dan (2000) "Public Policies on National Minorities in Romania (1996–1998)". In Lucian Nastasă and Levente Salat (eds.) *Interethnic Relations in Post-Communist Romania*. Cluj-Napoca: Ethnocultural Diversity Resource Centre.

OSCE (1997) *Report on the OSCE Implementation Meeting on Human Dimension Issues*. Paris: OSCE. http://www.ihf-hr.org/OSCE1997/minoriti.htm#Romania.

PER (1997) *Schools, Language, and Interethnic Relations in Romania: The Debate Continues*. Project on Ethnic Relations. http://www.perusa.org/romania.htm.

PER (2001) "Political Will: Romania's Path to Ethnic Accommodation". Project on Ethnic Relations. http://www.perusa.org/romania.htm.

Rokkan, Stein and Derek W. Urwin (1983) *Economy, Territory, Identity: Politics of West European Peripheries*. London: Sage.

Rothschild, Joseph (1993) *Return to Diversity: A Political History of East Central Europe Since World War II*. Second edition. Oxford and New York: Oxford University Press.

Schöpflin, George (1993) *Hungary and its Neighbours: Chaillot Paper 7*. Paris: Institute for Security Studies, Western European Union.

Schöpflin, George (2000) *Nations, Identity, Power: The New Politics of Europe*. London: Hurst and Co.

Tsukimura, Taro (1998) *Politics of Ethnic Coexistence: Internal Division and External Pressure in Eastern Europe*. Hokkaido: The Slavic Research Centre.

van der Stoel, Max (1993) "Letter from the OSCE High Commissioner on National Minorities to the Romanian Foreign Minister, Theodor Melescanu". Paris: OSCE. http://www.osce.org/recommendations/romania/index.htm.

van der Stoel, Max (1995) "Statement on Romania". Paris: OSCE. http://www.osce.org/pres_rel/1995/09/818-hcnm.html.

Venice Commission (2001) "Report on the Preferential Treatment of Ethnic Minorities by their Kin-State". Venice: Venice Commission. http://venice.coe.int/site/interface/english.htm.

Language Corpus and Language Politics: The Case of the Standardization of Romani

Ian F. Hancock

Language Corpus and Language Politics: The Case of the Standardization of Romani

Ian F. Hancock[122]

INTRODUCTION

The debate over the standardization of Romani is above all political. Its subject is the language of a people who, lacking a national, governmental structure and economy, are still very much dependent upon the non-Romani world for the things necessary to participate in the global community. This means that issues of language planning (among other things) have been, and continue to be, dealt with mainly by non-Romani specialists—an anomaly especially significant for a people desiring to be in control of its own affairs. And even if the necessary means were available, the problem would still exist, because the Romani language is very unevenly represented, in terms of the variety of its dialects, the numbers of speakers of those dialects and what the governments of the countries in which those dialects are spoken are prepared to offer by way of support. The standardization of the Romani language is, more than most other languages in a similar position, in the hands of outsiders.

In the first essay ever to address the question, Bernard Gilliat-Smith maintained that "[b]asic [i.e., common standard] Romani is in my opinion theoretically possible, but in the present state of development of the Gypsies of Europe it stands but little chance of being accepted, or even generally understood, by those for whom it is primarily intended" (Gilliat-Smith, 1960: 34). More recently, Donald Kenrick observed that "with no standard written language, and between fifty and a hundred dialects, Romani dialects are not mutually comprehensible except at very basic levels" (Kenrick, 2000: 7). Together, these statements—the earliest and the most recent—pinpoint two fundamental problems facing the creation of a standardized language: the diversity which exists among Romani dialects[123] and the general acceptance of such a formalized variety should it ever become established. The statements also underscore the fact that the creation of a general standard has not been successfully achieved in the forty years which separate them.

---

[122] The author is of Hungarian Romani and British Romani descent, and has regularly taught the Romani language at the University of Texas since 1976, where he is Director of the Romani Archives and Documentation Center.

[123] Romani dialects fall into four main groups: Northern, Central, Vlax and Balkan. Each is further divided into smaller dialects, altogether about sixty in number. These groups are broadly geographical, but speakers from each are found widely dispersed outside of the original areas. For various classifications of these, see Hancock (1988b).

In a monograph which appeared in 1975, I examined factors bearing upon:

> ... the problems attending the standardization of [Romani], especially ortho-
> graphic standardization. This of necessity takes into consideration several related
> issues: the prevailing non-Roma attitudes towards Roma and Romani, and the
> consequent effects upon the attitudes of the speakers themselves towards their
> language. It is also necessary to decide whether, because of the diversity of dialects
> a composite union variety should be created, or just one existing dialect selected
> for the international standard. A problem also exists for Romani groups no longer
> speaking Romani *per se*, but restructured forms of the language (as do, for ex-
> ample, sections of the Romani populations in the United States, Britain, Spain,
> Finland, etc.), and for whom Romani morphology and syntax are quite foreign.
> Hinging upon these considerations is the question of literacy, and of Romani at-
> titudes towards it, and to 'formal' education generally (Hancock, 1975: 8–9).

The issues remain the same a quarter-century later, and are examined in new detail
in the present chapter. They are: (1) attitudes towards Romani identity and language, both
among Romanies and non-Romanies, (2) competence and performance, and (3) the nature
of the proposed standard dialect.

1.   ATTITUDES

In order to feel good about one's language, one must feel good about oneself. The negative
attitudes that Romanies encounter in the outside world do nothing to inspire a good sense
of self; indeed, antigypsyism is all too often internalized and the resulting anger and frustra-
tion can, in extreme cases, manifest themselves in destructive behaviour within the home. It
can make parents instil a sense of ethnic shame in their children, and tell them not to reveal
their identity as Romanies to the outside world; it is often the case that they will even with-
hold the ethnic language from them, believing it to be a liability rather than an asset. The
same children can readily provide examples of antigypsyism they have encountered outside
the home, particularly at school, either overtly from teachers and classmates, or unintention-
ally in the reading materials provided, which almost uniformly present 'gypsies' in a negative
light (Hancock, 1988a; 2002). In schools, multicultural curricula which incorporate sections
of Romani history and culture and Romani contributions to society are only now becoming
a reality, though still in disappointingly few places; it is still much more commonly the case
that Romani children are not even in the same classes as their non-Romani schoolmates,
but are kept in separate groups for the 'disadvantaged'. In Bulgaria, "the Gypsy schools were
officially dubbed 'schools for children with inferior lifestyle and culture'" (Tagliabue, 2001:
A3). A Czech study "found that a Gypsy child was 23 times more likely to be placed in a
school for the mentally retarded than a white Czech child, even when of normal intelligence"
(Ledgard, 2001: 29).

Ilona Lacková (1999: 64) writes of being ridiculed by the non-Romanies in Slovakia for
speaking her own language:

I wrote in Slovak, and it never occurred to me that you could write in Romani as well. The peasants made fun of us for speaking cant, gibberish, Pharaoh talk; Romani had no place in school, I had never seen a printed word in Romani in my life, and I thought that Slovak was the only language appropriate for literature (1999: 64).

Academics, too, diminish the worth of Romani, most often claiming that it cannot express abstract or philosophical notions but only the most basic of ideas. Linguist Jules Bloch in his book on Romanies, referred to the language as merely an "argot" (1969: 113), while another linguist, Paul Wexler, believes it to be a composite of the linguistic registers of various marginalized and disenfranchised populations, and furthermore that "Romani is not of Indic origin and did not acquire its Asian component by direct contact with, or by inheritance from, Indic languages" (Wexler, 1997: 16). Sociologist Judith Okely, whom Wexler cites, had already supported a similar position some years earlier:

The Sanskrit linguistic link may also have been over-constructed ... The [Romanies'] Indian connection has been used as what Malinowski calls a 'mythical charter' to give cultural respectability (Okely, 1990: 7–8).

The prevalent notion that Romani lacks the refinements which characterize more civilized languages, and which therefore reflect the same characteristics in its speakers, is found in Isabel Fonseca's widely influential book *Bury Me Standing*, where she says that it:

has a small basic vocabulary ... a store of mostly 'domestic' words, those relating to home and hearth and mostly of Indian origin ... more pervasive is the 'spirit' of the language, or that which it seems especially well suited to express—hyperbolic, gregarious, typically expressive of extreme emotion ... With the simple addition of the ancient Indic suffix *pen*, like 'hood' or 'ness', one can create abstract nouns, such as *Romipen*, 'Gypsiness' ... *But among Romani speakers, these big-concept, encompassing words are not much needed* (Fonseca, 1995: 56–58; emphasis added).

To prove the 'inadequacy' of Romani in her book, Fonseca used a portion of Shakespeare's Romeo and Juliet, which had previously been translated into Romani by a non-Romani lacking native fluency in the language, and then had that same person translate it literally back into English (Fonseca, 1995: 56–57), in order to compare it with the original and demonstrate its shortcomings. One would be hard put to find a contemporary British or American author writing in English who had the skills to match William Shakespeare's, let alone one writing in Romani. She would certainly have been able to provide a better translation had she asked native-speaking poets such as Rajko Djurić or the now deceased Leksa Manush to provide one—writers known for the beauty and power of their Romani verse—and who would certainly have had a sense of the 'big concept' of 'Gypsiness'.

The Swedish Lutheran minister Christfrid Ganander went one better, believing that Romani by itself was so inadequate a means of communication that it required supplementing with hand gestures before it could be understood. In words reminiscent of those of Isabel Fonseca, who calls the language a "highly aspirated, raucously guttural vernacular" (Fonseca, 1995: 58), Ganander wrote in 1780 that the Romani's mouth and lips were:

... big, wide and thick, convenient for the pronunciation of their language, which is rather aspirated and full of 'schz' or 'Sclawonska' words, calling for strong aspiration and a lot of spittle before they can be pronounced. Their pronunciation or sounds and voices are peculiar, loud, sharp, rough and harsh, and also demand twitches of the body and gestures with the hands, before they can be articulated.[124]

Contemporary prejudice at the popular level, exemplified by Ilona Lacková's real-life experience and Isabel Fonseca's naïve journalistic observations, originates in long-standing stereotypes about Romani language and identity which gain additional support at the academic, and hence the administrative, level. The works of Okely and Fonseca are very frequently listed as sources of information in governmental and other official documentation dealing with Romanies—reports which sometimes lead to policy decisions.

A fundamental requirement for instituting a positive attitude towards Romani amongst its speakers, and thereby a positive native-speaker attitude towards the possibility of creating a written literary standard and the literature it would support, must be an overall increased awareness of Romani identity and the Romani experience.

2. COMPETENCE AND PERFORMANCE

Fluency in Romani varies greatly from place to place, and the capabilities of the dialect likewise vary greatly, reflecting the vitality with which the mother tongue has been preserved in the community. In parts of the Balkans, for example, it survives with vigour and some of the dialects spoken there are rich in lexical and grammatical resources. But in other communities it has lost so much of its vocabulary and grammar that it has become a register of the surrounding non-Romani language.

Romani speakers are aware of which dialects are rich and which are poor, and almost universally favour their own over any other:

> Most Gypsies look down on speakers of dialects other than their own, and their prejudices are often taken over vigorously by any *gaujos* [non-Romanies] who learn one dialect. At Epsom in 1970 I heard the visiting speaker of an East European dialect attack all British Gypsies for letting Romani fall into disuse. Even the best 'Welsh' Romani speakers, he assured me, though they might be able to take a fish out of the river in Romani, couldn't use it to take an engine out of a motor[-car] (Acton, 1974: 55).

---

[124] Neither aspiration (the accompaniment of the sound by breath during its articulation) nor the need for excess spit is an especially Slavonic characteristic, and Romani is probably *less* 'aspirated' than English, which does not have an aspirated/non-aspirated phonemic distinction, but aspirates initial voiceless stops *wherever* they occur before vowels as a phonetic feature; and if by 'guttural' the uvular [a] sound is meant, then this is lacking in almost all Romani dialects, being a characteristic particularly of Kalderash Vlax.

Interdialectal bias is one manifestation of the discrimination that exists among different Romani populations, where individual groups generally regard their own members as 'real' Romanies and all others as 'less real'. This has an historical basis, and is reflected in the different self-ascriptions. Thus a Mačvano Vlax would never call himself a Sinto or a Romanichal, and *vice versa*; nor would he call a Sinto or a Romanichal a *Rom*; greater commonality is evident among Romani groups saying what they are *not*—a Sinto may not be a Mačvano, but neither is he regarded by other Romani groups as a *gadžo*, a non-Romani.

This multiplicity of names and self-perceptions underlies the problems which journalists and others encounter in selecting an all-encompassing name to cover all peoples of Romani descent. While *Rom* (plural *Roma*) is being increasingly used by Romani activists, and *Roma* as both a singular and a plural noun and even as an adjective by those writing in English,[125] the label is by no means everywhere favoured, and use of 'gypsy' or 'Gypsy' remains common, despite growing objection to it. Still, a trend is in place; in November 2000, the United States government declared that it was abandoning 'gypsy' as a Library of Congress subject heading because it was "viewed as offensive by some Romani people", and has replaced it with 'Romani' (plural 'Romanies'); other exonyms such as *Zigeuner* or *Cikán* or *Yiftos* have likewise been declared politically incorrect in different European countries, and are being replaced in print by *Roma* or *Romi*.

It is here that education and sense of self come together in the context of standard language. Most Romanies neither know nor care much about the communities outside their own, let alone know about the distant origins in India or what Indian legacy survives in daily life and language. While the first Romanies to arrive in Europe were able to say that they had come from India, that history was lost over time and now has to be learnt anew. Fearing what this regained knowledge might mean politically, some administrators, scholars and journalists have sought to dismiss it as either being false history (cf. Wexler, 1997) or over-glorified history (cf. Okely, 1990); still others argue that, while the roots may be in India, a lot has happened in the millennium since leaving that part of the world, and Romanies are permanent inhabitants of the West now, and much mixed with Europeans, so the point is a moot one and not worth pursuing. But what option does this leave?

2.1 Integration vs. Assimilation

A people with a strong sense of identity and worth may desire to remain separate, or they may want to integrate into a larger society, becoming a part of it yet retaining its distinctiveness. A people with a poor sense of identity and worth, on the other hand, may want to abandon its identity altogether, and assimilate completely into another society, becoming one with it or, distressingly, taking on a completely new identity, like the *Egjiptani* in Macedonia and Kosovo. In some countries, ethnic minorities are encouraged to participate in the larger society, while at the same time being allowed to foster their individuality; in others, efforts

---

125   While both terms 'Roma' and 'Romani' may be used to refer to persons who identify themselves as such (the term 'Romani[es]' is more accurate), the term 'Romani' (pl. 'Romanies') will be used here in reference to a person and as an adjective.

are made to eradicate ethnic minorities through policies which might, for example, forbid use of the mother tongue, traditional dress or ethnic family name. Maria Theresa's and Archduke Joseph's efforts in Hungary over two centuries ago did irreparable harm to the Romani population there, for which their descendants are still paying. If a minority population remains distinctive because of a combination of factors such as complexion, clothing, occupation and the area in which it lives, it continues to be visible and different, even though its language and culture and name have been taken from it. The tragedy is that while such deracinated populations are still discriminated against by the greater population despite forcible efforts to assimilate them, they now also lack the linguistic and cultural wherewithal to enable them fully to function in their original community. They are caught between two worlds, not fully a part of either.

A population can only be a part of a group if that group wants to let it in and, for Romanies, this has so far not been much in evidence in Europe. While a majority of Romanies would like to live in the same neighbourhoods as the non-Romanies and share with them the same educational, employment and health-care facilities, poll after poll make it clear that most non-Romanies do not want this. Integration is a much-desired goal, but nowhere in Europe is it likely to happen soon, leaving a vast Romani population—numbering in the millions—marginalized and having to find a way to explain to their children why things are the way they are, and why people hate Romanies so much. This is a very difficult and painful thing to have to explain to a child.

Hopelessness and despair destroy the will to strive for better things, and to take pride in one's home or appearance. They destroy one's very sense of worth. As long as families in *Kali Oropa* (Romani Europe)—where the language is most widely spoken and the Romani population the densest, must deal on a daily basis with problems of racism, unemployment, housing and health-care, then abstract issues such as language standardization and the details of the Asian origins rank absolutely nowhere on their list of priorities. Interest in language comes with improved schooling and social conditions, and both can only come with improved civil and social rights (Hancock, 1992)—but these must originate with the non-Romani governments in whose lands Romanies live. Romani input into governmental programmes is essential, but remains under-represented because of the lack of sufficiently qualified Romanies, and because of a reluctance driven by prejudice to employ and promote even those Romanies who are qualified. And so the wheel of under-achievement and under-representation and under-empowerment continues to turn in a self-perpetuating cycle.

2.2 Moving Ahead

Knowing who Romanies are and where they came from is fundamental to knowing where the population is going and what its place in the global family in [Until now, Romani] history has not been made a part of the educational system anywhere in the world, and while European nations glorify their own histories, popular Western culture perceives 'gypsies' to be a people *without* a history, whose church was made of cheese, and who steal (or wander) because they stole (or made) Christ's nails. The widespread insistence on spelling 'Gypsy' in English without a proper name's capital initial letter also denies us some humanity: As Kaplan and

Bernays say, "it's interesting how much weight a large initial letter carries. A noun or adjective is a frog until you give it a capital first letter, at which point it becomes a prince, that is, a proper name" (1997: 71).

It is not 'fanciful' to promote the Indian origins of the Romani people, which contemporary genetic studies (most recently Bernasovský and Bernasovská, 1999; and Gresham *et al.*, 2001) confirm; indeed, the positive aspects of gaining a global identity are immeasurable. The Human Genome Project team at the Center for Human Genetics in Perth, after comparing genetic material from large numbers of both Romani and Indian groups, concluded that

> [t]he Roma are genetically closer to Asians than to surrounding Europeans. This conclusion can hardly be described as exciting news; it has taken genetics 70 years and several thousand blood samples to confirm what has been known to linguists for the last 200 years (Kalaydjieva *et al.*, 1999: 13).

Mastana and Pahipa's serological research determined that "gypsy populations of eastern Europe still have greater genetic affinity with Indian nomadic groups" than with the white population (1992: 50), while Siváková found that "the lowest genetic distance value" was between Romanies and Indians, "suggesting a relatively low degree of genetic assimilation of Gypsies with their surrounding [European] populations" (1983: 98). Bhalla found that "[t]he Rajputs occupy the position nearest the gypsies ... the gene pool of East European gypsies is markedly different from that of the surrounding non-gypsy population [while ...] measures of divergence reveal least distance between East European gypsies and the stock of people in India represented by the Jat–Sikh–Punjabi–Hindu–Rajput complex" (1992: 331–332).

If a permanent module on Romani origins, history and culture were to become a part of the educational offerings throughout Central and Eastern Europe and elsewhere, both Romanies and non-Romanies would gain a better sense of Romani ethnic identity. If it were demonstrated that 'all' populations of Romani descent speak (or at one time spoke) varieties of the same original language and retain more or less of a common culture, and if it were shown that where Romani groups throughout Europe differ from each other it is because of influences from outside, both Romanies and non-Romanies would gain a better sense of Romani historical unity and legitimacy. And if it were taught that the ancestors of the Romanies left India as warriors in a unified group (Hancock *et al.*, 1998; Hancock, 2000) and arrived in Europe in the same way (Marushiakova and Popov, 2001), and subsequently fought in different national armies, and introduced new musical styles and instruments, and produced such notable individuals as Charlie Chaplin, Sonja Kovalevskaja, Matéo Maximoff, Papuša (Bronisława Wajs), Carmen Amaya, Philomena Franz, Cinka Panna, Carlos Montoya, Django Reinhardt, Bob Hoskins, Ceferino Giménez Malla, Birelli Lagrene, Manitas de Plata, Miroslav Holomek, Rita Hayworth and her grandfather Antonio Cansino, Lafcadio Hearne and others, and maintain a language and culture which are remarkably intact despite slavery, despite deportations and pogroms, despite the Holocaust, despite repeated attempts to eradicate us as a people, then a sense of pride, and even wonder, must be engendered within the Romani population, and perhaps the seeds of respect and understanding planted among the *gadžé*. But until this begins to happen, questions of language standardization will not receive much attention from the overwhelming majority of Romanies throughout the world.

2.3   Objections to Standardization

We can learn a great deal by comparing the Romani situation with the situations of other speech communities which have had to tackle the problems of standardization. A common charge, for example, is that any standardized dialect is in one sense the property of a small elite, and serves only to distance those without access to it from the spheres of influence even further. This has been proven to be so in many instances, but if it is true in the Romani case, then the same must be said for competence in the non-Romani national tongue. Romanies with a good command of Czech, say, or Bulgarian or Hungarian, are at a distinct advantage over those lacking such fluency. And whether or not the charge of elitism is true, the fact remains that on practical grounds alone, a written standard is necessary and has been for all emerging nations.

There are those who say that creating a standardized dialect would rob Romani of its spontaneity and 'soul', and even that it should not be written at all in *any* form. This is a subjective argument, and one already lost, given the abundance of publications now being produced in different Romani dialects. The expense of producing the same materials in many dialects would be considerable, and creating literacy programmes for each of them would be just as much a problem. And instead of having to expand the lexicon for just one new stand-ard dialect, the other dialects would also have to address this need, not necessarily creating the same new words for, say, 'hard drive' or 'digital' or 'phylum'; thus the problems of miscommunication would simply be perpetuated.

2.4   Which Dialect to Learn?

In countries where Romani has disappeared, a dilemma faces those who seek to bring about its revival. In England, for example, where a Romani-influenced register of English is now the ethnolect,[126] the moribund British Romani described by Sampson (1926) would be the most obvious choice for reintroduction on both emotional and historical grounds. In Spain, it is Caló, a para-Romani variety of Spanish that has become the ethnolect. Here, lacking a complete description of any earlier inflected Iberian Romani, a dialect has been artificially reconstructed piecemeal, not unlike Cornish in Cornwall, and its propagation has already met with some success; in 2000 the European Commission held workshops in Perpignan, Lisbon and Valladolid entitled *Recuperación del Romano-Kaló: Un Idioma Gitana Universal* (The Revival of Romano-Kaló: A Universal Gypsy Idiom). But the question arises: If a Romani population is to learn its lost ethnic language for the first time, should this in fact be the ancestral dialect (or, as in Spain, a newly-created dialect) limited to the area in which it was once spoken or, since the language is being approached for the first time anyway, should a variety be learnt which will allow much wider communication, such as Kalderash Vlax, or a yet-to-be constructed standard? Ideally perhaps both the lost ancestral dialect *and* a new common dialect should be taught, for while practicality argues against it, even most natural

---

[126]   An 'ethnolect' is a variety of a language associated with a particular ethnic community and is usually distinct in its phonology and lexicon, and often also its structure.

dialects still require orthographies. One of the first things acknowledged in the grant proposal drawn up for a Romani school in the town of Tacoma, Washington, in the United States, was that "a strong basic linguistic research component ... will lead to the creation of an alphabet and grammar for Romani, as the first step in the creation of a bilingual education package" (*Anon.*, 1975: 5; Hancock, 2002). Already existing local dialects are not after all meant to be replaced by a new standardized Romani, merely supplemented with it.

3. NATURE OF THE STANDARD

There are two choices in the selection of a standardized Romani: to elaborate an existing natural dialect and bring it into general use, or else to create a completely new, levelled (or *koinéised*)[127] dialect out of several. The answer would seem to be a combination of each: Romani linguist Kochanowski (de Gila-Kochanowski, 1995) believes that a standardized variety, which he has referred to as *Khetani Romani* (Kochanowski, 1983, 2003), should be based on his own Baltic dialect, which belongs to the Northern group, arguing that it retains more of the original grammar and lexicon, unlike dialects in the Central, Vlax and Balkan groups, which have been more heavily influenced in all areas by the surrounding European languages. He further believes Romani to have between fifteen and twenty million speakers (Kochanowski, 1971: 76), and he has advocated its adoption as an international auxiliary language by the world community because it is not associated with any existing government.[128] The Occitan linguist Marcel Cortiade's proposed standardized dialect—the only other real attempt besides Kochanowski's and a far more extensive one—is more eclectic, but is based especially on Balkan and Vlax models.

Determining what group of dialects should constitute the basis of a new standard is the initial stage of language planning according to Einar Haugen's approach (Haugen, 1973: 3), and for national, territorial languages, this rests primarily upon political and social considerations. In the case of Romani, however, these are outweighed by linguistic arguments.

Romani dialects all share a high proportion of common grammar and lexicon; where they differ from each other, it is because of both internal and external factors. In a number of cases, these have been so far-reaching as to produce completely restructured and rephonologized languages, the so-called para-Romani varieties (Hancock, 1975; Boretzky and Igla, 1994; Bakker, 1995 and 1998; Bakker and Cortiade, 1991). Since these are typologically no longer Romani *per se*, they do not bear upon the present discussion, except where they might provide retrievable lexical material.

External factors are the result of interference from the various non-Romani languages with which all Romani speakers are in ongoing (and usually overwhelming) contact. These

---

[127] *Koïné* (from the Greek κοϊνή for 'common', 'general') is the linguistic term for the speech which emerges when numbers of speakers of very closely related languages, or of widely differing dialects of the same language, find themselves together for an extended period of time, and work out amongst themselves a kind of 'compromise' or levelled speech as a commonly shared means of communication. It is characterized by both the generalization and loss of forms peculiar to individual languages or dialects within the mix.

[128] Kochanowski publishes under both the name of Jan Kochanowski and Vania de Gila-Kochanowski.

include modification of native phonology, such as the loss of the phonemic aspirate/non-aspirate contrast[129] in the speech of some speakers of French and Italian Sinti, or the neutralization of voiced and voiceless stops[130] in Finnish Romani, as well as extensive syntactic and idiomatic calquing.[131] It is this latter which Gilliat-Smith focused upon in his 1960 article, and which he believed to be the greatest obstacle, along with Romanies' "present state of development" as a people, for the success of a standardized dialect.

Sometimes, in the absence of information on the pre-European character of Romani, external factors are not always easily identifiable: Did, for instance, the definite articles emerge during the *tradipe*, the period between India and Europe, being traceable to Old Indo-Aryan pronominal forms? Or are they later accretions from Medieval Greek? Does the fact that they are absent in Baltic Romani reflect an earlier, article-less Romani, or have they disappeared during the European period under influence from Slavic and Baltic languages?

Many Romani nouns have extended meanings that may or may not be inherited. We know that the Romani word for 'lungs' is simply a translation of the southern Slavic 'white liver' (*parno buko* in Romani); but we cannot be so sure, for example, about *mačho* ('fish') which also means 'bicep' or 'calf (of the leg)'; does the word for 'fish' also mean these things in any of the coexisting European languages? Does the word for 'walnut' also mean 'stye' anywhere else, as *akhor* does in Romani?

Internal factors are those that have occurred within Romani, distinguishing it from other Indian languages but not resulting from identifiable external influences. They also occur within individual Romani dialects, distinguishing one from the other. In Romani, *besh-* is the verb meaning 'reside', as well as its primary meaning of 'sit'; but in no Indian language do its related forms share this secondary meaning. Sometimes changes in Romani are matched by distinctions in India itself, thus the [s] ~ [h] ('Sind-Hind') split, exemplified by Sinti *har*, *hom*, *hi*, for *sar*, *som*, *si* 'how', 'am', 'is' in other non-Sinti dialects, or the collapse of [s] and [š] to [s] in some varieties of Vlax (*manus, saj*, for *manuš, šaj*, 'man', 'able'), a widespread and low-prestige alternation also found in languages such as Kumauni and Panjabi; was this inherited, or is it an innovation?

---

[129] 'Aspiration', or the accompaniment of a speech sound by a puff of air, can be *phonemic*, which is to say essential to the actual meaning of a word. Thus in Romani, *per*, without a puff of air following the [p], means 'fall', while *pʰer*, which does have it, means 'fill'.

[130] 'Voicing' is the quality in speech production achieved by allowing the vocal cords to vibrate during the articulation of a sound. This can be heard by making a prolonged hissing 'ssss' sound (which does not have voice) and comparing it with a prolonged buzzing 'zzzz' sound (which does).

[131] A 'calque' is the direct translation of an idiom or of the meaning of a word from one language into another language. An example would be the use of *papel* ('paper') in Spanish to mean 'newspaper' because 'paper' can mean 'newspaper' in English. In Spanish, *papel* is only the material to write on, while a newspaper is a *diario* or a *gaceta*. American Romanies will sometimes say *sar de phuro san*? Literally, 'how old are you?' copying the English phrase, instead of *sodengo san* ('of how many [years] are you') in the Romani way. Calquing is common among bilinguals and second-language learners.

3.1 Orthography

Haugen calls his second stage "codification", which he defines as "the activity of preparing a normative orthography, grammar and dictionary for the guidance of writers and speakers in a non-homogeneous speech community" (Haugen, 1973). Just one concerted effort has been made to create a standard orthography, and this was the system introduced at the Fourth World Romani Congress held in Serock, Poland, in 1990, and which is summarized in Hancock (1995). Created mostly by Cortiade, its implementation won a majority vote with the proviso that its success or failure would be evaluated at the end of ten years. While a number of publications have appeared in this orthography, including several children's books, a newsletter, a computer programme and some technical linguistic material, so far it has not been generally successful. Members of the Romani community who correspond with each other regularly in the language, including the past and present presidents of the Roma National Congress and the International Romani Union, have simply not availed themselves of it. Its weaknesses have been most directly addressed by Kochanowski (de Gila-Kochanowski, 1995).

Does this reflect a general lukewarm attitude towards orthographic conformity, or is it this specific spelling system which has failed? Perhaps both; there is no denying that different dialect speakers, either as a group or as individuals, can have strong feelings about formalization, particularly if it is based upon the speech of an outside group. In the Romani-language preface to a report prepared recently by one human rights organization, the grapheme [rr], representing a particular phoneme in Romani and one of the orthographic recommendations of the 1990 commission, was used in the preliminary version submitted to the publisher. It was removed from the final version on a whim, simply because the editor "didn't like it". The phonemic distinction, in that case originally represented by [r] and [rr], was not incorporated into the published text.

This particular distinction in fact serves very well as a test case. Some dialects distinguish between two [r] phonemes, usually a dental [ɾ] and a uvular [ʁ],[132] which have developed historically from different underlying sounds in Old Indo-Aryan. Many dialects have collapsed these to a single, undifferentiated phoneme, but the two sounds nevertheless reflect two separate origins in Old Indo-Aryan and continue to be distinguished in some Romani dialects today—including Kalderash Vlax, the dialect with more speakers than any other. Thus in that dialect [tʃɔɾimɔs] and [tʃɔʁimɔs], or [ɾaj] and [ʁaj], mean quite different things ('theft', 'poverty'; 'gentleman', 'twig'). The distinction may not always be specifically dental vs. uvular, but this historical distinction is nevertheless maintained in many dialects, and should therefore be acknowledged orthographically.

How it is represented is another matter. Cortiade recommended [rr], no doubt because the same graphemic distinction ([r] and [rr]) exists in Albanian, which he has to some extent been influenced by. Spanish is another language which has it, and it seems to have been the

---

[132] 'Dental' sounds are made by bringing the front of the tongue against the back of the top teeth in their articulation, as in the French pronunciation of *tu* or *de*. 'Uvular' sounds are made by vibrating the uvula—the piece of flesh that hangs down in the back of the throat. The common French pronunciation of the [r] in *restaurant* contains this sound.

only orthographic recommendation to have gained a measure of wider acceptance, perhaps because it requires no special font or diacritic. Cortiade's other symbols include, *inter alia*, [θ], [ç], [ă] and [ɨ], not generally present on most typewriters, and while they are accessible easily enough on a modern computer, most Romanies own neither a computer nor a typewriter.

Since 1990 there has been a proliferation of Romani-language periodicals from all over Europe. A very useful overview of these has been provided by Dragoljub Acković (1997), who reproduces sample pages of several of them. Here, even a cursory examination reveals that there is still a tendency to use orthographies which draw upon the conventions of the coexisting non-Romani language, but where most do employ a common diacritic, it is the wedge accent or *haček* (called a *čhiriklorro* in Romani). This is used with <c>, <s> and <z> to represent [tʃ], [ʃ] and [ʒ], thus (<č>, <š> and <ž>). In some systems it is even placed over [r] to represent [ʁ], thus <ř>. The first three graphemes are found in Serbian, Slovenian, Czech and Slovak, while <ř> is found in Czech, though with a different value.[133]

Aspiration in Romani is most commonly represented in the samples by <h>, thus <čh>, <kh>, <ph>, <th>, but sometimes by an <x> or an apostrophe. Palatalization[134] is most commonly represented by a <j>, though publications in Czech Romani inconsistently use either an apostrophe, or a wedge accent with [n]: <d'>, <l'>, <ň>, following Czech convention. Taking a consensus from majority use, a workable orthography would employ the wedge accent, represent aspirated stops with an <h>, and palatalization with a <j>, and not represent differently allophonic variants such as the centralized vowels which reflect, for example, interference from Romanian in the Vlax dialects. However, since the use of electronic mail to communicate in Romani has increased, even the use of one diacritic has given way to using no accents at all, English graphemes taking their place. Thus <č>, <š> and <ž> are represented by <ch>, <sh> and <zh>, the letter <h> in these positions not conflicting with its occurrence in the aspirated stops and elsewhere. While this spelling is not ideal from a narrowly phonetic perspective, for example not distinguishing between the retroflex vs. non-retroflex[135] or the palatalized vs. affricated[136] sounds in some Vlax dialects, it is functional, and has already been adopted in some Romani-language publications in Hungary. Constructed, non-Latin alphabets for Romani, such as the one devised by Andrzej Mirga on an Indian model (1989: 3), or actual Devanagari (Indian)-based systems, which have occasionally been used, are of academic interest only, but do reflect an awareness of Romani's historical Asian connection.

---

[133] In that language, it represents a kind of [r] made with the tongue curled back (an 'apico-postalveolar median fricative' in phonetic terms).

[134] 'Palatalization' is made by bringing the blade of the tongue up towards the roof of the mouth in the articulation of a sound, so that (for example) [k] will sound like [ky] ('cute', as opposed to 'coot').

[135] 'Retroflex' sounds are made by curling the tongue back towards the roof of the mouth while articulating the consonant. They are common in Indian languages, although the specific Indian retroflex sounds are not shared by Romani.

[136] An 'affricated' sound consists of a stop consonant (i.e., one in which the air-stream from the lungs is completely stopped at some point, such as [t] or [d]), followed immediately by the correspondingly-placed fricative sound (i.e., one where the air-stream is constricted but not stopped) made in the same place in the mouth, such as 'sh' ([ʃ]), giving a double sound, thus 't' + 'sh' ([t] + [ʃ]) makes the fricative [tʃ], 'ch'.

The only serious recommendation that an Indian alphabet be used for writing Romani was made by Joshi, who says that Romani requires "a script which can scientifically represent all its phonetic forms. The Devanagari script which is being used for Sanskrit and Hindi best suits as a solution to the problem" (Joshi, 1991: 3).

3.2 Lexization

Haugen calls the development of a standardized lexicon 'lexization'. Both Kochanowski and Cortiade agree that this should incorporate new items by drawing upon Hindi, which both have done in their respective work (e.g., Cortiade's *lekh-* and *pustik* for 'write' and 'book'). Kochanowski justifies this because, he says, "the basic vocabulary of Romani and Hindi-Rajasthani is 60 per cent the same" (Kochanowski, 1971: 76–77), and he supplies a substantial list of such recommendations in his *Parlons Tsigane* (de Gila-Kochanowski, 1994). Petrovski and Veličkovski have similarly introduced some Hindi words in their Macedonian-Romani dictionary, and Šaip Jusuf and George Sărau have both done the same in their respective Romani handbooks, though in each case without identifying them as being lexical adoptions rather than legitimate retentions. This is disconcerting for those working on natural dialects, and sometimes proves to be incorrect; Kochanowski, for example, lists recommendations for "*les mots sanskrits déjà introduits en hindi*" ("the Sanskrit words already introduced in Hindi") to be brought into his own standardized dialect, but includes the new Romani feminine noun *almar*, 'cupboard' from Hindi *ālmārī* (de Gila-Kochanowski, 1994: 191). Hindi, however, adopted this from Portuguese '*almario*' some five centuries after the *teljaripe*—the time when the ancestors of the Romanies were already leaving India.

Drawing directly upon Sanskrit to supplement the Romani lexicon has also been suggested, but the question then arises if such words were to remain in their Old Indo-Aryan form, or be modified to incorporate the phonological changes which have taken place in Romani, a New Indo-Aryan language.[137]

Cortiade also agrees with Kochanowski who wants "to replace the technical words by the international vocabulary", e.g., *televizija*, *komputeri*, etc., and while Kochanowski says this should be "mainly by words common to the French and English languages, of course adapting all these words to Romani phonology" (de Gila-Kochanowski, 1994: 76), things have changed in Europe in the thirty years since he wrote that; items common in Eastern European languages would now have to be considered, too.

The role of Greek was fundamental to the emergence of modern Romani—its contribution to the core lexicon is second only to words of Indic origin, and it has also contributed significantly to Romani grammar; indeed, Romani itself seems only to have finally taken shape in the Byzantine Greek-speaking environment. It can therefore be seen as a legitimate part of Common Romani (i.e., Romani as it existed at the time of the *aresipe*, or arrival in Europe). With the exception of Istriani Romani which has oddly just a handful, all dialects

---

[137]   Thus would a neologism, say for 'fine hair, down', keep the shape *bhūva* as in Sanskrit, or be rephonologized to a form such as *phum* in Romani in accordance with the corresponding sound changes?

281

contain Greek-derived items, and thus words from that language might also be brought in to supplement a standardized, expanded Romani vocabulary.

The first task, however, might be to scour all the recorded varieties of Romani in order to find legitimate words lost in other dialects. For example Vlax no longer has the original word for 'tree', and uses the word for 'wood' (*kašt*) to substitute for it, or an adoption from Slavic or Romanian; but other dialects still have the Indic word (*rukh*), which can therefore be brought into a constructed standard. Likewise, while most dialects retain words for 'hot' and 'cold' (*tato-šudro/šileno*), only a few retain the original word for 'warm' (*tablo*), which could be legitimately introduced. Some dialects have generalized the verb *phen-* to mean both 'say' and 'tell', where others still have *phuker-* for the latter.

Resources for lexical augmentation already exist in the language, but their use depends upon the richness of the dialect in question, and the fluency in it which its speakers command. One of the first grammatical distinctions to be lost in the process of attrition is that of derived verb forms.[138]

3.3 Grammization

The creation of a standard grammar, for which Haugen, following Ferguson (1968), suggests the term 'grammization,' should make maximum use of the original resources, retrieving them from the dialects in which they survive and bringing them together into the new standard. Thus Kochanowski argues that more than any other, his own Baltic dialect retains all the morphological oppositions, those between the optative and the subjunctive,[139] between the transitive, intransitive and transitional verbs;[140] between the aorist and the perfect,[141] between

---

[138] Causatives (verb forms expressing causation, e.g., 'to cause to fall' = 'drop'), inchoatives (verb forms expressing 'becoming', e.g., 'to become red' = 'redden') and passives can produce such extended lexical entries as *puterd-jol* 'it becomes undone', from *putrel* 'it opens (something)', *ankerdjol* 'it calms down', from *ankerel* 'it holds', *bisterdjol* 'it becomes obsolete', from *bisterel* 'it forgets', *dikhjol* 'it seems, it is regarded', from *dikhel* 'it sees', *hamisavel* 'it is involved', from *hamol* 'it mixes', *prindžardjol* 'it introduces', from *prindžarel* 'it recognizes', and so on. Use of thematic constructions instead of adopted foreign forms: *dav anglal* instead of *atvetiv* for 'I answer', *sosko* or *savestar* instead of *če fjalo* for 'what kind of', *sa gado* plus the noun instead of *adapat*, *mizmo* or *isto* to express 'same', *maškar koleste* for 'meanwhile' instead of *dotle* or *intratimpu*. Extended meanings using productive suffixes, such as *vazdari* 'elevator' (from *vazd-* 'lift'), *cirdari* 'drawer' (from *cird-* 'pull'), *avrjaluno* 'outer' (from *avri* 'out'), or *avutno* 'next' or 'subsequent' (from *av-* 'come'). Semantic distinctions between words sharing the same root could similarly be made using different productive suffixes: *vučipe* 'elevation', *vučimos* 'altitude', or by lexical selection: *šajipe* 'possibility', *dastipe* 'ability'. The augmentative possibilities of metaphor are limitless: e.g., *drakhin* ('grapevine') for 'internet', or *čhiriklorro* ('little bird') for the wedge accent.

[139] 'Optative' is a verbal mood expressing the intention or d... ... ... action, the subjunctive' mood indi... ... ... to hypothetical, or dependent upon a previous action.

[140] 'Transitive' verbs are verbs that can govern a noun object, such as 'lay' or 'set', while an 'intransitive' verb cannot, e.g., 'lie' or 'sit'. 'Transitional' verbs can do either, e.g., 'smell' or 'wash'.

[141] The 'aorist' is a past tense in which the time of the action is not specific; the 'perfect' is also a past tense, but expresses a single, completed action.

the present and the future; between the gerund and the absolutive,[142] and between the infinitive[143] and the optative (de Gila-Kochanowski, 1995: 98).

These are in fact found in other dialects too, but not one has retained all of them, or other grammatical features such as the native comparative ending {-der} (baro, bareder, 'big', 'bigger'), using instead a construction calqued on European languages and using an adopted comparative particle (maj baro in Vlax, meg baro in some Central dialects). Only a very few dialects have kept the earlier first and second person emphatic pronominal forms (maja, tuja, amaja, tumaja), which would enrich a constructed grammar.

Before a core grammar and lexicon can be abstracted and all of these scattered grammatical features codified, complete linguistic descriptions need to be made of all retrievable Romani dialects. We still lack such a massive study, though work in this direction is in progress. Once these data have been collected, the following suggested procedure might be followed to begin the task of codification:

1. all foreign material—lexical, phonological, syntactic, etc.—be removed from the natural dialect;
2. a comparison be made of the remaining corpus of material for each dialect;
3. their differences identified and extracted;
4. selection be made of the most suitable non-shared native grammatical and lexical features to be retained; and
5. lexical augmentation be made to supplement the existing reconstructed vocabulary.

CONCLUSION

For political reasons, most of the work on the standardization of Romani should be undertaken by Romanies, ideally native speakers of Romani, rather than by non-Romanies; of the twenty-two different people who have published on Romani standardization over the past forty years, only five have been Romanies, and this has kept the management of the language in mostly non-Romani hands. The creation of a mixed, but Romani-dominant, team of specialists would redress a long-standing imbalance of representation, but until educational and social conditions improve drastically, achieving the standardization and the practical implementation of the language will continue to be the concern of just a handful of individuals, and remain largely in the academic domain.

---

[142]   A 'gerund' is a noun formed from a verb, such as 'they're doing the washing'. An 'absolutive' is the basic, underived form of a noun or a verb: 'they're doing the wash'.

[143]   The 'infinitive' is the form of the verb which has no subject: 'to run' as opposed to the 'indicative' 'I run'.

REFERENCES

Acković, Dragoljub (1997) *Čitajte Ljudi—Ginavnen Romalen—Read People*. Belgrade: Rrominterpress.

Acton, Thomas A. (ed.) (1971) *Current Changes amongst British Gypsies and their Place in International Patterns of Development*. Oxford: Romanestan Publications.

Acton, Thomas A. (1974) *Gypsy Politics and Social Change*. London: Routledge and Kegan Paul.

Anon (1975) *Gypsy Education and Development Program: Grant Proposal*. Tacoma, Washington: Metropolitan Development Council.

Bakker, Peter (1995) "Notes on the Genesis of Caló and Other Iberian Para-Romani varieties". In Yaron Matras (ed.) *Romani in Contact. The History, Structure and Sociology of a Language*. Amsterdam: John Benjamins, pp.125–150.

Bakker, Peter (1998) "Para-Romani Languages versus Secret Languages: Differences in Origin, Structure and Use". In Yaron Matras (ed.) *The Romani Element in Non-Standard Speech*. Wiesbaden: Harrassowitz, pp.69–96.

Bakker, Peter and Marcel Cortiade (eds.) (1991) *In the Margin of Romani: Gypsy Languages in Contact*. University of Amsterdam: Institute for General Linguistics Publication No. 58.

Bernasovský, Ivan and Jarmila Bernasovská (1999) *Anthropology of Romanies (Gypsies): Auxological and Anthropogenetical Study*. Prešov: University of Prešov Minority Research Centre.

Bhalla, V. (1992) "Ethnicity and Indian Origins of Gypsies of Eastern Europe and the USSR: A Bio-Anthropological Perspective". In K.S. Singh (ed.) *Ethnicity, Caste and People*. Manohar and Moscow: Institute of Ethnography, pp.323–346.

Bloch, Jules (1969) *Les Tsiganes*. Paris: Presses Universitaires de France.

Boretzky, Norbert and Birgit Igla (1994) "Romani Mixed Dialects". In Peter Bakker and Marten Mous (eds.) *Mixed Languages: 15 Case Studies in Language Intertwining*. Amsterdam: Institute for Functional Research into Language and Language Use, pp.35–68.

de Gila-Kochanowski, Vania (1994) *Parlons tsigane: histoire, culture et langue du peuple tsigane*. Paris: L'Harmattan.

de Gila-Kochanowski, Vania (1995) "Romani Language Standardisation". *Journal of the Gypsy Lore Society*, 5(2): 97–108.

de Gila-Kochanowski, Vania (2000) *Précis de la Langue Romani Littéraire*. Paris: L'Harmattan.

Ferguson, Charles A. (1968) "Language Development". In Joshua A. Fishman, Charles A. Ferguson and Jyotirindra Das Gupta (eds.) *Language Problems of Developing Nations*. New York: John Wiley and Sons, pp.27–35.

Fonseca, Isabel (1995) *Bury Me Standing: The Gypsies and their Journey*. New York: Random House.

Ganander, C. (1780) *Undersökning om de så kallade Tattare eller Zigeuner*. Stockholm: Kongl. Svenska Vitterhetsakademien.

Gilliat-Smith, Bernard (1960) "Basic Romani?" *Journal of the Gypsy Lore Society*, Third Series, 39(1): 30–34.

Gresham, David *et al.* (2001) "Origins and Divergence of the Roma (Gypsies)". *American Journal of Human Genetics*, 69: 1314–1331.

Hancock, Ian (1975) *Problems in the Creation of a Standard Dialect of Romanés - I (Orthography)*. Working Papers in Sociolinguistics, No. 25. Austin: 65.

Hancock, Ian (1988a) "Gypsies in our Libraries". *Collection Building* 8(4): 31–36.

Hancock, Ian (1988b) "The Development of Romani Linguistics". In Ali Jazyery and Werner Winter (eds.) *Languages and Cultures*. The Hague: Mouton, pp.89–110.

Hancock, Ian (1992) "The Roots of Inequity: Romani Cultural Rights in Their Historical and Social Context". In David Mayall (ed.) (1992) *Gypsies: The Forming of Identities and Official Responses*. Special issue of *Immigrants and Minorities*, 2(1): 2–17.

Hancock, Ian (1995) *A Handbook of Vlax Romani*. Columbus: Slavica.

Hancock, Ian (2000) "On the Emergence of Romani as a koïné Outside of India". In Thomas A. Acton (ed.) *Scholarship and the Gypsy Struggle: Commitment in Romani Studies*. Hatfield: The University of Hertfordshire Press, pp.1–13.

Hancock, Ian (2002) "The Schooling of Romani Americans: An Overview". *The Patrin Web Journal*, http://www.patrin.com/Paris/5121/schooling.htm. In Kyuchukov (2002), pp.30–51.

Hancock, Ian, Siobhan Dowd and Rajko Djurić (eds.) (1998) *Roads of the Roma*. Hatfield: University of Hertfordshire Press.

Haugen, Einar (1973) "Language Planning: Commentary". Session on Language Planning at the Eighth World Congress of Sociology, Toronto, 1974.

Joshi, Aravind K. (1991) "Some Suggestions for the Standardisation of Romani Language". *Roma*, 33–34: 38–48.

Kalaydjieva, Luba, David Gresham and Francesc Calafell (1999) *Genetics of the Roma (Gypsies)*. Human Genome Project Special Report. Perth: Cowan University Centre for Human Genetics.

Kaplan, Justin and Anne Bernays (1997) *The Language of Names*. New York: Simon and Schuster.

Kenrick, Donald (2000) "Inflections in Flux". In *Lingua Fracas*, an In Focus special issue of *Transitions Online*, April 2000. http://archive.tol.cz/apr00/inflflux.html.

Kochanowski, Jan (1971) "The Future of Romani". In Thomas A. Acton (ed.) *Current Changes amongst British Gypsies and their Place in International Patterns of Development*. Oxford: Romanestan Publications, pp.76–77.

Kochanowski, Jan (1983) "Romani koyni (Khetani Romani)". *Studia Indo-Iranica*, 57–63.

Kyuchukov, Hristo (ed.) (2002) New Aspects of Roma Children Education. Sofia: Diversity Publications.

Lacková, Ilona (1999) *A False Dawn: My Life as a Gypsy Woman in Slovakia*. Hatfield: University of Hertfordshire Press.

Ledgard, J. (2001) "Europe's Spectral Nation". *The Economist*, 12 May 2001: 29–32.

Marushiakova, Elena and Vesselin Popov (2001) *Gypsies in the Ottoman Empire*. Hatfield: University of Hertfordshire Press.

Mastana, Sarabjit S. and Surinder S. Papiha (1992) "Origin of the Romany Gypsies: Genetic Evidence". *Zeitschrift für Morphologische Anthropologie*, 79(1): 43–51.

Matras, Yaron (ed.) (1995) *Romani in Contact. The History, Structure and Sociology of a Language*. Amsterdam: John Benjamins.

Mirga, Andrzej (1989) "Romani kripta". Unpublished document.

Okely, Judith (1990) "The Invention and Inventiveness of Gypsy Culture". Paper presented at the Leiden University Fund Congress conference The Social Construction of Minorities and their Cultural Rights in Western Europe, Leiden.

Sampson, John (1926) *The Dialect of the Gypsies of Wales*. Oxford: The Clarendon Press.

Siváková, Daniela (1983) "Estimation of the Degree of Assimilation of the Gypsy Population Based on Genetic Distance Calculations". *Anthropologia*, 28–29: 95–102.

Tagliabue, John (2001) "Bulgaria's Gypsies Fighting for their Education". *International Herald Tribune*, 28 November, 2001: A1, A3.

Wexler, P. (1997) "Could there be a Rotwelsch Origin for the Romani Lexicon?" Paper presented at the Third International Conference on Romani Linguistics, Prague.